O9-BTM-514

GRAND OPERA IN DIGEST FORM

By the Author

THE BOOK OF HOLIDAYS

INDIAN HEROES

GRAND OPERA IN DIGEST FORM
(formerly *Operas and Musical Comedies*)

PIONEER HEROES

STORIES FROM DICKENS

SHAKESPEARE'S PLAYS IN DIGEST FORM
(formerly *Shakespearean Synopses*)

GRAND OPERA IN DIGEST FORM

J. Walker McSpadden

THOMAS Y. CROWELL COMPANY

New York · Established 1834

To

The memory of my beloved wife whose devotion to my work lasted for half a century and whose name, as formerly, is merely inscribed as
"MAC"

Originally published by the
Thomas Y. Crowell Company
under the title
Operas and Musical Comedies

Library of Congress Catalog Card Number: 54-13112

PRINTED IN THE UNITED STATES OF AMERICA
APOLLO EDITION 1961

INTRODUCTION

That "great oaks from little acorns grow" is exemplified in a work for which I am again privileged to write the introduction. A third of a century ago, a modest, pocket-size volume appeared with J. Walker McSpadden as author, and with the title *Opera Synopses*. Since then it has been continually reprinted, each time larger as it has kept pace with stage productions old and new. It was for the fifth edition of the book (representing the fifteenth printing) that I wrote an introduction, and I began by remarking that when a book has survived for so many years, and repeated editions have been required to supply the public demand for it, we may be sure that it continues to fill a real need. During its long period of usefulness the frequently revised and enlarged editions of the book have kept it abreast of the changing repertoire of the leading opera companies. With the coming of the radio back in the 1920's it acquired many more readers, who kept it beside their radios and consulted it before, and often during, the weekly opera broadcasts. Since World War II later editions have brought the contents up-to-date. Finally this Apollo Edition puts a famous book into an inexpensive format, suitable for wide distribution to students and opera lovers everywhere.

The usefulness of Mr. McSpadden's book and the real need for it are not to be questioned. It is true that various types of music lovers enjoy different features of an opera performance, and in varying degrees. To some the music is the principal attraction. They would as soon hear operatic music in the concert hall. Others enjoy the visual aspects, the scenic and the lighting effects, the costumes and the ballet. Still others, perhaps the majority, regard opera as drama. They like to know what the singing actors are saying and doing. To these people, listening to an opera in a strange language is an incomplete experience, and many of them are advocates of translating the texts into English. But even a familiar tongue is inadequate unless the singers have excellent diction, and the words they sing are easily understood.

It is, of course, to the latter group that a book like Mr. McSpadden's is most useful, but it is safe to say that anyone who listens to any opera, or to any operatic selection, will gain more from hearing it if he has at least a general idea of what it is all about, of the emotions the music expresses, and the action it portrays. Thus, the person who consults this new volume will inform himself briefly and clearly of the outlines of the drama act by act, and scene by scene. When he sits in the opera house he will not have to strain his eyes in a darkened auditorium trying to follow a badly translated libretto while his favorite tenor is singing "Celeste Aida." He will know already that Rhadames, the warrior, is singing of Aida, the slave, and he will realize that the music is describing a beautiful maiden and expressing the hero's admiration of her.

This latest edition has still another newly added feature which increases its value and usefulness. In the accounts of many of the more familiar operas, frequent phrases of music are inserted to illustrate the principal arias and to show where they occur. These thematics, as they are called, give musical outlines of the operas to supplement the dramatic outlines of the texts.

As for the contents, the new volume contains all the old favorites that were included in previous editions—the standard operas of the Italian repertoire, the German and Austrian masterpieces from the time of Gluck and Mozart, representative works of the French School, and the outstanding operas of other nations. And once again the works that have been added keep the volume fully up to date. The modern *Wozzeck* of Alban Berg and Krenek's *Johnny Plays On* were included in the previous edition, but now are added Hindemith's *Mathis der Maler, Goyescas* by Granados, Hageman's *Caponsacchi*, as well as numerous other operas, which are widely discussed and performed either in opera houses or on the radio.

In the new edition the author continues the arrangement he devised for a former edition, of grouping the operas according to the nationalities of their composers in chronological order. Each national group is preceded by a brief account of the development of the opera in that country. Thus the book is actually a condensed history of opera throughout the world, and by reading it the student may trace its development from the ancient Greeks through the era of Italian *bel canto,* of the Wagnerian leitmotif, right down to the realism of the ultramodernists. And if he's interested in the dates of first performances, he'll find them too, together with the names of singers who appeared in the premieres.

As a personal friend and neighbor of J. Walker McSpadden, I know at first hand of the intense thought and planning that has been put into this book of his. Various criteria were set up to show which operas qualified for inclusion, and why. And since the book contains so many different kinds of operas, and is the only one now in print that does do so, those who buy it will probably do with it just what I do—put it right in the middle of the nearest bookshelf, where we keep the works we consult most often.

John Tasker Howard

AUTHOR'S PREFACE

I wish to repeat my thanks given in the earlier work to the assistant librarians in the New York Public Library, the Newark Public Library, the Montclair Public Library; Mrs. Robert Bartlett, daughter of Victor Herbert; the late Harry B. Smith who was most helpful; the private collections of programs of the late Alvin L. Powell, of Glen Ridge, and of A. Ray Wilkerson, of Richmond, Virginia; John Tasker Howard, author of *Our American Music* and in charge of that division of the New York Public Library; George W. Watson, of that library, whose forte is grand opera programs and librettos; George Freedley, curator of the Theatre Division; Albert Ellis, of New York, for constructive criticism; and others for friendly advice and suggestions.

J. W. McS.

AUTHOR'S PREFACE

To Later Editions

During the years this book has constantly expanded, keeping pace with the musical life of this very fruitful period. One important feature added to the 1951 edition is a comprehensive index of characters in grand opera. For example, Rhadames can be immediately identified as a tenor lead in *Aida*. Opera-goers and radio and television listeners have appreciated this added aid.

And now another printing is necessary to keep the work still more closely in line with productions—a goal which both my publishers and I have kept in mind. New material and data have been included from the stages of the Metropolitan and the City Center.

To the long list of those to whom I have previously been indebted I wish to add the Music Department of the Boston Public Library, the New York City Center of Music and Drama, Daniel McNamara of ASCAP, and other music lovers whose messages throughout the years have been a constant inspiration.

J. W. McS.

CONTENTS

GERMANY AND AUSTRIA

ITALY

FRANCE

RUSSIA

OTHER NATIONS

THE UNITED STATES

RECENT AND REVISED GRAND OPERAS

GERMANY AND AUSTRIA

HISTORICAL PREFACE

Because they are linguistically allied and the works of these neighboring composers were often performed in Vienna as in Berlin, the composers of Germany and Austria are here grouped together. The roots of Grand Opera, however, were not originally in Teutonic soil. They may be traced through Italy as far back as ancient Greece. For many centuries in Greece the classic drama had flourished. Music with it was incidental, but it had its Prologue and Chorus which, though spoken, were based upon the same stage mechanics. Musical accompaniments gradually crept in. And the dance was a time-honored partner.

The Renaissance brought to Europe a renewed regard for the fine arts, and its first expression was found in Italy. Here in the sixteenth century a group of Florentine noblemen introduced what is regarded as the first of the operas. For further notice of this and other Italian works the reader is referred to that section.

Teutonic opera, however, is given precedence in this book for the reason that the works of at least four major composers from this country, beginning with Gluck, head the list in the beginnings of modern opera. But numerous composers antedated Gluck. We are told of a certain Reinhard Keiser (1679–1739) who wrote over one hundred operas; and of another, Johann Adolph Hasse, who also had a hundred to his credit. Nevertheless, Gluck's "Orpheus and Eurydice," produced in 1762, remains the earliest of such works still holding its place in modern repertory. Those other giants, Mozart (an Austrian), Beethoven, and Weber, were all born before the end of the eighteenth century. Spontini, born in 1774, was of Italian parentage, but his achievements in opera made no lasting impression upon his native soil. His chief work, "The Vestal Virgin," was brought out in Paris and later in Berlin, where for twenty years he was a musical director.

Both Gluck and Mozart were genuine pioneers. While the former studied in Italy and his first operas were produced there, they were experimental and he soon lost patience with the so-called Greek methods and struck out boldly for himself. His efforts to found a new school met with the same violent opposition which greeted Wagner of a later day. Mozart, on his part, was an antithesis of Gluck and was the first to inject pure singing melody in its simplest form into dramatic production.

It would require a volume in itself to trace all the sources of modern opera. Literally hundreds of attempts were made by Italian, French and German composers dating as far back as the thirteenth century. Some of these works won fair success in their day. But the operas of Gluck and Mozart are the only ones of this formative time to linger on. Beethoven's single opera, "Fidelio," was not produced until nearly a quarter of a century after Mozart's death.

With the dawn of the nineteenth century German opera was definitely launched on a national basis. Louis Spohr (1784–1859) aided to bridge the gap from the early masters, and was closely followed in point of time by Weber, whose delightful works revealed the springtime blossoming of the new school. A score of imitators arose, one of the most important being Heinrich Marschner (1795–1861), some of whose works are still produced in Germany. Then came Lortzing, Cornelius, Nicolai, and other noteworthy names. Our list could be prolonged to considerable length. It even includes such great names as Mendelssohn, Schubert, Schumann, and Liszt, but their forte was not that of opera. Liszt in a sense passed on the torch to a blazing genius who was to dominate German opera—Wagner.

Wagner's art was diametrically opposed to that of the prevailing school. He did not view opera as a vehicle merely for some singer, nor yet for some melody. He regarded it as a dramatic work into which all elements should be co-ordinated—the story, the melody, the singer, working together to express the motif of the drama. As a part of his plan he developed a system of *leit-motives,* or leading themes, which should serve to label the characters and even their emotions and thoughts. It was a sort of musical cue. He also chose folk and native German themes, writing his own librettos. Naturally his revolutionary methods and no less radical orchestrations aroused the most determined opposition, but eventually prevailed. So profound has been his influence that German opera now falls into two divisions—before Wagner and since Wagner.

Since Wagner the outstanding composer in Germany has been Richard Strauss. His "Der Rosenkavalier" had the distinction of being performed twice in the first week of the Metropolitan opera season, November, 1945. Some half-dozen other operas in addition to many orchestral suites have given him assured position. D'Albert of "Tiefland" did not realize his first promise. Leo Blech, Alban Berg, Eric Korngold, and Ernst Krenek, are other latter-day figures.

However, the impact of two world wars has snuffed out the divine flame in that unhappy country, perhaps for years to come. The nation under its Nazi leaders turned materialistic, and all the arts suffered, wellnigh to extinction. It will doubtless require an entirely new generation to retake the torch in arts and letters; and meanwhile in the field of opera we shall have to continue to enjoy the fruits of the past.

CHRISTOPHER W. GLUCK

Gluck may be regarded as the great-grandfather of modern opera. He is the earliest composer whose works are still found in the present-day repertory. Born in Weidenwang, Palatine, July 2, 1714, he was from the outset of his career a musical reformer who aroused as intense opposition as did Wagner later. He studied in Milan and thus came under the Italian influence, but his first operas presented in Italy met with scant success. His first successful work was "Helena and Paris." In 1774 he went to Paris, where he presented his masterpieces, among them "Orpheus and Eurydice," "Armide," "Iphigenia in Aulis," "Iphigenia in Tauris," and "Alcestes." The composer, Nicola Piccini, was a bitter rival of his, and adherents of the two frequently came to blows. Gluck died in Vienna, November 15, 1787.

ORPHEUS AND EURYDICE

(Orf'-use and Yoo-rid'-i-see)

(Orfeo.) Legendary Opera in Four Acts. Music by Christopher Gluck. Book by Raniero di Calzabigi. Vienna, October 5, 1762. At New York, the Metropolitan, 1891.

SCENE: Greece and the Lower World.
TIME: Antiquity.

CAST ORPHEUS, *a sweet singer* (Contralto).
EURYDICE, *his bride* (Soprano).
AMOR, *god of love* (Soprano).
Furies, Shades, Friends of Orpheus, etc.

ARGUMENT "Orpheus and Eurydice" is based upon the ancient Greek legend of the musician who went into the depths of Hades to rescue his dead wife.

Act I *The Tomb of Eurydice.* Eurydice, the bride of Orpheus, who charms all things by his music, has perished from the bite of a serpent. After a brief, dirgelike prelude the curtain rises as Orpheus and his friends lament her loss in a touching aria and chorus, "Thou whom I loved." He prays to the gods to restore her to him. He is ready to make any sacrifice, even descend into Hades itself in order to rescue her. Touched by his grief, the god Amor is sent to tell him he may make the journey, trusting only to his powers of song; but that he must on no account turn to look upon the face of his wife, else Death will again seize upon her. "The will of the gods fulfill with joy," sings Amor as Orpheus departs.

Act II *Hades, the Abode of the Departed.* The shades and furies swarm around the entrance to Hades reviling Orpheus for having attempted to enter; but he sings so sweetly of his grief and present quest that they stand aside and allow him to enter. His aria, "A thousand griefs," and recitative, "What pure light," finally win over the furies, who respond with, "Welcome, sweet singer."

Act III *Valley of the Blest.* In the midst of Hades is the Valley of the Blest, where dwell the pure in heart. Here Orpheus on his journey finally finds his wife. The others cannot understand why she wishes to return, but touched by his song lead her to him. He does not turn to look at her, but with averted face takes her hand and leads her from the valley. She, of course, is puzzled and his efforts to reassure her lead to the lovely duet, "On my faith rely."

Act IV *A Forest before a Cave.* After a long upward journey, Orpheus leads his wife through a cave, finally emerging into a dense forest. Still he does not look at her, but calling back urges that she follow him quickly. She complains that he is indifferent to her; that he has not given her so much as a single glance. Without his love she would prefer death. She continues this plaint until he can resist no longer and turns to reassure her. Immediately she sinks to the ground lifeless. Then it is that Orpheus bitterly reproaches himself in the lament which is best remembered: "I have lost my Eurydice!"

The god Amor is touched, he again appears to Orpheus and says that since he has suffered and toiled greatly he will be forgiven. With a touch he restores Eurydice to life and to her husband's arms.

ARMIDE

(Ar-meed)

Romantic Opera in Five Acts. Music by Gluck. Book by Quinault, founded upon Tasso's "Jerusalem Delivered." Académie Royale de Musique, Paris, September 23, 1777. Metropolitan, New York, November 14, 1910, with Caruso, Fremstad, Gluck, Rappold, Homer.

SCENE: Damascus and Environs.
TIME: The First Crusade, 1098 A.D.

CAST
ARMIDE, *a sorceress* (Soprano).
PHENICE, *her friend* (Soprano).
SIDONIE, *her friend* (Soprano).
HIDROAT, *King of Damascus* (Baritone).
ARONT, *his chief of staff* (Basso).
RINALDO, *Commander of Crusaders* (Tenor).
ARTEMIDOR, *a Crusader* (Tenor).
UBALDO, *a Knight* (Baritone).
A DANISH KNIGHT (Tenor).
Demons, Naiads, Knights, Courtiers, Servants, etc.

ARGUMENT "Armide" is a legendary episode connected with the Crusade under Godfrey of Bouillon. His chief officer falls under the power of a beautiful sorceress.

Act I *The Palace of Armide.* The Princess Armide is famed both for her beauty and her powers of magic. She has remained unmarried, although Hidroat, the King, wishes her to choose a husband. But she cannot free her mind from the thought of Rinaldo, the victorious Crusader. At every new word of his conquests her heart is torn by hatred of him as an enemy of her country, and love for him as a hero. Tidings are received that the Saracen host is at last victor in a battle, but this is disproved by a later messenger and the arrival of Aront's army which has again suffered defeat. All swear vengeance against the Christian army.

Act II *An Enchanted Garden.* Rinaldo, the Crusader, while wandering in the desert, suddenly finds himself in an enchanted garden, conjured up by the wiles of Armide. Naiads rise up before him and sing him to sleep. While reclining under a bower of roses, insensible, the sorceress advances toward him with drawn dagger. At last she has her country's enemy within her power. But the sight of the man of her dreams once more kindles love in her heart; the sorceress is lost in the woman, and she clasps him in her arms.

Act III *The Palace of Armide.* Again in her palace, Armide is torn among the mingled feelings of love, hate, pride, and remorse. Instead of striking her enemy she has yielded to him. She summons before her the Demon of Hate, who warns her that for this indecision Rinaldo will yet escape her. Instead of nerving her fury, this only redoubles her love, and the Demon in anger disappears.

Act IV *The Enchanted Garden.* Rinaldo has continued under the power of the sorceress. The Crusaders, alarmed by his absence, send Ubaldo and a Danish knight in search of him. At their approach Armide bars their path, but is compelled to fall back powerless before a consecrated scepter borne by Ubaldo. Other visions appear at Armide's command, but are dissipated by the scepter.

Act V *The Palace* (*sometimes combined with the Garden scene*). Armide conveys her lover to the palace and seeks to entertain him by ballets and tableaux. He forgets his past life while subject to her wiles. She leaves the room for an interval, and Ubaldo and the Danish knight enter, carrying the scepter and a highly polished shield which when held up before Rinaldo reveals to him the warrior he formerly was. Roused to action by this vision, he grasps his sword just as Armide returns. She implores him to remain with her. When he refuses and departs with the Crusaders she sets fire to her palace and perishes in the flames.

Two memorable arias in "Armide" are: "Ah! si la liberté!" and "Plus j'observe ces lieux."

IPHIGENIA IN AULIS

(If-ee-zhee-ny'-a in Ah'-lis)

Legendary Opera in Three Acts. Music by Gluck. Book by du Roullot. Paris, April 19, 1774.

SCENE: Aulis.
TIME: After the Trojan War.

CAST
AGAMEMNON, *King of the Greeks* (Basso).
CLYTEMNESTRA, *wife of Agamemnon* (Contralto).
IPHIGENIA, *daughter of Agamemnon* (Soprano).
CALCHAS, *the High Priest* (Baritone).
ACHILLES, *a warrior* (Tenor).
Soldiers, Courtiers, Priests, etc.

ARGUMENT Although this opera does not rank with "Iphigenia in Tauris," it is yet worthy of preservation on its own account. And its plot may be regarded as the first part of the tragedy. Its overture is still frequently played.

Act I *Camp of Agamemnon.* After the Greek victory at Troy, the victorious soldiers seek to return home, but an unfavorable wind detains them. The High Priest states that the gods can be appeased only by an innocent offering. Agamemnon is urged to sacrifice his daughter, Iphigenia. The king is torn between his mistaken sense of duty and his love for his child. Iphigenia is betrothed to Achilles, and the two prepare for their wedding, unmindful of the secret danger.

Act II *Portico of the Temple.* Iphigenia is adorned for her wedding, and Achilles comes to lead her to the altar, when Agamemnon's messenger informs them that death awaits Iphigenia.

Clytemnestra, in despair, appeals to Achilles, and the bridegroom swears to protect Iphigenia. She alone is resigned in the belief that it is her father's will that she should face this dreadful duty. Achilles reproaches Agamemnon and leaves the unhappy father a prey to mental anguish. At last he decides to send mother and daughter to Mycene, and to hide them there until the wrath of the goddess is appeased.

Act III *Before the Tent of Agamemnon.* The soldiers crowd before the king and demand the sacrifice. While Achilles implores Iphigenia to flee with him, she stands ready to offer herself on the bloody altar. Her mother in turn offers to take her place, but the girl will not consent. Just as the priest is ready to plunge his knife in the victim, the goddess Diana appears and saves her; declaring that she does not want her blood, but her life and service as priestess in a foreign land.

Two arias most often heard are: "Diana impitoyable!" and "O toi, l'objet le plus amiable."

IPHIGENIA IN TAURIS

(If-ee-zhee-ny'-a in Taw'-ris)

Legendary Opera in Four Acts by Gluck. Book by François Guillard. Académie de Musique, Paris, May 18, 1779. At New York in the Metropolitan, November 25, 1916, with Kurt, Rappold, and Sundelius.

Scene: Tauris.
Time: After the Trojan War.

CAST IPHIGENIA, *priestess of Diana* (Soprano).
ORESTES, *her brother* (Baritone).
PYLADES, *his friend* (Tenor).
THOAS, *King of Scythia* (Basso).
DIANA (Soprano).
Scythians, Priestesses of Diana.

ARGUMENT An opera which takes very high rank among early compositions. Both book and music are classic and so harmonious that Herder called the opera "sacred." The plot follows "Iphigenia in Aulis," in point of time.

Act I *Before the Temple of Diana.* Iphigenia, King Agamemnon's daughter, who has been saved by the goddess Diana from death at the altar of Aulis, has been carried in a cloud to Tauris, where she serves as high-priestess in the Scythian temple. Here we find her, after having performed her cruel service for fifteen years. Human sacrifices are required, but more than once she has saved her victims.

She is troubled by a dream in which her father is fatally wounded by her mother, and she herself is compelled to kill her brother Orestes. Thoas, King of the Scythians, orders her to sacrifice two strangers who have been thrown on his shores. They are Orestes and his friend Pylades.

Act II *Temple of Diana.* Orestes bewails his fate. Pylades sings of his undying friendship for him. Pylades is separated from Orestes, who temporarily loses his mind. Iphigenia questions him. Orestes refrains from disclosing his identity. He tells her that he is from Mycene, that Agamemnon has been slain by his wife, and that her son, Orestes, has slain her in revenge, and is himself dead. Of the once great family only a daughter, Electra, remains.

Act III *Temple of Diana.* Iphigenia is struck with the resemblance of the stranger to her brother and, in order to save him from the sacrifice demanded by Thoas, charges him to deliver a letter to Electra. He declines to leave Pylades. The latter agrees to take the letter only because he hopes to bring aid to Orestes.

Act IV *Altar of the Temple.* Orestes is led to the sacrifice. Iphigenia vainly tries to lift her dagger against this stranger but an inner voice forbids. At last when on the point of striking, Orestes reveals himself to her. A touching scene ensues, and Iphigenia declares to the King that she will die with her brother. At this moment Pylades at the head of a rescue party enters the temple. A combat ensues in which Thoas is killed. Diana appears, pardons Orestes, and returns to the Greeks her likeness which the Scythians had stolen when they built their infamous temple.

Two arias still sung: "Unis dès la plus tendre enfonce" and "O malheureuse Iphegénie."

WOLFGANG AMADEUS MOZART

If ever there was "a born musician," Mozart was that one. Stories are still current of his precocity. Born in Salzburg, Austria, January 27, 1756, his extraordinary musical genius early came to public attention. At the age of four he played the clavichord and composed minuets which are still extant. At six we find him and his gifted sister, also a child, playing before the courts at Munich and Vienna. At seven, Mozart took his place in a stringed orchestra and played a difficult score at sight. At the mature age of thirteen he was appointed director of concerts at Salzburg, and made a concert tour with his father to Italy, whither his fame had preceded him. But despite this early popularity Mozart was destined to a life of deprivation and want, due to the pittances which he received for his musical works. His first opera, "Mithridates," was composed at fourteen (1770) and produced in Milan the same year. Ten years later came "Idomeneus" (1780); followed by "The Marriage of Figaro" (1786); "Don Giovanni" (1787); "Cosi Fan Tutte," a comic opera (1788); "The Seraglio," a light opera (1789); "Titus" (1791); and "The Magic Flute" (1791). This does not take into account his quartets, masses, and other compositions, possibly the most noteworthy being his celebrated "Requiem Mass" left unfinished at the time of his decease. That Mozart was "a genius by the grace of God" is revealed by the fact that his career ended at the age of thirty-five. He died in Vienna, December 5, 1791.

THE MARRIAGE OF FIGARO

(The Mar-riage of Fee'-gah-roh')

(Le Nozze di Figaro.) Comic Opera in Four Acts. Music by Mozart. Book by Lorenzo Da Ponte, founded upon the comedy of Beaumarchais.

National Theatre, Vienna, May 1, 1786. At New York, the Metropolitan, 1895, with Eames, Nordica, De Tusson, Maurel, Carbone.

SCENE: Seville.
TIME: The Seventeenth Century.

CAST COUNT ALMAVIVA, *a nobleman of Seville* (Baritone).
COUNTESS ROSINA, *his wife* (Soprano).
FIGARO, *valet to the Count* (Basso).
SUSANNA, *his betrothed* (Soprano).
DOCTOR BARTOLO, *a physician* (Basso).
BASILIO, *a music-master* (Tenor).
CHERUBINO, *a page* (Soprano).
MARCELLINA, *the housekeeper* (Contralto).
ANTONIO, *a gardener* (Basso).
BARBARINA, *his daughter* (Soprano).
DON GUZMAN, *a judge* (Tenor).
Members of the Count's household, Friends, Citizens, etc.

ARGUMENT "The Marriage of Figaro" is a direct continuation of "The Barber of Seville," Rossini's tuneful opera, both being founded upon the uproarious comedy by Beaumarchais.

The sparkling overture represents Mozart at his happiest. It does not depend upon later arias for its appeal, but blazes a path of its own of riotous, rollicksome melody. As for the story, the curtain rises to disclose Count Almaviva at last the husband of the fair Rosina, whom he courted under such difficulties with the aid of the "Barber." But having obtained the lady he proves fickle and susceptible to other beauties who may chance to come his way. His latest flame is Barbarina, the pretty daughter of his gardener, but he has a rival in the persistent page, Cherubino, whom he seeks to get rid of by placing him in the army. Figaro, the barber, has entered the Count's service and is looking forward to marriage with Susanna, a ward of the Countess. Susanna also has been pursued by the Count, unsuccessfully.

Act I *A Room in the Count's Castle.* Preparations are forward for the marriage of Figaro and Susanna. He is discovered busily arranging the furniture, while she is trying on a bridal wreath before the mirror. They plan for the future and she says she will be glad thus to escape the Count's attentions. Dr. Bartolo, the physician, arrives and is told by Marcellina, the old housekeeper, that Figaro was formerly engaged to marry her. The doctor agrees to help her win justice, and is also glad to have this chance to even up some old scores. Marcellina and Susanna now engage in a war of words: "Go first, I entreat you, Miss, model of beauty!" The page, Cherubino, now appears upon the scene—a fickle youth who finds every petticoat desirable. (This role is taken by a soprano.) He thinks he is once more enmeshed in the grand passion: "Ah, what feelings now possess me!"

His outpourings are halted by the entrance of the Count himself. The page jumps behind a chair. Susanna seats herself before him. The Count makes advances, but is disturbed by the entrance of Basilio, and in turn goes behind the chair. The page slips like an eel into the chair and is covered by a dress which Susanna throws over it. After some further confusion, both the Count and Cherubino are discovered and the page is ordered to depart forthwith.

Act II *Apartments of the Countess.* Cherubino still lingers around the premises, and the Countess decides to use him as a tool to unmask her husband's perfidy. She and Susanna plan to dress him in woman's attire, and he is nothing loath, as this will enable him to remain for the wedding and be near Barbarina.

One of the famous arias of the opera emerges as Cherubino sings the exquisite: "What is this feeling which makes me so sad?"

The Count comes to the door and demands admittance. Cherubino jumps out of the window and the Count is baffled. But when the gardener comes in to complain that his flower-pots beneath the window are broken, the Count's suspicions are again aroused. The gardener also produces Cherubino's commission in the army, which has been dropped in the leap. But Figaro, who has entered meanwhile, shoulders all the blame, saying that he had come to see Susanna and also had the letter. Marcellina, the housekeeper, now appears to enforce her claim against Figaro.

Act III *Apartments in the Castle.* Susanna is persuaded by the Countess to meet the Count in the hope of untangling the marital difficulty. The Count is obdurate, until it is found that Figaro is actually the son of Marcellina and so could not possibly marry her. This apparently removes the last obstacle to his happiness. But the Countess and Susanna had agreed to change clothes for the evening in order to confuse the Count still further. The ruse is so successful that Figaro also is fooled and becomes furiously jealous.

In this Act during the concoction of a letter between the Countess and Susanna comes one of the loveliest numbers: "The Song to the Zephyr," a duet which "brought down the house" when the opera was first presented:

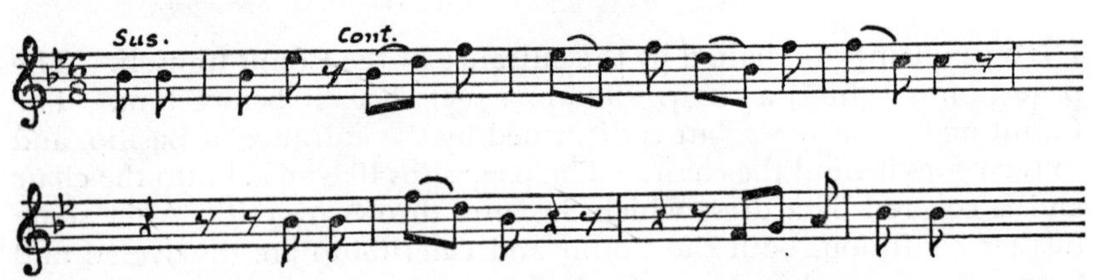

Act IV *The Garden.* The last act becomes a farce of confused identities. The Countess and her maid have changed clothes, fooling both the Count and his servant. Barbarina is also in the general mix-up, but it is Figaro who comes in for cuffing whenever he or his master makes a mistake—which is frequently. Finally, lights are brought on, the Count realizes that he has been well punished, and the marriage of Figaro is approved.

DON GIOVANNI

(Don Jo-vahn'-nee)

(Or, The Marble Guest.) Opera Bouffe in Two Acts. Music by Mozart. Book by Da Ponte, after a Spanish tale by Tirso de Molina. Prague, October 29, 1787. Special performance in honor of Mozart's birth, at the Metropolitan, New York, January 27, 1906, with Nordica, Sembrich, and Scotti.

SCENE: Seville.
TIME: The Seventeenth Century.

CAST DON GIOVANNI (JUAN), *a Castilian dandy* (Baritone).
DON PEDRO, *the Commandant* (Baritone).

ANNA, *his daughter* (Soprano).
ELVIRA, *a former sweetheart of Juan* (Soprano).
DON OCTAVIO, *the fiancé of Anna* (Tenor).
LEPORELLO, *servant of Juan* (Basso).
MASETTO, *a peasant* (Basso).
ZERLINA, *his betrothed* (Soprano).
Spanish Nobles, Ladies, Guests, Guards, Servants.

ARGUMENT Among the many operas on the subject of Don Juan and his amours, none has the merit or the continuing popularity of this of Mozart.

Act I *Scene 1. The Garden of the Commandant's Palace.* Don Juan, a notorious libertine of Seville, goes by night to enter the apartments of Don Pedro's daughter, Anna, who is betrothed to Octavio. As soon as she discovers the intruder's presence she cries for help, and her father hastens to her aid. He is mortally wounded by Don Juan, who escapes in the darkness unrecognized.

Scene 2. Public Square in Front of Don Juan's Palace. Returning from this bloody adventure, Don Juan and his servant Leporello calmly discuss new conquests. While they consult, a former discarded sweetheart, Elvira, appears and upbraids Don Juan for his cruelty. He retreats, leaving the girl with his servant, who reveals to her the amazing list of his master's villainies.

Leporello's recital to Elvira contains the lofty arias, "Madamina" (Gentle Lady) and "Nella Bionda" (Fair One). The former begins thus:

Don Juan's next piece of rascality is an attempt to seduce Zerlina, a peasant girl, on the very eve of her wedding with Masetto, a villager. He is foiled, however, by the entrance of Elvira, who shows the girl her danger. Meanwhile, Octavio and Anna have been searching for the murderer of Anna's father, and come to ask Don Juan to aid them in their search, but they soon begin to suspect the libertine of the deed. Preparations proceed for the peasant wedding, and Don Juan's servant aids him to hoodwink Masetto and Zerlina. The jealous bridegroom is pacified by his bride, while the libertine conducts both to a gaily decorated apartment prepared for them. Masked guests arrive.

Scene 3. The Ball Room. While all the guests engage in a dance, Leporello devotes himself to Masetto, and Don Juan conducts Zerlina to a private room. She resists his advances and her cries attract the masked guests who prove to be Anna, Elvira, and Octavio. Don Juan draws his sword, fights his way through the crowd and escapes. This scene introduces the stately, graceful minuet:

Act II *Scene 1. Before Elvira's House.* Don Juan still pursues Zerlina, who is in the service of Elvira. He exchanges cloaks with his servant, who goes to call upon the mistress while the master devotes himself to the maid. Masetto comes upon the latter, in the midst of a serenade, but is beaten by Don Juan, who again gets away.

Scene 2. Elvira's Apartments. The pretended Don Juan is unmasked by Elvira, Anna and Octavio, and found to be Leporello. Their suspicions are further confirmed as to Don Juan's guilt. Octavio sings the classic aria for tenors, "To my beloved":

Scene 3. A Graveyard, in which stands a statue of the slain Don Pedro. Leporello, who has escaped, comes to tell his master of what has occurred, but the latter's spirits are still gay and he plans further deeds of violence. At this juncture a hollow voice warns him to repent before it is too late. It is the statue of the murdered nobleman speaking to him. The libertine, unabashed, jeers even at this, and invites the statue to attend a banquet which he is to give.

Scene 4. The Apartments of Donna Anna. Love scene between Anna and Octavio (sometimes omitted).

Scene 5. Don Juan's Dining Hall. True to his word, Don Juan has spread a sumptuous meal, and in the midst of it a heavy tread is heard. The marble statue of the Commandant enters and bids the libertine accompany him. The floor opens and both descend into the infernal regions.

THE MAGIC FLUTE

(Il Flauto Magico. Die Zauberflöte.) Fantastic Opera in Two, or Four Acts. Music by Mozart. Book by Emanuel Schickaneder and Gieseke. Vienna, September 30, 1791. New York, the Park Theatre, in English, April 17, 1833. At the Metropolitan, in German, January 11, 1904, with strong cast headed by Sembrich, Gadski, and Ternina.

SCENE: Egypt.
TIME: Antiquity.

CAST SARASTRO, *Priest of Isis* (Basso).
THE QUEEN OF NIGHT, *a sorceress* (Soprano).
PAMINA, *her daughter* (Soprano).
TAMINO, *a Prince* (Tenor).
PAPAGENO, *his attendant* (Basso).
PAPAGENA, *the latter's sweetheart* (Soprano).
MONASTATOS, *a Moor* (Tenor).
Priests, Ladies, Pages, Fairies, and Wild Creatures.

ARGUMENT "The Magic Flute" is an allegorical fantasy showing the reward of constancy. It relates the adventures of a Prince and an imprisoned maiden. The bewildering array of scenes is wedded to sensuous music and the effect of the whole is heightened by strange scenic effects. The two acts into which the opera was originally divided have become three or four acts in modern presentations. The overture beginning with a series of stately chords, continuing with a lordly adagio, then a vivacious fugue, again illustrates Mozart's versatility as a composer.

Act I *A Forest.* Prince Tamino has lost his way in a dense forest and is moreover pursued by a gigantic serpent. His outcries bring three fairies to his aid, who slay the serpent with their spears. Tamino now sees a strange being who walks like a man but is clad in birds' feathers. It is the fantastic Papageno, who claims that this is the proper way to catch birds. Papageno is a great braggart and at once claims the honor for having slain the serpent. The fairies fasten a padlock on his lips in punishment for the lie. They show the Prince the portrait of a lovely maiden, Pamina, who is in the power of Sarastro, at the Temple of Isis. Her mother, the Queen of the Night, now appears and invokes his aid to rescue the maiden. The Prince gladly consents to enter upon the adventure, and is given a magic flute which will ward off danger. Papageno is to accompany him; the padlock is removed and he is given a chime of bells.

Act II *Scene 1. The Palace of Sarastro.* The Moor, Monastatos, has persecuted Pamina with his attentions. Angered by her disdain he drags her into an apartment, but is frightened away by Papageno, who has been transported thither by her mother to announce the coming of the Prince. Pamina plans to flee with them.

Scene 2. Entrance to the Temple. Tamino approaches the Temple of Isis, conducted by three pages. At two of its doors he is denied admittance, but at the third a priest appears and tells him he is mistaken in his opinion of Sarastro. The maiden is really being protected in the Temple to keep her out of the power of her mother's sorceries. Pamina and Papageno now appear, but the Moor prevents their escape. Sarastro enters and having heard all the story orders that the Moor be punished. The two lovers he greets kindly, telling the Prince he must show himself worthy by passing through an ordeal of the Temple.

Act III *Scene 1. A Palm Grove.* The priests meet to consider the case of the two lovers, and agree that they shall be united if the Prince can successfully undergo the ordeals. This will also prevent Pamina from falling under the evil influence of her mother. The chorus of priests with its deep harmony from the orchestra is unforgettable:

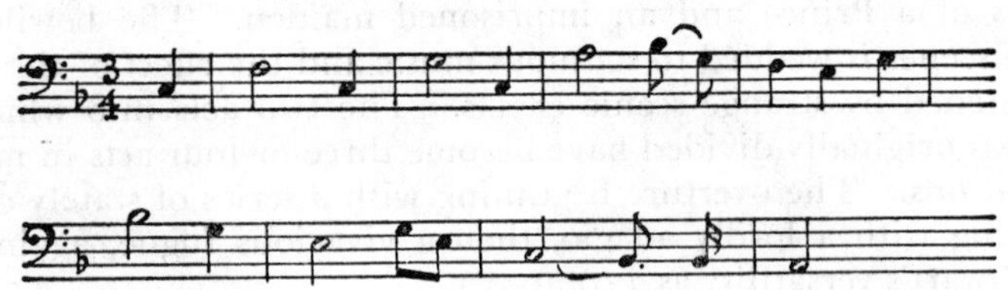

Scene 2. A Courtyard. The first ordeal is that of silence. Tamino and Papageno must not utter a word. The three attendants of the Queen of the Night now appear and tempt them, but they remain firm, though at great cost to Papageno.

Scene 3. A Garden. While Pamina is asleep the Moor approaches her, then conceals himself when her mother appears with a dagger, which the girl is commanded to employ against Sarastro. When the Queen is gone, the Moor returns and threatens Pamina, but is again foiled by Sarastro.

Scene 4. A Corridor in the Temple. Papageno and his master still continue under the ordeal of silence, which finally becomes too great a strain for the former. The Prince remains silent even when Pamina neets him and addresses endearing remarks. She is deeply wounded hat he does not reply.

Act IV *Scene 1. The Pyramids.* The Prince is commanded to wander out into the desert. He parts sadly from Pamina. Seeng the delights as well as the sorrows of love Papageno wishes for a little wife" of his own. An old hag appears before him. As he is bout to run away she changes into the young and pretty Papagena. But he, too, must first prove his worth.

Scene 2. The Desert. Pamina believes the Prince to be faithless nd is about to kill herself with the dagger, when she is prevented by he three pages. Papageno likewise is in the depths of despair over the oss of Papagena, but when he finds he can summon her by ringing his hime of bells his sorrow is turned into joy.

Scene 3. A Fiery Cavern. Tamino is seen undergoing the last of his rdeals. He is menaced by great waterfalls and tongues of flame. Beond these he beholds Pamina and calls to her, his lips now being unaled. The lovers are reunited and a few strains from the magic flute ause the remaining dangers to vanish.

This opera, which is full of difficult vocal passages, has none more xacting than that of Pamina: "All is vanquished"—

Scene 4. The Temple of Isis. Despite the interference of the Queen f the Night, the lovers have overcome their trials. The High Priest olemnly blesses them. While the clownish Papageno also finds hapiness in winning Papagena, the bird woman. The opera ends amid a laze of joyous melody.

LUDWIG VAN BEETHOVEN

Although Beethoven is recognized as one of the greatest, if not the eatest, musical composers of modern times, he produced only one era. He was born at Bonn, Germany, December 16, 1770. He died at Vienna, March 26, 1827. His works are numerous and in every vari ety of style—oratorios, chamber music, orchestral suites, vocal music and compositions for the pianoforte. It was Schikaneder, the librettis of Mozart's "Magic Flute," who first suggested to Beethoven that h compose an opera. The completed work, however, was produced unde the patronage of Baron Von Braun, who was then manager of th Theatre An Der Wien, Vienna, where the opera, "Fidelio," was firs sung.

FIDELIO

(Fee-day'-lee-o)

Dramatic Opera in Two Acts. Music by Ludwig Van Beethover Book by Joseph Sonnleithner, after Bouilly's "Leonore." Theatr An Der Wien, Vienna, November 20, 1805. In revised form, in Vienna May 23, 1814. In New York at the Park Theatre, September 9, 183 At the Metropolitan, January 11, 1891.

SCENE: A Prison near Seville.
TIME: The Eighteenth Century.

CAST
DON FERNANDO, *minister of state* (Baritone).
DON PIZARRO, *governor of prison* (Baritone).
DON FLORESTAN, *a noble prisoner* (Tenor).
LEONORA, *his wife, known as "Fidelio"* (Soprano
ROCCO, *jailer* (Basso).
MARCELLINA, *his daughter* (Soprano).
JACQUINO, *turnkey* (Tenor).
CAPTAIN OF THE GUARD (Basso).
Prisoners, Guards, Citizens, etc.

ARGUMENT "Fidelio" is of great interest not merely for i score during the action, but also for its overture Beethoven constantly experimented with these, writing four in al Three were entitled "Leonore," his original choice of name for th opera. All four are still in the active repertory of orchestras, and if th opera had been forgotten, they alone would show his mastery in th field. The theme itself is a touching story of conjugal love and fidelit

Act I *Courtyard of the Prison.* Don Florestan, a Spanish noblema incurs the hatred of Don Pizarro, governor of the prison, ar soon disappears from the world. Florestan's wife, Leonora, suspec that his enemy has hidden him away in one of the prison dungeons, ar disguises herself as a young man known as "Fidelio," and undertakes dangerous mission to rescue him. In an aria of sublime courage sl commits herself to this quest: "Sweet hope, forsake not this abiding heart!"

he enters service with Rocco, the jailer, and soon finds her husband, as he had feared. Meanwhile, she is in danger of discovery, as she wins he approval of the jailer and his daughter, Marcellina, and the latter alls in love with the handsome "young man," much to the sorrow of the urnkey Jacquino, who loves Marcellina. Fidelio cannot refuse the roffered match as she desires to keep on good terms with the jailer. Vord is received that the minister, Don Fernando, is coming to inspect he prison. This fills Pizarro with alarm and he resolves to put Flo-estan out of the way before that time. Rocco refuses to kill the pris-ner, but finally consents to dig the grave. Fidelio overhears the plans nd is in despair. She obtains the jailer's permission for the prisoners o file out into the courtyard to get the fresh air. She hopes thus to get ome message to her husband, but he does not appear with the rest, so he accompanies Rocco to dig the grave.

ct II *Scene 1. Florestan's Dungeon.* In one of the lowest cells of the prison, Fidelio finds her husband weak from exhaustion. Ie does not recognize her. She gives him food and drink, and with mulated cheerfulness helps to dig the grave. Before the task is ended izarro comes down eager to get his dangerous prisoner out of sight. 'he minister is coming. Pizarro is about to stab the prisoner, when idelio, or Leonora, throws herself in front of him crying: "First slay is wife!" She threatens him with a pistol and the cowardly governor ees. Trumpets from without announce the arrival of Don Fernando, hile Florestan clasps his wife in his arms and Rocco scratches his head bewilderment. The trumpet call, the climax to this scene, is lofty nd dramatic.

Scene 2. The Courtyard. Fernando quickly frees Florestan, and the chains are ordered upon Pizarro instead. The minister felicitates with the rescued man in having a "Fidelio" for his wife. Marcellina decides that Jacquino will make her a better husband, after all, greatl to the turnkey's delight.

CARL MARIA VON WEBER

A German composer, born in Eutin, Germany, December 18, 1786 His father was a musician and the boy inherited not only this talent, bu also painting and engraving. However, music was his grand passion and he began composing as early as twelve years of age. He went on tour with his father, and about 1803 paid his first visit to Vienna, wher he met Haydn. He became successively director of the opera at Pragu and Dresden. In 1821 he produced "Der Freischütz" at Berlin, wit great success. Five years later he superintended the première o "Oberon,"at London. But his career was cut short, this same year, b death, June 5, 1826. His other operas include "The Forest Maiden, and "Euryanthe."

DER FREISCHÜTZ

(*Dair Fry'-sheets*)

(The Sharpshooter.) Romantic Opera in Three Acts. Music b Weber. Book by Friedrich Kind, after an old legend in "Popular Tale of the 'Northern Nations.'" Berlin, June 18, 1821. At New York i the Park Theatre, in English, March 2, 1825. At the Metropolitan March 11, 1910, with Gadski, Alten, Jadlowker, Muhlmann, and Witherspoon.

SCENE: Bohemia.
TIME: Seventeenth Century.

CAST OTTAKAR, *Duke of Bohemia* (Baritone).
KUNO, *his head game-keeper* (Basso).
AGNES, *his daughter* (Soprano).

ANNA, *her friend* (Mezzo-Soprano).
MAX, *a ranger* (Tenor).
CASPAR, *a ranger* (Basso).
KILIAN, *a wealthy peasant* (Basso).
A HERMIT (Basso).
ZAMIEL, *the evil one* (Speaking part).
Foresters, Villagers, Followers of the Duke, Servants.

ARGUMENT The story of "Der Freischütz," or "The Sharpshooter," is based upon a Teutonic legend that magical bullets may be cast which never miss their mark.

The overture, an abiding concert favorite, is more widely known than the opera itself. It is full of singing melodies.

Act I *Estates of the Prince of Bohemia.* The advancing years of Kuno, head ranger of the Duke of Bohemia, make the choice of a new head ranger necessary. Max, who is in love with Agnes, Kuno's daughter, is a candidate for the place, but in order to obtain it he must win in a sharpshooting contest. At a preliminary trial, Max is unsuccessful, the peasant, Kilian, being the better marksman. Max is much cast down and therefore disposed to listen to the evil counsels of Caspar, who has already sold himself to the devil and who hopes to obtain respite by furnishing this new victim. Max is invited to try Caspar's gun, and is astonished to find that he can bring down an eagle from a great height. Caspar then tells him that he can obtain seven magical bullets which will hit any mark, but he must sell his soul for them. Max, undaunted, agrees to meet him at the Wolf's Glen at midnight.

Act II *Scene 1. Agnes' Room.* Agnes is filled with forebodings over the coming contest. She has met a hermit in the forest, who has warned her of impending danger. Then, while she and Anna are in her room, at the very moment when Max tries the magic bullet, an ancestral portrait falls to the floor. Anna tries to calm her fears. She is reassured by the appearance of her lover and sings the exulting melody first heard in the overture: "Ah, how my pulse is beating!"

However, the joy of their meeting is brief. Max confesses that he is under an obligation and must hurry away to an appointment at the Wolf's Glen.

Scene 2. The Wolf's Glen. Caspar awaits the arrival of his victim, and meanwhile tells Zamiel, the evil one, of his success. When Max arrives, the incantations are under way, and amid scenes of terror the magical bullets are cast.

Act III *Scene 1. Agatha's Room.* Agatha is being prepared for her wedding with Max. She is still filled with foreboding, which is not lessened by finding that a box of flowers contains a funeral wreath. She is comforted, however, by a bridal wreath which the holy hermit has blessed.

Scene 2. Duke Ottakar's Camp. The marksman's tourney is in progress, and is introduced by a rousing chorus in praise of hunting: "What so fine as a huntsman's life?"

Max amazes all the others by his skill. Only one remains of his store of magical bullets, and this one the fiend has in personal charge. The Duke orders Max to shoot at a dove flying through the forest. He obeys and a woman's shriek is heard. Agnes, in her wedding finery, has been struck; but she revives and it is found that the wreath blessed by the hermit has turned the bullet aside. The fiend, cheated of his prey, seizes upon the cursing Caspar, whose day of grace has expired. The horrified Max tells the story of the bullets and confesses his fault, whereupon the Duke imposes a year of penance before he can receive the post of head ranger or the hand of his bride.

EURYANTHE

(Yoo-ree-ahn'-thee)

Romantic Opera in Three Acts. Music by Weber. Book by Helmine von Chezy. Vienna, October 25, 1823. At New York, the Metropolitan, December 23, 1888, with Lehmann, Brandt, and Alvary.

SCENE: Castle Premery and Burg of Nevers, France.
TIME: 1110 A.D.

CAST Louis VI, *King of France* (Basso).
Adolar, *Count of Nevers* (Tenor).
Euryanthe of Savoy, *his betrothed* (Soprano).
Lysiart, *Count of Forest* (Baritone).
Eglantine von Puiset, *the captive daughter of a mutineer* (Mezzo-Soprano).

ARGUMENT The story of Euryanthe is adapted from an old French romance, entitled "The Story of Gerard of Nevers and the beautiful and virtuous Euryanthe." It is reminiscent of Shakespeare's "Cymbeline." The overture, which is divided into two parts, remains in active repertory and is better known than the opera; the theme of the latter being inane, the music "spotty."

Act I *Scene 1. A Hall in the King's Palace.* In the court of King Louis of France, Count Adolar pays a glowing tribute to the beauty and virtue of Euryanthe, his betrothed. All present applaud except Count Lysiart, who sneers at the chastity of women, and boasts that he could win Euryanthe. Adolar dares him to make the test, staking his fortune on the outcome. The King attempts to dissuade him from the foolish wager, but in vain.

Scene 2. The Palace Garden of Nevers. Euryanthe is discovered alone, but is soon joined by Eglantine, a captive maiden who is secretly in love with Adolar. In a moment of confidence, Euryanthe tells her the secret of a neighboring tomb, in which rests the body of Emma, her sister, who had poisoned herself, and whose ghost can find no peace until tears of innocent distress have been shed upon her ring. Eglantine decides forthwith to make use of this secret against Euryanthe, and takes Lysiart into her confidence when he presently arrives.

Act II *Scene 1. The Same Garden.* Lysiart has tried vainly to win the favor of Euryanthe, and now deplores his failure. When hope of winning his evil wager seems lost, Eglantine brings him Emma's ring from the tomb, to use as evidence of Euryanthe's infidelity.

Scene 2. The King's Palace. Euryanthe and Adolar appear at court. They are confronted by Lysiart, who claims to be the victor. He displays Emma's ring, and Euryanthe is visibly confused at this evidence that she could not keep the secret of her sister's death. Her confusion is taken by Adolar to be evidence of her guilt with Lysiart. He forfeits his lands and leaves the court in humiliation, taking Euryanthe with him.

Act III *Scene 1. A Forest.* Adolar has taken Euryanthe to the wilderness to slay her, but on the way is attacked by a huge serpent. The maiden tries to shield him with her own body. He kills the snake, and renounces his intention of harming her. However, he deserts her in the forest. The King and a band of hunters arrive and rescue her. To him she tells the whole story of Eglantine's treachery. The King takes her back to the palace.

Scene 2. Garden of the Castle of Nevers. Adolar repents his hasty belief in the guilt of Euryanthe, and returns to Nevers to challenge Lysiart. He meets the wedding procession of Eglantine and Lysiart, and in the encounter Eglantine confesses her duplicity and passion for Adolar. In a rage, Lysiart turns and stabs her. The King appears upon the scene, vindicates Euryanthe, orders Lysiart to the scaffold, and restores Adolar to his possessions. The two lovers are reunited, and the soul of Emma is at peace, as tears of innocent distress have been shed upon her ring.

OBERON

(Oh'-ber-on)

(Or, the Elf-King's Oath.) Fairy Opera in Three Acts. Music by Weber. Book by James R. Planché. Covent Garden, London, April 12, 1826. At New York, the Metropolitan, in English, December 28, 1918, with Althouse, Rosa Ponselle, Martinelli.

SCENE: Fairyland, France, Tunis, and Arabia.
TIME: Eighth Century.

CAST OBERON, *the Elfin King* (Tenor).
TITANIA, *his Queen* (Mute Character).
PUCK, *his messenger* (Contralto).
DROLL (Contralto).
HUON DE BORDEAUX (Tenor).
SCHERASMIN, *his esquire* (Baritone).
HAROUN EL RASCHID (Baritone).
REZIA, *his daughter* (Soprano).
FATIMA, *her slave* (Soprano).
PRINCE BABEKAN (Tenor).
EMIR ALMANSOR (Baritone).
ROSCHANA, *his wife* (Contralto).
ABDALLAH, *a pirate* (Basso).
CHARLEMAGNE (Basso).
Fairies, Soldiers, Pirates, Courtiers, Ladies of the Harem, etc.

ARGUMENT Weber's success with "Der Freischütz" had been so immediate, that he was asked to write "Oberon" for Covent Garden. The elfin theme with its graceful music gives no hint of the physical handicap under which he labored. His health had been steadily failing under the ravages of tuberculosis, and by the time of "Oberon's" first performance he was too ill to wield the baton as he and his countless admirers had hoped. The opera was a great success, the audience being captivated from the start with the fairylike overture, which is still a favorite with orchestras. But Weber survived its opening by less than two months. The story deals with elves and fairies.

Its melodious overture is still a prime favorite with orchestras: "Ocean, thou mighty monster!" has been sung most recently by Kirsten Flagstad.

FRIEDRICH VON FLOTOW

A German composer, born in Mecklenburg-Schwerin, April 26, 1812. He studied music in Paris but did not meet with success there in his early operas. At the age of twenty-seven he finally achieved recognition with "Medusa's Shipwreck." This was followed by "Camoen's Slave" (1843), and "The Soul in Pain" (1846). "Alexander Stradella," one of the few operas by which he is still remembered, had its première at Hamburg in 1844, and his most successful work, "Martha," at Vienna in 1847. He wrote several other operas, and was director of the court theatre in his native duchy from 1855 to 1863. He died in Darmstadt, January 23, 1883.

STRADELLA

(*Strah-del'-la*)

Romantic Opera in Three Acts. Music by Flotow. Book by W. Friedrich. Palais Royale Theatre, Paris, 1837; in revised form as "Alessandro Stradella," in Hamburg, December 30, 1844. At New York, the Metropolitan, also in the New Theatre, February, 1910.

SCENE: Venice and Rome.
TIME: Circa 1675.

CAST ALESSANDRO STRADELLA, *a musician* (Tenor).
LEONORA, *his bride* (Soprano).
BASSI, *a wealthy nobleman, her guardian* (Baritone).
MALVOLIO } *two desperadoes*
BARBARINO } (Baritones).
Priest, Friends, Servants.

ARGUMENT This opera preceded "Martha" in time, but was greatly overshadowed by the latter. It is remembered chiefly today as being by the composer of the more popular work.

Act I Stradella, a musician with a lovely voice, wins the hand of Leonora, ward of a wealthy nobleman, Bassi, who has planned to marry her himself. Aided by friends, Stradella captures the girl during a carnival and flees with her to Rome, where they are married. The infuriated grandee hires two desperadoes to find the singer and kill him. They secrete themselves in his home and later are admitted, posing as pilgrims.

Act II A tuneful quartet opens this Act, by Leonora, Stradella, and the two ruffians, in praise of Italy. So moved are the two villains by Stradella's wonderful voice, that they haven't the heart to murder him.

Act III Bassi, however, follows them up and tries to bribe them still further to carry out their evil project. Again they conceal themselves in his house. When he returns he rehearses a "Hymn to the Virgin," which he is to sing publicly, the next day. His melting tones again are too much for them. They implore forgiveness, and Bassi himself relents. The amazed Leonora, who now enters, unites with the group in a chorus of rejoicing.

MARTHA

Romantic Opera in Four or Five Acts. Music by F. von Flotow Book by St. Georges and Friedrich. Imperial Opera House, Vienna, November 25, 1847. In Italian and in English, London, 1858. At New York in Niblo's Garden, November 1, 1852, in English. At New York, the Metropolitan, April, 1887, with Patti.

SCENE: Richmond, England.
TIME: Reign of Queen Anne.

CAST LIONEL, *a farmer* (Tenor).
PLUNKETT, *his foster brother* (Basso).
LORD TRISTAN, *a courtier* (Basso).
LADY HENRIETTA DURHAM, *a maid-of-honor* (Soprano). *Also called* HARRIET.
NANCY, *her attendant* (Contralto).
SHERIFF OF RICHMOND (Basso).
Lords, Ladies, Farmers, Servants, Citizens.

ARGUMENT "Martha" at the end of a century of service is still one of the best loved operas. It is a "hardy perennial," delighting millions in the past and probably will continue to delight millions yet unborn. From the tuneful overture with its rounded horn solo as a dominant theme through to the last curtain the opera is a sure escape from the cares of the day. "Martha" is more Light than Grand, but the greatest singers have not disdained it. The plot is an old one—love opposed to pride, and pride finally vanquished.

Act I *The Queen's Court at Hampton.* Lady Henrietta, a maid-of-honor to Queen Anne, has become weary of humdrum court life and seeks a new diversion. She talks it over with her saucy maid, who tells her "of the knights so true and charming," but does not fall in with any of the latter's fancies. "That is really too distressing!" is the theme of a lively duet. Lord Tristan, an old admirer, meets with as little success when he proposes entertainments for the day. At this moment a group of villagers and servants pass singing gaily on their way to a county fair.

"Come away, maidens gay, to the fair let's repair!" they sing and their gay abandon strikes a responsive chord in the bored lady's heart. That's the very thing, she decides. She and her maid shall go also dressed as servants. What a lark! The shocked Tristan tries to dissuade her, but the willful lady persists; and he finds himself pressed into service as their unwilling escort.

Act II *The Richmond Market.* A chorus of villagers greets the girls seeking service: "Maidens bright and fair, draw near."

While they sing, two well-to-do farmers, Lionel and Plunkett, enter, in quest of servants. A mystery clouds Lionel's birth, as he indicates in his song, "Lost, proscribed."

The sheriff arrives and proclaims that all contracts for domestic servants shall be binding upon both parties for a full year, if money is advanced. Just after this announcement is made, Tristan arrives with the two girls dressed as servants, who immediately capture the fancy of the two farmers. In spite of Tristan's efforts to draw them away, they allow the farmers to haggle with them over terms and finally accept an advance payment for salaries. A pleasing quartet ensues: "Now indeed our love we may be taking."

Without knowing it, they have bound themselves to service for a year. When the farmers now insist upon an immediate departure, objections are raised by the other three. But the crowd prevents Tristan from rescuing the girls, and the sheriff declares that they must go with their new masters.

Act III *The Farm House.* Henrietta has taken the name of Martha; and Nancy that of Julia. Lionel and Plunkett try to introduce them to their duties as farm servants. Both are so ignorant, however, of the simplest tasks, that Lionel and Plunkett are in despair. The men try to teach them spinning, but are forced to seat themselves at the wheel, while Harriet admiringly sings, "What a charming occupation!" The Spinning Wheel quartet at this point is one of the gems of the opera. "Presto, presto!" whirls the melody.

But when the men ask, "Do you understand?" Nancy says, "Yes, we do," overturns the wheel and runs out, pursued by Plunkett. When "Martha" makes as if to follow, Lionel restrains her with, "Art afraid?" Then ensues a duet, "To his eye mine kindly meeting." She sees that despite her clumsiness in household matters he is falling in love with her. At first amused, she softens a little, and then sings the crowning aria of the opera, " 'Tis the last rose of summer."

The touching melody has a temporary effect, and the four bid one another a demure good night, in a quartet of rich harmony. The young women, however, by this time realize the predicament they are in. They must get away, and now. The faithful Tristan appears, with a waiting carriage. Out the window they go, to safety and their former station. The farmers find their servants gone and are overcome with grief and fury.

Act IV *A Country Tavern.* While Plunkett is drinking with some of his friends, a party of hunters from the court enter, and he recognizes among them his lost servant girl, "Julia," as she sings "Huntress fair." He demands that she go home with him and complete her contract, but her calls for help bring her friends about her and they chase Plunkett out into the forest. Next Lionel enters, greatly dejected over the loss of "Martha," when whom should he see among the hunters but the girl herself as a court lady. His song, "M'appari" (Like a dream) remains one of the most popular tenor arias.

Lionel stubbornly continues to claim "Martha," and she reproaches him for being an impertinent bumpkin. The others think him a madman, and she is glad to escape in this fashion. He sings in despair, "May Heaven grant you pardon."

Act V *Scene 1. The Farm House.* Lionel's long-standing claim to the earldom of Derby is decided in his favor, but he takes no interest in the matter. He is almost insane with grief. Henrietta is persuaded to visit him, but he does not recognize the "Martha" of his dreams. Nancy and Plunkett come to an understanding and arrange a little scene to restore Lionel's reason.

Scene 2. The Fair at Richmond. Another fair is being held, and Plunkett brings his friend to the square where they had first met the girls. Lo! there they are again, dressed in their servant's attire. Memory and reason return to Lionel, and when "Martha" sings again to him the ballad of the rose his cup of happiness is full. She is willing to become his wife.

RICHARD WAGNER

This foremost German composer, who created a school all his own, was born at Leipsic, May 22, 1813. When eight years of age he had acquired a passable knowledge of the pianoforte; and as a schoolboy he was fond of versifying—Shakespeare being his grand passion. At the age of twenty Wagner began his career as a professional musician, becoming chorus-master at the Wurzburg Theatre. Here he wrote his first opera, "The Fairies," which, however, was not produced until after his death. His next engagements were Königsberg and Riga, and in the latter city he began work on his first great success, "Rienzi," which was produced in Dresden (1842). Not long thereafter the composer was appointed one of the conductors of the Dresden Royal Opera. "Rienzi" was followed by "The Flying Dutchman" (1843); "Tannhäuser" (1845); "Lohengrin" (1850); the "Nibelung" dramas; "Tristan and Isolde," and "Die Meistersinger." Political and other troubles prevented Wagner from producing some of the later operas at the time when written. In fact, so different was his music from the accepted types, that his life was a crusade. His work is remarkable also from the fact that he wrote his own librettos, which reveal a dramatic skill and imagination of high order. His final opera was "Parsifal" (1882). Wagner died in Venice, February 13, 1883.

RIENZI

(Ree-en'-zee)

Grand Opera, in Five Acts. Words and Music by Wagner, after the historical novel, "Rienzi, the Last of the Tribunes," by Bulwer-Lytton. Dresden Opera House, October 20, 1842. At New York in the Academy of Music, 1878; the Metropolitan, February 5, 1886.

SCENE: Rome.

TIME: The Fourteenth Century.

CAST COLA RIENZI, *Roman Tribune and Papal Notary* (Tenor).

IRENE, *his sister* (Soprano).

STEFFANO COLONNA (Basso).

ADRIANO, *his son* (Mezzo-Soprano).

PAOLO ORSINO (Basso).

RAIMONDO, *Papal Legate* (Basso).

BARONCELLO } *Roman citizens* { Tenor.
CECCO DEL VECCHIO } { Basso.

MESSENGER OF PEACE (Soprano).

Ambassadors, Nobles, Priests, Monks, Soldiers, Messengers, and Citizens.

ARGUMENT This first opera of Wagner's, and one which he himself later turned his back upon, is yet a work of great force and beauty. Its theme is semi-historical.

The overture, which remains in repertory, sounds in a long trumpet tone the theme of popular uprising. This is followed by a quieter melody denoting the prayer of Rienzi; then the thunder of revolt; their interplay outlines the turbulent plot.

Act I *A Street in Rome.* Rienzi, a notary of lofty ideals, cherishes the hope of one day freeing his beloved city from the power of the insolent nobles. His anger against them is heightened by an attempted abduction of his sister Irene by Orsino, a patrician. Orsino is balked by Adriano, son of Colonna, another patrician, and of a family which has already wronged Rienzi's house. Adriano, however, is in love with Irene. During the tumult, Rienzi appears upon the scene, and urges the people to take up arms against the nobility. His cause is espoused by the Church, and is successful. The nobles are driven into flight.

Act II *The Capitol.* Rienzi is created Tribune, and the nobles are forced to pledge their allegiance. They secretly despise him, and Orsino, one of their party, tries to stab Rienzi. The latter's coat of mail thwarts the blow. The nobles who have taken part in this plot are condemned to death, but Adriano, who belongs to the Tribune's party, pleads for them, and Irene joins in his petition. They are pardoned.

Act III *A Public Square.* The nobles, far from experiencing a change of heart, are stirred on to fresh excesses. Although Rienzi is again victorious over them, it is at heavy loss of his own men. Adriano feels compelled to turn against the Tribune and side with his own family.

Act IV *A Public Square.* Adriano denounces Rienzi as a traitor. The credulous people begin to fall away from him. Irene alone clings to her brother, and scornfully repulses her lover when he tries to draw her from Rienzi's side. When the Tribune presents himself at the doors of the cathedral, he is met with a ban of excommunication, instead of a blessing.

Act V *The Capitol.* The Tribune is now in danger of his life. Adriano, seeing this, once more visits Irene to urge her and her brother to seek refuge in flight. But they will not do so. Rienzi appears on a portico to make one last appeal to the populace. The mob fires the building with torches, and hurls stones at Rienzi and his sister. When Adriano sees that they are doomed to death, he rushes into the blazing building, to perish with them.

THE FLYING DUTCHMAN

(Der Fliegender Hollander.) Romantic Opera in Three Acts. Music by Wagner. Book by the Composer, after Heine's version of the legend. Dresden, January 2, 1843. At New York in the Academy of Music, January 26, 1877. The Metropolitan, December 31, 1890.

SCENE: A Norwegian Fishing Village.
TIME: The Eighteenth Century.

CAST A DUTCH SEA CAPTAIN (Baritone).
DALAND, *A Norse Sea Captain* (Basso).
SENTA, *his daughter* (Soprano).
MARY, *her servant* (Contralto).
ERIC, *a huntsman* (Tenor).
DALAND'S STEERSMAN (Tenor).
Chorus of Maidens, Seamen, Villagers, etc.

ARGUMENT The legend of "The Flying Dutchman," condemned to sail the high seas for many centuries, finds a worthy musical and dramatic setting in this work of Wagner. According to this legend, a Dutch captain, foiled by contrary winds when rounding the Cape of Good Hope, takes a sacrilegious oath that he will succeed if he has to take eternity for it. Thereafter, for long centuries his ship is in charge of demons, who make it the sport of wind and wave. The opera deals with the lifting of the curse.

Like all of Wagner's operas, the overture is one of the dominant parts of the work. Here the composer gives a musical foreword to the piece: the stormy seas, the stubborn Dutchman laboring under a curse, the hint of redemption in Senta's voice, the final victory—all are foreshadowed.

Act I *A Bay in Norway.* Daland, a Norwegian sea captain, is driven by a violent storm to the shelter of a port. During the storm a strange-looking vessel also arrives, riding high upon the waves, and casts anchor alongside. The captain, a man of wild aspect dressed in black, steps ashore. He is the famous Flying Dutchman, whom all mariners fear and dread. By the terms of his oath, he is allowed to go ashore once in seven years, and if perchance he find a wife who will leave all for love of him, the spell will be released. He speaks with Daland, and finding that the latter has a daughter, asks permission to court her, at the same time offering Daland gold. The father's cupidity overcomes his scruples and, the storm having abated, the two vessels set sail in company.

Act II *The Home of Daland.* The curtain discloses a scene in sharp contrast to the preceding. Senta and her friends are busily spinning, the hum of the wheels blending with their voices in the most pleasing chorus of the opera.

Senta is a dreamy, romantic girl, who is already familiar with the strange story of the Flying Dutchman, and feels in her heart that she, at any rate, would be willing to give up all to save him. She tells the others of her wild resolve in a descriptive ballad:

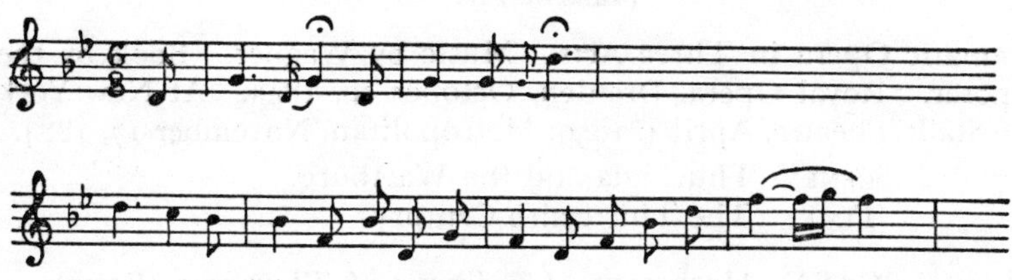

Eric the huntsman, who loves her, enters at this moment and warns her against her dangerous whim. He also tells her that a mysterious stranger is approaching with her father, but Senta is delighted and Eric leaves in dejection. Daland enters with the Dutchman, who gazes fixedly at the maiden and she at him. She readily accepts her father's plan for an early marriage, as she believes herself to be divinely appointed the savior of this sea rover. The two exchange vows of eternal fidelity, and the Dutchman believes his hour of liberation is at hand.

Act III *The Harbor.* The sailors on board Daland's ship give themselves over to merry-making. Girls bring them hampers of refreshments. The Dutchman's ship lies hard by, dark and silent, although his crew has been invited to share in the festivities. Finally they sing a mocking song of their captain's adventures, while the others listen in superstitious fear. Senta comes down to the shore followed by Eric, who makes one last plea for her to relinquish her folly and love him as she had formerly done. The stranger overhears this, and believing himself betrayed, bids her farewell and hastens on board his ship, ordering the anchor raised and all sails set. He admits publicly that he is the Flying Dutchman, upon whom a curse rests, and while Daland and the rest shrink back in horror the ship heads toward the open sea. But Senta tears herself away from Eric and her father, who would restrain her, and rushing to a cliff under which the vessel is passing, throws herself into the sea. Over the roar of the waves her last words ring out:

"Praise thou thine angel, for what he saith:
Here stand I faithful, even unto death!"

Instantly the curse is lifted, the phantom ship sinks beneath the waves, and from its shadow a tableau discloses the Dutchman and Senta ascending heavenward.

TANNHÄUSER

(Tahn'-hoy-zer)

Dramatic Opera in Three Acts. Music by Wagner. Book by the Composer. Royal Opera, Dresden, October 20, 1845. At New York in the Stadt Theatre, April 4, 1859; Metropolitan, November 17, 1884.

SCENE: Thuringia and the Wartburg.
TIME: The Thirteenth Century.

CAST HERRMANN, *Landgrave of Thuringia* (Basso).
TANNHÄUSER, *a knight* (Tenor).
WOLFRAM VON ESCHENBACH, *his friend* (Baritone).
WALTER VON DER VOGELWEIDE, *a knight* (Tenor).
BITEROLF, *a knight* (Basso).
REIMAR VON ZWETER, *a knight* (Basso).
HEINRICH, *a scribe* (Tenor).
ELIZABETH, *niece of the Landgrave* (Soprano).
VENUS, *goddess of love* (Soprano).
Retainers, Lords, Ladies, Bacchantes, Shepherd, etc.

ARGUMENT "Tannhäuser" deals with a legend of the Venusberg, a magic grotto in the mountains of Germany. Here the beautiful goddess of love holds court and beguiles any mortals who come her way. Tannhäuser, a Knight of Song, has fallen under her evil spell and dwelt several months with her in luxury and dissipation. But the remembrance of his former high station and the ties of earth still hold him, and when the scene opens he wishes to return to the light of day.

The overture, one of the loftiest, most descriptive, of the Wagnerian suite, interprets the theme: the solemn chant of the pilgrims; the voluptuous strains from Venusberg; the vision of the goddess herself; the minstrel's song of love; the far-off strains of the pilgrim's song, as of warning; the hint of repentance from the flesh—all prepare the auditor for the opening scene.

Act I *Scene 1. The Grotto of Venus.* Tannhäuser is growing weary of the blandishments of Venus and of the elaborate pageants which she prepares to entertain him. Amid the enchanting strains of the Bacchanale, the minstrel nevertheless strives to break away, to return to the world of men and women, but his request only makes her the more jealous of her waning power. She shows him new spectacles of beauty and luxury, but he only insists the more. Seeing that she cannot hold him an unwilling prisoner, she exacts from him a promise that he will sing her praises only, as against the merits of any earthly love. He gives this pledge as a means of escape, and the grotto and its occupants vanish from sight.

Scene 2. The Valley of Wartburg. Tannhäuser finds himself alone in the mountains of the Wartburg. In the distance a shepherd lad plays upon his pipe. By a mountain path stands a rude wayside cross, and presently a throng of pilgrims are heard singing as they go on their mission. After they have passed by, the Landgrave of the country and some of his nobles, among them Tannhäuser's loyal friend, Wolfram von Eschenbach, enter upon a hunting expedition. They recognize Tannhäuser and ask him many questions regarding his long disappearance. He evades their questions. Wolfram urges him to return to court, saying that Elizabeth, the Landgrave's niece, has long held his memory dear. The erring knight is filled with shame at the thought of this pure love which he has cast aside, and promises to return with his friends.

Act II *Hall of Wartburg Castle.* Elizabeth's joyful song of greeting opens this Act, "Dich teure Halle!" All is in readiness for the festival.

Wolfram enters bringing the errant knight, and Tannhäuser is delighted to find her still faithful to his memory. They pledge their love anew in a duet. Then comes one of the musical high spots, the Procession of Guests:

The minstrel knights are the last to enter, and the contest begins. Wolfram sings of love ennobling and spiritual, the highest type of bliss. But Tannhäuser, bound by his unholy promise to Venus, answers scornfully that such love is paltry compared with other delights which he might perchance reveal. Being pressed for an explanation by other angered knights, he launches into a wild song in praise of Venus. The court is horrified. The ladies leave in haste, and the knights press around the daring minstrel with drawn swords ready to kill him. Elizabeth throws herself before him and pleads for the unhappy man's life. They finally allow him to go unscathed on condition that he join the pilgrims, who now pass by on their journey to Rome, and there obtain the forgiveness of the Pope. The repentant Tannhäuser sets forth, amid the recurring strains of the Pilgrims' Chorus:

Act III *The Valley of Wartburg.* Several months have passed by without news of Tannhäuser. Both Elizabeth and Wolfram await him. Wolfram's friendship is unselfish, as he himself has long loved the maiden who pines over the wanderer's departure. The pilgrims return from Rome, and she comes to the wayside cross to look for him among them. But he does not appear, and, brokenhearted, she returns to the castle and soon dies. Wolfram enters, comparing her pure bright spirit to the evening star which shines upon him.

A haggard stranger now appears, who proves to be Tannhäuser returning without the Pope's forgiveness. The latter refuses to pardon him until his pilgrim's staff blossoms with leaves. Tannhäuser is ready to return to the haunts of Venus, and she now appears and beckons him. But Wolfram pleads with him and prevails upon him to deny her. He does so, and the vision vanishes. Mourners bring forward the bier upon which rests the body of the maiden, and while the troubled Tannhäuser kneels beside it, he dies. At this moment messengers come from the Pope, bearing the pilgrim's staff. A miracle has happened. The staff has put forth green leaves.

LOHENGRIN

(*Lo'-hen-grin*)

Romantic Opera in Three Acts. Music by Wagner. Book by the Composer. Weimar, Germany, August 28, 1850. At New York, Stadt Theatre, April 3, 1871; Metropolitan, November 23, 1885.

SCENE: The Scheldt, Flanders.
TIME: The Tenth Century.

CAST HENRY I, *King of Germany* (Basso).
FREDERICK OF TELRAMUND, *a nobleman* (Baritone).
ORTRUD, *his wife* (Contralto).
ELSA OF BRABANT (Soprano).
LOHENGRIN, *the Knight of the Swan* (Tenor).
HERALD (Baritone).
Courtiers, Soldiers, Citizens, Servants.

ARGUMENT The basis of "Lohengrin" is a legend connected with one of the Knights of the Holy Grail. These knights are pledged to aid the oppressed at any time, and it is in an adventure of this sort that the Knight of the Swan appears.

The music of this inspiring opera fits it "like a glove." The auditor is at once placed in rapport with the story from its opening theme in the Prelude or Vorspiel, which is repeated with many orchestral variations:

Working gradually up to a magnificent crescendo, the final chords crash as the curtain rises.

Act I *The Banks of the Scheldt.* According to ancient custom, the King of Germany holds a public outdoor court in which he hears complaints and tries all cases which may be brought before him. Frederick of Telramund, an unscrupulous nobleman, appears before this court and claims the Duchy of Brabant. He has been acting as regent during the minority of Godfrey and his sister Elsa, and now claims that the maiden has made away with her brother in order to seize the dukedom. Elsa is summoned to defend herself and declares her innocence. She is willing to leave the merits of her cause to a trial by combat, stating that she has seen in her dreams a resplendent knight who promised to come to her assistance. The arrogant Frederick says that he is ready to meet any champion and shakes his head scornfully while the Herald stations his trumpeters and Elsa sinks on her knees in prayer. Here occurs again the lovely, flowing melody known as the Elsa Motif:

The trumpets blare and the Herald announces: "He who by right of Heaven will come to fight for Elsa of Brabant, let him stand forth!" Silence. All watch in awe for any outcome. Elsa calls out imploringly: "My champion bides afar." Then a shout goes up. A swan is discerned in the distance, drawing a boat on which a figure stands erect. Nearer and nearer it comes until it stops near the throng, and a knight, clad in glittering armor, steps forth and announces himself as Elsa's champion. He speedily overcomes Frederick, but grants him his life, and asks Elsa's hand in marriage. Only one condition is interposed. She is not to ask the knight's name and whence he came. She consents and all rejoice at the happy outcome of events.

Act II *The Courtyard and Cathedral.* On the night before the wedding of Elsa and her champion, Frederick and Ortrud, his wife, wander into the deserted courtyard. They have been banished from the country, but Ortrud revives her husband's drooping spirits by her plans to deceive Elsa, whom she is to persuade to ask the forbidden questions. Elsa receives Ortrud out of pity and grants her shelter.

Morning dawns and the people assemble. When all is ready for the ceremony and Elsa and her attendants are about to enter the church, Ortrud steps forward and accuses the knight of being a magician. Frederick also mounts the church steps and proclaims his wrongs. But the knight is undaunted, and, Elsa once more declaring her confidence in him, the procession continues.

Act III *Scene 1. The Bridal Chamber.* This brilliant Act is preceded by the widely known "Introduction," a favorite piece with orchestras. It leads naturally to the famed, "Bridal Chorus," the procession of maidens seen as the curtain rises singing, "Brightest and best, we lead thee on!" Countless thousands of brides have gone to the altar with this lovely melody in their ears. The maidens are followed by Elsa and her knight. But the happy scene is marred. Elsa has been troubled by Ortrud's scoffing accusation, and she now begins to chide her husband for concealing his identity from her. He tries to prevent her from asking the fatal questions, but she persists. At this moment a band of conspirators, headed by Telramund, rush into the room, but the knight easily defeats them all and strikes Telramund dead. He then directs the attendants to carry the body to the king, and promises to follow and tell all.

Scene 2. The Banks of the Scheldt. The court of the king is again assembled as the monarch prepares to set forth for war. The body of Frederick is borne in, and the knight follows it. He defends his act and then in an aria of haunting loveliness at last reveals his identity. He is Lohengrin, a Knight of the Holy Grail and the son of Parsifal. Now he must return to the brotherhood, despite the tears of the penitent Elsa. The swan boat reappears, and as the knight kneels in prayer the swan disappears in the stream, and in its place steps forth Godfrey, Elsa's lost brother. Ortrud confesses that it was her magical arts which caused him to assume this shape. A fluttering dove takes the place of the swan and conveys the boat and Lohengrin on their return journey, while Elsa clasps her brother in her arms, but weeps for the loss of her husband.

THE NIBELUNGEN RING

(Der Ring des Nibelungen—"Nee'-bel-oong-en")

The "Ring" comprises four music-dramas: "Das Rheingold," "Die Walküre," "Siegfried," and "Götterdämmerung." Wagner, who wrote his own books, was familiar with the "Eddas" of Icelandic writers, but probably got his basic idea from another cycle, known as the Saga of Thedrek. The Nibelungen myth based on Teutonic mythology first began to take shape in his mind and on paper, in 1848. However, it was over twenty years until the first opera was produced, and with such revolutionary handling of orchestration and theme that it set a new and an advanced standard.

The entire cycle was first produced at Baireuth, August 13 to 17, 1876. In America it had its first complete presentation at the Metropolitan Opera House, during the week beginning March 4, 1889.

I

DAS RHEINGOLD

(Dahs Rine'-gold)

(The Rhine-Gold.) A Music-Drama in Four Acts. Music by Wagner. Book by the Composer. Munich, August 25, 1869, and authoritatively at Baireuth, August 3, 1876. American premiere at the Metropolitan, January 4, 1889, with Fischer, Alvary, and Moran-Olden.

SCENE: Germany and Upper and Nether worlds.
TIME: Antiquity.

CAST
WOTAN, *the mighty* (Basso).
FRICKA, *his spouse* (Mezzo-Soprano).
DONNER, *god of thunder* (Basso).
FRÖH, *god of rain* (Baritone).
LOKI, *god of fire* (Tenor).
FREYA, *goddess of love* (Soprano).
ALBERICH, *a dwarf* (Baritone).
MIME, *a dwarf* (Tenor).
WOGLINDE, WELLGUNDE, FLOSSHILDE, *Rhine-maidens*: Soprano. Soprano. Contralto.
FAFNER, FASOLT, *giants*: Basso. Basso.
ERDA, *spirit of the Earth* (Contralto).
Gods and Goddesses, Dwarfs, and Spirits.

ARGUMENT "Rheingold," the first of the four operas forming the "Ring" series, tells the story of how the magic ring came to be made, and how its curse rested upon all who came in contact with it, whether gods or men.

A Prelude of masterly musical description opens the work, its central notes the Motif of the Rhine. The horns and 'cellos give their mellowness to this strain, as the curtain rises to an underwater scene.

Act I *The Bottom of the River Rhine.* Down in the bed of the River Rhine a mass of pure gold has been hidden. It is magic treasure, conferring upon its owner boundless power, but whoever possesses it must forswear love. The three Rhine-maidens have been entrusted with the duty of guarding the gold, and they turn the task into a sport, singing and dancing among the grottoes beneath the water, but never venturing far from their charge. Their joyous cry, "Rheingold!" rings out through the waves:

But their careless boasts are short lived. Their song and the glitter of gold attract Alberich, lustful of wealth and power. He knows that once a Ring is fashioned from this precious metal, its owner would be master of the world. The music interpolates this in the Ring Motif. The foolish maidens coquet with him, but he pretends to be indifferent to their charms and to the treasure. Then come the sharp notes of the Nibelung Motif; the dwarf suddenly springs down, lays hands upon the gold, and scales the cliff. "Hark, ye fools!" he cries. "Love I renounce forever!" Amid screams of anguish from the Maidens, rock and waters vanish, leaving the dwarf triumphant.

Act II *The Gardens of Walhalla, Abode of the Gods.* The giants Fasolt and Fafner have built the beautiful castle Walhalla for the abode of the gods. Loki, the god of fire, who is the embodiment of deceit, has persuaded Wotan the mighty to accept the giants' terms for their labors. The Loki Motif which recurs is characteristic:

However, Wotan is dismayed to learn that the giants demand Freya, goddess of love, as their reward, and they now proceed to carry her off despite the entreaties of all the other immortals. Without the presence of Freya the flowers wither and die, the trees refuse to bear fruit, and the gods begin to grow old. The only way in which the giants can be induced to restore the goddess is by a bribe of the magic gold. Wotan and Loki go in search of this treasure, which is now jealously guarded by the dwarfs in the earth caverns.

Act III *The Dwarfs' Caverns.* Alberich gloats over his treasure, and to watch over it more carefully he has commanded Mime, the smith, to fashion for him a tarnhelm or invisible cap which enables him to assume any shape he pleases. He has also fashioned from the gold a Ring which confers upon its wearer power over gods and men. Wotan and Loki enter to confer with Alberich and he boastingly displays his powers by changing himself first into a dragon and then into a toad—the last at a sly suggestion from Loki. Wotan then quickly places his foot upon the toad, and will not release his squirming victim until he has given up all his treasures, including the cap and the Ring. Alberich, however, puts a curse upon all who shall hereafter wear the Ring.

Act IV *The Gardens of Walhalla.* The gods carry the gold in triumph to Walhalla, and the giants are summoned to the parley. They return with Freya, and the treasure is heaped before her to excite their cupidity. Wotan secretly hopes to retain the cap and the Ring but they insist upon these also and threaten otherwise to carry off the goddess again. Wotan is compelled to yield, although he foresees in the terms the ultimate destruction of the gods. The curse of the Ring is shown in an immediate quarrel between the giants, in which Fafner kills Fasolt. While the gods pass over a rainbow bridge to their new mansion of Walhalla, the voices of the Rhine-maidens are heard below lamenting their loss.

II

DIE WALKÜRE

(Dee Vahl-kee'-reh)

(The Valkyrie.) Music-Drama in Three Acts. Music by Wagner. Book by the Composer. Munich, June 24, 1870, and authoritatively ıt Baireuth, August 14, 1876. At New York, the Metropolitan, Januıry 30, 1885.

SCENE: The Forests of Germany.
TIME: Antiquity.

CAST
WOTAN, *the mighty* (Basso).
FRICKA, *his spouse* (Mezzo-Soprano).
HUNDING, *a warrior* (Basso).
SIEGLINDE, *his wife* (Soprano).
SIEGMUND, *her brother* (Tenor).
BRUNHILDE, *a Valkyr* (Soprano).
OTHER VALKYRIE (Sopranos and Contraltos).

ARGUMENT In order to understand the plot of "Die Walküre" as related to the "Ring," a certain amount of narative is necessary which is not represented upon the stage.

Wotan, foreseeing the doom of the gods because they are pledged to espect the power of the magic Ring, endeavors to protect Walhalla by reating a band of Valkyrie or warrior-maidens whose duty it is to carry n their winged steeds the bodies of the noblest warriors, slain upon the eld of battle, to the abode of the gods, where these warriors will live gain, a mighty race to defend Walhalla. Upon the earth, also, Wotan as begotten two children of his own, Siegmund and Sieglinde, who row up in ignorance of each other.

The tumultuous nature of the scenes about to unfold is evidenced by ıe musical Introduction, which depicts the fury of the elements. ightning flashes, thunder roars, and a wild wind sweeps around the ıt in the forest, upon which the curtain rises.

ct I *The Forest Hut of Hunding.* The abode of the warrior, Hunding, is built around the great trunk of a tree, which erces the center of the roof. Here Hunding dwells with his wife, eglinde, whom he has carried away from her home in childhood, against her will. She has been promised a protector, however, by a mysterious stranger who drives his sword up to the hilt in the ash; and the protector will be known by his ability to withdraw the weapon.

On the night when the scene opens, Hunding is away, and Sieglinde opens the door to an exhausted stranger who begs for food and drink. It is Siegmund, a mortal enemy of Hunding, who has taken refuge here against his foes. Hunding, returning, finds him here and allows him to stay for the night, but challenges him to combat the next morning. Meanwhile Siegmund and Sieglinde feel irresistibly drawn to each other. The Love Motif which recurs throughout the scene is its dominant theme:

They hide their affection, but as soon as Hunding retires, Sieglinde gives him a drug which induces deep sleep. The two, who have dis-covered that they are really children of Wotan, plan flight; but Sieg-mund is weaponless. "My father did promise me a sword," he cries As the Sword Motif rings out, a gleam of light from the dying fire fall upon the tree trunk within the hut—and there gleaming is the hilt o a sword! The Sword Motif gives way to a Song of Victory, as the war-rior with a triumphant shout easily draws the weapon from the oak (where it had been placed by Wotan). Again comes the Love Motif a a rush of wind sweeps wide the door, and the lovers flee into the night

Act II *A Mountain Pass.* The Prelude to this Act is a fusing of the themes in the preceding, then musical passages denoting the flight of the pair, and finally the ride and hail of the Valkyrs.

It has been the will of Wotan that his two earth children shall mee and mate, but he finds unexpected opposition to his plan from Fricka his wife. She is scandalized by this infraction of marital laws, and de-mands that he punish the guilty pair. He is finally prevailed upon t summon Brunhilde, his favorite among the Valkyr maidens, and h charges her to deliver over Siegmund to his enemy. The joyous shout o the Valkyrs: "Hoyo to ho! Hyah aha!" echoes through the pass, and th wild ride of the war maidens is heard, while clever stage setting depict their unearthly parade.

The courageous Brunhilde pleads with her father for the warrior, but in vain; she must on no account disobey this mandate even though she knows it is against the wishes of Wotan himself. She encounters the lovers in a mountain pass, whither they are being pursued by Hunding, and warns Siegmund of his fate; but resolves to shield him at any cost. Hunding now engages him in battle. The Valkyr protects Siegmund. Wotan appears and shivers Siegmund's sword, and the latter is slain by Hunding, who is struck down by Wotan. Brunhilde flees from the wrath of Wotan, carrying with her Sieglinde, whom she conceals.

Act III *Haunt of the Valkyrie.* Wotan goes forth to seek and punish his disobedient Valkyr. Brunhilde implores her sisters to help her, but they are fearful of Wotan's anger. They promise, however, to watch over Sieglinde. The latter is comforted by Brunhilde and told that she shall have a son who will prove the greatest of heroes; meanwhile she is to hide from gods and men, and preserve the broken bits of the sword of Siegmund. Wotan approaches and orders Brunhilde to stand before him. A stormy and pathetic scene ensues, in which he at first consigns her harshly to a fate worse than death. Her pleadings and his harsh answers afford some of the most dramatic musical passages of the opera. Then he mitigates her sentence. Touching her with his staff she falls into a deep slumber. High on a cliff he places her body and summons Loki, the tricky god of fire. "Loki! Loki!" he shouts, "hear me and heed!"—and strikes the rock with his sword. Instantly little tongues of flame appear and circle upward until at last the sleeping war maiden is completely encircled by the fire. "Only a hero will dare this fiery height," is Wotan's last decree. The curtain falls

amid the strains of the lovely Fire Music—in the opinion of many, one of the supreme melodies of the great composer.

III

SIEGFRIED

(Seeg'-freed)

Music-Drama in Three Acts. Music by Wagner. Book by the Composer. Baireuth, August 15, 1876. American premiere, at the Metropolitan, November 9, 1887, with Brandt, Alvary, Ferenczy, and Fischer.

SCENE: The German Forests.
TIME: Antiquity.

CAST WOTAN, *the Wanderer* (Basso).
SIEGFRIED, *the hero* (Tenor).
MIME, *the smith* (Tenor).
ALBERICH, *the dwarf* (Basso).
FAFNER, *the dragon* (Basso).
BRUNHILDE, *a Valkyr* (Soprano).
THE WOOD BIRD (Soprano).

ARGUMENT "Siegfried" continues the story of the Ring at a period some twenty years later than the events of "Die Walküre."

As Brunhilde has foretold, Sieglinde bears a son to the slain Siegmund, and she also dies at the child's birth. He is sheltered by Mime the dwarf, who teaches him the smith's trade. But Siegfried, as he is called, has the blood of warriors and hunters in his veins, and soon domineers over the craven fellow.

The quieter music which precedes this third part of the Ring is in welcome contrast to the stormier music of "Die Walküre." Now we listen to the voices of nature; and intermingled with them, the familiar motives of the Ring, the Sword, the Curse, the dawning Love.

Act I *The Forest Forge of Mime.* On Siegfried's reaching manhood, one of the first tasks which he imposes upon Mime, the dwarf, is to forge for him an unbreakable sword. This the coward tries vainly to do; every one he offers his young master is shivered. As the scene opens, the horn of Siegfried is heard in the distance:

In dashes the hunter with the carcass of a bear, to the dismay of the dwarf, who sees more trouble. The musical theme changes to the Joy of Life Motif. "How have you done?" demands Siegfried; and when the smith timidly brings out another sword, his master shatters it also upon the anvil. Meanwhile, the fragments of Siegmund's sword have been preserved, and the next time the young hunter is absent, Wotan appears and informs Mime that Siegfried himself must forge the new weapon. The dwarf, more frightened than ever, decides that he cannot withstand the hand of fate. He gives over the smithy to the hunter, tells him the secret of his birth, and yields the sword fragments. Now at last the hero knows the task before him. Joyously he fashions his sword from the pieces of the old, singing lustily as he labors the Sword Song: "Nothung! Nothung!—Helpneed! Helpneed!"

Act II *The Forest before the Dragon's Cave.* During all these years Fafner has guarded the magic gold jealously. To do so better, he has assumed the form of a dragon, who dwells within a cavern in the depths of the forest. On the outside loiters Alberich, the greedy dwarf, still trying to regain the treasure. Wotan finds him here and warns him that a hero is coming who is stronger than them all. Meanwhile Siegfried has been told of the dragon by Mime, who endeavors thus to frighten him, but the news only fires the young man's spirit, and he resolves to christen the new sword in a combat with Fafner. On his way thither the Wood Bird sings to him warningly, but Siegfried does not understand and goes on his way. The orchestra meanwhile plays a pleasant interlude of "Forest Murmurs." He summons Fafner from his lair and in the fight kills him. A drop of the dragon's blood touches his tongue, and instantly he understands the wood voices. The Bird has told him that Mime is trying to poison him. He is also told of the magical properties of the Ring, which he puts on. He kills Mime, and follows the Bird, who tells of other adventures in store. "Ho, Siegfried, hero, listen!" the Bird chants. "A glorious maid lies sleeping on a mountain top! Only a hero may break through the fire that encircles her." "Oh, Bird, lead on!" challenges Siegfried. And together they make their way up the mountain.

Act III *A Mountain Pass.* Erda, the earth spirit, has warned Wotan of the impending doom of the gods. He therefore resolves to stop Siegfried in his journey up the mountain. But the latter, undaunted, shivers the great Wotan's spear with his sword, Helpneed, and Wotan stands aside, knowing that the progress of events cannot be stayed. Neither is Siegfried deterred by the wall of flame which encircles the peak. He pushes through it and it dies away, leaving him unscathed. He finds Brunhilde in her warrior's garb, and awakens her. The music of this climactic scene culminating in Brunhilde's awakening rises to sublime heights:

It is followed by Motives of Greeting, Passion, and Peace, denoting the mutual rapture of meeting. The awakened Brunhilde, delighted with the identity of her rescuer, willingly foregoes her immortal qualities to become his wife.

IV

GÖTTERDÄMMERUNG

(Gur-ter-dem'-mer-oong)

(The Dusk of the Gods.) Music-Drama in a Prelude and Three Acts. Music by Wagner. Book by the Composer. Baireuth, August 16, 1876. In America with the "Ring" at the Metropolitan, 1889.

SCENE: The German Forests.
TIME: Antiquity.

CAST
SIEGFRIED, *the hero* (Tenor).
BRUNHILDE, *the Valkyr* (Soprano).
GUNTHER, *a king* (Baritone).
GUTRUNE, *his sister* (Soprano).
ALBERICH, *the dwarf* (Basso).
HAGEN, *his son* (Basso).
VALTRAUTE, *a Valkyr* (Mezzo-Soprano).

THE NORNS, *spinners of fate* (Mezzo-Sopranos).
THE RHINE-MAIDENS (Sopranos).

ARGUMENT The last of the Ring, "Götterdämmerung," brings to a close the adventures and fates of the hief characters. The downfall of the gods, long foretold, is at hand, nd the Ring of the Curse completes its fatal mission.

relude The Norns, who control the fates of both men and gods, weave their thread of life, and it breaks. They know by this oken that the destruction of all things is near. Siegfried departs from Brunhilde in order to go upon new adventures, but meanwhile gives er the Ring to wear while he is gone. He takes with him the Tarnelm, or invisible cap, and Helpneed, the sword, and Brunhilde lends im her horse to ride.

The interwoven music is reminiscent of much that has gone before. Ve hear the Siegfried Motif, and that of Brunhilde. The leave-taking etween the two is long and tender, and as he rides on his further mision, the notes of his horn are heard.

ct I *Scene 1. Gunther's Court.* Siegfried proceeds to the court of Gunther, a powerful king, who welcomes him cordially. Haen, the cunning son of Alberich, is one of the court, and knowing of iegfried's deeds, he brews the hero a drink which causes him to forget ll his past. The Motif of Forgetfulness is sounded by the French orns. It gives way to the Gutrune Motif. The memory of Brunhilde ades away, and he asks of Gunther the hand of his fair sister Gutrune n marriage. The King consents on condition that Brunhilde is secured or himself, and the forgetful Siegfried agrees to go with Gunther and ompel her to yield.

Scene 2. A Mountain Pass. While Brunhilde awaits the return of er warrior, Valtraute, another Valkyr maiden, comes to plead with her restore the Ring to the Rhine-maidens. Thus only can the gods be pared from destruction. But Brunhilde answers scornfully that the ods have not been kind to her, and besides the Ring is not her own. y means of the Tarnhelm, Siegfried assumes the shape of Gunther, and omes to claim Brunhilde as his wife. She struggles against him but is verpowered, and he wrests the Ring from her finger. She is compelled follow him back to Gunther's court.

ct II *Gunther's Court.* The King publicly proclaims Brunhilde as his Queen, and gives Siegfried the hand of Gutrune. Brunlde cannot understand this arrangement and suspects treachery when e sees the Ring on Siegfried's hand. She upbraids him for fickleness d falseness, but he is still under the influence of the drug and pays little heed to her. Her former love turns to rage and she listens will ingly to Hagen's plots to kill Siegfried. Hagen believes that he can thu secure the Ring for himself. They falsely tell Gunther that Siegfrie has been unfaithful with respect to Brunhilde; and the King finall agrees to his destruction.

Act III *Banks of the River Rhine.* While Siegfried is out upon hunting expedition, the Rhine-maidens beseech him to re store the Ring to them, telling him that thus only can he escape death But Siegfried is fearless and will not yield it up under a threat Gunther, Hagen, and other hunters join him, and while they rest the ask Siegfried to relate his adventures. The drug has begun to wea off and Siegfried tells of his past. When he comes to the meeting wit Brunhilde, he stops, puzzled, to watch the flight of some ravens. A this moment Hagen drives his spear in between Siegfried's shoulder and the latter falls dying. But his memory is clear and he calls fo Brunhilde. Both Hagen and Gunther try to seize the Ring, and in th struggle the King is killed. The retainers are in an uproar. Gutrun bewails the loss of her husband and her brother. But Brunhilde, wh has learned the truth, comes in and bids the tumult cease. She orde a funeral pyre to be built, and the body of Siegfried to be placed upon i Mounting it, she also is consumed. The waters of the Rhine rise an engulf all, including Hagen, who has tried to seize the Ring, and th cursed emblem is at last restored to its rightful owners. In the sky great blaze is seen. It is the destruction of Walhalla with all the god

Throughout these closing scenes of tragedy, the music skillfully ai the description. Theme after theme interplays, even the lighter not of the Rhine-maidens, while distant rumblings of thunder herald th Twilight of the Gods. Then as they sit in solemn array awaiting the doom, the music mounts with the flames. It is the Downfall of Wa halla.

This in turn gives way to a more peaceful note. "A new day is hand!" announces the arpeggio notes of the orchestra. ("The Dawn Peace.")

TRISTAN UND ISOLDE

(*Tris'-tahn oont Ee-sohl'-deh*)

Tragic Opera in Three Acts. Music by Wagner. Book by the Com-oser. Munich, June 10, 1865. At New York, the Metropolitan, De-mber 1, 1886.

SCENE: Cornwall, Brittany, and the Sea.
TIME: Antiquity.

CAST
MARK, *King of Cornwall* (Basso).
ISOLDE, *his Queen* (Soprano).
TRISTAN, *a knight* (Tenor).
KURVENAL, *his servant* (Baritone).
MELOT, *a knight* (Baritone).
BRANGAENE, *Isolde's servant* (Contralto).
STEERSMAN (Tenor).
SHEPHERD (Tenor).
Courtiers, Knights, Servants.

ARGUMENT The story of "Tristan and Isolde" is adapted from a romance by Gottfried of Strasburg, telling of the nflict between love and duty in the hearts of two lovers of medieval ys.

As in the preceding dramas of the Ring, the music is an integral part the theme. The Prelude prepares the auditor for the plot—a series highly emotional passages dwelling upon mutual love, confession, sire, renunciation. It shares with the concluding love scene in pop-ar appeal.

t I *On Shipboard.* Tristan, a valiant knight, has been involved in many adventures. In Ireland he has met the beautiful Princess lde, and incurred her enmity by killing Morold, an unworthy knight, o was her betrothed. Tristan also was wounded, and the maiden's art softened toward him as she nursed him back to life. He after-rds gives so glowing an account of her charms, that his royal master,

King Mark of Cornwall, desires her for his wife; and Tristan is sent t conduct her to Cornwall. The Princess comes most unwillingly as sh secretly prefers Tristan, but his lips are sealed on account of his missio On shipboard he treats her with the most scrupulous courtesy, but wi not allow himself to come under her influence. She sends her attend ant, Brangaene, to summon him, but he makes excuses. Angere Isolde orders Brangaene to brew a deadly poison for Tristan, and whe he finally appears in answer to her repeated requests, she asks him t drink a toast. Tristan neither knows nor cares as to the nature of th drink, but takes it without protest. She purposes to drink also and thu perish with him. But Brangaene has brewed a love potion instead and the two, after drinking, look into each other's eyes with their mu tual passions increased tenfold. (Love Theme.)

Act II *The Castle of King Mark.* Tristan despairingly complete his mission and conducts Isolde to the King. But the tw lovers plan a last meeting, and Melot, who has pretended to be Tristan friend, arranges a hunting expedition, in order to draw the King an his retainers from the castle. It is night, and Tristan is summoned b a torch in Isolde's window. Brangaene keeps watch from the towe In the midst of their bliss, the lovers are warned by her that the King returning; and Kurvenal, Tristan's servant, also rushes in warning hi to flee. But it is too late. Melot has betrayed his friend, and Kin Mark confronts the guilty pair in dignified surprise. Tristan is ove whelmed with shame, but when Melot makes a sneering remark, h draws his sword. The two fight and Tristan falls wounded.

The high point in this scene is the love duet: "Nacht der Liebe"-

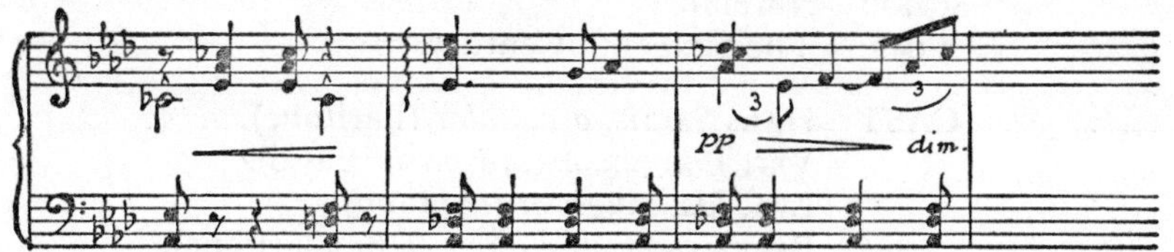

Act III *Scene 1. A Castle Ruin in Brittany.* The wounded knight is allowed to depart by the generous King, and is conveyed by Kurvenal to a deserted castle on the coast of Brittany. But his anguish of soul and desire for Isolde prevent his wound from healing. In despair, Kurvenal sends to Isolde, who is also skilled in drugs. She answers that she will come in person, and the sick man is buoyed up by this hope. At last her ship is sighted—it nears the shore—and she lands. With a final effort Tristan rises to meet her, only to sink down exhausted and die in her arms.

The Liebestod, or Death Music, of this scene, where Isolde pours out her grief over the dead Tristan, is now considered the supreme achievement of the composer. Its recurring theme of a love that can triumph over death itself is a classic of sublime pathos:

Scene 2. The Same (usually omitted). King Mark and Melot follow Isolde. Kurvenal opposes their entrance and kills Melot, himself receiving a death wound. The King learns from Brangaene of the love potion and hopeless passion of the two lovers whom he has separated, and feels only remorse for their fate.

DIE MEISTERSINGER

(Dee My'-ster-singer)

(The Master-Singers.) Comic Opera in Three Acts. Music by Wagner. Book by the Composer. Munich, June 21, 1868. At New York in the Metropolitan, January 4, 1886.

SCENE: Nuremberg.
TIME: The Sixteenth Century.

CAST
HANS SACHS, *a cobbler* (Baritone).
VEIT POGNER, *a goldsmith* (Basso).
EVA, *his daughter* (Soprano).
BECKMESSER, *the town clerk* (Baritone).
KOTHNER, *a baker* (Basso).
WALTER VON STOLZING, *a Knight* (Tenor).
DAVID, *apprentice to Sachs* (Tenor).
MAGDALENA, *maid to Eva* (Contralto).
WATCHMAN (Baritone).
Master-singers, Villagers, Servants, etc.

ARGUMENT "Die Meistersinger" is the only comic opera that Wagner wrote. It deals with a historic time in Nuremberg when all the tradespeople wrote verses and indulged in singing contests, and may be regarded as Wagner's protest against artificiality.

The "Prize Song" is undoubtedly the mainmast which holds up the swelling canvas of "Die Meistersinger." The overture contains hints of it; it is rehearsed in the Third Act, as both an aria and a quintet; and its closing notes form the climax of this pleasing opera.

Act I *Interior of St. Catherine's Church.* The whole town of Nuremberg is music-mad. The master-singers, or head men in this noble profession, hold public contests governed by rigid rules, and the victors are richly rewarded. Veit Pogner, the goldsmith, finally announces that at the next contest he will bestow his daughter's hand upon the successful man. Beckmesser, the town clerk, is overjoyed at this, as he has long courted the fair Eva, and thinks he can easily win the contest. But Eva has had no eyes for the clerk. She has noted the respectful attentions of a young nobleman, Walter von Stolzing, who has met her at the Church and elsewhere. Hearing of the contest, Walter resolves to enter it and is instructed in the rules by David, the apprentice of Hans Sachs. But when Walter first appears before the master-singers, Beckmesser keeps the score and marks down so many mistakes that the young man is ruled out. Hans Sachs, the cobbler, is the only one who speaks in his favor.

Act II *A Street in Nuremberg.* On one side is Sachs' cobbler shop; on the other, Pogner's house. Eva finds an opportunity to meet Walter and console him for his lack of success. She says that she will not abide by her father's wishes, if some one else wins, but will elope with him. They hasten to conceal themselves as Beckmesser comes out to sing a serenade under Eva's window. But the serenader is interrupted by the hammering and singing of Sachs in his shop. Then David appears and mistaking the attentions of Beckmesser as being directed to his own lady-love, he pounds the clerk over the head. Their cries draw the whole village upon the scene and a small-sized riot is in progress, which ends as suddenly as it began, when the watchman's voice is heard down the street.

Act III *Scene 1. The Cobbler's Shop.* While Sachs and his apprentice are at work, Walter comes in greatly elated. He says that he has dreamed a song so beautiful that, if he can set it down, it will win the prize. As he voices it, Sachs is enchanted. "Wonderful!" he exclaims, and proceeds to write it down. Beckmesser learns of this famous song and steals the manuscript, planning to sing it as his own. Eva comes in to try on some new shoes, and all plan for the coming contest.

Scene 2. An Open Field. The morning of the songfest has arrived, and the different trade guilds bring forward their noted singers. Sachs alone champions Walter, who is not concerned over the loss of his manuscript. His song is superior to the master-singers' rules anyway. Beckmesser tries to sing the stolen song, but his memory proves treacherous and he makes a laughable jumble of it. Walter is grudgingly allowed to follow and speedily wins all his hearers by his song. He is accorded the prize, and Pogner bestows upon him the hand of the happy Eva. (Prize Song.)

PARSIFAL

(Par'-tsee fal)

Music-Drama in Three Acts. Music by Wagner. Book by the Composer after the epic by Wolfram von Eschenbach. Baireuth, July 22, 882. At the Metropolitan Opera House, New York, December 24, 903.

Scene: Montsalvat, in the Mountains of Spain.
Time: The Middle Ages.

CAST Amfortas, *Keeper of the Grail* (Baritone).
Titurel, *his father* (Basso).
Gurnemanz, *Keeper of the gate* (Basso).
Parsifal, *the guileless one* (Tenor).
Klingsor, *a magician* (Basso).
Kundry, *his accomplice* (Mezzo-Soprano).
Knights of the Grail, Flower Maidens, Servants, Villagers.

ARGUMENT This closing work of Wagner's is the most deeply religious of all. For a period of years it was held sacred to the precincts of Baireuth; in fact, save in concert form it was not given elsewhere until its New York presentation, in 1903 (a "Christmas piece")—over twenty years after its initial performance.

The title "Parsifal" is familiar to hearers of "Lohengrin," for that knight finally tells Elsa that he is Parsifal's son. The present story is embedded in the legend of the Holy Grail, the cup which Christ blessed and which caught the blood from his wounded side. Both the cup and the spear which wounded him were found by Titurel and his Knights of the Grail, who founded a temple for their service at Montsalvat, in the mountains of Spain.

In his old age, Titurel appointed his son, Amfortas, as Keeper of the Grail. Klingsor, a magician, angered at not being elected a Knight, created an enchanted castle and garden near by. He compelled Kundry, a woman who had laughed at Christ and was condemned to wander until her sin was expiated, to aid him. Kundry tempted Amfortas, who turned aside and was wounded by Klingsor with the sacred spear.

The overture is based upon three religious motifs which recur in the work: the Sacrament, the Grail, and Faith. Later it becomes agitated foreshadowing the remorse of Amfortas.

Act I *The Forest at Montsalvat.* Gurnemanz, keeper of the gate tells of the grievous condition of Amfortas. The wound made by Klingsor refuses to heal and is doubly painful when Amfortas tries to celebrate holy communion. For this reason the Temple service is being neglected. Amfortas is borne in on a litter in search of healing springs and Kundry, who has repented her share in his woe, comes in bearing a balsam which she has obtained with great difficulty. But it is written that he can find relief only from the touch of the sacred spear in the hands of the Guileless One, and him they await. Gurnemanz repeat the prophecy of the oracle: "By pity lightened, the guileless fool; wait thou for him, my chosen tool" (The Prophecy):

The song is interrupted by a cry of dismay from the near-by lake; then a wounded swan falls to the ground. A half-grown lad, unmindful of the anger he has caused by this desecration of the sacred grounds, comes in blithely to claim his quarry. The fine Parsifal Motif, lofty and joyous, heralds his entrance:

The boy's triumphant mood changes to one of penitence when Gurnemanz reproves him, telling him that he is little better than a murderer. The old keeper then relents and, struck by the boy's demeanor, takes him into the service of the Temple. Now follows a dramatic scene portrayed by both action and music. The lovely Bell Motif is heard, also that of Amfortas' Contrition. The latter again shrinks from his duty of uncovering the Grail, but when he finally does so, an unearthly light streams down from the dome above. Again in a chant the words of the oracle are heard: "By pity lightened, the guileless fool—" The strange lad, however, stands silent, unmoved through the rites. "Don't you know what it is all about?" demands Gurnemanz. The youth shakes his head. "Oh, you are only a fool!" exclaims the old knight in disgust. "Begone, and instead of hunting swans, join the geese where you belong!"

Act II *The Castle of Klingsor.* Several years have passed. The magician is greatly alarmed over tidings that a fearless young knight is coming, who has put his enemies to flight on every side. It is Parsifal grown to manhood. Klingsor summons Kundry to his aid, who obeys him most unwillingly. The castle sinks from view and in place of it are seen enchanting gardens in which the Flower Maidens dwell. As Parsifal comes by the garden, they sing to him seductively; but he turns a deaf ear to them. The Parsifal Motif, again heard, gives way to a lovely Flower Melody:

Then Kundry appears, a dazzling vision of loveliness, and bids him stay until she tells him of his parents, whom he does not remember. He tarries and she relates that he is the son of King Gamuret, slain in battle, and that his mother brought him up as an ignorant peasant in order to keep him from becoming a warrior. His mother—says Kundry—entrusted her with a last message and kiss. With this the enchantress leans over and presses a burning kiss on the young knight's lips; it was in this way that she had formerly betrayed Amfortas. Realizing his danger, Parsifal springs to his feet. Kundry summons the magician to her aid. Klingsor hurls the sacred spear at the knight, but he seizes it in mid-air and strikes Klingsor dead. The gardens vanish and only Kundry is left, an old woman, crouching upon the ground in terror.

Act III *Scene 1. Montsalvat.* Years pass by. Gurnemanz, though grown old, is still the keeper of the gate, and Amfortas is still a sufferer from his grievous malady which will not heal nor let him die. The penitent Kundry lingers about the Temple as a hewer of wood and drawer of water. A strange knight appears, faint and weary from his journeys. It is Parsifal who has completed his self-imposed mission. He kneels in prayer, the sacred spear thrust before him in the soil. Gurnemanz recognizes in him the Guileless One whom he thrust rudely out of doors as a boy, and now ministers to him; while Kundry kneels and washes his feet. He baptizes her. The Temple bells sound for the noonday service, and they array Parsifal in the white robes of a Knight of the Grail.

Scene 2. The Temple Interior. The aged Titurel, father of Amfortas, wishes to see the Holy Grail unveiled once more before he dies, but the pain-racked King shrinks from the task. He begs his knights to kill him and thus remove the curse. At this moment Parsifal enters bearing the spear. He touches the wound of Amfortas and it heals immediately. Parsifal then announces that he has been sent to take charge of the Grail, and he proceeds with the services. As the Grail is uncovered and held aloft, the aged Titurel expires with a smile upon his lips. The Temple is flooded with light, and a dove descends and alights upon Parsifal. Kundry, who has crept in unnoticed, falls at his feet and also dies—redeemed.

The music of this entire scene, with its floating, exquisite arpeggios, lifts the hearer literally up "on wings of song." The heavenly strains persist and die softly in the heights, as the final curtain slowly descends upon the lofty Motif of Faith:

VICTOR NESSLER

Nessler was widely popular during his lifetime, but has since become almost forgotten, unless in Germany. He was born in Baldenheim, Alsace, January 28, 1841, and died in Strassburg, May 28, 1890. He wrote many songs and choruses, chiefly for male voices. Of his operas, beginning with "Fleurette" (1864), only two are now in occasional repertory: "The Piper of Hamelin" (1879) and "The Trumpeter of Säkkingen" (1884).

THE PIPER OF HAMELIN

An Opera in Five Acts. Music by Nessler. Book by Fr. Hofmann, from the legend by Julius Wolff. The story is somewhat similar to Robert Browning's later "Pied Piper of Hamelin," where the piper undertakes to rid the town of a plague of rats. He does so by playing on his pipe, and the rats follow him in droves to the river and are drowned. But when Hunold Singuf, the piper, claims his reward and a kiss from the lips of the Burgomaster's daughter, Regina, they condemn him to death as a sorcerer. Hunold then plays one final aria. The citizens dance in spite of themselves; and the children follow him, just as the rats had done. Piping, he leads them straight into a mountain-side which opens and swallows them up forever.

THE TRUMPETER OF SÄKKINGEN

(Der Trompeter Von Säkkingen.) Opera in Prologue and Three Acts. Music by Nessler; text by Rudolf Bunge, after Victor von Scheffel's poem with the same title. Produced, Leipzig, May 4, 1884. At New York, the Metropolitan, 1888.

SCENE: Germany.
TIME: Recent.

ARGUMENT This plot follows the familiar lines of a mysterious hero, who is found to be a missing nobleman Werner, an unknown trumpeter, wins the favor of Maria, daughter of the Baron von Schonau. Her aunt, Countess of Wildenstein, is also attracted by the young man, but is also suspicious of him. She watches the two young people zealously, while Werner gives Maria music lessons. Damian, the Count's son, a cowardly fellow, has been destined to be Maria's husband; but after a peasant uprising in which he plays the coward, and Werner, the hero, the latter is found to be the long-lost son of the Countess, and he and Maria are united.

The bright music relieves a somewhat stodgy story. The Prologue and First Act bring in a serenade and trumpet strains; a stirring chorus by students and troopers; festival dances; and a charming lyric by Maria: "How proud and grand his bearing!"

In the Second Act we hear: an aria sung by Werner, "On shore played me a merry tune"; a duet between him and Maria, "Sun, has th light not grown in splendor?"; a quintet, "Must so soon the sunshine vanish?"; and Werner's sentimental farewell, "Oh, it is sad!"

The Third Act introduces these numbers: Maria's song, "My Love rode out to the wide, wide world"; the Maytime song, "There comes a youth of sweet renown"; the Maytime pantomime and dance; a duet between Maria and Werner, "True love, I give thee greeting"; and a particularly strong final chorus, "Faithful love and trumpet blowing!"

ENGELBERT HUMPERDINCK

This German composer achieved an instant popularity in Germany on the occasion of the production of his fairy opera, "Hänsel and Gretel." It speedily crossed the channel into England, and was also performed in Holland, Belgium, Italy, and America—all within two years. In a sense it violates operatic traditions in substituting for the somber atmosphere and tragic close a simple naïveté that is delightfully refreshing. The success of this opera was repeated in "Koenigskinder," of a slightly later date. Humperdinck was born in Siegburg on the Ahme, September 1, 1854, was educated in the German school, and devoted his life to orchestral and other musical work. His scores reveal the influence of Wagner. He died, September 27, 1921.

HÄNSEL AND GRETEL

(Hen'-sel and Gray'-tel)

Fairy Opera in Three Acts. Music by Engelbert Humperdinck. Book by Adelheid Wette. Weimar, December 23, and at Munich, December 30, 1893. Two years later, at Daly's Theatre, New York, in English. At the Metropolitan, in German, November 25, 1905, with Alten, Abarbanell, Weed, Homer, and Goritz.

SCENE: A German Forest.
TIME: The Seventeenth Century.

CAST PETER, *a broom-maker* (Baritone).
GERTRUDE, *his wife* (Contralto).

Hänsel, *their son* (Mezzo-Soprano).
Gretel, *their daughter* (Soprano).
The Crunch Witch (Mezzo-Soprano).
The Sand Man (Soprano).
The Dew Man (Soprano).
Fourteen Angels, Children, Elves, etc.

ARGUMENT "Hänsel and Gretel," adapted from a fairy tale by the brothers Grimm, loses nothing of its verve and freshness in this delightful musical setting. The haunting charm of the opera, which while classed as "children's" has no less appeal to adults, begins with the overture. The French horns sound out the Prayer Theme that recurs in the story, followed by that of the Witch and other themes.

Act I *The Broom-Maker's Cottage.* The two children of Peter, the broom-maker, are trying to finish their stint of work while awaiting the return of their parents with supper. But they finally grow so hungry that they lay aside their tasks and dance about to forget their appetites. Their mother, a hasty-tempered woman, finds them thus wasting time and by way of punishment packs them off into the woods of Ilsenstein, to pick berries for supper. After they have run away in terror, Peter comes in greatly pleased over having sold all his brooms. He brings food in plenty. But when he learns that the children have gone to Ilsenstein, where the bad Crunch Witch dwells, he and Gertrude hasten in search of them.

The music throughout is charming. The two children in the first scene while away the time by singing. Gretel asks, "Susy, pray what is the news?"; and her brother joins in, "Pray, what's to be done?" Then the girl sings, "Brother, come dance with me!" And they suit the action to the word. After the children are sent out into the forest, their mother repents and becomes alarmed. "An old witch within that wood doth dwell," she sings; and then tells in song the fate of children that fall into the witch's hands.

Act II *In the Forest.* The children wander about picking berries but are so hungry that they eat them as fast as they are picked. They are therefore afraid to return home, and besides it is growing dark. They sink down weary beneath a large tree and the Sand Man comes and sprinkles his sand of slumber in their eyes. Then, in accordance with their childish prayer, fourteen angels descend a staircase from Heaven and assume guard about them.

Both music and setting form one of those unforgettable unions, which have done so much to keep this opera a perennial favorite with all ages of opera-goers. The lost children try to comfort each other, but with poor success. "What's glimmering in the darkness?" they ask. The Sand Man sings, reassuringly, "I send the children happy dreams." As they fall asleep, celestial strains herald the angels. The lovely Prayer Theme, first heard in the Overture, is the dominant one here:

Act III *The Witch's Gingerbread Hut.* The next morning the Dew Man arouses the children and they are surprised to find themselves in front of the Gingerbread Hut of the Crunch Witch. This is her trap to lure children whom she wishes to devour, but Hänsel and Gretel do not know it. They are hungry and break off bits of the delicious house to nibble. "Nibble, nibble, mousekin, who's nibbling at my housekin?" sings a voice from within. And out pops the witch and seizes them.

"Come, little mousey, come into my housey!" she cackles. "Hocus, pocus, witch's charm!" she chants. Hänsel she locks up in a cage to fatten, but Gretel, who is plump enough, is made to bring water and fuel to help the witch prepare her feast. The witch is impatient for Hänsel to fatten and meanwhile stirs up her oven fire. As she looks in at the oven door, Hänsel escapes from the cage, and he and Gretel give the witch a sudden push, sending her headlong inside the oven. The children dance about with glee, eating their fill of sweetmeats. "Hocus, pocus, elder bush!" chants Hänsel, in imitation of the witch's charm. Then the oven cracks open, and at the same time a row of gingerbread children, who stood along the façade of the hut, turn into real live children, who thank their deliverers for their escape from the witch's spell. The witch herself is burned to a crisp. Peter and Gertrude now enter, overjoyed to find their children alive, and the opera ends in a general dance and merrymaking.

KOENIGSKINDER

(Kur'-nigs-kin-der)

(The King's Children.) Fairy Opera in Three Acts. Music by Humperdinck. Book by Ernst Rosmer, after the fairy tale by Elsa Bernstein. World premiere at the Metropolitan, New York, December 28, 1910, with Farrar as the "Goose Girl," and Homer, the "Witch."

SCENE: Hellabrun, in the Mountains of Germany.
TIME: The Middle Ages.

CAST
THE KING'S SON (Tenor).
THE GOOSE GIRL, *also of royal descent* (Soprano).
THE WITCH (Contralto).
THE FIDDLER (Baritone).
THE WOODCUTTER (Basso).
THE BROOM-MAKER (Tenor).
THE INN-KEEPER (Baritone).
THE INN-KEEPER'S DAUGHTER (Soprano).
THE COUNCILLOR (Basso).
A LITTLE CHILD (Soprano).
Villagers and Country People.

ARGUMENT "Koenigskinder" is something more than a fairy opera; it is an allegory upon love which unlocks the eyes of those who have it in their hearts, causing them to see what is denied to ordinary mortals.

The musical themes have been developed in the Wagnerian school, but without imitation; and the story, based on myth, lends itself to this musical structure. The overture and two or three excerpts were known to orchestras some years before the opera's premiere. That event, interestingly enough, was upon the stage of the Metropolitan Opera House. Geraldine Farrar added to her fame as the "Goose Girl."

Act I *The Witch's Hut and Garden.* In a secluded valley a witch has kept a young girl prisoner. She has grown up in ignorance of her parents, and the witch has cast a spell upon the forest round about so that she may not escape. The girl tends her geese and dreams of the sunny world without; but the witch chides her for idling, telling her that there is more evil in the world than good, and bidding her come in and knead the magic bread which is never to grow stale but will some day carry death to the eater. The girl obeys against her will while the witch departs. When the girl returns to the sunshine she is amazed to see a man—the first who has penetrated the forest. It is the King's son who is now in exile. Both having hearts of love, they recognize each other as "King's Children." He tells her to come with him into the world, and she would willingly go but cannot for the witch's spell. He does not understand and departs in anger. Meanwhile the King has died and the citizens of Hellabrun send a delegation—the fiddler, the woodcutter, and the broom-maker—to the witch to ask her who shall be the next ruler. She replies that it will be the one who shall come to the city gates the next day at the stroke of noon. The fiddler alone understands her and lingers behind to talk to the goose girl in whom he also recognizes one of kingly descent. She departs with him despite the witch's curse.

Act II *Gates of the Town of Hellabrun.* The town councillors decide to put the witch's prophecy literally to the test, and all the people gather near the city gates to await the coming of their new ruler. Among the throng is the King's son, clothed in rags and unnoticed. He has been working in menial tasks, no one recognizing his rank. The innkeeper's daughter loves him selfishly but he disdains her. Then a little child with open heart sees him as he is and becomes his friend. The bell strikes the hour of noon and all await feverishly for the gates to open. As they do so, behold! only the goose girl surrounded by her geese and followed by the faithful fiddler. With a cry the King's son springs forward. "My queen!" he cries. But the others laugh them both to scorn and drive them from the city. They cannot accept rulers who come in rags and tatters. Only the little child sobs in grief and tells the chief councillor that they have turned away their King and Queen.

Act III *The Witch's Hut, in Winter.* The witch has been burned by the people in their rage, and now all is cold and desolate around the hut. The fiddler, old and lame, has taken up his refuge there. To him comes the little child who had known the Prince, with her playmates, and asks him to go with them to find the King's children again. He hobbles out to join them. After they are gone, the two lost ones appear, wearied and faint with hunger. The Prince goes to the hut for shelter, but finds the woodcutter there, who denies them admittance. Finally he sells the Prince a loaf of bread for his crown. It is the poisoned bread which has remained always fresh. They eat and are overcome with stupor, falling in the snow. The fiddler and the children presently return from their search and find them cold in death.

Heartbroken, the fiddler bids the children make a grave for the pair upon the summit of the mountain. There they can lie and dream of the many other children of the King who go through the world unrecognized save by those whose hearts are touched with love.

WILHELM KIENZL

An Austrian composer, born in Weitzenkirchen, January 17, 1857. Of his operas, "The Evangelist," "Urvasi," "Der Kuhreigen," and "Don Quixote," only the first has been produced in this country. Kienzl died in Vienna, October 3, 1941.

THE EVANGELIST

(Der Evangelimann.) Musical Drama in Two Acts. Book and Music by Wilhelm Kienzl. After the work by Meiszner. Berlin, 1895. At New York, the Metropolitan, in 1923, but was not retained in repertory.

SCENE: Benedictine Convent, Vienna.
TIME: Latter part of the Nineteenth Century.

ARGUMENT The story of this drama of village and convent life in Austria is that of a hidden crime and its long-drawn-out expiation.

Act I *Courtyard of the Convent of St. Othmar.* Martha, the pretty niece of Engel, head of the Benedictine brotherhood, is beloved by Matthias, the clerk of the convent. Engel is informed of this fact by Yohannes, Matthias' brother, who is also in love with the maiden, and takes this method of getting Matthias out of the way. Yohannes watches the lovers, who are planning to elope, and sets in action a plot for their ruin. A fire breaks out in the convent buildings. Matthias is accused of having set them on fire, and is arrested and sentenced to a long prison term.

Act II *Scene 1. A Courtyard in Vienna.* Thirty years pass by. Matthias, having served his prison term, turns evangelist, and goes up and down the country on preaching missions. Martha meanwhile has drowned herself. Magdalena tells him that she is taking care of Yohannes, now on his death-bed, who wishes to see a minister before he dies.

Scene 2. Yohannes' Bedroom. Matthias goes unrecognized to his brother's bedside. Yohannes, not knowing to whom he is confessing, makes a last statement in which he acknowledges that he is the real incendiary. Matthias pardons his brother, who then dies.

LUDWIG THUILLE

A German composer, born November 30, 1861, at Bozen, and died, February 5, 1907. He studied in German schools and wrote numerous shorter pieces. He is known outside his own country for a single opera, "Lobetanz."

LOBETANZ

(*Loh'-buh-tahnts*)

Fairy Opera in Three Acts. Music by Ludwig Thuille. Book by Otto Julius Bierbaum. Mannheim, Germany, February 6, 1898. At New York, the Metropolitan, November 18, 1911, but did not remain in repertory.

SCENE: Germany.
TIME: The Middle Ages.

CAST LOBETANZ, *a wandering minstrel* (Tenor).
THE KING (Baritone).
THE PRINCESS (Soprano).
FORESTER (Basso).
HEADSMAN (Baritone).
JUDGE (Basso).
Prisoners, a Youth, Maidens, Minstrels, Poets, Courtiers, Huntsmen, Peasants.

ARGUMENT A pleasant, old-fashioned fairy tale of a princess dying of an illness, who can be healed only by the strains of a wandering minstrel's song, is the theme of this melodic opera. After much misadventure, Lobetanz is sentenced to be hanged. A crowd gathers on Hangman's Hill. The Princess is borne in, almost lifeless, and Lobetanz craves permission to play his violin for the last time. The sweet strains sound, and at their first echo the Princess begins to recover. When they have ended, she is sitting upright, stretching out her arms to the minstrel. The King pardons him and accepts him as a son. The lovers join hands and lead the dance, in which all join merrily—even the King and the hangman.

EUGENE D'ALBERT

A pianist and composer of mixed English and German stock. He was born in Glasgow, Scotland, April 10, 1864, but obtained most of his schooling on the Continent. He studied the pianoforte under Liszt, at Weimar, early showing marks of genius. At eighteen he became a concert performer. At twenty-five he first visited the United States, where he met with a flattering reception. In 1895 he was appointed royal pianist at the Court of Saxony. "Tiefland" represents his first successful opera. D'Albert died in Riga, Latvia, March 3, 1932.

TIEFLAND

(Teef'-land)

(Martha of the Lowlands.) Dramatic Opera in Prologue and Two Acts. Music by Eugene d'Albert. Book by Rudolph Lothar, after the story by A. Guimera. Prague, 1903. At New York, the Metropolitan, November 23, 1908.

SCENE: The Pyrenees and Valley of Catalonia.
TIME: The Present.

CAST SEBASTIANO, *a wealthy landowner* (Baritone).
TOMMASO, *a village patriarch* (Basso).
Others below are servants of Sebastiano:
MARTHA, *a village girl* (Mezzo-Soprano).
PEPA, *a village girl* (Soprano).

Antonia, *a village girl* (Soprano).
Rosalia, *a village girl* (Contralto).
Nuri, *a village girl* (Soprano).
Moruccio, *a miller* (Baritone).
Pedro, *a shepherd* (Tenor).
Nando, *a shepherd* (Tenor).
Priest, Villagers, etc.

ARGUMENT The simple but strong story of the displacing of dishonest love and deception by honesty is here woven into a musical theme of vigor and beauty.

Prologue *A Rocky Fastness in the Pyrenees.* All his life long Pedro the shepherd has lived among the heights of the Pyrenees. He sees few faces except that of his fellow-shepherd, Nando, and women almost not at all; but he dreams of the day when the Blessed Virgin will send him a wife. Beyond this dream he lives carefree among his beloved hills. As if in answer to his prayer, his wealthy employer one day brings to him a beautiful lowlands girl, Martha, and tells him that she shall be his wife if he will go to the lowlands and live with her at the mill. Unknown to Pedro, Martha has been the mistress of Sebastiano, who is taking this means to keep her in respectable society.

Act I *Interior of the Mill.* All of Sebastiano's servants except Pedro know of Martha's relations with their employer, and have much sly fun at the simple shepherd's expense. Sebastiano himself is about to contract marriage with an heiress. Martha views her own approaching marriage bitterly. She is at heart an honest girl, who has been forced into her present position, and she dislikes to delude Pedro, whom she has come to admire. But she is powerless to hinder the course of events, and the marriage takes place, while Pedro accepts at full value the boisterous congratulations of the villagers. It is Sebastiano's intention to continue his relations with Martha, but she avoids him by not going to her room. She also avoids Pedro, who is becoming puzzled by the turn of events.

Act II *Same Scene. Early Morning.* Nuri, a peasant girl, who has taken quite a fancy to Pedro, enters singing and knitting. She finds him alone and disconsolate. He tells her that he is going away. Martha comes from her room and finding them talking, becomes suddenly jealous for her husband's regard and orders Nuri out of the house. Pedro goes with her, and Martha, not knowing what course to pursue, confides in old Tommaso, who advises her to tell Pedro the truth. This she does not want to do; she feels that Pedro really loves her, and her own regard is awakening. Pedro returns and tells her that he does not belong in the lowlands; his place is away from men, among the hills. "Ah, take me with you, then!" she pleads, but he in a rage advances with a knife to kill her. Love and remorse prevent the deed, and the two are reconciled and determine to fly together. They are prevented by the entrance of Sebastiano and the villagers who wish to make merry over the wedding. Sebastiano mockingly thrums on a guitar and bids Martha dance for them. Pedro springs at him, and the villagers interpose to prevent a fight between the two men.

Act III *Same Scene.* Sebastiano's conduct has reached the ears of his fiancée, and she rejects him. He returns to Martha for consolation, and is amazed when she also turns from him. In scorn he seeks to force his attentions upon her, when she calls aloud for Pedro. He has escaped from the villagers and now bounds into the room wild with just anger. At first he draws a knife, but seeing that Sebastiano is unarmed he throws it away and meets him on equal terms. After a furious struggle, Pedro shakes and throws his rival aside, helpless. The crowd gathers, and Pedro defies them all. "Why don't you laugh now?" he demands. Then picking up Martha in his strong young arms he escapes with her to freedom among the hills.

RICHARD STRAUSS

A modern German composer whose work has revealed more vigor, breadth and originality than any other composer of this school since Wagner. Strauss was born in Munich, June 11, 1864, and studied there first under his father, a member of the Royal Opera Orchestra, and in other German schools, before taking up orchestral work. He began composing at so early an age—seeming to take to it naturally—that on the first performance of a work by him, he came out as a mere lad to receive the plaudits of the audience. Strauss is famed in Germany as the composer of many beautiful short pieces and orchestral numbers. His operas include: "Fire Famine" (1901); "Guntram" (1894); "Salome" (1905); "Elektra" (1909); "Der Rosenkavalier" (1911); "Ariadne auf Naxos"; "The Egyptian Helen" (1928); and "Arabella," which was performed at Berlin, in 1933, but has not yet reached America. Strauss died near Berlin, September 8, 1949.

SALOME

(Sa-lo'-meh)

Tragic Opera in One Act. Music by Richard Strauss. Book adapted from the romance by Oscar Wilde. Court Opera, at Dresden, December 9, 1905. At New York, the Metropolitan, January 22, 1907, with Fremstad as "Salome." Also at Manhattan Opera House, with Mary Garden as "Salome"—one of her famous roles.

SCENE: Tiberias, the Capital of Herod, in Galilee.
TIME: 30 A.D.

CAST
HEROD, *Tetrarch of Galilee* (Tenor).
HERODIAS, *his wife* (Mezzo-Soprano).
SALOME, *her daughter, and the King's stepdaughter* (Soprano).
JOHN THE BAPTIST, *a prophet* (Baritone).
NARRABOTH, *a Syrian captain* (Tenor).
A PAGE (Contralto).
Jews, Courtiers, Soldiers, Priests, Servants.

ARGUMENT One of the most revolutionary of modern composers, Richard Strauss did not hesitate to shock his public, and in "Salome" he administered the greatest shock of all—but, this time, not so much on account of his score as of his theme. It is one of sadism and sensuality that even the amoral courts of the Orient cannot quite explain or excuse. The story is based upon a romance by Oscar Wilde, who took his text from the New Testament tale of the death of John the Baptist.

The Palace of Herod. Salome, the beautiful but unprincipled stepdaughter of King Herod, falls passionately in love with John the Baptist, the prophet of the wilderness. Because of his bold speech against Herod and Herodias, John has been cast into a deep dungeon. There the King holds him, not caring to take further action for fear of displeasing the Jews. Salome is filled with an unholy desire to kiss the prophet's lips and fondle his long uncut tresses. She persuades Narraboth, a captain who is in love with her, to bring the prisoner before her. When the captain finds that she loves only John, he kills himself; but Salome gives little heed to this in the joy of having the prophet in her clutches. John, however, rejects all her advances, bidding her repent. Filled with rage she has him cast again into the dungeon and bides her time for revenge.

The music, which meanwhile has added to this growing intensity of passion, here depicts through the orchestra the prophet's descent into the well.

Herod the king is also troubled. His problems with the Jews are mounting; he has squabbles with Herodias; he is filled with lust for Salome; and, now that he finds his young captain dead at her feet, he pleads with the girl to show him some favor. She consents to dance for him at a feast for his guests if he will grant her a boon in return. The distracted monarch agrees and Salome then gives the famous Dance of the Seven Veils. The sensuous music follows her lithe body as she removes one by one the diaphanous coverings. Amid the applause, the dancer now demands her reward: it is the head of John the Baptist. The horrified king objects; he is fearful of an uprising; he offers her, instead, his treasures or half his kingdom; but she is obdurate. In desperation the King gives the fatal signal. A dull blow is heard and a moment later the executioner appears with the gory head. Salome is wild with delight. She fondles the trophy as though it were alive, kissing the lips. In disgust and horror the King orders her to be put to death, and the soldiers crush her beneath their shields.

Other musical numbers include a favorite aria for sopranos: "Thou wouldst not suffer me to kiss thy mouth"; and a descriptive aria, "Thy body was a column of ivory."

ELEKTRA

(*E-leck'-trah*)

Dramatic Opera in One Act. Music by Strauss. Book by Hugo von Hofmannsthal. Dresden, January 25, 1909. The same year in the Manhattan Opera House, New York, with Mazarin as "Elektra."

SCENE: Greece.
TIME: Antiquity.

CAST
QUEEN KLYTEMNESTRA, *widow of Agamemnon* (Mezzo-Soprano).
ÆGISTHUS, *her paramour* (Tenor).
ORESTES, *the Queen's son* (Baritone).
ELEKTRA, *the Queen's daughter* (Soprano).
CHRYSOTHEMIS, *the Queen's daughter* (Soprano).
Messenger, Waiting Women, Soldiers, Courtiers.

ARGUMENT In "Elektra," a modern continuation of an ancient Greek story, the death of King Agamemnon at the hands of the Queen and her paramour is avenged by the crazed daughter. The story is unpleasant but powerful, and lends itself to the unconventional musical treatment given by the composer. The action is confined to a single act, which takes place in an inner court of the royal palace at Mycene.

As servants tell of the strange behavior of the grief-crazed, revenge-driven Elektra, daughter of the murdered Agamemnon, she appears and tells of her plans of vengeance in which she shall be aided by Orestes, her brother. Chrysothemis, her sister, who is actuated by softer, more womanly feelings, now enters and urges Elektra to abate her hatred, lest harm come to them all, and warns her especially against their mother. The Queen appears at a lighted window, and as she and her wild daughter rail at each other, news is brought that Orestes is dead. Elektra, however, states that she alone will slay "the woman and her husband."

But the report as to Orestes proves false, as he presently returns to the court in disguise. At first Elektra does not know him, but when she recognizes him her joy is almost savage. The tragedy from this point rapidly reaches its consummation. Urged on by the implacable sister, Orestes enters the palace and slays both his mother and Ægisthus, while Elektra waits outside in a perfect frenzy of impatience. When she is assured that the bloody revenge is accomplished, she dances madly until she falls prone upon the ground. Chrysothemis runs to her, only to find her dead.

DER ROSENKAVALIER

(Dair Ro-zen-cav-ah-leer')

(The Rose-Knight.) Comic Opera in Three Acts. Music by Richard Strauss. Book by Hugo von Hofmannsthal. Dresden, January 26, 1911. At New York, the Metropolitan, December 9, 1913.

SCENE: Vienna.
TIME: The early years of the reign of Maria Theresa.

CAST PRINCESS VON WERDENBERG (Soprano).
BARON OCHS OF LERCHENAU (Basso).
OCTAVIAN, *a young gentleman of noble family* (Mezzo-Soprano).
HERR VON FANINAL, *a rich merchant, newly ennobled* (High Baritone).
SOPHIA, *his daughter* (High Soprano).
Attendants, Servants, Orphans of Noble Family, Couriers, Musicians, Watchmen, Children, Various Personages of suspicious appearance.

ARGUMENT As if to make amends for his two earlier works, which shocked both the ears and the morals of some of his hearers, Strauss now rewarded them with a light opera abounding in gaiety and charm. Some critics rank it as the best of its type since "Figaro." So tuneful is it that complete recordings have been made of "Der Rosenkavalier."

The overture gives a foretaste of the work. It is by turns capricious, impassioned, tender, and romantic. Waltz music abounds, recalling the school of Johann Strauss, although here perhaps more robust.

Act I *Boudoir of the Princess.* During her husband's absence the Princess von Werdenberg amuses herself by encouraging the devotion of Octavian, a young cavalier, seventeen years of age. An ardent love scene is interrupted by the entrance of the impecunious and disreputable old Baron Ochs. Octavian, having no time to escape, and thinking it to be the Princess' husband, hurriedly dons the clothes of her maid. The Baron is anxious to consult the Princess in regard to a proposed match with Sophia, the daughter of a recently ennobled merchant, but his story is much interrupted by his amorous attentions to the supposed maid, "Mariandel," whom he ogles violently. The Princess is urged to suggest a suitable messenger to bear to Sophia the Baron's *gage d'amour,* a silver rose. She names Octavian.

The introduction to this Act is a delightful medley and is often used as an orchestral number. The action itself is so interwoven with elusive melody, as, for instance, the flute solo which entertains the princess, that it is hard to particularize.

Act II *A Room in the House of Faninal.* Faninal takes leave of Sophia and departs, promising to return with her noble bridegroom. Meanwhile Octavian enters with the silver rose. The inevitable happens—Octavian and Sophia fall madly in love with one another, and the beauty and elegance of the young cavalier only make Sophia the more disgusted with the disreputable old Baron, who is ceremoniously presented to her by her father. His coarse manners and attempted familiarities offend Sophia and enrage Octavian, who challenges the Baron to a duel and succeeds in wounding him slightly. A tremendous hubbub ensues. The Baron thinks himself in a dying condition, various people rush to minister to him, Sophia declares that nothing will induce her to marry the Baron, while Faninal insists that she shall do so. Sophia and Octavian concoct a plot, the object of which is to place Ochs under compromising circumstances. A letter is delivered to him purporting to come from "Mariandel," who has attracted him.

The "Letter Scene and Waltz" are here heard, while the amorou

Baron thinks he is making headway in his suit. In this Act is also heard one of the most sparkling numbers, "The Presentation of the Rose" in dance rhythm.

Act III *A Private Room at an Inn.* Octavian appears, dressed as "Mariandel," the maid. Various suspicious-looking persons are disposed about the room in hiding-places. Finally Baron Ochs appears to keep his appointment. His enjoyment, however, is marred, first by the resemblance of "Mariandel" to Octavian, the young cavalier who wounded him, then by the appearance of the various spies, of the landlord and waiters, of a woman who claims him as her husband, and four little children who hail him shrilly as "papa," of the Commissary of Police, of the enraged Faninal, and finally of the Princess. The Baron at last departs in the midst of a clamorous host presenting bills. The Princess gracefully gives Octavian his freedom and the young lovers are made happy.

In the closing Act strains of the "Presentation of the Rose" recur; with other memorable music—"Breakfast Scene," and trio sung by the Princess, Octavian and Sophie.

ARIADNE AUF NAXOS

Legendary Opera in One Act. Music by Strauss. Book by Hugo von Hofmannsthal. Written as an interlude to Molière's comedy, "Le Bourgeois Gentilhomme." Zurich, December 5, 1912. Berlin, February 27, 1913. In English by the Juilliard School, New York, December 5, 1934.

SCENE: Island of Naxos.
TIME: Antiquity.

CAST
ARIADNE (Soprano).
BACCHUS (Tenor).
NAIAD (Soprano).
DRYAD (Contralto).
ECHO (Soprano).
ZERBINETTA (Soprano).
Four Clowns: Harlequin, Scaramouche, Truffaldin, and Brighĕlla.
Three characters from Molière's "Le Bourgeois Gentilhomme," as spectators.

ARGUMENT In order to understand this "play within a play," some explanation is necessary. Strauss first wrote some incidental music to accompany Molière's comedy, in which the action there was stressed. In a second version (1916) references to the Molière play were dropped, and a scenic prelude substituted. In the original story, Jourdain, of the bourgeois, strives to break into the uppercrust of society and for this purpose puts on an elaborate entertainment in his own home, to which he invites among others, Marquise Dorimene and Count Dorantes. Jourdain has engaged a ballet troupe but decides to give a play instead—and "Ariadne auf Naxos" is thi play. However, in his ambition to outshine, he has also engaged a troupe of clowns and insists upon their performance, also; so thes comedians give a brief performance on the stage, and then make thei exit. Despite all these confusing preliminaries, the story of Ariadn follows.

A Cave on a Desert Island. The lovely Ariadne is asleep, whil Naiad, Dryad, and Echo sing a charming ballad to soothe her restles spirit; for Ariadne feels herself forsaken, bereft. On awaking she bewails her unhappy lot and says she is only awaiting the coming of Death An interruption occurs, but instead of the dread guest, four characters from an ancient comedy come dancing across the stage, headed by Zerbinetta, who sings and dances with them—their theme, let us be gay an enjoy life while we may. The disconsolate Ariadne does not appear t notice them, and they whirl off again. Naiad, Dryad, and Echo now announce another visitor. He is youthful and handsome. His tuneful aria is heard in the distance. Ariadne listens eagerly. If this b Death, he is indeed welcome. But when he comes on stage, he is seen t be the god Bacchus. Not oblivion, he tells her, but renewed joy in life his mission. Eagerly she questions him, then quite as eagerly sinks int his arms.

THE EGYPTIAN HELEN

Dramatic Opera in Two Acts. Music by Strauss. Words by Hug von Hofmannsthal. Dresden, June 6, 1928.

SCENE: Egypt and Morocco.
TIME: Homeric Antiquity.

CAST
MENELAUS (Tenor).
ALTAIR (Baritone).
DA-UD, *his son* (Tenor).
THE ALL-KNOWING MUSSEL (High Tenor).
HELEN, *wife of Menelaus* (Soprano).
HERMIONE, *their young daughter* (Soprano).

AITHRA, *an Egyptian princess and sorceress* (Soprano).
FIRST HANDMAIDEN (Soprano).
SECOND HANDMAIDEN (Mezzo-Soprano).
FIRST GOBLIN (Soprano).
SECOND GOBLIN (Soprano).
THIRD GOBLIN (High Tenor).
Elves, Slaves, Soldiers, Eunuchs, etc.

ARGUMENT The plot of this opera was suggested by the passage in the "Odyssey" describing how Telemachus visited Lacedæmon, and found Menelaus and Helen living amicably together, the Queen plying the King with draughts of nepenthe whenever he began to remember the awkward history of the Trojan war. The music is more direct and simple in its emotional and sensuous appeal, more comprehensible and more melodious than "Elektra."

Act I *In the House of the Royal Sorceress Aithra.* Aithra is awaiting her divine lover, Poseidon, in company with a mysterious-talking Mussel, a gift from the gods. A ship is approaching, with Menelaus and Helen, homeward bound from Troy. The Mussel announces that Menelaus is about to stab Helen to death in her sleep, and urges Aithra to intervene. Aithra promptly conjures up a violent storm, which she appeases when Menelaus takes Helen in his arms and swims with her through the fierce waves. Guided by a torch, the royal travelers make their way to the house of the princess. Helen is anxious to win back the love of her much-wronged husband, but he is proof against all her wiles. He thinks of all the valiant men, Greeks and Trojans, whom her beauty has done to death. He tells her how near he came to killing her on the ship, with the same dagger that slew Paris: that she shall never see again their daughter Hermione. Just as he raises his dagger to smite her, Aithra, by her magic art, stays his hand. She calls up a horde of spirits to bemuse and perplex him and lead him away. She gives the Queen a magic potion. A similar drink is given Menelaus, and the two are conveyed to an island.

Act II *A Tent in an Oasis under the Shadow of Mount Atlas.* In a series of four scenes the tangled fortunes of the pair are unraveled. While they are still under the spell of the magic draught, the first interruption to their bliss comes in the person of Altair, a desert chief. He like others falls under the spell of Helen's beauty; his son Da-ud also swears his allegiance; while the bemused Menelaus imagines the young man to be Paris, come to life again. They ride away on a hunting expedition. Helen implores Aithra to give her a second potion for Menelaus, but before it can be administered, Da-ud falls a victim to his sword. The body of the slain prince is borne in, followed by the distraught Menelaus. To divert him a feast is spread and Helen at last persuades him to drink of the second cup. As he does so, remembrance comes back to him; he recognizes her as his true wife; a white horse is seen bearing their child, Hermione; and as the three, long parted, meet in happy reunion, the curtain falls.

"Helen's Awakening" and "The Funeral March" are memorable numbers.

FIRE FAMINE

(Feuersnot.) Legendary Opera in One Act. Music by Strauss. Book by Ernest von Wolzogen. Dresden, November 21, 1901.

SCENE: Munich.
TIME: Thirteenth Century.

ARGUMENT Following an old superstition, the citizens of Munich go from door to door collecting wood for the fire in honor of the winter solstice. They proceed to one gloomy, shuttered house, in which lives Kunrad, a student of magic. Kunrad bids them take all his wood, but seeing a beautiful girl in the crowd, Diemut, daughter of the burgomaster, he embraces and kisses her. Although she finds the young man's love interesting, she is angry at the public caress; and when he comes later to her house to plead his love, she traps him in an order basket hanging from the window. In a rage he makes use of his magic art to invoke an icy cold upon the town. Instantly cold and darkness descend and grip them until the townsfolk in dismay beseech Diemut to relent. She has, in fact, decided to do so on her own account; and her love for Kunrad is a signal for the welcome light and warmth to return.

The "Love Scene" is an orchestral number from this opera.

ALBAN BERG

Alban Berg was born in Vienna, February 7, 1885, and spent most of his life there. He showed musical talent early and was self-taught until nineteen, when he became a pupil of Arnold Schoenberg. He wrote many pieces for the piano, voice, and instrumental quartets; and one opera, "Wozzeck," said by some critics to be "the first extended opera freed from the bonds of tonality." It has, indeed, roused partisan discussion by reason of its radical departure from accepted tonal methods. Berg died in Vienna, December 24, 1935.

WOZZECK

(Voht'-zek)

Tragic Opera in Three Acts and Fifteen Scenes. Music by Alban Berg. Book by the composer, after the drama by Georg Büchner. Berlin Staatsoper, December 14, 1925. At New York, the Metropolitan, November 24, 1931, by the Philadelphia Opera Co.

CAST WOZZECK, *a poor soldier* (Baritone).
MARIE, *his mistress* (Soprano).
THEIR YOUNG SON.
CAPTAIN OF WOZZECK'S COMPANY (Basso).
ANDRES, *a soldier* (Baritone).
A DRUM MAJOR (Baritone).
AN ECCENTRIC DOCTOR.
MARGARET, *neighbor of Marie* (Contralto).
Soldiers, Townspeople, etc.

ARGUMENT A musical drama of military life, this opera has no particular locality or time. It relates to the affairs of a poor soldier, Wozzeck, who is a primitive sort of fellow living from day to day and hand to mouth. He is the father of a child, by a mistress, Marie, and though not legally obligated, he strives to provide for them. The only way he can do this is to yield his own body to a medical crank, who makes all sorts of experiments upon him.

Despite his sacrifices on her behalf, Marie is untrue. She has an affair with a Drum-Major, who boasts of his conquest to Wozzeck, and there is further evidence in some earrings she is wearing. Wozzeck surprises the couple dancing together at an inn, and later takes the girl on a woodland stroll and slashes her throat. He comes back to the inn seeking to forget his crime in drink, but instead in a frenzy of fear and remorse, throws the fatal knife into a pond, then in further dread of its recovery wades in after it and is drowned.

PAUL HINDEMITH

Hindemith, who has been called "the playboy of modern music," was born in Hanau, Germany, November 16, 1895. He came of poor Silesian stock, his father being a craftsman, but at an early age showed pronounced musical talent. His father taught him to play the violin, beginning at four, and by thirteen he had mastered the instrument and, two years later, went on a concert tour with his sister as accompanist. In 1936 he was banned by the Nazis, and was invited to come to the United States as performer and guest conductor. He has resided here since 1939. He wrote symphonies, string quartets, an oratorio, "The Eternal," and various operas: a "tabloid," "Hin und Zuruck" (There and Back), 1927; "Cardillac," 1927; "Neues vom Tage" (News of the Day), 1929—an "ingenious and diverting piece" which won added notice by reason of an aria sung in a bathtub; and "Mathis der Maler" (see below).

MATHIS DER MALER

(Matthias the Painter.) Opera in three movements. Music by Hindemith. Book inspired by life and work of Grünewald. Berlin, March 12, 1934, in concert form; same in New York by Philharmonic, Carnegie Hall, October 6, 1934. As an opera, Zurich, May 28, 1938.

ARGUMENT This work was first presented as a symphony, or synthesis, of three stylistically related excerpts. Its radical modernism so nettled German officialdom that Hindemith's music was subsequently banned from that country. In its finished form as an opera it was based on the story of Mathis Grünewald, a noted sixteenth-century artist. In a peasant uprising he sympathized with the people. His painting was a forerunner of "classic realism" and for this reason appealed to the composer.

The three movements of the opera were inspired by three panels of the artist's masterpiece, a poliptych painted for the Isenheim Altar at Colimar: I. "Angelic Concert"; II. "Entombment"; and III. "The Temptation of St. Anthony." The musical development has been spoken of by critics as clear and definite. From a festive and happy chorus of the angels, the music descends gradually to a more somber tone and an elegy marks the entombment scene. The ordeal of the saint with spirited and ılmost tumultuous strains leads up to a finale with a "Hallelujah Hymn" ınd vision of celestial exultation.

ERIC WOLFGANG KORNGOLD

Korngold was born in Brünn, May 29, 1897, the son of Julius Kornold, well-known music critic. He early showed his versatility, both omposing and conducting, church music, symphonies and operas. Ie came to America in 1936, residing a few years later in Los Angeles ·here he composed for films. His works include: "The Ring of Polycates," "Die Tote Stadt" ("The Dead City"), and "Violanta." Kornold died in 1957.

DIE TOTE STADT

(*Dee toh-ta staht*)

(The Dead City.) Opera in Three Acts. Music by Eric Korngold. ook by Schott, after the story by Rodenbach, "Bruges la Morte." Both ıamburg and Cologne, December 4, 1920. At New York, November), 1921, when Jeritza made her début in America.

SCENE: Bruges.
TIME: End of Nineteenth Century.

CAST PAUL, *a young citizen of Bruges.*
MARIETTA, *a dancer.*
COUNT ALBERT, *of Brussels.*
FRANK, *a friend of Paul.*
A boating party, players, dancers.

ARGUMENT "Die Tote Stadt" has a haunting quality, a commingling of the past with the present, which is flected in the music. From the opening notes of the overture, the ditor is prepared for the unusual. Even the final note of tragedy is :tened into a dream.

Act I *A Room in Paul's House.* Paul is living in seclusion, nursin the memory of his deceased wife, Marie. A company of player comes to his city, and Marietta, a dancer, looks so much like Marie tha Paul thinks it must be his wife restored to him. He invites her in an Marietta, to humor him, puts on one of Marie's dresses and sings one o her songs. Paul in a transport of delight fancies that it is really his los wife, who has stepped out of her pictured likeness on the wall.

Act II *A Street.* Paul is walking along a moonlit street near th dancer's home, when he is hailed by a merry party of boatme led by Count Albert. They hold an improvised street carnival; Mar etta entering into the gaiety, who acts a ghost visitor, a nun in her win ing sheet. Paul, horrified, rushes forward and tears the sheet off he The boatmen protest, but Marietta quiets them and persuades Paul take her to his home.

Act III *Paul's Room.* Once more the distraught man battles wi the image of Marie and this strange woman who threatens take her place in his affections. While he strives to reconcile the tw Marietta, to tease him, winds a lock of Marie's hair about her throat ar dances madly about the room. In a rage, Paul throttles her—only awake to discover he has been the victim of a nightmare. The actu Marietta now enters, but he repulses her and departs with his frie Frank to another city, to begin life anew.

ERNST KRENEK

Of Czech parentage, Ernst Krenek was born in Vienna, Austr August 23, 1900, but came to America and became a naturalized citiz in 1945. The opera which made him famous was "Jonny Spielt Au a work so radical that it was shopped around before being produced Leipzig, in 1927, and two years later at the Metropolitan, New Yo He was for a time professor of music at Vassar. He was a composer great fertility, with seven operas, four symphonies, and numerous ot works to his credit.

JOHNNY PLAYS ON

(Jonny Spielt Auf.) Jazz Opera in Two Acts. Words and Music y Ernst Krenek. First produced at the Neuen Theater, Leipzig, February 18, 1927. At New York, the Metropolitan, January 19, 1929, but ot continued in repertory.

SCENE: An Alpine resort, a large town in Central Europe, Paris.
TIME: The present.

CAST MAX, *a composer* (Tenor).
NIGGER JOHNNY, *a performer in a Jazz Orchestra* (Baritone).
DANIELLO, *a celebrated violinist* (Baritone).
ANITA'S MANAGER (Basso).
A HOTEL PROPRIETOR (Tenor).
A STATION EMPLOYEE (Tenor).
FIRST POLICEMAN (Tenor).
SECOND POLICEMAN (Baritone).
THIRD POLICEMAN (Basso).
ANITA, *a prima donna* (Soprano).
YVONNE, *a chambermaid* (Soprano).
Servants, Guests in Hotel, Travelers, etc.

ARGUMENT This opera enjoys the distinction—if distinction it can be called—of being the first composed in the aracteristically modern idiom of jazz. The plot and action are as ;hly colored, violent and grotesque as the music.

t I The action is complete in four scenes—the first, an Alpine plateau; the second, Anita's room; the third and fourth, a hotel Paris. Max, a melancholic composer, at first seeks distraction in the pine scenery; then in Anita's society. She leaves him for a musical eer in Paris, where she is to sing the chief role in his opera. In Paris, wever, a rival appears in Daniello, a famous violinist, who is besieged admirers clamoring for his autograph. Later Johnny, a saxophone yer, forces Daniello's lock and steals his precious violin. The next rning there is a lively scene between Anita and the violinist. She s him "she is another's." When he tries to placate her by playing on violin, he finds it gone.

Act II Seven involved scenes with a jumble of both characters an music further bewilder all but the most determined hearer The action shifts from an Alpine hotel, where Max impatiently awai the return of the erring Anita, to a glacier, where the distracted com poser hears her voice singing an aria from his opera over the radic The melody is suddenly interrupted by a lively jazz band. "That Johnny's band!" some one exclaims, and a lively dance follows. In th next, a scene in a town, Johnny has the center of the stage, but doesn fancy it. Detectives are seeking the lost violin and suspect him. The follow him to a railway station; he catches sight of them and hides th instrument on top of Max's luggage and "makes himself scarce." Th police think Max the thief. A general mix-up follows, with farce com edy worthy of Hollywood. In the final scene, the railway statio Johnny, who has again purloined the violin, is seen on a footbridg fiddling away at his jazz. As a clock points to twelve it blurs, the who scene changes, a terrestrial globe begins to revolve, and there at the to of the North Pole stands Johnny—still playing jazz.

ITALY

HISTORICAL PREFACE

In point of time, Italian opera ranks among the earliest. Modern opera is said to have had its remote beginnings in Greece and was transplanted thence by way of Italy into Europe. Down in the French court at Naples, about the year 1285, Adam de la Halle brought out a dramatic pastoral entitled "Le Jeu de Robin et de Marion," which was but one of many early attempts to string ballads together into a loose plot. They bore the same relation to opera as did the traveling players of the fifteenth century to modern drama.

It was not until the end of the sixteenth century that any concerted attempt was made toward a union of music and drama. Then a coterie of Florentine music lovers known as La Camerata banded themselves together. They enlisted a poet, Rinuccini, and a musician, Jacopo Peri, who wrote "Dafne"—now usually considered the first opera to have been performed in Europe and indeed the first work of this definite type. "Dafne" was privately performed in the Palazzo Corsi, Florence, in 1597. It met with such an enthusiastic reception on the part of the little group and their friends that the librettist and composer were commissioned to write a second piece, "Euridice," which was publicly performed at the wedding festivities of Henry IV of France and Maria de Medici. This performance at the Pitti Palace, October 6, 1600, is a very definite milestone in opera.

During the next fifty years many composers essayed their wings in the new empyrean. Most of them are only names now, but left their mark. We note such men as Claudio Monteverde (1567–1643) and his pupil, Caletti-Bruni, known as Cavalli; Provenzale, Cesti, and many another as this fruitful century drew to its close. The first opera house, the Teatro di San Cassiano, opened its doors in Venice, in 1637. Within the next thirty years eleven opera houses were opened in Venice alone. In Florence, Milan, Rome, and other cities the new form of entertainment flourished.

One would think that from this productive era would have descended a whole flock of operas to sing to modern ears. But such is not the case. Another century was to elapse before Spontini (born 1774) and the greater Rossini (born 1792) were to usher in the succession of famous composers and compositions now known as Italian opera. Meanwhile in the formative years the Italian school undeniably exerted a profound influence upon both Germany and France.

Rossini is the earliest bright, particular star on the Italian horizon. His was a pen of prodigious fertility. No less than fifty operas are placed to his credit, but only two or three are still produced, "The Barber of Seville," "Semiramide," and "William Tell." Hard on his heels follows a brilliant line—Donizetti, Bellini, Verdi, Ponchielli, Ricci, and Boito belonging by birth to the first half of the nineteenth century.

Verdi stands out head and shoulders above his contemporaries and indeed all other Italian composers. He is the proponent of Italian opera as definitely as is Wagner that of the German. He was both a prolific writer and a progressive one. His earlier works, such as "Rigoletto," "Il Trovatore," and "La Traviata," are in the approved melodious style of their period, when plot was subordinated to singer—the *bel canto* (good song). Florid solos were inserted without reference to theme. But in middle life Verdi began to strive for more consistency and dramatic freedom. "Aida" is the first example, to be followed later by such dramatic works as "Othello" and "Falstaff." Verdi's influence upon later composers has been profound.

Following him came such masters as Puccini, Leoncavallo, and Mascagni. The fame of the two latter rests upon only one or two works but Puccini has attained a position second only to that of Verdi. Of the work of these and others, such as Franchetti, Leoni, Giordano Montemezzi, and Wolf-Ferrari, record is found in succeeding pages Among the most recent composers a tendency has been manifest to emphasize the brutal and gruesome, rather than the romantic and lovely. But Italian opera as a whole proves conclusively that this is singing nation.

GASPARO LUIGI P. SPONTINI

An outstanding, early composer who, even in his lifetime, was the storm center of opposing schools, Spontini had a humble origin. Born of peasant stock at Majolati, near Jesi, Italy, November 14, 1774, he was destined for the priesthood, but ran away from home. Later reconciled to an uncle who had opposed his musical passion, he went, in 1791, to conservatory in Naples. His first works were church music, but again rebelling he went to Rome where his first opera was put on—"I Puntigli delle Donne"—now forgotten with others that followed. His remembered ones include "La Vestale," "Olympia," and "Cortez." Spontini conducted orchestras in Paris, Berlin, and other cities. He died in 1851.

LA VESTALE

(The Vestal Virgin.) Romantic Opera in Three Acts. Music by Gasparo Spontini. Book by Etienne Jouy. The work was dedicated to Empress Josephine and produced by Napoleon's order at the Tuileries, December 14, 1807. At New York, the Metropolitan, November 12, 1925, with Rosa Ponselle, Johnson, De Luca, Mardones, and Matzenauer.

SCENE: Rome.
TIME: Ancient days.

CAST LICINIUS, *a Roman General* (Tenor).
JULIA, *a Vestal Virgin* (Soprano).
CINNA, *Captain of the Legion* (Baritone).
PONTIFEX MAXIMUS (Basso).
HIGH PRIESTESS (Mezzo-Soprano).
A CONSUL (Basso).
Vestals, Priests, Senators, Consuls, Soldiers, Gladiators, Citizens.

ARGUMENT "La Vestale" is of historic as well as musical interest. It foreshadows some of the glow and romance which later entered so largely into Italian composition. It also reveals elements which represent both the older and the newer schools of that nation's music. It was regarded and is still so regarded as one of the most significant pieces of its day.

Act I *The Roman Forum.* Licinius has covered himself with glory in his campaign against the Gauls. He had hoped by his prowess to win the hand of Julia, a patrician's daughter, but after five years of absence learns that she has taken the veil of a Vestal Virgin. At his triumph she is chosen to place a laurel wreath on his brow and, seeing in her glance that she still loves him, he manages to whisper to her that he will meet her that night before the altar in the Temple.

Act II *Interior of the Temple of Vesta.* The High Priestess leaves Julia in charge of the sacred flame, and warns her of the fate of such as are untrue to the trust. While the virgin kneels and implores grace to withstand her new-found passion, Licinius enters. As he pleads his love to not unwilling ears, the altar's flame dies out! The goddess is wrathful and inevitable discovery follows. Worshipers and soldiers rush in, in tumult. Cinna, a captain, rescues his friend, Licinius. The Pontifex Maximus bids the lictors tear off the virgin's white veil, and place upon her a black veil, the symbol of death.

Act III *The Field of Infamy.* Cinna has told Licinius that his friends would rescue the Vestal; but, despite their efforts, plans for the execution go forward. A large pyramidal tomb is seen, and into its depths Julia must descend to be entombed alive. She is resigned to her fate. Licinius now hastens forward and offers to die with her. As the throng closes in about them and prevents a rescue, a storm comes up. Amid the crash of thunder a bolt of lightning ignites the Vestal's veil, lying on the altar; then the sky clears. The people, taking this as an omen that her sin is forgiven, rejoice in the lovers' happiness.

GIOACCHINO ANTONIO ROSSINI

An Italian composer, called the "Swan of Pesaro," from the town of his birth (February 29, 1792). In 1807 he entered the Liceo (conservatory) at Bologna, studying 'cello under Cavedagni and composition with Padre Mattei. By 1810 he had written and brought out in Venice, and with applause, a one act comedy opera, "La Cambiale di Matrimonio." During 1812 he received commissions for no less than five light operas scoring, in 1813, with his "Tancredi" his first success. There was scarcely a year now that did not see a work from his pen, sometimes two until his "William Tell" was produced in Paris, 1829. This was an entire change of style from his earlier works, possibly, however, foreshadowed by his "Comte d'Ory." No less than fifty are credited to him. During the remaining thirty-nine years of his life, Rossini turned aside from opera. He resided in Bologna and Florence until 1855, then in Paris, dying at Ruelle, November 13, 1868.

THE BARBER OF SEVILLE

(Il Barbiere di Siviglia.) Comic Opera in Two Acts. Music by Rossini. Book by Sterbini, founded on a comedy by Beaumarchais. Argentina Theatre, Rome, February 5, 1816. In London at the King's Theatre, March 10, 1818. In New York, in English, at the Park Theatre, May 3, 1819. At the Metropolitan, December 15, 1883, with Sembrich as "Rosina."

SCENE: Seville.
TIME: The Seventeenth Century.

CAST COUNT ALMAVIVA (Tenor).
FIGARO, *the barber of Seville* (Baritone).
DOCTOR BARTOLO, *a physician* (Basso).
BASILIO, *a music teacher* (Basso).
ROSINA, *a ward of Bartolo* (Soprano).
BERTHA, *a duenna* (Contralto).
FIORELLO, *the Count's servant* (Baritone).
AMBROSIO, *the doctor's servant*.
Musicians, Citizens, Guards, etc.

ARGUMENT "The Barber of Seville" is a light opera of more than usual interest. It was written by Rossini at top speed in less than three weeks, but is the only one of his works which has persisted continuously in repertory. While it has not the grandeur of his "William Tell," it is a little masterpiece of its kind. Before the curtain rises the bright and merry overture prepares us for the musical feast that is to follow.

Act I *Scene 1. A Street in Seville.* Count Almaviva, who has fallen in love with Rosina, the ward of Dr. Bartolo, goes to sing a serenade beneath her balcony. His aria, "Dawn with her rosy mantle," is one of the most beautiful. While there Figaro the town barber, a droll, self-important fellow, comes along to tell all and sundry what a fellow he is. "Figaro here! Figaro there!" he rattles off his patter song at break-neck speed, with the orchestra working valiantly to keep the droll pace (Factotum Song):

The Count observes him and decides he is the man he needs to aid in the nobleman's suit. Figaro tells him that he goes every day to shave the old doctor, who is insanely jealous over his ward and wants her to marry him. She is a virtual prisoner. Rosina drops a letter from the balcony, which her guardian cannot find, but it is picked up by the Count, who is overjoyed to see that his attentions are welcome. He pours out his heart to his beloved in another serenade: "Who 'neath thy window sighing." The wily barber then suggests that the Count impersonate the colonel of a passing regiment and demand a billet in Bartolo's house.

Scene 2. A Room in Bartolo's House. As the curtain rises, Rosina is seen at her desk just finishing a letter to her unknown admirer. Her soliloquy is one of the best known coloratura arias for sopranos: "A little voice I hear" (Una voce poco fa):

While Rosina is grumbling at her imprisonment and promising herself to lead her guardian a merry dance, Bartolo enters. He is determined to marry his ward, and invokes the aid of Basilio, the music teacher. While the two men go to draw up a contract, Figaro enters and Rosina entrusts him with a letter to "Lindoro" (which she supposes to be the Count's name). Their duet begins, "Am I his love, or do you mock me?" The doctor returns and accuses her of writing letters. At this point the Count staggers in disguised as a drunken officer. An amusing series of incidents follow among all the principals including the wily barber. An officer enters and arrests the Count for disorderly conduct, but on privately learning his true rank he releases him and arrests the doctor instead. A trio, "Awestruck and motionless" leads up to the rousing final chorus.

Act II *Music Room in Bartolo's House.* Count Almaviva returns to the doctor's home, this time disguised as a music master, sent in place of Basilio who is supposed to be sick. Bartolo views him with suspicion and, to prevent his being alone with Rosina, orders Figaro to shave him (Bartolo) in the same room. Rosina enters and the strange combination proceeds amusingly. At this juncture Basilio appears but is bribed to pretend that he is really ill. During the music lesson the two lovers arrange to elope at midnight, being aided by the tricks of the barber.

The confusion is heightened in this scene by the fact that Rosina still does not know the identity of her suitor, whom she still calls "Lindoro." When she at last learns that he and the Count are the same person, she joyfully accepts him. Bartolo, meanwhile, has hastened to a notary to draw up a wedding contract in favor of himself; but when Basilio later appears with the notary, the Count and the barber intercept them and have it changed to read in the Count's favor. At the final curtain, the lovers are blissful; the doctor grudgingly yields to the inevitable; while the garrulous Figaro showers all with his good wishes. He has been the one indispensable person (so he thinks) all along!

The Act opens with a musical soliloquy by Bartolo, who voices his suspicions of people and things. Then comes the famous "music lesson," beginning with the false teacher's greeting, "Heaven send you peace and joy!" But his actions are not peace inspiring. The music here is a riot of melody. A dialogue quintet is followed by a lengthy aria by the watchful duenna, Bertha. When the lovers finally take their leave of Basilio, they sing the duet, "Fare you well then, good Signore!" (Zitti, zitti.) A melodious finale brings the curtain down.

SEMIRAMIDE

(Say'-me-rah'-me-day)

Tragic Opera in Two Acts. Music by Rossini. Book by Gaetano Rossi, based on Voltaire's tragedy, "Semiramis." Fenice Theatre, Venice, February 3, 1823. At New York, in 1826, in 1855; and at the Metropolitan, April 13, 1887, with Patti.

SCENE: Babylon.
TIME: Antiquity.

CAST SEMIRAMIDE, *Queen of Babylon* (Soprano).
ARSACES, *Commander of the Assyrian Army* (Contralto).

GHOST OF NINUS (Basso).
OROE, *Chief of the Magi* (Basso).
ASSUR, *A Prince* (Baritone).
AZEMA, *a Princess* (Soprano).
MITRANUS } *of the royal household* { (Baritone).
IDRENUS } *of the royal household* { (Tenor).
Magi, Guards, Satraps, Slaves.

ARGUMENT "Semiramide" is one of those "forgotten" operas which has enough good music to deserve a better fate. In the days of Patti and Scalchi its brilliant arias for the soprano voice were prime favorites; and for many years after the work had left the boards its stately overture with its sweeping, hymnlike opening bars remained a pièce de resistance with orchestras. The story is oriental dealing with the machinations of a queen in mixing politics with love. The First Act introduces an especially difficult and brilliant aria, in which Queen Semiramide sings "Bright ray of hope" (Bel raggio lusinghier).

Act I *Babylon.* Queen Semiramide has put her consort, Ninus, out of the way, in order to aid the usurper Assur, who is also her lover. Meanwhile, her son Ninia, who has grown to man's estate, enters her service under the assumed name of Arsaces and speedily wins high rank. When he returns a victor from the wars, his mother, ignorant of his identity, falls in love with him and asks him to marry her. But Arsaces refuses because already in love with the Princess Azema.

Act II *A Temple.* During a gathering of the Babylonians in the temple, while Semiramide is announcing to her people her choice for their future King, the gates of Ninus' tomb suddenly open, and his ghost appears in their midst, asserting that Arsaces will be his successor to the throne, and commanding him to avenge his death upon the enemy who shall visit the tomb that night. In the meantime the Priest Oroe has revealed to Arsaces the true circumstances of his birth, whereupon he discloses his story to his mother. The repentant Queen declares that he shall be the successor to the crown, and warns him against Assur. At midnight Arsaces descends to the tomb of his father, and is followed by Assur, who has planned to murder him. Semiramide, fearful for the life of her son, follows Assur into the tomb, and Arsaces, who is lying in wait for him, hears the footsteps of his mother approaching, and thinking her to be Assur stabs her. She dies in his arms. Assur is seized, and Arsaces weds Azema, and is proclaimed King.

WILLIAM TELL

Romantic Opera in Three Acts. Music by Rossini. Book by Hippolyte Bis and Etienne Jouy, after the drama by Schiller. Académie, Paris, August 3, 1829. In New York, 1857, and at the Metropolitan, season of 1888–89.

SCENE: Switzerland.
TIME: Fourteenth Century.

CAST GESSLER, *a tyrant* (Basso).
RUDOLF DE HARRAS, *his lieutenant* (Tenor).
WILLIAM TELL, *a patriot* (Baritone).
WALTER FÜRST, *a patriot* (Basso).
MELCHTHAL, *a patriot* (Basso).
ARNOLD, *his son* (Tenor).
LEUTHOLD, *a patriot* (Tenor).
MATHILDE, *daughter of Gessler* (Soprano).
HEDWIG, *wife of Tell* (Mezzo-Soprano).
JEMMY, *son of Tell* (Soprano).
RUODI, *a fisherman* (Tenor).
Peasants, Huntsmen, Soldiers.

ARGUMENT "William Tell" is still another Rossini opera which is far better known for its overture than for the complete work. Who even among non-opera-goers is not familiar with the lovely melodies in this introduction, beginning with the quiet bars denoting an Alpine calm? Then comes a storm, in which we can almost see the lightning as with a roar it crashes down upon the trees. It has hardly died away in the distance when we hear the horns of huntsmen, and then a trumpet call—a call to arms for the Swiss peasantry to uprise against their Austrian oppressors. This gives the opera's theme, a story well-known to all the Swiss, be it history or legend, of a patriot who successfully stirred up his countrymen in the cause of freedom.

Act I *The Shores of Lake Lucerne, in front of Tell's House.* William Tell, his wife, and little son are making merry by the shores of Lucerne when their aged countryman, Melchthal, and his son, Arnold, come to greet them. Arnold is torn between two desires: He wishes to aid Tell and the patriots against the tyrant Gessler, but he is also in love with the latter's daughter, Mathilde, whose life he has saved. Tell pleads with him to put his country first. Presently Leuthold, a villager, rushes in, imploring assistance. He has killed a soldier who tried to abduct his daughter, and he must flee across the lake to escape his enemies. The fisherman, Ruodi, does not dare venture in the face of an approaching storm, but Tell leaps into the boat with Leuthold and rows him across. The soldiers appear led by Rudolf and, in revenge, set fire to Tell's house and other cottages, and seize Melchthal as a hostage.

The most popular musical number in this Act is Arnold's greeting to his sweetheart, "Oh, Mathilde!"—a tour de force for any ambitious tenor.

Act II *Scene 1. A Forest.* The horns of a party of huntsmen sound through the wood, and are answered by a chorus of shepherds. Arnold meets Mathilde and declares his passion for her and learns that she also loves him. But Tell and Fürst enter at this moment to inform Arnold that the soldiers have slain his father. The young man bids his sweetheart a sorrowful farewell and casts in his lot with his country.

Scene 2. The Open Country. Following the call of Tell, Fürst, Arnold, and other patriots, the villagers and shepherds assemble from the various cantons. All take the oath of allegiance to Switzerland and prepare to battle against the tyrant's forces.

The musical climax of the Second Act is the trio of the three leaders, followed by a rousing chorus of the Swiss taking oath to conquer or die: "May glory our hearts with courage exalt!"

Act III *The Open Square at Altdorf.* Gessler has erected a pole in the market place at Altdorf and commanded that all shall bow before the cap, placed thereon, as a recognition of his authority. Tell refuses to do so and is seized by Rudolf. The tyrant has heard of Tell's skill with the crossbow, and will release him only on condition that he give an exhibition of this skill by shooting an apple off of his son's head. Tell does so, but when questioned as to a second arrow which is in his possession, he states that it was intended for Gessler's heart, had the first arrow harmed the lad. For this bold speech Tell is still held prisoner, although Mathilde intercedes for him.

Scene 2. The Shore of Lake Lucerne. Hedwig, Tell's wife, grieves for her husband and child who are both in the hands of the soldiers. Mathilde enters bringing the boy, whom she has aided to escape. The father also soon appears, having made good his own escape. He lies in wait for Gessler and kills him with an arrow from his bow. The patriot army is victorious over the enemy, and Arnold enters at the head of the joyous patriots. All unite in thanksgiving and a prayer that Switzerland may continue to be free.

The final Act brings in a striking tenor aria by Arnold, where he views the ruins of his own home: "O, silent abode!" (O muto asil). As the curtain descends we hear an inspiring hymn to liberty, and to the peaks of their land which typify it: "I boschi, i monti!"

GAETANO DONIZETTI

The Italian composer, Donizetti, was born in Bergamo, Italy, November 29, 1797. His father was a weaver, and wanted his son to study law. But neither the loom nor the bar attracted the young man, who early showed musical ability. He was at last allowed to enter the conservatory in his native town. His father, however, had no intention of continuing his tuition further than to fit him for teaching music; so Gaetano enlisted in the army. While in the service he composed his first opera, "Enrico di Borgogna," which was produced in Venice, 1818, but is now forgotten. Donizetti first came prominently into notice in 1830, when his opera, "Anna Bolena," was produced in Rome. "Belisarius" was produced in Vienna (1836). One opera followed another during his busy life, his total being about seventy. Of these only some half dozen are in the modern repertory, "Lucia di Lammermoor" being by far the most popular. Donizetti was equally facile in serious and lighter operas. Of the latter he is best known by his "L'Elisir d'Amore" (1832); "La Figlia del Reggimento" (1840); and "Don Pasquale" (1843). Donizetti suffered a paralytic stroke in 1845, and died in his native town, April 8, 1848.

LUCREZIA BORGIA

(Lu-cree'-tsia Borzh'-ya)

Tragic Opera, in a Prologue and Two Acts. Music by Donizetti; words by Felice Romani, after Victor Hugo. La Scala, Milan, 1834; Théâtre des Italiens, Paris, 1840; London, 1839. At New York, the Metropolitan, December 5, 1904, with Caruso, Maria de Macchi, Walker, and Scotti.

SCENE: Venice and Ferrara.
TIME: Early Sixteenth Century.

CAST ALFONSO D'ESTE, *Duke of Ferrara* (Baritone).
LUCREZIA BORGIA (Soprano).
MAFFIO ORSINI (Contralto).

GENNARO	*Young noblemen in the service of the Venetian Republic*	Tenor.
LIVEROTTO		Tenor.
VITELLOZZO		Basso.

GAZELLO (Bass).
RUSTIGHELLO, *in the service of Don Alfonso* (Tenor).

GUBETTA	*in the service of Lucrezia*	Basso.
ASTOLFO		Tenor.

Gentlemen-at-arms, Officers, and Nobles, Ladies-in-waiting, Capuchin Monks, etc.

ARGUMENT Based upon Hugo's story of the celebrated poisoner of history, "Lucretia Borgia," is one of the earliest of the tragic operas which has had a permanent place.

Prologue *Terrace of the Grimani Palace, Venice.* During a night festival, Gennaro, a young nobleman, becomes weary and falls asleep on a bench. Lucrezia Borgia, passing by, masked, is struck with the comeliness of the youth and while wondering if this can be her own son by an early marriage, he awakens. He in turn is interested in this fascinating woman, and when other friends arrive and she is unmasked, he is still more attracted by her beauty. But his friends lose no time in revealing her true character as a murderess. He turns from her in hatred, and she swoons away.

Act I *A Public Square, Ferrara.* Don Alfonso, Duke of Ferrara, and the present husband of the notorious Lucrezia, is jealous of her interest in Gennaro. Like the young man himself, the Duke is ignorant of the fact that Gennaro is really Lucrezia's son. Gennaro now comes to Ferrara with a party of his friends, and in order to show his loathing for her crimes, he hacks her name off the shield on the gates of the palace. The Duke orders his arrest, glad of this excuse to get a possible rival under surveillance.

Lucrezia, ignorant of the offender's identity, demands that he be put to death for this insult. Alfonso cynically consents. Gennaro is brought in, and the now horror-stricken woman pleads for his life; but her husband is adamant. With exquisite cruelty he commands that she herself shall prepare the poisoned cup—a draught in which she is an adept. She does so, but also secretly administers an antidote which saves Gennaro's life. She implores him to flee the city.

Act II *Banquet Hall of the Negroni Palace.* Lucrezia has not forgotten the other young men who were with Gennaro in his attack upon the palace, and determines to revenge herself by poisoning them. She invites them to a banquet and drugs their wine. She then appears before them and announces this fact. What is her horror, however, to find Gennaro again among them. He threatens to kill her. She reveals to him the secret of his birth, but he turns from his mother and dies. The Duke enters to find the hall filled with dead or dying, and Lucrezia herself expiring from remorse.

Recorded arias from this opera: "Il segreto per essere felice," "Come e bello quale incento," "M'odi, ah, m'odi!" and "Vieni la mia vendetta."

LUCIA DI LAMMERMOOR

(Lu-chee'-ah dee Lam'-mer-moor)

Tragic Opera in Three Acts. Music by Donizetti. Book by Cammerano, after Scott's "Bride of Lammermoor." Produced at San Carlo Theatre, Naples, September 26, 1835; in London three years later; and in English at the Park Theatre, New York, November 17, 1845. The most celebrated sopranos of the past century have sung "Lucia." Sembrich made her American debut in it, at the Metropolitan, October 24, 1883.

SCENE: Scotland.
TIME: 1700.

CAST HENRY ASHTON, *of Lammermoor* (Basso).
LUCY ASHTON, *his sister* (Soprano).
EDGAR, *of Ravenswood* (Tenor).
LORD ARTHUR BUCKLAW, *friend of Ashton* (Tenor).
NORMAN, *a follower of Ashton* (Tenor).
RAYMOND, *chaplain to Ashton* (Basso).
ALICE, *attendant to Lucy* (Soprano).
Friends and retainers of the Ashtons, Villagers, etc.

ARGUMENT The story of "Lucia di Lammermoor" follows closely the well-known novel of Scott dealing with the tragic fate of two lovers separated by family strife. Although generally regarded as Donizetti's masterpiece, some modern critics have scoffed at it, saying that it was merely the vehicle for some prima donna. Nevertheless, the opera remains a favorite for its freshness of melody, the skillful interplay of the music with its tragic theme, the rich coloratura passages, and the fine ensembles including the famed Sextet, which is still unchallenged as near the topmost flights of all Italian opera.

Act I *Scene 1. A Grove outside Ashton's Castle.* Lucy Ashton is being urged by her brother to accept the hand of Bucklaw, who will restore their family fortunes, but she persists in refusing him. Henry Ashton is further enraged by learning that she is in love with Edgar of Ravenswood, his worst enemy, and that she has been meeting him secretly. Henry's confidant Norman, has sent his huntsmen to discover the truth of the matter. They return and tell in a brisk chorus, that, "Long they wandered o'er the mountain"—and that the suspicion is correct. Then comes Henry's defiant aria: "From my breast I mercy banish."

Scene 2. A Fountain in the Grove. It is evening and a moon shines on a peaceful scene. A harp breathes the quietude in lovely melody. Lucy enters with her companion, Alice, and sings the "Legend of the Fountain." Edgar appears and the two again pledge their troth. He is seeking safety in France, but says he will return for her. A second aria by Lucy, one of the best-known numbers, "Then swift as thought," is followed by their no less well-known duet, "My sighs shall on the balmy breeze" (Verranno la sull' aure)

Act II *Scene 1. Lucy's Apartments.* Ashton makes preparations for the marriage of his sister with Bucklaw, never doubting that he will obtain her consent at the final moment. The girl is in deep dejection. Letters between her and Edgar have been intercepted and she is told that he is faithless. A forged letter from Edgar is shown in proof of this. Finally she yields to her brother's entreaties and the arguments of Raymond, her spiritual adviser, and agrees to sign the wedding contract.

Scene 2. Hall of the Castle. A brisk chorus of guests assembled to witness the signing of the wedding contract opens this climactic scene. Bucklaw is being congratulated by his friends. Lucy is a sad and passive figure. Just as she takes the pen to sign the fatal document, Edgar rushes wildly into the hall. Then with an orchestral prelude ensues that finest of Italian ensembles, the Sextet. Edgar sings: "What restrains me at this moment? Why my sword I do not draw?" Because

Henry sees his sister "as a rose 'mid tempest bending," he is moved to exclaim: "To my own blood I'm a traitor!" One after another take up the melody until it is a glorious volume of sound with Lucy's despairing voice rising above the rest:

Ashton triumphantly shows Edgar the contract signed by his sister. Edgar loads her with reproaches and leaves the room before Ashton's retainers can interpose.

Act III *Scene 1. Hall of the Castle.* The wedding has been celebrated despite Edgar's interposition, and he has made an appointment to fight a duel with Ashton. The bride and groom have been shown their apartments, and while the guests still make merry the news is circulated that Lucy has gone mad and stabbed Bucklaw. She appears among the horrified guests raving insane. The "mad scene," another pivotal one in the opera, is favored by great prima donni as it challenges their best both in vocalization and in acting. Lucy by turns is reminiscent of her first happy hours with Edgar; then her mood turns ("Shed thou a tear of sorrow"); then comes a brilliant bit of coloratura work, "Yet shall we meet at the altar, dear Edgar"; then grief-stricken ravings with the orchestra in rapid tempo.

Scene 2. A Churchyard. (*Sometimes omitted.*) Edgar awaits his enemy and dreams of his lost love. A bell tolls and he hears that Lucy is dead, and to the last was faithful as she had promised. "Why lament ye?" he demands of the mourners. When told that she is no more he voices a final plaint: "Thou hast spread thy wings." A 'cello strain accompanies his final prayer, as he stabs himself.

LA FAVORITA

(Lah Fav-o-ree'-ta)

(The King's Favorite). Romantic Opera in Five Acts. Music by Donizetti. Book by Royer and Waëtz, after the drama, "Le Comte de Commingues." Académie Royale de Musique, Paris, December 2, 1840. At New York, Park Theatre, October 4, 1848; and at the Metropolitan, November 29, 1905, with Caruso, Walker, Scotti, and Plançon.

SCENE: Castile.
TIME: 1340.

CAST ALFONSO XI, *King of Castile* (Baritone).
FERNANDO, *an officer of the guard* (Tenor).
BALTHASAR, *Prior of the Monastery of St. Jacob* (Basso).
GASPARO, *an officer* (Tenor).
LEONORE DE GUZMAN, *the King's favorite* (Mezzo-Soprano).
INEZ, *her companion* (Soprano).
Officers, Soldiers, Courtiers, Ladies, Servants, Monks.

ARGUMENT The theme of "La Favorita" is simple but dramatic, treating of lost illusions and blighted hopes. A young anchorite forsakes his vows for the sake of a pretty face, only to find that the promised happiness is a mirage.

Act I *Hall of a Monastery.* Fernando, a novice in orders, of the Monastery of St. Jacob, has shown such earnestness and insight that he is spoken of as the next prior. But between him and his vows comes the vision of a beautiful woman, an unknown whom he loves and who, he finds, loves him in return. He confesses his attachment to his best friend, Balthasar, the present prior, who endeavors to warn him against the snares and pitfalls of the world. But finding that the young man is determined, he releases him from the monastic orders and bids him go in peace.

The "high note" in this Act is the tenor aria by Fernando in which he describes to the prior his lady love: "A virgin, an angel of God" (Una vergine):

Act II *A Palace Garden.* Fernando decides to seek service in the royal army. He comes blindfolded into the palace garden, where ladies of the court who have heard his story, entertain him graciously. Among them, he finds his unknown love, Leonore; but while she reciprocates his affection, she begs him to go away and forget her. She will not even tell him her name and station. She is the King's "favorite" and is afraid Fernando will despise her if he learns her true station. The scene opens with a pleasing solo and chorus of Leonore and her attendants: "Bright sunbeams, lightly dancing," which is followed by the women's chorus: "Gentle zephyr," as Fernando's boat nears shore. Her strange attitude only adds fuel to the flame. While she tries to send him away, Inez enters to announce the approach of King Alfonso. The mystified young man now thinks that his lady is of too high rank for him to presume to address her. Leonore leaves him, after presenting him with a document which proves to be a royal commission as officer in the King's army. Ferdinand resolves to win the King's favor and the lady's hand in the wars.

The Act closes with the martial strain: "Oh, fame, thy voice inspiring!"

Act III *The King's Court.* King Alfonso is delighted with news of his army's victories over the Moors, and with the brilliant conduct of his young officer, Fernando. The latter dreams of happiness at last with Leonore, but he is still ignorant of the fact that she is the King's favorite, and Alfonso does not intend to give her up. A spirited scene ensues between monarch and mistress in which the former reiterates his devotion and the latter reproaches him for putting happiness out of her reach. Before the court she finally hurls defiance at him, being aided by Balthasar, who comes with a message from the Pope threatening the King with excommunication unless he relinquishes Leonore in favor of Fernando. He is given one day in which to decide. Fernando hears nothing of this, but Leonore is cast into the depths of sorrow at the prospect of deceiving her lover.

The two leading arias in this Act are: Alfonso's own plea of passion, "Come, Leonore"; and the prior's vigorous denunciation of the King, "Call not down the wrath of God."

Act IV *A Palace Apartment.* Alfonso decides to yield to the papal pressure and reward Fernando. He tells the young officer that he will give him Leonore in marriage. (Aria, "Thou flower beloved!") While the officer is overjoyed, the lady is a prey to misgivings; she feels that their happiness will not be assured unless she tells her betrothed the truth about her relations with the King. Her plaint, "O, my Fernando!", is one of the best-known songs for the mezzo voice in Italian opera:

She writes a letter to him and entrusts it to Inez, but is stopped on her way by Gasparo. The King ennobles Fernando and orders an immediate marriage, which ceremony is performed. But during the festivities the bridegroom overhears slurring remarks from Gasparo and the courtiers, and returns to the King demanding an explanation. When he learns the truth, he renounces his bride and honors, breaks his sword, and casts its fragments at the feet of the King. This dramatic scene is the climax of the work. Amid conflicting voices of protest, irony, grief, Fernando departs, while the courtiers salute him with the stirring chorus: "Fernando, the truly brave, we salute and pardon crave!"

Act V *The Monastery Hall.* Fernando returns to the monastery and resumes his study for the priesthood. On the day when he is to receive holy orders, Leonore comes to beg his forgiveness. She tells him of the undelivered letter in which she had confessed the truth and which she thought he had received. He forgives her and says that he loves her still, but now the Church calls him. He leaves her swooning and joins the procession of monks.

The closing Act also abounds in melody, beginning with the song of Balthasar and the monks, "Behold the stars in splendor celestial"; and continuing with Fernando's song of renunciation, "Spirit of Light!"—another gem of this school of opera.

LINDA DI CHAMOUNIX

(*Linda dee Shah'-moo-nee*)

Romantic Opera in Three Acts. Music by Donizetti. Book by Rossi. Vienna, May 19, 1842. At New York, the Metropolitan, 1890, with Patti; and, on February 4, 1919, with Galli-Curci.

SCENE: Chamounix and Paris.
TIME: 1760.

CAST MARQUIS DE BOISFLEURY (Basso).
CHARLES, VISCOMTE DE SIRVAL, *his nephew* (Tenor).
PREFECT (Basso).

PIERROT (Contralto).
LINDA, *a village girl* (Soprano).
ANTONIO, *a farmer, her father* (Baritone).
MADELEINE, *his wife* (Soprano).
INTENDANT (Tenor).
Peasants, Savoyards, Servants, etc.

ARGUMENT A tuneful opera with a thin and implausible story. In its first act is one of the famed arias for the soprano voice, "Oh, star that guidest!"

Act I *The Village of Chamounix.* Linda's parents are poor peasants who are in fear of being dispossessed from their home by the Marquis. Meanwhile an ardent and pure love affair has sprung up between the Marquis' nephew, Charles, and the girl, who does not know his real rank, but thinks him only a poor artist. The Marquis and his Intendant arrive, and the old nobleman (who is very much of an old roué) assures Linda's parents that they will be undisturbed. His kindness however, is only a cloak to get possession of the girl for himself.

Act II *A Paris Apartment.* Linda has been set up amid luxurious surroundings in Paris. It develops that, not the Marquis, but Charles himself, has thus sought to shield her—but without sin! The old nobleman now enters and tries to win her, but is repulsed. He laughs sardonically when she tries to explain the true situation. Charles, meanwhile, is being pressed by his mother to make a brilliant match, but still loves his village sweetheart. Her parents have been turned out of doors by the Marquis, and her father enters her apartment seeking alms. He does not recognize her at first, but when he does, hurls her money at her feet. When she realizes her impossible situation, she goes mad.

Act III *The Village of Chamounix.* Pierrot alone of her friends has been faithful to Linda. He has come to Paris for her and brings her back home. His singing soothes her. In the meantime, Charles has at last persuaded his mother to allow him to marry Linda; and he has also restored their farm to her parents. When she learns all this, her reason is restored and there is a joyful reunion.

The music throughout is sprightly, the few more dramatic passages giving contrast to soft, seductive melodies. Chief among these are: "Ambo nati ni questa valle," "O luce di quest' anima," and "Romanza di Pierotto."

VINCENZO BELLINI

Bellini was one of those unfortunate examples of a musical genius cut off in his first rich maturity. Born in Catania, Sicily, November 3, 1802, he died in the village of Puteaux, France, September 23, 1835, at the age of thirty-three. He was educated at Naples, under Zingarelli, and when only twenty he had composed an opera, "Bianca and Fernando," which was successfully produced. Several others followed, of which "Il Pirata," "La Sonnambula," "Norma," and "I Puritani" have sufficed to make his fame permanent.

LA SONNAMBULA

(Lah Son-nahm'-boo-lah)

(The Sleepwalker.) Romantic Opera in Three Acts. Music by Vincenzo Bellini. Book by Felice Romani. Carcano Theatre, Milan March 6, 1831. In English at Drury Lane, London, 1833; and at Park Theatre, New York, in 1835. At the Metropolitan, in 1892; and December 15, 1906, with Sembrich, Jomelli, and Plançon.

SCENE: A Village in Switzerland.
TIME: Early Nineteenth Century.

CAST Count Rodolpho, *Lord of the Castle* (Basso).
Teresa, *owner of the Mill* (Soprano).
Amina, *her foster daughter* (Soprano).
Lisa, *owner of the Inn* (Soprano).
Elvino, *a young farmer* (Tenor).
Alessio, *a villager* (Basso).
Notary, villagers, etc.

ARGUMENT "La Sonnambula" is a simple, human story, written into an opera full of tenderness and color. Its appeal to the sympathies, because of an unmerited punishment falling on the head of a young girl who walks in her sleep, and its dramatic climax, made it widely popular, a century ago. Its arias were prime favorites with sopranos, among them Jenny Lind and Adelina Patti. Then came the more robust school of German opera culminating in Wagner, and the lighter, more delicate melodies of Bellini went int eclipse. "La Sonnambula" is now seldom heard, yet its melodies retain their old-fashioned charm.

Act I *The Village Green.* The villagers make merry, for they celebrate the betrothal of Amina, the pretty foster daughter of Teresa, who owns the mill, and Elvino, a landowner of the neighborhood. Only one person, however, does not enter into the merry-making —Lisa, the proprietress of the tavern, for she also is in love with the young farmer. Alessio, a villager who is in love with her, is repulsed. Presently the two lovers enter, and a notary brings in the contract, which is duly signed. Just at this moment, a stranger drives up, who is on his way to the castle hard by, but first seeks shelter at the tavern. He addresses a polite speech to Amina, much to her lover's annoyance. Teresa, however, warns him against the castle, which is said to be haunted.

Amina has two pleasing songs in this Act: "How for me brightly shining" (Come per me sereno); and "With this heart its joy revealing" (Sovia il sen la man mi posa). There is also a pleasing betrothal duet between her and Elvino, "Take now the ring."

Act II *A Room in the Inn.* The stranger proves to be Rodolpho, who is lord of the castle. He is conducted to his room in the inn by Lisa, who is not averse to flirting with him. They are interrupted by some of the villagers without, and Lisa runs away, dropping her handkerchief in her haste. Shortly afterward, Rodolpho is astonished to behold the figure of Amina, clad in a white nightdress, raise his window and enter his room. He soon sees that she is walking in her sleep, and it is this apparition that has given rise to the village superstition. Rodolpho considerately leaves the room, and the sleeping girl falls upon the bed. Lisa, however, sees in this situation an opportunity to wean away Elvino from his sweetheart. She brings Elvino into the room and points out the sleeping girl. The latter, awakened by the noise, as others have entered, is covered with confusion, and cannot explain her conduct to Elvino, who casts her off in scorn.

The most striking number in this Act is the duet, before the curtain falls, between the two young people—Amina's protestations of innocence, and Elvino's wrath.

Act III *Scene 1. A Valley.* The villagers try to reconcile the lovers, but Elvino, meeting Amina, still scorns her. He snatches his ring from her finger. She is heartbroken, for she still loves him.

Scene 2. Near the Mill. Lisa has lost no time in making Elvino promise to marry her, instead of Amina. Preparations for the wedding are afoot. Rodolpho tries to dissuade Elvino from this step. He tells him about somnambulism, but Elvino is incredulous. Teresa confronts Lisa with her handkerchief, which was found in Rodolpho's room. At this moment the attention of all is directed to Amina, who emerges from a window upon the roof of the mill. She is again walking in her sleep, and she proceeds to cross a rickety foot-bridge near the turning wheel, while the villagers fear for her life. At last she crosses in safety and as she reaches the ground, she speaks of her lost love. Elvino, convinced and touched, gently replaces his ring on her finger, while her friends crowd around her in congratulation.

The last Act sparkles with melody. Amina's sleepwalking song, "Ah scarce could I believe how soon my blossoms would wither!", is followed by the joyful greeting of Elvino, "Mingle not an earthly sorrow" —which for many years was a tour de force with tenors.

NORMA

Dramatic Opera in Two Acts. Music by Bellini. Book by Felice Romani. Milan, 1831 In New York, Park Theatre, 1841; and sung at the opening of the Academy of Music, October 2, 1854, with a notable cast. At the Metropolitan, 1890, as a "benefit performance" for Lilli Lehmann.

SCENE: Gaul.
TIME: Circa 50 B.C.

CAST OROVESO, *chief of the Druids* (Basso).
NORMA, *his daughter the High Priestess* (Soprano).
ADALGISA, *a priestess* (Contralto).
POLLIONE, *Roman proconsul* (Tenor).
FLAVIUS, *his friend* (Tenor).
CLOTILDA, *friend of Norma* (Soprano).
Two Children, Priests, Soldiers, Druids.

ARGUMENT "Norma" is an opera of tragic intensity, written around the theme of a woman's scorn. A Druidic priestess, forsaken by her Roman lover, brings down vengeance upon his head, but is yet willing to share his fate. "Norma" appeared the year after "La Sonnambula" and was no less successful. Its technique is that of the earlier Italian school, relying upon directness and simplicity, rather than severe declamation. Nevertheless it is of high emotional quality and its arias tax the ability of the best coloratura. For this reason it has remained a favorite with the greatest of prima donni for a hundred years and more. The overture gives a foretaste of its changing moods. The first strains are martial, followed by a tense, minor theme and leading up to a chorus of Druids, which in turn leads logically to the first curtain.

Act I *Grove of the Druids.* Norma, the High Priestess of the Druids, is charged with the duties of the Temple, and she alone can declare war or peace. By cutting the sacred mistletoe she can give the signal for war, and this she is urged to do in order that the Roman invaders may be expelled; but she stays her hand. Despite her vows to the Temple, she has secretly wedded Pollione, the Roman proconsul, and has had two children by him. But the Roman is faithless and is even now planning to abduct Adalgisa, another virgin of the Temple. The latter, however, resists his pleas and finally confesses her temptation to the priestess. Norma is disposed to pardon her, remembering her own weakness, until she learns that the proconsul is the man involved; then she turns upon Pollione, who has entered, and reproaches him.

This Act is filled with fine music of the older tradition: the opening chorus and march of the Druid soldiers, "With thy prophetic oracle" (Dell' aura); then the famous aria by Norma, "Queen of Heaven" (Casta diva)—

This is followed by "Beloved, return unto me" (Ah! bello) in slower tempo. The Act ends with a melodic trio for Norma, Adalgisa, and Pollione, "O, how his art deceived you!" (Oh, di qual.)

Act II *Scene 1. Norma's Apartments.* While the two children of Norma's secret union with the Roman lie asleep upon a couch, the Priestess enters, resolved to kill them. But maternal love proves stronger than anger, and she asks Adalgisa, who now enters, to take charge of the children and conduct them to the proconsul. They may thus escape to Rome, while she herself remains to expiate her sin upon the funeral pyre. The duet between the two, "Hear me, Norma!" (Mira, O Norma!) is one of the gems of the opera:

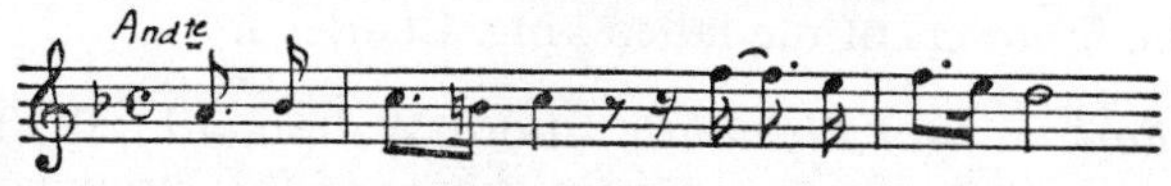

Adalgisa, however, will not aid Norma in her plan; instead she goes to Pollione to urge him to make amends.

Scene 2. (*Sometimes presented as a separate Act*) While Adalgisa is ministering at the altar, the Roman impiously attempts to seize her by force. Norma enters and strikes upon the sacred shield, summoning all her warriors. She declares that the time has come to make war and drive out the invaders. They seize the proconsul and bring him before her for judgment. Norma condemns him and then tears off the wreath from her brow, saying that she also has been guilty. The proconsul recognizes too late the worth of the woman he has scorned. He begs to die with her. The Druids make ready the funeral pyre and Norma ascends it with her lover, both perishing in the flames.

The impassioned scene between the two lovers, reunited in death, is finely outlined in the music. Another fine passage is the basso aria sung by Oroveso, with chorus of soldiers: "Haughty Roman!" (Oh del Tebro.)

I PURITANI

(*Ee Poo-ree-tahn'-ee*)

(The Puritans.) Romantic Opera in Three Acts. Music by Bellini. Book by Count Pepoli. Théâtre des Italiens, Paris, January 25, 1835. At New York, 1844, and in 1883, at the Metropolitan, with Sembrich as "Elvira."

SCENE: Near Plymouth, England.
TIME: Circa 1635.

CAST
LORD GAUTIER WALTON, *a Puritan* (Basso).
SIR GEORGE WALTON, *his brother* (Basso).
LORD ARTHUR TALBOT, *a Cavalier* (Tenor).
SIR RICHARD FORTH, *a Puritan* (Baritone).
SIR BENNO ROBERTSON, *a Puritan* (Tenor).
HENRIETTA OF FRANCE, *widow of King Charles* (Soprano).
ELVIRA, *daughter of Lord Walton* (Soprano).
Puritans, Soldiers, Guards, Women, Pages, etc.

ARGUMENT A slight historical background is offered for this opera, in the wars between the soldiers of Cromwell and the followers of the fallen king, Charles I.

Act I *A Fortress near Plymouth.* Lord Walton, a loyal adherent of Cromwell the Protector, is in charge of this stronghold, which contains political prisoners, among them Queen Henrietta, widow of

Charles I. Lord Walton's daughter, Elvira, is enamored of Lord Arthur Talbot, a Cavalier, and follower of the Stuarts, but her hand has been promised by her father to Sir Richard Forth, a Puritan. Yielding to her entreaties, however, he allows her to betroth herself to Talbot, and her uncle, Sir George Walton, arranges for the safe conduct of the Cavalier.

Talbot arrives, and then discovers that Queen Henrietta is a prisoner there. As a loyal follower, he plots her escape. He obtains Elvira's bridal veil and drapes it over the form of the Queen. As they pass out they are intercepted by Forth, the disappointed suitor. He halts them, believing the lady to be Elvira, but when her features are partially disclosed, and he sees that it is another woman, he permits them to pass. When the escape is discovered, Elvira is so wrought up over her lover's apparent faithlessness, that she loses her reason.

Three notable musical numbers in this Act are: Sir Richard's cavatina, "Ah, forever I have lost thee!"; Lord Arthur's impassioned, "To thee, Beloved!"; and Elvira's sprightly, "I am a blithesome maiden."

Act II *Another Part of the Fortress.* Elvira seems hopelessly mad. She wanders around like one distraught. Her uncle, Walton, and her Puritan lover, Forth, declare that they will meet Talbot in battle, and avenge her distress.

Here we have the mad scene of Elvira, beginning, "It was here in sweetest accents"; followed by her lovely aria, "Come, dearest love"; and a closing duet between Sir Richard and Sir George, in lusty martial vein.

Act III *A Grove.* Having accomplished the safety of his Queen, Talbot once more becomes the lover. He risks his personal safety to come to a grove near the fortress, in the hope of seeing Elvira. He meets her in the woodland, and is able to lighten her darkened mind no little by his presence and renewed words of love. But she is still in a disturbed state. While he is trying to recall her memory and reason, he hears men approaching. He knows that capture means death, but he will not forsake her. He is arrested and speedily sentenced to death. The execution is about to take place, when word is received that the Cavalier forces have been signally defeated, and Cromwell has proclaimed amnesty for all prisoners. Talbot is accordingly set free, and the sudden joy operates to restore Elvira's full reason. She and Talbot are united.

A charming song by Elvira graces this Act: "Sad and lonely by a fountain." Other good bits are Arthur's plea, "Still to abide"; and her reply, "All words are wanting."

GIUSEPPE VERDI

This supreme master of Italian opera was born at Roncole, near Busseto, Lombardy, October 9, 1813. Verdi early showed a predilection for music, at ten being the village organist, but when at eighteen he applied for admission to the Italian Conservatory, he was refused on the score that he did not reveal sufficient musical talent. Yet this was the composer who a few years later was to astonish the world by his brilliance and sustained excellence of his operas. His first opera, "Oberto," is reminiscent of Bellini. Others appeared until, in 1844, when he was thirty-one, his first really successful opera, "Ernani," was produced. A few years later came "Rigoletto," "Il Trovatore," and "La Traviata," titles which are still household words in every operatic repertory. "The Masked Ball" (1859), "The Force of Destiny" (1862), and "Don Carlos" (1867), which also belong to this middle period, have recently been revived in America. When fifty-eight, he gave evidence of still greater mastery of his art with "Aida." At a still later period came "Othello" (1887), and "Falstaff" (1893), which more nearly resemble music-drama than opera and reveal the influence of Wagner. Verdi passed away at Milan, January 27, 1901.

ERNANI

(*Air-nah'-nee*)

Dramatic Opera in Four Acts. Music by Giuseppe Verdi. Book by Francesco M. Piavé, after Hugo's "Hernani." Fenice Theatre, Venice, March 9, 1844. New York, Astor Place Theatre, 1846; Academy of Music, forty years later. At the Metropolitan, January 28, 1902, with Sembrich, Bauermeister, De Marchi, Scotti, and Edouard de Reszke.

SCENE: Aragon, Aix-la-Chapelle, and Saragossa.
TIME: 1519.

CAST
DON CARLOS, *King of Spain* (Baritone).
DON RUY GOMEZ DE SILVA, *a Spanish grandee* (Basso).
DONNA ELVIRA, *his niece* (Soprano).
JOHANNA, *her nurse* (Contralto).
ERNANI, *an outlaw* (Tenor).
DON RICCARDO, *royal armor-bearer* (Tenor).

IAGO, *armor-bearer to Gomez* (Basso).
Lords, Ladies, Soldiers, Outlaws, Servants.

ARGUMENT The story of "Ernani" originally followed Hugo's tragedy, "Hernani," so closely that the poet ac-
used the composer of literary piracy and demanded that the libretto be hanged. The title of "Il Proscritto" was therefore given the opera or a time.

ct I *Scene 1. A Mountain Retreat.* Ernani, the son of a Spanish duke, has been outlawed by the King and becomes chief of a obber band. He has fallen deeply in love with Donna Elvira, a noble ady, and hearing that she is betrothed to Don Gomez de Silva, a wealthy randee, he plans to abduct her.

The opening chorus of the bandits is the drinking song, "Haste, clink e the glasses," is followed by the tenor aria, "Unhappy one," and one a faster tempo, "Adoring soul."

Scene 2. Donna Elvira's Apartments. During the preparations for lvira's marriage, a cavalier enters her apartments and tries to persuade er to fly with him. Her cries for assistance bring Ernani upon the ene, who recognizes the King in her assailant. Carlos, on his part, cognizes the outlaw whom he has formerly defrauded of his lands nd titles, and a heated dispute arises in which Ernani hurls defiance at e monarch. Silva now interposes, and the enraged outlaw offers to ght them both, but is restrained.

Elvira's opening song, a rich, coloratura piece, has long been a vorite with prima donni. Beginning in a tone of despair, it works up a climax of brilliant cadenza: "Ernani, fly with me!" (Ernani, involami)—

ct II *Hall of Silva's Mansion.* Ernani returns to the grandee's home, disguised as a pilgrim, in order to frustrate the wedding ans of Silva with his niece. He pretends that he is in danger, and lva, not discovering his identity, grants him safe harbor so long as he under his roof. Later, Silva surprises him in an interview with Elvira d recognizes him, but the grandee's pledge of safety holds good, and postpones his personal vengeance till a later time. Silva will not en yield up the bandit to the King, who now appears before the castle lls. The monarch is appeased only by the surrender of Elvira as a stage. When the royal troops are withdrawn, Silva releases Ernani and immediately challenges him to a duel. Both agree, however, t postpone their personal differences until they have rescued Elvira. Th outlaw, on his part, pledges himself to appear at any time that Silv shall sound his hunting horn.

An impassioned duet between Ernani and Elvira is a high point i this Act: "Ah, to die would be a blessing!" (Ah, morir!)—

The King's baritone solo, "Come with me," the sounding of the huntin horn, and the spirited chorus, "To horse, to horse!" are other musica features.

Act III *Charlemagne's Tomb, at Aix-la-Chapelle.* While Carlos visiting the tomb of the great emperor, he chances to overhea a conspiracy against him. Among the conspirators are Silva and E nani. The royal guard appears and the King steps forth and orders th arrest and execution of all present. Ernani then declares that he Don Juan of Aragon, a proscribed nobleman, who has been urged o to this course by his wrongs. The King's magnanimity is touched, an yielding to Elvira's supplications, he forgives the conspirators and als bestows the lady's hand upon Ernani.

Musical numbers include: Carlos' solemn soliloquy at the tomb; th chorus of the conspirators, "Let the lion roar"; and the stirring final "Oh, noble Carlos!"

Act IV *Don Juan's Castle.* Ernani has been restored to his rank an ancestral estates. His cup of bliss is filled by his marriage Elvira. The ceremony has just been completed, when the omino sound of a bugle is heard. It is Silva come to exact his pledge. Th stern old grandee silently enters and hands a dagger to Ernani, wh takes it without protest and stabs himself to the heart.

The farewell songs of the lovers: Ernani's plea to Silva, "To linger misery"; and Elvira's wish to share his fate, "Stay thee, my lord," bri the work to a close.

LUISA MILLER

Tragic Opera in Three Acts. Music by Verdi. Book by S. Camm rano. San Carlo Theatre, Naples, December 8, 1849. New Yo Academy of Music, October 20, 1886. At the Metropolitan, Decemb 21, 1929, with Ponselle, and De Luca.

Scene: A Tyrolean Village.
Time: The Seventeenth Century.

CAST Count Walter (Basso).
Rodolfo, *his son* (Tenor).
Frederica, Duchess of Ostheim, *the Count's niece* (Contralto).
Wurm, *the Count's steward* (Basso).
Miller, *a retired soldier* (Basso).
Luisa, *his daughter* (Soprano).
Laura, *a peasant girl* (Contralto).
Ladies, Pages, Archers, Servants, Villagers.

ARGUMENT A morbid tale set to melodious music. The subtitles originally given the opera outline its gloomy end. The plot ends in stark tragedy. A tenor aria, "Quando le sere al placido," is well known.

Act I. Love *Exterior of Miller's house. Early morn.* Rodolfo, son of the Count, incognito has been courting Luisa Miller, daughter of an old soldier of humble station, and is loved in return. Their love affair, however, is beset by difficulties. Wurm, the Count's servitor, is a rejected suitor of Luisa, and threatens revenge by telling all. Meanwhile, the Count himself has been planning to have his son wed the widowed Duchess of Ostheim. When Rodolfo defies him, the Count in a rage threatens to imprison both Luisa and her father; but is deterred by his son's threat to reveal a past crime on his father's part.

Act II. Intrigue *Interior of Miller's house.* Despite Rodolfo's threat, old Miller is put in prison by the Count's orders. Luisa is then told that in order to save her father's life she must write a letter avowing that she has never really loved Rodolfo, but only wanted his wealth and station; and that she is ready to flee with Wurm. Rodolfo is deceived by this note and in both sorrow and anger says he is ready to marry the Duchess. He secretly resolves, nevertheless, to kill both Luisa and himself.

Act III. Poison *Same as Act II.* Luisa likewise has determined on death, but Rodolfo forestalls her by paying her a last visit and confronting her with the fatal letter. Then he pours out a drink, himself quaffs it, and offers it to her. He then tells her that both are facing death. Feeling the effects of the poison creeping over her, she tells him that death has released her from her promise; she can tell all; she had written the letter at Wurm's instigation, to save her father. As the now reconciled lovers clasp each other despairingly, to die together, Miller, the Count, Wurm and the villagers rush in to view the double tragedy with horror. Luisa sinks in death. Rodolfo with a last effort runs his sword through the body of Wurm before he dies

RIGOLETTO

(Ree-go-let'-to)

Tragic Opera in Four Acts. Music by Verdi. Book by Francesco M Piavé, after Hugo's "Le Roi S'amuse." Fenice Theatre, Venice, Marc 11, 1851. Two years later, at Covent Garden; New York, Academy c Music, November 4, 1857. At the Metropolitan, November 17, 188 with Sembrich as "Gildá." A later performance at "the Met," Noven ber 23, 1903, is noteworthy as marking the début here of Enrico Carus as the Duke. Sembrich again sang "Gilda," and Scotti, the Jester.

SCENE: Mantua.
TIME: The Sixteenth Century.

CAST THE DUKE OF MANTUA (Tenor).
RIGOLETTO, *his jester and attendant* (Baritone).
GILDA, *daughter of Rigoletto* (Soprano).
COUNT MONTERONE (Basso).
COUNT CEPRANO (Baritone).
COUNTESS CEPRANO (Soprano).
SPARAFUCILE, *an assassin* (Basso).
MADDALENA, *his sister* (Mezzo-Soprano).
GIOVANNA, *friend of Maddalena* (Contralto).
BORSA, *a Courtier* (Tenor).
Officers, Courtiers, Ladies, Attendants, Servan

ARGUMENT "Rigoletto" is an intense tragedy of unbridled c sires and retributive vengeance. Based up Hugo's powerful drama of medieval court life, "The King Amuses Hi self," it is unrelieved by pleasant themes, but has been lastingly succe ful because of the closely knit plot and the brilliant music with whi Verdi has invested it. "Rigoletto" is remarkable in having been wr ten at top speed, forty days, but is still ranked as one of the four b operas produced by Verdi and, after nearly a century of repertory, o of the Italian works most frequently presented. Its quartet in Fourth Act is of almost universal familiarity. The brief overt sounds a warning note of tragedy in swift contrast to the opening sce

Act I *An Open Court in the Duke's Palace.* The Duke of Mant one of the most profligate of rulers, devotes his leisure mome to the pursuit of ladies, and no house high or low is safe from his att tions. The courtiers are embittered, and especially so against Rigoletto, his jester and familiar, who aids him in these adventures. Rigoletto, though deformed, has a keen mind. His own daughter, a beautiful young girl, has been kept carefully hidden away (so he thinks). He can therefore laugh loudly with the Duke when the latter tells of having fallen in love with a fair face he has seen at church, and promises his master another rare adventure. At the same time the Duke is planning an intrigue with the Countess Ceprano. When he is warned by one of the courtiers that her husband might overhear him, he shrugs his shoulders indifferently. Here is heard the first of the tenor arias, as the Duke sings, " 'Mid the fair throng" (Questa o quella). A graceful minuet danced by the courtiers forms a foil for this ironic confession of the Duke's morals. The lively music is broken into by the sudden entrance of Count Monterone. His daughter, also, has fallen a victim to the Duke's lust. As he voices his grief and wrath, Rigoletto treats it as a great jest. Monterone, enraged, turns and hurls a father's curse against both. The Duke treats the matter lightly, but the jester cannot get the curse out of his mind.

Act II *A Secluded Street in Front of Rigoletto's House.* Still thinking of the curse, the jester has an interview with Sparafucile, a hired assassin, who promises to aid him. In a soliloquy cleverly outlined by the music, Rigoletto voices his shifting moods; first the Count's curse—"Yon assassin is my equal. He stabs in darkness—I in daylight" —then a note of scorn for the Duke and his own share in his amours—then an attempt at philosophy, to take things as they are. He is pleasantly interrupted by his daughter, Gilda, the joy of his heart, whom he guards jealously. She answers his questions as to her coming and going, but conceals from him the fact that she has seen a young man at church who has shown her marked attention. It was the Duke, posing as a student. He has found out where she lives, and his men are planning to abduct her this very night. No sooner has the jester gone than the Duke enters, his first greeting a soft melody, "Love in the sun." Meanwhile, Gilda has been singing to herself, "Ah, this is the dear voice!" She desires to know his name. He replies, "Walter." In an emotional duet they pledge their love and part. Alone again, she sings one of the best-known of Italian arias, "Dearest name" (Caro nome)—

Even while she muses tenderly of him, the Duke has put his nefarious plot into action, and his men do not spare his jester. They think that Gilda is his mistress, and encountering him in the street plan a trick at his expense. He is informed that they are after the Countess Ceprano, and he is to accompany them blindfolded. He agrees, and while blinded they place a scaling-ladder against his own house and carry off Gilda. He discovers the ruse too late to rescue her, and again remembers the curse.

Act III *An Apartment in the Palace.* When the curtain rises, the Duke is brooding because he thinks his plot has failed. He had returned to the jester's home, only to find his bird had flown. He laments his loss in a very effective song, "Each tear that falls" (Parmi veder le lagrime). Then his fellow conspirators enter to reassure him In a lively, amusing chorus they relate the night's adventures, where they have stolen Rigoletto's "mistress"—"On mischief bent" (Scorrendo) The Duke joins in their merriment and goes at once to meet his new sweetheart. Now ensues one of the most dramatic bits of this or an other opera. Rigoletto comes to the palace to rescue Gilda, but i prevented from reaching the Duke by the laughing courtiers. At firs he disguises his gnawing anxiety by an airy "Tra-la-la," meanwhile seek ing a device to get past them. When he finds he cannot succeed, h turns upon them in a rage: "Race of courtiers, vile rabble detested!" Then in an agony of despair: "She is my daughter. Oh, my lords Will you not have compassion?" His pleas fall on deaf ears; they hav grown hardened to abductions. At the height of their merriment an his despair, Gilda rushes in. The others retire, leaving father an daughter alone. His worst fears have been realized. She has been dis honored. Monterone passes by, and Rigoletto tells him his curse ha been effective. "Not so," says Monterone: "the Duke is still happy! "I join you in vengeance against him!" exclaims Rigoletto.

Act IV *A Retired Street.* Rigoletto shudders to learn that Gilda sti loves the Duke and would shield him from vengeance. H therefore hastens to the home of the murderer, Sparafucile, and ba gains with him that he shall slay the first person who enters the hous regardless of whom it may be. The bandit agrees. The jester the lures the Duke to the house by means of the bandit's sister, Maddalen The fickle Duke is ready for another adventure. In his famous aria h charges womankind with his own failing: "All women are fickle" (La donna è mobile)—

Gilda and her father outside the house listen to the flirtation going on between Maddalena and the Duke. Gilda is loath to believe her lover faithless, despite the evidence of her ears. Then comes the wonderful quartet—the voice of the Duke: "Fairest daughter of the graces"; Maddalena's coquettish: "All you say is but to flatter"; Gilda's tearful: "Ah, to speak of love thus lightly"; and Rigoletto's stern reproof: "Silence! Thy tears avail thee naught." (Bella figlia)—

The singing over, Sparafucile comes out to get half his fee for killing the Duke. Rigoletto gives it to him, but has meanwhile ordered his daughter to leave the city. Instead, she continues to linger near the house. The Duke has gone upstairs to sleep, while Maddalena pleads with her father to spare him. The rising storm gathers in intensity. The assassin, who has been drinking deeply, stabs Gilda, who in boy's clothes has come to impersonate her recreant lover, and places her body in a sack. Rigoletto comes to claim the remains of his victim, but while gloating over his vengeance he opens the sack only to find the corpse of his beloved Gilda. "Ah, the curse!" he cries.

IL TROVATORE

(*Eel Troh'-vah-toh'-ray*)

(The Troubadour.) Romantic Opera in Four Acts. Music by Verdi. Book by Salvatore Cammerano after a Spanish drama by Gutiérrez. Apollo Theatre, Rome, January 19, 1853. At Covent Garden in 1855, and, a year later in English, as "The Gypsy's Vengeance" at Drury Lane, London. In Philadelphia, in 1856; and at the Academy of Music, New York, February 25, 1857. At the Metropolitan, 1888.

SCENE: Biscay and Aragon.
TIME: The Fifteenth Century.

CAST COUNT DI LUNA (Baritone).
COUNTESS LEONORA (Soprano).
AZUCENA, *a Gypsy* (Contralto).
MANRICO, *the Count's brother, a wandering troubadour* (Tenor).
FERRANDO, *servant of the Count* (Basso).
INEZ, *friend of Leonora* (Soprano).
RUIZ, *a Gypsy* (Tenor).
Gypsies, Gentlemen, Ladies, Servants.

ARGUMENT "Il Trovatore" is the romantic tragedy of a high-born child kidnapped by Gypsies—to this extent a parallel with "The Bohemian Girl." Its tragic denouement, which seems forced, does not detract from the brilliant color of its scenes or the pleasing quality of its music. In fact, "Il Trovatore" may be said to have succeeded in spite of its plot, which has been called "jumbled" and "absurd." A great deal of the action is supposed to have taken place before the first curtain, being narrated by Captain Ferrando in the opening scene; but unless one understands Italian, it would go over the heads of many in the audience. This is his tale: The former Count di Luna had two sons. In their childhood the younger one, an infant, was stolen from its cradle by an old Gypsy woman, who was caught and burned at the stake. Her daughter, Azucena, had seized the child and at first intended to kill it for vengeance, but, instead, slew her own infant and brought the Count's son up as her own. When the stage action begins, this son grown to manhood is a leader of the Gypsies, known as Manrico the Troubadour.

As for the music it has been so perennially popular that it is as widely known, whistled and sung by non-opera-goers, as by the elect. Who does not know the "Anvil Chorus" or the "Miserere"?

One further word—each of the Four Acts has been given a title: I, "The Duel"; II, "The Gypsy"; III, "The Gypsy's Son"; and IV, "The Penalty."

Act I *Scene 1. Interior of the Count's Castle.* The present Count di Luna is in ignorance of the fact that his younger brother still lives. The story of the kidnapping is related by Ferrando in a ballad, "The Gypsy Hag sat there." His melodious story and the chorus of horrified listeners form a good prelude of what is in store.

Scene 2. Balcony of the Castle. The Countess Leonora has become enamoured of a minstrel, who comes nightly to sing beneath her window. She describes her sensations in a lovely aria, "Peaceful was the night."

While awaiting his appearance one evening, Count di Luna, also a suitor, arrives and she mistakes him for the minstrel. The surprise is general a few moments later when Manrico appears. The two men quarrel and cross swords. Manrico is wounded, but escapes before the Count can summon his attendants.

Act II *Scene 1. A Gypsy Camp.* Manrico is being nursed back to health by Azucena, his supposed mother. She confesses to him that she is not his real mother, but refuses to tell anything more. Ruiz, Manrico's follower, brings word that Leonora, believing him dead, is about to take the veil in order to escape from the Count, and that the latter is pursuing her with his soldiers. Manrico dons his armor and despite his weakened condition hurries to the rescue.

The music in this scene strikes the high note of the work. The opening chorus, a lusty song to the rhythm of beats upon the anvils, tells of the joys of Gypsy life and especially of their maidens: "Who cheers the life of the roving Gypsy?" (Anvil Chorus)—

Azucena's wild song, "Upward roll the flames," (Stride la vampa) is almost equally famous:

Scene 2. A Convent. It is the day when Leonora is to take the veil. Di Luna is encamped without, to prevent her from doing this. The nuns march slowly by singing, with Leonora among them. Di Luna attempts to abduct her, but is in turn surprised by Manrico and his band, who now rush in. The Count's forces are outnumbered and he is compelled to withdraw. Leonora is overjoyed to find her lover alive, and renounces the veil in his favor.

Di Luna's song, "The radiant gleaming of her smile," is so engaging that one is tempted to sympathize with him. The chorus of nuns within is also effective: "Ah, when the shades of night!"

Act III *Scene 1. The Camp of Di Luna.* The Count has captured Azucena, and is overjoyed to learn that she is his rival's reputed mother. Ferrando charges her with having murdered the Count's brother. She denies it stoutly, but will say nothing more, and the Count orders her to the torture chamber.

Scene 2. The Convent. Preparations are forward for the marriage of Leonora and Manrico, but before the ceremony occurs, Ruiz enters with the tidings that Azucena is in the Count's power and about to be tortured. Manrico is loyal to his foster mother, and at once sets forth to rescue her, bidding his tearful bride-to-be a hasty farewell.

Manrico's lyrical address to Leonora, in which he tries to quiet her alarm, "Oh, come, let links eternal," a rich melody, is followed by his still more famous challenge to his enemies: "Tremble, ye tyrants!"

Act IV *Scene 1. Outside the Prison Tower.* This time the Count's men are too strong for Manrico, and he is overpowered and made prisoner. The Count condemns him to death as an outlaw, and he is shut within the fatal tower. Leonora, on the outside, hears the mournful strains of the Miserere, or death chant, and her voice forms an obligato:

As the solemn strains peal forth, one can also hear the heartbroken cry of Leonora, while rising above it the farewell of Manrico in the tower: "Ah, how death still delayeth!" (Ah, che la morte!)—

These climactic passages alone would make the opera famous. Leonora pleads with the Count, who now enters, to spare the life of her lover, and finally in desperation offers herself to him for this boon. The Count agrees to sign a reprieve on these terms, and Leonora furtively drinks poison to avoid becoming his victim.

Scene 2. Within the Prison. Azucena, worn and exhausted, lies upon a pallet in troubled sleep. Manrico watches over her, awaiting his own summons to the block. This is a final, highly effective musical scene between the two, when he attempts to comfort her and their voices join in still another unforgettable duet: "Home to our mountains" (Ai nostri monti).

The door opens and Leonora, wild-eyed and panting, rushes in to bid him save himself. He at once suspects that she has sold herself for him, but sees the whole of her sacrifice as she falls dying. The Count arrives to find his triumph short-lived, and in a rage orders Manrico at once to execution. As the blow of the headsman is heard, the dying Gypsy rises up on an elbow. To the Count's triumphant cry, "It is ended!" she replies: "Your victim was your own brother!"—then: "Mother, you are avenged!"—and falls back dead. The Count, horrified at his act, exclaims: "And I still live!"

LA TRAVIATA

(*Lah Trah-vee-ah'-tah*)

(The Castaway.) Lyric Opera in Three Acts. Music by Verdi. Book by Francesco M. Piavé, based upon "La Dame Aux Camellias" (Camille), by Alexandre Dumas, the younger. Fenice Theatre, Venice, March 6, 1853. New York, 1856, and in 1883 at the Metropolitan, with Sembrich as "Violetta." Also, in 1883, at the Academy of Music, with Patti.

SCENE: Paris.
TIME: Nineteenth Century.

CAST VIOLETTA VALERY, *a frivolous woman* (Soprano).
FLORA BELOIX, *of her set* (Soprano).
ANNINA, *a servant* (Contralto).
ALFRED GERMONT, *a young Parisian* (Tenor).
GERMONT SENIOR, *his father* (Baritone).
GASTON DE LETORIÈRES, *a Parisian* (Tenor).
BARON DOUPHAL, *a Parisian* (Baritone).
MARQUIS D'ORBIGNY, *a Parisian* (Baritone).
DR. GRENVIL, *a physician* (Basso).
JOSEPH, *a servant* (Baritone).
Members of the gay set, Servants, etc.

ARGUMENT "La Traviata" follows closely the story of "Camille" which tells of the awakening of a pure love in an abandoned woman's heart. Dumas' story is a picture of modern Parisian life; but the Italian libretto harks back to the days of Louis XIV. When first produced the opera was a failure, but on its revival with some changes, a year later, it became a pronounced success and ever since has ranked high in popularity among works of this Italian school. The overture is of soft and tender nature with strings predominating and a theme similar to the prelude which precedes the death of Violetta, in the last Act.

Act I *Banquet Room in Violetta's Paris Mansion.* Violetta Valery, one of the most beautiful and noted of the Parisian demi-monde gives a supper party to some of her set. Her latest conquest, Alfred Germont, is present, and finds himself taking a strange interest in this talented but dissolute woman. He questions her about her past life while the guests revel in this and an adjoining ballroom. The woman who has dallied with love all her life finds her better nature awakened by his interest and sympathy, and agrees to leave her folly and devote herself to him alone.

A jovial drinking song by Alfred, in which Violetta and her guests join, is an early feature. Then comes an avowal of love by him, and a response by her, culminating in the duet, "Rapturous Moment" (Un d felice). After her guests have gone, Violetta soliloquizes in two well known melodies, the first a realization of dawning love: "The one o whom I've dreamed" (Ah, fors' è lui); the other a brilliant coloratura "What folly! For me there's no returning" (Sempre libera)—

Act II *Scene 1. A Villa near Paris.* True to her word, Violetta retires from Paris and lives quietly but happily with Alfred in a little country place. Their money is spent freely and carelessly, and from time to time Annita, Violetta's maid, goes to Paris, whence she returns with fresh funds. Alfred finally learns from the girl that she has been disposing of all her mistress' property piecemeal in order to run this establishment. For the first time Alfred realizes his true position, and rushes off to the city to raise funds by his own efforts. While he is gone his father, who has just discovered this retreat, arrives to upbraid Violetta for leading on his son in a spendthrift and dissolute life. She smiles scornfully at this charge; but when Germont goes on to say that it is wrecking the young man's chances and also preventing the marriage of his sister, she begins to realize that perhaps she is standing in his way. The music mirrors the intensity of this dramatic scene. Germont's plea, in which he describes his daughter, "Pure as an angel," is followed by Violetta's, "Say to her that one unhappy heart has perished." She finds that the noblest love is unselfish and self-sacrificing, and she proves that this is the quality of her love for Alfred by promising to give him up. Penning a hasty note of farewell, she returns to her old life in the city. When Alfred returns, he pays no heed to the note or to his father's explanations, but hastens back to the city with rage and grief in his heart. His father's attempts to console Alfred and reclaim him to his former life are voiced in the familiar aria, "Thy home in fair Provence."

Scene 2. Flora's Apartments. Another scene of revelry is at its height in the mansion of one of Violetta's friends. A troupe of Gypsy women dance a lively ballet, while they sing, "We're Gypsies gay and youthful." Another group in Spanish costume sing of the matadors. Violetta enters upon the arm of Baron Douphal. Here Alfred finds her. He begins gambling recklessly and soon wins heavy stakes from the Baron. Alfred then upbraids Violetta for leaving him, and implores her to return. She refuses, though giving no explanation of her apparent faithlessness, and Alfred in anger hurls his winnings at her feet, calling them all to witness that he has paid her in full. The Baron interposes, and the two quarrel and challenge each other. Alfred's father now arrives and, chiding his son for his conduct, leads him away. The closing song in this climactic scene is Violetta's despairing, "Alfred, Alfred! Little canst thou fathom the love in my heart!"

Act III *Violetta's Bedchamber.* The pensive quality of the overture is again reflected in the prelude by the orchestra which heralds the rise of the last curtain. It foreshadows the fate which is overtaking the "castaway." Violetta is paying for her former gay life by suffering from tuberculosis and now with hope of a happy love gone, she sinks rapidly. She pines for Alfred, but will not send for him. As she senses the approach of death she sings the aria of haunting loveliness, "Farewell, bright vision!" (Addio del passato)—

Her grief is turned to joy when Annita comes with the tidings that Alfred is on his way to visit her. He has learned of her sacrifice. In the haven of his arms they sing of a new life together: "We shall fly from Paris, beloved" (Parigi, o cara)—

But their happiness comes too late. The doctor arrives with Alfred's father, the latter contrite as he witnesses this tragedy. Sorrowful but helpless, the little group stand about her bedside as the soul of Traviata takes its flight.

SIMON BOCCANEGRA

(See-mon Bo-kan-nay'-grah)

Tragic Opera in Prologue and Three Acts. Music by Verdi. Book by F. M. Piavé and A. Boïto. La Fenice, March 12, 1857. In a revision at Milan, March 24, 1881. At New York, the Metropolitan, January 28, 1932, with Tibbett, as "Simon," and Martinelli, as "Gabriele."

SCENE: Genoa.
TIME: Fourteenth Century.

CAST SIMON BOCCANEGRA, *Corsair, the Doge* (Baritone).
JACOPO FIESCO, *Nobleman* (Basso).
PAOLO ALBIANI, *Goldsmith* (Basso).
PIETRO, *a Follower and Courtier* (Baritone).
GABRIELE ADORNO, *Nobleman* (Tenor).
MARIA BOCCANEGRA, *Daughter of Simon, known as Amelia Grimaldi* (Soprano).
MAIDSERVANT (Mezzo-Soprano).

CAPTAIN OF THE GUARD (Tenor).
Soldiers, Seamen, Commoners, Senators, Courtiers, Servants, etc.

ARGUMENT A tale of personal enmity and intrigue based upon the struggle between the Guelphs and the Ghibellines in northern Italy, in the middle of the Fourteenth Century.

Prologue *A Public Square in Genoa.* Paolo and Pietro, two ambitious citizens, are discovered perfecting a plot to elevate Simon Boccanegra to the Doge's throne. Simon has formerly been a corsair, but has extended the sea power of Genoa and therefore won a wide following. He has also had a secret union with Maria, daughter of Fiesco, a nobleman, and a daughter is the result. Simon now consents to the plot as a means of getting possession of Maria and their child. He confronts Fiesco with a plea for this recognition, but the haughty lord spurns him. Maria dies soon after, and their child disappears. While the populace hail Simon as their new Doge, he is grief-stricken.

Act I *Scene 1. The Grimaldi Garden.* Twenty-five years elapse. Simon's daughter has been living under the assumed name of Amelia Grimaldi, as the ward of Fiesco. The latter, however, does not know her true name. The nobleman has never relinquished his enmity for Simon and is secretly plotting to overthrow him. One of his aides is the young Guelph, Gabriele Adorno, who has fallen in love with, and is loved by, Amelia. The Doge himself pays her a visit and learns by accident that she is his long-lost daughter. The two are overjoyed at the reunion; but Paolo, who is also in love with her, plots to abduct her.

Scene 2. The Council Chamber. While the Doge is busy with affairs of state, a riot is fomenting in the streets of Genoa. Amelia has been carried off, and Gabriele is led to believe that the Doge himself is guilty. With a band of followers he dashes into the Council Chamber and tries to stab Simon, but Amelia enters at this moment and throws herself between them. The Doge by his dignity awes the crowd, and Paolo, the real culprit, is forced to repeat a curse upon the head of the scoundrel—himself.

Act II *Doge's Chambers in Ducal Palace.* Both Adorno and Fiesco are being kept as political prisoners. Paolo, now plotting against his master, pours poison into his cup; then unlocks the cells in which the two prisoners are confined and seeks to enlist them in his own nefarious projects. He tells Gabriele that the Doge has evil designs upon Amelia and that the latter loves him. When Amelia enters,

Gabriele accuses her of this. She admits it, but says their love is without sin. As Simon nears the room, she conceals Gabriele and then pleads for his life. He grants her prayer on learning of her love for Gabriele, then dismisses her, wearied by all these conflicting interests. He drinks of the poisoned cup and falls into a stupor. Adorno comes from his hiding place and is about to kill him, when Amelia again saves her father from his vengeance. She tells the young man that the Doge is her father; and Gabriele begs forgiveness and says that henceforth he will fight at Simon's side.

Act III *Interior of Palace Court, with view of City.* The last Guelph uprising has been quelled and voices again hail the Doge. Fiesco is given amnesty, and Paolo is sentenced to death. On his way to execution he confesses to Fiesco that it was he who abducted Amelia, and that even now the poison he gave her father is taking effect. Fiesco, a prey to conflicting emotions, watches his lifelong enemy, the Doge, totter feebly to his chair. But when the lord learns at last that Amelia is his own granddaughter he is stricken with remorse. She now enters with Gabriele, and with his failing breath the dying Doge gives them his blessing.

Memorable music: the [illegible], "Il lacerato spirito," and [illegible] quartets, "Figlia tal nome palpita" and "Piangi su voi."

UN BALLO IN MASCHERA

(The Masked Ball.) Tragic Opera in Three Acts. Music by Verdi. Book by Somma, based on Scribe's libretto for an opera by Auber. Apollo Theatre, Rome, February 17, 1859. At New York, the Metropolitan, in 1889.

SCENE: Naples.
TIME: The Eighteenth Century.

CAST RICCARDO, *Duke of Olivares and Governor of Naples* (Tenor).
AMELIA (Soprano).
RENATO, *secretary to the Governor and husband of Amelia* (Baritone).
SAMUEL } *Enemies of the Governor* { (Basso).
TOMMASO } { (Basso).
SILVAN, *a sailor* (Soprano).
EDGARDO, *a page* (Soprano).

ULRICA, *a fortuneteller* (Contralto).
A Judge, a Servant of Amelia, Populace, Guards, etc., Conspirators, Maskers, and Dancers.

ARGUMENT For political reasons, the scene of this opera was first laid in Boston, but with these reasons removed, the scene shifts more logically back to Italy, as librettist and composer originally intended.

Act I *Scene 1. Reception Hall in the Governor's House.* Riccardo, the Governor, is popular with the people, but detested by the nobility, who plan to get rid of him. When the action begins, the Governor is giving a public audience. He is shown a list of guests to be invited to a masked ball; and notes with satisfaction the name of Amelia, who is the wife of his secretary. During the audience, a judge is announced, who brings in for signature a warrant against an aged Negress, who is said to be a sorceress.

Scene 2. Ulrica's Hut. Before signing a decree of banishment against the Negress, Ulrica, the Governor decides to pay her a secret visit and test her powers of divination. He goes in disguise, followed by two of his enemies, Samuel and Tommaso. Unknown to him, Amelia has also come on a visit, and, concealed behind a curtain, he hears her confess to the fortune-teller her sinful love for himself, and implore aid to conquer it. The sybil tells her to pluck a magic herb which grows beneath the gallows tree. Amelia shudders but consents. Riccardo is secretly overjoyed at her confession, and resolves to protect her on her quest. After she departs he asks to have his own fortune told. Ulrica predicts that he will be slain by a friend—the first one that shall shake him by the hand. At this moment his faithful secretary, Renato, enters and greets him with a handshake. Riccardo laughs at the prophecy.

Outstanding musical numbers in this Act are: the chorus in praise of the Governor, "Our welfare is his sole desire"; and the barcarolle by the disguised sailor, Riccardo, "Declare if the waves will faithfully bear me."

Act II *Midnight, beside the Gallows.* Amelia, deeply veiled, comes to pluck the magic herb. The Governor arrives to protect her. Amelia is unable to conceal her love for him. But during their rendezvous a third person approaches. It is Renato. Concern for his master has called him to the spot. The conspirators also are lying in wait near by. Riccardo exacts from Renato a promise to escort back to the city the veiled lady, without making an attempt to learn who she is, while he himself returns by another path. Renato and his companion fall into the hands of the conspirators. The latter do not harm the secretary, but want at least to learn who the Governor's sweetheart is. They lift the veil and Renato sees his own wife. Rage seizes him, and he bids the leaders of the conspiracy meet him at his house the following morning.

It is at the opening of this Act that Amelia sings one of the best known arias, "When at last from its stem I shall sever."

Act III *Scene 1. Room in Renato's House.* Believing his wife guilty, Renato bids her prepare for death. He listens to her pleas and allows her to tell her little son farewell. He finally determines not to slay her, but to wreak vengeance instead upon Riccardo. During her brief absence the conspirators arrive, and they decide that the slayer of Riccardo shall be determined by lot. On Amelia's return she is instructed to draw a name from among others in an urn. Not knowing its purport, she draws her husband's name.

Renato's change of heart is finely shown in his song, "Is it thou?" (Eri tu che macchiavi.)

Scene 2. A Ballroom in the Palace. This festive scene, which gives the opera its name, reveals the revelry of a masked ball. The gay music is itself a mask for the impending tragedy, just as the costumes lend their aid to the conspirators. Riccardo has come to the party despite Amelia's warnings. He has determined to send Renato and his wife abroad on a diplomatic mission, and thus remove temptation from his own path. He informs Amelia of this purpose, but while they talk, Renato again surprises them and plunges his dagger in the Governor's breast. With his dying breath the latter pardons his misguided friend, assures him of his wife's innocence, and tells him of his own intentions now frustrated by death. He begs that no one will seek to avenge him. A crash of music contrasting these conflicting emotions brings the final curtain.

LA FORZA DEL DESTINO

(Lah Fort-zah del Des-tee'-no)

(The Force of Destiny.) Tragic Opera in Four Acts. Music by Verdi. Book by Francesco M. Piavé, based on the play "Don Alvaro," by the Duke of Rivas. St. Petersburg, November 10, 1862. At New York, the Metropolitan, November 15, 1918, marking the début of Rosa Ponselle; also in the cast were Caruso, De Luca, and Mardones.

SCENE: Spain and Italy.
TIME: End of the Eighteenth Century.

CAST THE MARQUIS OF CALATRAVA (Basso).
DONNA LEONORA, *his daughter* (Soprano.)
DON CARLOS DI VARGAS, *his son* (Baritone).
DON ALVARO, *a gallant* (Tenor).
PREZIOSILLA, *a Gypsy maiden* (Soprano).
PADRE GUARDIANO } *Franciscan Friars* { (Baritone).
FRA MELITONE } *Franciscan Friars* { (Baritone).
CURRA, *maid to Leonora* (Soprano).
MASTRO TRABUCO, *a peddler* (Baritone).
A Magistrate, a Surgeon, Muleteers, Peasants, Soldiers, Friars, etc.

ARGUMENT A tragedy of involved plot, in which the motifs of deception, revenge, and magnanimity alternate. They are illustrated by a musical setting of great flexibility.

Act I *Home of the Marquis, Seville.* Leonora, the dearly beloved daughter of the Marquis of Calatrava, has hidden from her father the fact that she has a lover, Don Alvaro. Knowing that her father will not consent to their nuptials, because Alvaro is suspected of being of mixed blood, she agrees to elope with her knight. But just at the moment when the couple are escaping, the Marquis enters. A stormy scene ensues, and he is slain by the accidental discharge of Alvaro's pistol.

Act II *Scene 1. A Village Inn.* Leonora dons male attire and stops at a village inn on her way to the mountains, whither she is fleeing. Her brother, Don Carlos, has sworn to avenge his father's death, and to hunt the wide world over until he finds the guilty pair.

Scene 2. Exterior of a Cloister. Leonora finally reaches a secluded church and, still in male disguise, becomes a recluse. She is protected by Father Guardiano, to whom she tells her story.

Act III *A Wood in Italy, near Velletri.* Don Carlos and Don Alvaro, under assumed names and unknown to each other, are serving in Italy. The former is saved from assassination by the latter, and they vow a lasting friendship. Soon after this Alvaro is wounded in battle, and Carlos discovers, from a portrait of Leonora in his friend's possession, that he is none other than his sister's lover, and the slayer of his father. They fight, but are separated by soldiers. Alvaro announces his intention of entering a monastery.

Act IV *A Monastery.* As Father Raffaello, Alvaro enters a monastery near the cloister where Leonora dwells. Don Carlos, however, follows him and again compels him to draw his sword. Carlos falls, this time mortally wounded. Leonora enters at this moment, and the three recognize each other. The dying man asks his sister to embrace him before he dies, and seizes this opportunity to stab her. Leonora pardons Alvaro with her last breath, and he falls weeping and penitent at her feet.

(In another version of this opera, a final scene is appended, in which Alvaro casts himself from a precipice.)

This opera also has an abundance of good music, too seldom heard: the soprano aria, "Madre, pietosa Vergine"; the duet, "La Vergine degli angeli"; and the tenor arias (sung at various times by Caruso, Martinelli, and Gigli) "O tu che in seno agli angeli," "Solenne in quest ora," and "Sleale! il segreto!"

DON CARLOS

Tragic Opera in Four Acts. Music by Verdi. Book by Mery and Du Locle, after the tragedy by Schiller. Grand Opera, Paris, March 11, 1867. "Revived" to open the Metropolitan season, as "Don Carlo," November 6, 1950.

SCENE: Spain.
TIME: The Sixteenth Century.

CAST
PHILIP II OF SPAIN (Basso).
DON CARLOS, *his son* (Tenor).
RODRIGO, *Marquis de Posa* (Baritone).
GRAND INQUISITOR (BASSO).
ELIZABETH DE VALOIS, *the Queen; also stepmother of Don Carlos* (Soprano).
PRINCESS EBOLI (Soprano).

ARGUMENT "Don Carlos" is scarcely remembered today within five years it was to be completely eclipsed by Verdi's masterpiece, "Aida." Indeed, it is hard to realize that the two works are by the same composer; yet the "Don" contains some fine passages. Its scene is laid in Spain in the time of Philip II.

Act I *Convent of St. Just.* Don Carlos, the heir apparent to the Spanish throne, has long been enamored of Elizabeth de Valois but for reasons of state her hand is bestowed upon Don Carlos' father King Philip. While the Prince is bewailing his hopeless passion, his friend Rodrigo counsels him to be prudent and seek solace in a foreign country. He resolves to go on a mission to Flanders, but in an interview with the Queen he again breaks down and declares his love

Elizabeth reproaches him. The King enters and misunderstands the situation. He charges Rodrigo, his favorite, to keep a watch over the Queen.

Act II *Royal Gardens of Madrid.* In a masked fête, Don Carlos sees a lady whom he mistakes for the Queen, and pours out his tale of love again. The lady, however, proves to be the Princess Eboli, who has been secretly in love with the Prince, and she now turns her thoughts to revenge. She gets possession of a casket from the Queen, containing the Prince's portrait, and shows it to the King. The latter finds a pretext, in the religious wars, to throw his son into prison.

Act III *Scene 1. The Queen's Apartment.* Elizabeth searches for her casket, and is accused of infidelity by the King. She is at a loss to explain matters until the Princess Eboli comes to her rescue and confesses her share in the intrigue. The Queen's innocence is proved, and the Princess is banished from court.

Scene 2. A Prison Cell. While the Prince languishes in prison, he is visited by his friend Rodrigo, who had taken his sword away from him on his arrest. Rodrigo tells Don Carlos that this measure was for the Prince's protection. Meanwhile he himself has taken the blame for the uprising in Flanders, and soon pays the penalty for this pious fraud. He is shot by order of the King. When the latter comes to the prison to return his sword to Don Carlos, the latter turns from him, and tells him he has put an innocent man to death.

Act IV *Convent of St. Just.* Once again the Prince seeks an interview with Elizabeth, and again she meets him, but actuated only by lofty motives. The jealous King again surprises them, and, yielding to the counsel of the Grand Inquisitor, he consigns his son to the tender mercies of the Inquisition.

Best musical numbers: a duet (made famous by Caruso and Scotti) "Dio, che nell' alma infondere"; an aria for contraltos, "O don fatale"; two for bassos, "Ella giammai m'amo" and "Domiro sol nel manto mio regal"; and two for baritones, "Per me giunto" and "O, Carlo, ascolta!"

AIDA

(*Ah-ee'-dah*)

Romantic Opera in Four Acts. Music by Giuseppe Verdi. Book by Antonio Ghislanzoni, from the French of Camille du Locle. Written for the Khedive of Egypt, and first produced at Cairo, December 24, 1871. In La Scala, Milan, with Verdi conducting, February 8, 1872. At the Academy of Music, New York, November 26, 1873; and, in 1883, with Patti as "Aida." At the Metropolitan, November 12, 1886, in German.

SCENE: Memphis and Thebes.
TIME: Rule of the Pharaohs.

CAST THE KING OF EGYPT (Basso).
AMNERIS, *his daughter* (Contralto).
RHADAMES, *a General* (Tenor).
RAMFIS, *the High Priest* (Basso).
AMONASRO, *the King of Ethiopia* (Baritone).
AIDA, *his daughter, a slave* (Soprano).
Soldiers, Courtiers, Citizens, Tire-women, Dancers, etc.

ARGUMENT "Aida" is considered Verdi's masterpiece, and one of the most brilliant of all operas. It has remained continuously in favor with the public. The story, which is full of color, has an ancient Egyptian setting, being a romance woven around a beautiful slave girl, who later proves to be the daughter of a rival king.

Musically the work is of interest as being the first example of Verdi's "mature" style. It has been likened to the Wagnerian operas in theme and treatment. This is not exact as it is still of the more florid Italian school, but of more modern pattern. Verdi was here again exhibiting his great versatility. After a brief prelude which gives only a hint of the chief motifs, the curtain rises and the reader is transported back to ancient Egypt.

Act I *Scene 1. Interior of the Egyptian King's Palace, at Memphis.* The High Priest, Ramfis, delights the warrior, Rhadames, by informing him that Isis, the goddess, has decreed that he shall lead the army against the warring Ethiopians. Rhadames is madly in love with Aida, the slave, and sees in this prospective victory an opportunity to obtain her from the King as his bride. He gives vent to his passion in that magnificent aria beloved of all tenors, "Heavenly Aida" (Celeste Aida). The first soaring notes:

lead up to the climactic phrase:

His outpourings, however, are interrupted by the entrance of Amneris, the King's daughter, who has long loved the young soldier. As he is cold to her, she begins to suspect the truth, and she jealously watches Rhadames and Aida, when the slave appears. The King and his court enter, and Rhadames is formally invested with the command against the Ethiopians, who have advanced upon Thebes. All rejoice except Aida, who knows secretly that her lover is to meet her father, the rival king, in battle, and that one of them must fall. As the multitude give a great shout of farewell, "Return victorious!"

she expresses her conflicting emotions in the long and difficult aria containing her tender prayer:

Scene 2. The Temple of Ptah. Ptah is the war god of Egypt, and this short scene is occupied with the consecration of the arms of Rhadames. The music is of solemn character, the prayer of Ramfis, "God, guardian and avenger," being a dominant note.

Act II *Scene 1. The Apartments of Amneris.* By sharp contrast we next look into the luxury of a Princess' rooms. Slave girls sing in praise of their mistress, and a Moorish ballet follows. Some weeks have passed, and Amneris with the rest of the court has heard that Rhadames is returning victorious from war, and, desirous of winning him by her charms, she orders her women to deck her in her finest. Aida enters, and Amneris tricks her into revealing her love for the general by falsely announcing that he has fallen in battle. When Aida's grief betrays her secret, Amneris scorns her.

Scene 2. The Entrance to Thebes. Pharaoh summons his whole glittering court to do honor to his conquering general. The troops enter in formal review, and Rhadames is borne in, in triumph, on the shoulders of slaves. This superb scene where oriental color and display unite with the swelling strains of triumph is the "grand moment" of the opera, and it is a case-hardened auditor indeed who can listen and watch unmoved. The triumphal march in which one set of instruments after another takes up the strain: "Glory to Egypt!"

is succeeded by the shouts of the multitude (Chorus of Triumph):

The procession halts at the foot of the throne. Pharaoh himself comes down to greet his general and escort him up the steps to a place at his right hand. Amneris presents him with a crown signifying her own desires and as she glances meaningly at her father, he asks Rhadames to name his own reward. The captives of war are brought forward, and the populace demand that they be put to death. Aida recognizes the conquered King as her father, but he conceals his true rank. Rhadames now asks as his boon, that the lives of the captives may be spared. The King grants his request, and in addition bestows his daughter's hand upon him and proclaims him heir to the throne.

Act III *A Night Scene on the Nile.* Amneris, accompanied by the High Priest, goes to pay her vows to Isis, on the evening before her marriage. Aida follows secretly, to meet Rhadames for the last time. While she muses upon her own unhappy fate, another lovely song emerges: "Oh, native land!" (Oh, patria mia!). But instead of seeing Rhadames, Amonasro, her father, suddenly presents himself. In a tumultuous scene he alternately reproaches her and urges her to aid their country by betraying to him the next movements of the Egyptian army. This she will not consent to do. They are interrupted by the entrance of the young general and the mutual expressions of love are voiced in an exotic duet: "In ectasy the world forgotten." However, in the course of their talk Rhadames tells her his next plans, and Amonasro in hiding overhears them. The captive King now plays a bold stroke by presenting himself to Rhadames in his true rank, and urging him to take sides with Ethiopia. Aida's hand is pledged by way of reward. Rhadames will not yield to the temptation, and while they parley Amneris comes from the Temple to denounce them. Rhadames urges the father and daughter to flee, but himself remains to submit to the guards of Ramfis.

Act IV *Scene 1. Corridor in the Palace.* Amneris has repented her action against Rhadames, and now seeks to save him. She tells him that Aida's father was killed in the flight, but that Aida herself still lives. If Rhadames will renounce her, Amneris says that she will obtain the pardon of Pharaoh. Rhadames refuses, and the enraged Princess tells him to go to his doom. But when the tribunal of priests decree that the soldier shall be entombed alive, as the penalty of his supposed treason, Amneris turns upon them in redoubled fury.

Scene 2. Interior of the Temple, showing the crypt below. While the priests and priestesses perform the ceremonial temple service above, Rhadames is seen in the shadowy vault, resigning himself to death. Aida now steals to his side. She has come to die with him. As he sings the tender aria, "To die, so pure and lovely," she replies with, "Ecstasy of immortal love." Slowly the light recedes in the vault, in contrast to the lighted room above, where the penitent Princess vainly lifts her voice in prayer. But below all is peace. United in death the lovers sing a final duet of haunting loveliness: "Farewell, O earth! Farewell, thou vale of sorrow! Now opens to us the sky!" (O, terra, addio!)

OTHELLO

(*O-thel'-lo*)

Music Drama in Four Acts. Music by Giuseppe Verdi. Book by Arrigo Boïto, after the play by Shakespeare. La Scala Theatre, Milan, February 5, 1887. A year later, at the Academy of Music, New York. At the Metropolitan, March 24, 1891, with Tamagno as "Othello," and Albani, as "Desdemona."

SCENE: Cyprus.
TIME: The Fifteenth Century.

CAST OTHELLO, *a Moorish general in the service of Venice* (Tenor).

DESDEMONA, *his wife* (Soprano).
IAGO, *lieutenant to Othello* (Baritone).
EMILIA, *his wife* (Contralto).
CASSIUS, *lieutenant to Othello* (Tenor).
RODERIGO } *Venetian gentlemen* (Tenor).
LODOVICO } *Venetian gentlemen* (Basso).
MONTANO, *former governor of Cyprus* (Basso).
Soldiers, Sailors, Citizens, Servants.

ARGUMENT The story of "Othello" closely follows Shakespeare's play of the same name, except that it omits the first act of the play dealing with Desdemona's courtship and marriage. This work followed "Aida" after an interval of nearly sixteen years, and when the composer had reached the age of seventy-four. It astonished the musical world by the fire and continuity of its composition, no less than by Verdi's versatility. "Othello" is in the style of the Wagnerian music-dramas.

Act I *Open Square at Cyprus.* Othello, a noble Moor in the service of the Venetian state, has won the heart of Desdemona, a high-born Venetian lady, and has brought her with him on his expedition to Cyprus. The people welcome their arrival. Othello appoints Cassius as his first lieutenant in command, which act enrages Iago against them both. Iago is the servant and confidant of the general and had hoped to win this place for himself. His scheming mind now launches far reaching plans of revenge. He succeeds in his first purpose of getting Cassius drunk and embroiled in a quarrel with Montano, the retiring governor. Othello enters at this moment—as Iago hoped he would—and punishes Cassius by depriving him of the command.

Musical numbers in this Act include: Iago's drinking song, "Then let us quaff the noble wine" (Inaffia l'ugola); and the love duet between Desdemona and Othello, which she begins by the aria, "When thou didst speak" (Quando narravi).

Act II *A Room in the Palace.* Iago next endeavors to poison the mind of Othello against his lovely and virtuous wife. At first Iago carefully drops hints and innuendoes, some of which, however stick. He now makes use of Cassius as a pawn in this game, pretending friendship for him, and urging him to ask Desdemona to seek his pardon and reinstatement. Cassius does so, and Iago makes capital of this with the Moor. Othello finally becomes so suspicious that when his wife comes to intercede for the lieutenant, he can see in this only evi-dences of her guilt. He rebuffs her angrily. Her handkerchief ha allen, and Emilia, Iago's wife, picks it up; but Iago snatches it from her and keeps it to bolster up his flimsy chain of evidence. When alone with the Moor, he boldly charges Cassius with having had improper relations with Desdemona, and states that she has given her lover a handkerchief which will be found on his person. Othello vows vengeance against the pair.

In the early part of this Act is Iago's remarkable confession of his cynical creed, known as "Credo," a notable baritone aria; and his great duet with the indignant Othello, at its close: "Farewell, O sacred memories!" (Addio, sante memorie)—

ct III *A Room in the Palace.* Desdemona again intercedes for Cassius, but her very innocence leads to her undoing. Othello sees in it only further confirmation of his suspicions. Cassius now led in by Iago. Othello conceals himself, and Iago gives the harmless conversation such a turn as to make it appear in line with his accusations. The handkerchief is, of course, found as Iago predicted and arranged. Othello bursts into a torrent of rage, and as he confronts his wife with the proofs of her "infidelity" some of the finest dramatic-musical passages occur. Her tearful plea, "Upon my knees before thee" (Esterrefatta fisso), only brings a scornful rejoinder from him. He finally hurls her to the floor and is only prevented from doing her further harm by the arrival of an embassy from Venice. It brings the news that he is deposed as governor, and Cassius has been appointed in his place. When they depart, Othello commands Iago to slay Cassius, and himself wrought up to such a fury that he falls upon the floor. Their mingled voices finally merge into an impassioned sextet. The Act ends ironically with the shouts of the people outside: "Hail, Othello, thou lion of Venice!" "A fine lion!" sneers Iago.

ct IV *Desdemona's Bedchamber.* Desdemona sits weeping with Emilia. All her actions have been misjudged and she is in terror of her life. Her pathetic narrative to her maid takes the form of old Italian folksong, "The Willow" (Salce, Salce)—

After Emilia leaves her, Desdemona intones a lovely "Ave Maria" anc then retires. Othello enters and roughly bids her prepare to die. Sh pleads, but he is obdurate. He suffocates her. Emilia rushes in, bu too late to save her mistress' life. She alarms the palace and then re veals to Othello the whole extent of Iago's infamy, stating that he hac obtained the handkerchief from her. Othello, too late, sees the truth and overcome with remorse, stabs himself, falling by the bed of th slain Desdemona. His final outcry shows his grief and remorse: " kissed thee ere I slew thee!"

FALSTAFF

(Fal'-staff)

Comic Opera in Three Acts. Music by Verdi. Book by Arrig Boito, after "The Merry Wives of Windsor," by Shakespeare. Teatr Alla Scala, Milan, Feb. 9, 1893. At New York, the Metropolita February 4, 1895.

SCENE: Windsor.
TIME: The Fifteenth Century.

CAST
SIR JOHN FALSTAFF, *a soldier of fortune* (Baritone
FORD, *a citizen of Windsor* (Baritone).
MISTRESS ALICE FORD, *his wife* (Soprano).
ANNE FORD, *their daughter* (Soprano).
MISTRESS PAGE (Soprano).
MISTRESS QUICKLY (Contralto).
FENTON, *suitor of Anne* (Tenor).
DR. CAIUS, *a citizen* (Tenor).
BARDOLPH } *followers of Falstaff* { (Tenor).
PISTOL } *followers of Falstaff* { (Basso).
ROBIN, *a page*
Innkeeper, Townspeople, Servants, etc.

ARGUMENT "Falstaff" is noteworthy as being Verdi's single i cursion into Light Opera. Perhaps tempted his success with one of Shakespeare's tragic dramas, "Othello," he now turned his hand to this lighter medium. The music while pleasing does not measure up to the high standards which this master composer had set for himself. Shakespeare's comedy is closely followed as to plot in this musical version of the fat knight's misadventures.

Act I *Scene 1. A Room at the Garter Inn.* Falstaff, the doughty knight whose prowess has been tested on the battlefield (if his own word is to be believed), decides to try his skill in the lists of love. He therefore prepares two billets-doux for estimable wives of Windsor, and since his followers, Bardolph and Pistol, balk at taking them, he sends them by a page. He also quarrels with Dr. Caius, who complains of being robbed by Bardolph and Pistol.

In this scene Falstaff sings the praises of Mistress Ford: "O love with starlike eyes!"; and the monologue on "Honor," the words taken from Henry IV.

Scene 2. Ford's Garden. Mistress Ford and Mistress Page, the ladies who have received the epistles, meet and compare them, and with Mistress Quickly plan to revenge themselves upon the sender. Bardolph and Pistol confuse their plans by informing Ford of the affair. The latter is to meet Falstaff in disguise. Meanwhile, a plot of a different sort is afoot. Ford has planned to have his daughter Anne marry Caius, but she is in love with Fenton, who meets her clandestinely.

The reading of the letter by Mistress Ford is delightfully lyrical. This is followed by a quartet of women, unaccompanied, "He'll surely come courting," and a male quartet in sharp contrast, "He's a foul, a ribald thief," with a pleasing aria by Fenton.

Act II *Scene 1. The Garter Inn.* Dame Quickly comes to the inn to give Falstaff a note from Mistress Ford, apparently yielding to his wishes and making an appointment for that afternoon. After she departs, Ford is introduced under the name of Fountain, who pretends that he is a stranger seeking the love of Mistress Ford. Falstaff readily agrees to help him, and states complacently that he has an engagement with that lady for this very day. Ford has heard nothing of the women's plot, and is both astounded and jealous, but hides his feelings. His song is an excellent dramatic outburst, "Do I dream? Or is it real?"

Scene 2. Room in Ford's House. Falstaff arrives at Mistress Ford's and at once begins to make ardent protestations of love. At this moment, Dame Quickly bustles in to say that Ford and his friends are at hand. The fat knight is hastily thrust behind a screen, and a little later, when the search begins in earnest, he is persuaded to hide in a basket of soiled linen. Meanwhile, Fenton and Anne take refuge behind the screen for a little love-making on their own account. Ford returns and thinks he has discovered the villain behind the screen, and is greatly disgusted when the young lovers come to view. While the search proceeds, Falstaff is nearly suffocated in the basket. The women, ostensibly to rescue him, have the basket conveyed to the river brink and its entire contents dumped into the water.

This scene, which has to do with the ludicrous clothes-basket episode, is again utilized to the utmost by the instruments. Vocal numbers include: Mistress Quickly's droll description of her visit: " 'Twas at the Garter Inn"; and Falstaff's song, "Once I was a page."

Act III *Scene 1. The Garter Inn.* Dame Quickly again visits the crestfallen knight to express her sorrow and to make a new appointment. The knight again falls into the trap. As the doughty knight soliloquizes over his misadventures, one instrument after another in the orchestra seems laughing at him. A cacophony of mirth greets his song, "Ungrateful world! Wicked world!" Mistress Ford explains the whole hoax to her husband, and he promises to aid them this time. Dr. Caius is again promised Anne's hand, and Dame Quickly, who learns of it, runs to warn the lovers.

Scene 2. Windsor Park. Fenton is aided by the women, who disguise him as a monk. Falstaff again meets Mistress Ford, but is interrupted by a crowd disguised as witches, elves, and fairies, who belabor the knight soundly. He begs for mercy and, at his promise of good behavior, Ford pardons him. Meanwhile, Dr. Caius finds that he has captured the wrong person, and Anne, for whom he has sought, enters with Fenton. Ford is persuaded to relent and unite the two lovers.

This closing scene brings in Fenton's love song, "From those sweet lips"; and an equally pleasing melody by Anne, "We'll dance in the moonlight"; a dance by elves; and in a spirit of lightheartedness the music blends with the close, "All the world is jesting!"

AMILCARE PONCHIELLI

Ponchielli was born at Paderno Fasolaro, Cremona, August 31, 1834 He studied at the Milan Conservatory. In 1856 he brought out a Cremona an opera, "I Promessi Sposi" (The Betrothed), which, in a revised version, Milan, 1872, was his first striking success. His second opera, "I Lituani" (The Lithuanians), brought out in 1874, was revived ten years later, as "Alguna"; and, while "La Gioconda" (1876) did not wait so long for success, it, too, was revised and brought out in a new version before it received popular acclaim. Among his other operas are, 1880, "Il Figliuol Prodigo" (The Prodigal Son), and, 1885, "Marion Delorme." "La Gioconda," however, is the only one of his operas that has made its way abroad. Ponchielli died at Milan, January 16, 1886.

LA GIOCONDA

(Lah Jo-kon'-dah)

(The Street Singer.) Dramatic Opera in Four Acts. Music by Amilcare Ponchielli. Book by Tobia Garrio, after Hugo's Tragedy, "Angelo, the Tyrant of Padua." La Scala Opera House, Milan, April 8, 1876. At New York, the Metropolitan, December 20, 1883, with Nilsson, as the street singer, and Scalchi as the blind mother.

SCENE: Venice.
TIME: The Seventeenth Century.

CAST
LA GIOCONDA, *a street singer* (Soprano).
LA CIECA, *her blind mother* (Contralto).
ALVISE BADOERO, *an inquisitor* (Basso).
LAURA, *his wife* (Mezzo-Soprano).
ENZO GRIMALDO, *a Genoese noble* (Tenor).
BARNABA, *a spy* (Baritone).
ZUANE, *a boatman* (Basso).
ISEPO, *a scribe* (Tenor).
A PILOT (Basso).
Ladies, Senators, Masqueraders, Sailors, Monks, Citizens, Servants.

ARGUMENT "La Gioconda" is the sole opera upon which Ponchielli's fame rests today, and it had a stormy career both at home and abroad. Its first performance at the Metropolitan in New York, in 1883, was unsuccessful and it was withdrawn from the boards for the next fourteen years. Today it seems to have won a permanent and rightful place in repertory, its charming "Dance of the Hours" alone holding acclaim, even if one forgot its many other fine musical moments. As to the plot, it is a swiftly moving Venetian tale of love, intrigue, jealousy and crime—the sort of dish that many "Grand" operas seem to demand. Each Act was given a separate title, as here shown.

Act I *"The Lion's Mouth." Court of the Ducal Palace.* Called "The Lion's Mouth" because of a receptacle into which letters intended for the Inquisition are dropped. Leading her blind mother, the beautiful La Gioconda, a street singer, enters the ducal square just as a chorus of merrymakers have deserted it. She is in search of Enzo, a nobleman with whom she is in love. But the spy Barnaba bars her way, and when she repulses his advances he takes revenge by stirring up the populace against her mother, La Cieca, charging her with being a sorceress. The latter is rescued by Laura, the Inquisitor's wife, once the sweetheart of Enzo. The latter, who has come upon the scene, also recognizes Laura, and the spy, noting their exchange of glances, plots a new piece of villainy. He arranges a meeting between them on board Enzo's ship, and at the same time sends word to Laura's husband of the adventure. La Gioconda also learns of the meeting.

Chief musical numbers in this Act: the chorus by the populace, "Sports and feasting" (Feste e pane); an expressive aria by La Cieca, "Voice of woman or of angel" (Voce di donna); and the dramatic duet between Barnaba and Enzo, "Prince, thou art pensive" (Principe di Santa Fior).

Act II *"The Rosary." On Board Enzo's Ship.* This act is called "The Rosary" from the fact that La Cieca has given Laura a rosary in token of gratitude and it plays a further part in the action. While Barnaba gloats over the success of his scheme Enzo comes on deck and greets Laura, who arrives in a boat. The two renew their pledges of love. Gioconda who has hidden on board now comes forward with a dagger resolved to stab her rival, but Laura holds up the rosary given by Gioconda's mother, and the street singer, recognizing it, resolves to save rather than slay her. Gioconda advises her that Alvise, the outraged husband, is near at hand and aids her to escape in her (Gioconda's) boat. Seeing his ship surrounded, Enzo sets fire to it.

There is a very effective fisher's ballad sung by Barnaba in this Act: "Ah, fisher, lower now thy net!" (Ah, Pescator!)—

Also a still more famous song, favored of tenors, by Enzo. As he looks upon a scene of great beauty where the moon and stars are reflected upon the waters of the lagoon, he apostrophizes in the delightful melody which matches it: "Heaven and ocean!" (Cielo e mar!)—

Act III *"The House of Gold."* Alvise is determined to avenge himself upon his unfaithful wife and tells her she must die by poison. Deaf to her entreaties he hands her a vial and bids her drain it before his return. Gioconda enters and substitutes a sleeping potion, and Laura is soon stretched upon the couch pale and apparently dead. Alvise's song, "Yes, her doom is to die!" (Si, morir ella de'!) is noteworthy.

After the attempt on Laura's life, the scene changes to a sumptuous ballroom, which stages the magnificent ballet, "Dance of the Hours."

The dancers' costumes, the scenic and lighting effects, and the colorful music depict dawn, noonday, twilight, and night. The combined effect is almost overpowering and the ballet is justly regarded as one of the finest in opera. The furious gaiety of the ball, however, only brings into sharper contrast the calculated villainy of the plot. No sooner has the dance ended than Alvise draws apart the curtains concealing the death couch and reveals the form of Laura. Enzo rushes forward to attack Alvise but is disarmed. Barnaba is placed over him as a guard, and Gioconda now tells the spy that if he will release him, she will agree to his desires. Barnaba does so.

Act IV *"The Orfano Canal." A Ruined Palace.* While Gioconda sits alone and dejected, the unconscious form of Laura is borne in. Gioconda fights an inward battle as to whether she shall kill or resuscitate her helpful rival. She finally resolves to kill herself. Enzo comes in and she tells him that Laura has been saved. Overjoyed he hastens to the couch, hearing the voice of Laura. Barnaba enters to claim Gioconda as she has promised, and in reply she stabs herself, falling lifeless at his feet.

The music of the orchestra forms a wonderful foil for the conflictin emotions of this powerful Act. As the voices rise in protest a volume o pure melody pours forth. Laura, regaining her senses, calls out "Enzo!" A chorus offstage is heard in a serenade, a recurrence of a earlier theme. " 'Tis the rosary!" sings Gioconda. Enzo and Laur join their voices in thanks, "Upon thy hands tears are falling." An as Gioconda stabs herself it is with a defiant cry: "Gioconda is thine! With a yell of baffled rage the spy tells her deaf ears: "Thy mother, have strangled her!" But no one heeds him. The curtain falls.

ARRIGO BOÏTO

Arrigo Boïto was known as poet and librettist before turning his han to composing. He was the author of the books to Ponchielli's ope "La Gioconda," and Verdi's "Othello" and "Falstaff." Boïto was bor in Padua, Italy, February 24, 1842. From 1853 to 1862 he studied the Milan Conservatory, but lived so long thereafter in Germany as become Teuton in his musical tastes. He was an ardent admirer Wagner's music. He wrote and composed another opera, "Nerone but withheld it from production. "Mefistofele" is based on the tw parts of Goethe's "Faust." Boïto died in Milan, June 10, 1918.

MEFISTOFELE

(Mef-is-tof'-e-leh)

(Mephistopheles.) Dramatic Opera in Prologue, Four Acts, and E logue. Music by Arrigo Boïto. Book by Composer. After Goeth "Faust." La Scala, Milan, March 5, 1868. At New York, Academy Music, November 24, 1880. The Metropolitan, January 15, 18 when "revived" for Emma Calvé. Edouard de Reszke was the Evil Or

SCENE: Germany and Greece.
TIME: Middle Ages.

CAST MEPHISTOPHELES, *the Evil One* (Baritone).
FAUST, *a student* (Tenor).
WAGNER, *a student* (Basso).
NEREUS (Baritone).

PANTALIS (Tenor).
MARGUERITE, *a German girl* (Soprano).
MARTHA, *her mother* (Contralto).
HELEN OF TROY (Soprano).
Students, Townspeople, Spirits, Witches, Bacchanal Women, Greeks, etc.

ARGUMENT The plot of this opera is not unlike that of Gounod's "Faust," except that it delves more deeply into Goethe's theme, and shows the final redemption of Faust.

Prologue *The Court of Heaven.* As the angels prostrate themselves before the throne of the Most High, Mephistopheles appears and wagers that he can seduce the philosopher, Faust. He is bidden to make the attempt.

Act I *Frankfort.* It is Easter Sunday. Amid the merry throng of the streets, Faust and Wagner wander, observing the crowd, but holding themselves aloof from it. Their attention is finally attracted by a gray Friar, whom every one seems instinctively to shun. He follows Faust so persistently, that the latter enters his house to avoid him. However, the Friar also slips in, and presently reveals himself to Faust as the Evil One. He says that he will open to Faust the riches and happiness of the world, if Faust will serve him in the next world. Faust accepts the proposition, and Mephistopheles carries him away on his cloak.

Act II *Scene 1. A Garden.* Mephistopheles first offers Faust love, and introduces him to Marguerite, the village girl. The two walk arm in arm in a garden, while Mephistopheles keeps the coast clear by making love to Martha, her mother. Faust hands the girl a phial containing a powerful sleeping potion, which she is to give her mother

Scene 2. The Brocken. The witches' saturnalia is in full progress. Mephistopheles shows Faust their wild revels. During one incantation, they summon before his eyes the picture of Marguerite, suffering imprisonment because of crimes instigated by him.

Act III *Interior of a Prison Cell.* Marguerite is shown alone in a cell, crazed by grief and remorse. She has been condemned to death for poisoning her mother and killing her child. She can look only to Heaven for pardon. Through the power of Mephistopheles, Faust enters the prison and bids her escape with him, but she will not do so while he is associated with the Evil One. Until dawn they urge her to go, but they are forced to leave without her. She falls back lifeless, while an angelic choir chants that she is saved.

Act IV *A Scene in Ancient Greece.* In order further to show his power, Mephistopheles transports Faust to ancient Greece, and bestows upon him the hand of the most beautiful of women, Helen of Troy. She tells Faust her story and the events leading to the fall of Troy. Faust makes ardent love to her, and she accepts him.

Epilogue *Faust's Study.* Faust as an old man is seen reviewing his past life, which he regrets bitterly. He has not found happiness in the gratification of the senses. Mephistopheles appears, but finds that he has lost his power to tempt him. Sirens surround Faust and call to him seductively. He turns away and opens his Bible, reading therein that the vilest of sinners can repent and be saved. He prays for forgiveness, and Mephistopheles sinks into the earth, vanquished. Faust dies, and a shower of roses falls upon his body from above, in token that Heaven has accepted his soul.

Musical numbers include a soprano aria, "L'Altra notte in fondo a mare," and a quartet, "La notte del Sabba."

ALFREDO CATALANI

An Italian composer who was born in Lucca, July 19, 1854, and died in Milan, August 7, 1893. He wrote songs and instrumental pieces, but is known in this country for only one opera, "Loreley," which was presented in both Chicago and New York, but has not continued in repertory.

LORELEY

(Loh'-ray-lay'-ee)

Romantic Opera in Three Acts. Music by Catalani. Book by A. Zanardi and Carlo D'Ormville. Chicago, and New York, at the Metropolitan, February 13, 1919, by the Chicago Opera Company.

SCENE: The Rhine.
TIME: The Middle Ages.

ARGUMENT The traditional story of the Loreley is here interwoven into a romantic opera. While wandering along the banks of the Rhine, Walter, the governor of Oberwesel, meets the Rhine-maiden, or Loreley. Smitten with her charms, he loves her to her undoing, and his own as well as he forgets that he is already betrothed to Anna of Rehberg, niece of the Margrave. He later confides his dark secret to his friend, Herman, who, although himself in love with Anna, urges him to remain faithful to her. In the ensuing action Walter strives vainly to resist the siren. Anna pines away and dies. In the final scene Walter meets a procession of mourners and is told that Anna has not survived his falseness. He rushes remorsefully to the river and is again greeted by Loreley. She is about to embrace him, when voices from the deep bid her desist. She belongs to the river god. As she sings her song of enchantment and farewell, Walter throws himself into the torrent and perishes.

RUGGIERO LEONCAVALLO

A Neapolitan, born March 8, 1858, Leoncavallo is known as a pianist and man of letters, as well as dramatic composer. He was his own librettist. He studied at the Naples Conservatory, but early came under the influence of Wagner. His first opera, "Thomas Chatterton," was unsuccessful at first, but was later produced in Rome (1896). He then wrote "I Medici," produced in Milan in 1893; "La Bohème" (Venice, 1897); "Zaza" (Milan, 1900); "Roland in Berlin" (Berlin, 1904); "La Reginetta delle Rose" (Rome, 1912); and "Zingari" (London, 1912). It must be admitted, however, that none of these has had a lasting success, and Leoncavallo's claim to distinction, a very just one, rests upon his famous opera, "I Pagliacci." One other, "Zaza," has recently been revived with considerable success. Leoncavallo died, August 9, 1919.

I PAGLIACCI

(Ee Pah-lee-ah'-chee)

(The Players.) Dramatic Opera in Two Acts. Music by Leoncavallo. Book by Composer. Milan, May 21, 1892. At New York,

Grand Opera House, June 15, 1893. At the Metropolitan, Decembe 11, 1893, with Melba, De Luca, and Ancona. The role of "Tonio' has been a favorite with many baritones, because of the famous Pro logue.

SCENE: Near Montalto, in Calabria.
TIME: August 15, 1865.

CAST CANIO (Clown), *chief of a troupe of strolling players* (Tenor).
NEDDA (Columbine), *his wife* (Soprano).
TONIO (Taddeo), *a player* (Baritone).
BEPPO (Harlequin), *a player* (Tenor).
SILVIO, *a peasant* (Baritone).
Villagers.

ARGUMENT "Not how much, but how good," might be th motto of this gem of shorter operas. With tha other gem, "Cavalleria Rusticana," by a kindred spirit, Mascagni, Leor cavallo reached the heights in a single bound for a completely satisf ing evening at the opera. The theme is simple, but strongly develope in both text and music. The keynote is sounded in the Prologue: "W are all players." Before the curtain rises, it parts slightly and Toni comes forth in his "Taddeo" costume. He warns his audience that buffoon's heart is human; his tears may be real; and his jests may conce sadness.

His voice rises in its pleading: "Ah, think then, kind people . . . v are men like you!"—

He concludes with a signal to his company, "Come, then, let us begin

Act I *A Village in Calabria.* The curtain rises as villagers sing a joyous chorus, "They're here!" A troupe of players has come, and Canio, their chief, tells the crowd to be sure to be on hand for the night's performance. He then goes down street, leaving his wife, Nedda, alone. Tonio, another player, tries to make love to her, but she strikes him in the face with a whip, and he goes away vowing vengeance. He has suspected a secret love between her and Silvio, a villager. Tonio overhears them making plans, and steals away to summon Canio. Meanwhile as a troupe of bagpipers pass by, the villagers sing a charming "Chorus of the Bells." Nedda soliloquizes over her unhappy lot in an aria, "Ah, ye birds without number!" When Canio hastens back to intercept the lovers, Silvio runs away. Enraged he is about to lay violent hands upon his wife, when other members of the company interpose: the play must go on; they must jest to the end. He echoes their desire in a pathetic song, "On with the play!" (Vesti la giubba)—

Act II *Village Square, with Showman's Stage.* The voice of Beppo (Harlequin) is heard in a lively serenade, "O, Columbine, come to thy window!" Tonio beats a drum to summon the villagers. They bustle in, while Nedda collects the tickets. Silvio reminds her of their assignation, but she cautions him to be silent. The plot of the play, which now begins, deals with a jealous husband who surprises his wife with another man at supper. The unwelcome guest jumps out the window, while the husband loads his unfaithful wife with reproaches; the pair being presented by Canio and Nedda. As he forgets his lines in his own jealous rage, the music rises in ominous intensity: "No, Pagliaccio, no more!" he shouts. "I am a man again!" Nedda, still striving to conceal her emotions and keep the play intact, sings a teasing ditty, "I never knew you were such a tragic fellow." (Suvvia, cosi terrible)—

But her gay song is ended tragically. Canio roughly demands, "His name!"—then plunges his knife into her breast. The terrified Silvio tries to interpose, and Canio kills him also. He regards his victims for a moment, and a final, bitter cry wells from his throat: "The comedy is ended!" (La commedia è finita!)

ZAZA

(*Zah'-zah*)

Lyric Opera in Four Acts. Words and music by Leoncavallo, after the play by P. Berton and Ch. Simon. Milan, 1900. At New York, the Metropolitan, January 16, 1920, with Farrar, Amato, Crimi, and Howard.

SCENE: Paris.
TIME: The Present.

ARGUMENT "Zaza" avoids the tragic and reaches only the level of melodrama. It is on the familiar theme of a false love which does not bring happiness to either principal. The opera has achieved more success in Italy and Germany than in other lands. The music, while pleasing, lacks the dramatic force of "Pagliacci."

Act I *Side View of a Stage.* Zaza, a reigning music-hall favorite, has become smitten with Milio Dufresne, a man about town. The latter does not apparently notice her, and she is much piqued. She finally makes a wager with Bussy, a musical writer, that she will bring the cold Dufresne to her feet. She exerts all her powers of fascination and the latter succumbs.

Act II *Zaza's Living Room.* Zaza imperils her singing career because of her attachment for Dufresne. She is reproached by her mother and Cascart, her singing partner, for withdrawing from the music season, then at its height. Dufresne spends most of his time with her, but he finally returns to Paris under the plea of urgent business. In his absence, her mother and Cascart plot to break up this love idyl, and they tell her that her lover has gone to make an appointment with another sweetheart. Zaza, in a huff, departs at once for the city.

Act III *Dufresne's Home.* Dufresne has been leading a double life with Zaza, as he is already married and has a child. Zaza and her maid visit the Dufresne home, while monsieur and madame are away. Then it is that Zaza discovers the truth; but after she has seen Toto, the little girl, she departs without making a scene, as she had intended.

Act IV *Zaza's Home.* Zaza goes back home brokenhearted. Cascart tries to console her and win her back to the stage, but without success. The next time her lover comes, she hides her thoughts in order to find out the true state of his affections. When he still tries to keep up the deception she tells him she has seen Toto. She says, his secret is safe, and bids him farewell.

Musical numbers available in records: a duet for soprano and baritone, "Il bacio"; a soprano aria (Geraldine Farrar) "Mama usciva di casa"; tenor songs (Martinelli) "E un riso" and "O mio piccolo"; baritone song, "Buono Zaza" (Titta Ruffo); and another baritone aria, "Zaza piccola zingara" (John Charles Thomas).

GIACOMO PUCCINI

Puccini was born in Lucca, Italy, June 22, 1858, first studied music in his native place as a private pupil of Angeloni. Later at the Royal Conservatory, Milan, he studied under Ponchielli, composer of "La Gioconda." Puccini is generally regarded as the foremost modern composer of the Italian school, and the one man upon whom the mantle of Verdi fell. His work showed more variety and sustained effort than that of either Mascagni or Leoncavallo. He composed at least four operas which promise to become classic: "Manon Lescaut" (1870); "La Bohème" (1896); "La Tosca" (1900); and "Madam Butterfly" (1904). "La Fanciulla del West" (1910) has met with more favor in America than at home, and is better known here as "The Girl of the Golden West." Other works include an early two-act opera, "Le Villi," "Edgar," and "La Rondine." A final work, "Turandot," was incomplete at the time of his death, in Brussels, November 29, 1924.

MANON LESCAUT

(Mah-nohn' Les-co)

Tragic Opera in Four Acts. Music by Puccini. Book by composer, after the novel by Abbé Prévost, and with assistance of group of friends. Produced at Turin, February 1, 1893, and in the same year, in Buenos Aires; in Philadelphia, 1894, in English; and at the Metropolitan in

New York, in Italian, January 18, 1907, under the personal direction of the composer. In the latter cast were Caruso, Cavalieri, Scotti, and Rossi.

SCENE: Amiens, Paris, Havre, Louisiana.
TIME: Second half of Eighteenth Century.

CAST MANON LESCAUT (Soprano).
LESCAUT, *Sergeant of the King's Guards* (Baritone).
CHEVALIER DES GRIEUX (Tenor).
GERONTE DE RAVOIR, *Treasurer-General* (Basso).
EDMUND, *a student* (Tenor).
Guards, Students, Street Women, etc.

ARGUMENT A colorful opera, showing how a lifetime of devotion may work reformation in the character of even the most selfish and abandoned.

Act I *An Inn at Amiens.* Manon Lescaut, the pretty sister of a sergeant of the Guards, is blessed more with looks than with morals. Her brother, realizing her susceptible nature, determines to place her in a convent. He brings her to Amiens for this purpose, but on his arrival is inveigled into a gambling game. Another traveling companion, Geronte, has become infatuated with the girl en route, and now tries to seize this interval to abduct her. But on this same evening another suitor has appeared in the person of the Chevalier des Grieux, who falls in love with her on sight. She also likes his appearance and readily consents to meet him later. So, while her brother is engrossed at the gaming table, she and the Chevalier elope in the carriage which Geronte had placed in readiness for his own use. Geronte is furious when he discovers that his bird has flown with another, but cannot rouse the cynical brother into action. "She will soon tire of him and come back to you," the latter says.

The gay singing of the students heralds the curtain rise in this Act. Later when Des Grieux first meets Manon, his song in her praise is a notable one: "Never did I behold a maiden so fair" (Donna non vidi)—

Her clear voice joins him in a charming duet, as she promises to be faithful to this new love: "Behold me!" she sings.

Act II *Geronte's Mansion.* Manon, as her brother had predicted does not linger with her latest lover after his money is gone

She deserts Des Grieux for the wealthy Geronte, and is now discovered living at ease as the latter's mistress. Yet she is not happy. She finds that she has left her heart with her impecunious lover. Geronte is old and a bore; and although he entertains her with musicians and dancers, she soon tires of them all. During a free moment, the Chevalier enters surreptitiously, and at first reproaches her for her desertion. But soon, overcome by her charms, he renews his ardent vows. Geronte surprises them. He conceals his true feelings under a mask of sarcasm and leaves them. Lescaut enters to warn them to flee from Geronte's anger; he has gone to call the guards. Manon lingers long enough to seize her jewels, but the delay is fatal. The guards enter and seize her. Geronte has preferred charges against her as an abandoned woman, and she is to be deported to America in company with other undesirables. Des Grieux declares his intention to follow her to the end of the world.

The music reflects conflicting emotions. Manon is not happy in her new love nest. She sings of her former happiness with the Chevalier: "O, my little humble dwelling!" Geronte tries to entertain her with a troupe of singers—their madrigal: "Speed o'er the mountain summit, O, my Chloe!" is excellent. A minuet follows, as a dancing master teaches her steps. This gaiety soon gives way to approaching tragedy.

The journey to the port of embarkation is represented by an Intermezzo, a striking bit of orchestration inserted to prepare the auditor for the later action:

Act III *A Public Square near the Waterfront, Havre.* Manon is in prison pending her deportation. Her brother and her lover attempt to rescue her, but are foiled. The utmost that Des Grieux can do is to walk by her side as she makes her way to the waiting ship. The captain is so touched by their story, that he consents to take the Chevalier as one of the crew. Manon is almost reconciled to her lot when she learns that he is to be near her.

The chief musical moments are Des Grieux's plea to the captain, and a dramatic aria by the latter.

Act IV *"A Vast Plain on the Borders of the Territory of New Orleans" (then a French possession).* Night is falling. Manon and Des Grieux enter, poorly clothed and weary. Manon is exhausted and leans heavily on Des Grieux. They do not know where to find either food or shelter, or even water to drink. Des Grieux is beside himself with despair. He finds a resting place for her, and goes off to look for water. Manon, thinking he has forsaken her entirely, feels undone. Only the tomb, she cries, can release her. Des Grieux returns in time to be present at her last moments. She dies, declaring to the last her love for him. Des Grieux falls senseless by her side.

The gloom of this scene is again reflected by both voice and instrument. There is a lengthy duet by the two lovers, while she reclines, dying, in his arms.

LA BOHÈME

(La Bo-ame)

(The Bohemians.) Romantic Opera in Four Acts. Music by Puccini. Book by Giacosa and Illica, after Henry Murger's "Vie de Bohème." Teatro Regio, Turin, February 1, 1896. Covent Garden, in English, October 2, 1897. Also in English, in America, the next year; and at the Metropolitan, New York, in Italian, December 18, 1901. In the latter cast were Melba, Campanari, Gilibert, and Journet.

SCENE: Paris.
TIME: 1830.

CAST RUDOLPH, *a poet* (Tenor).
SCHAUNARD, *a musician* (Baritone).
MARCEL, *a painter* (Baritone).
COLLINE, *a philosopher* (Basso).
BENOIT, *a landlord* (Basso).
MIMI, *a flower girl* (Soprano).
MUSETTA, *a grisette* (Soprano).
PARPIGNOL, *a toy vender* (Tenor).
ALCINDORO, *a wealthy Parisian* (Basso).
Sergeant, Guards, Grisettes, Students, Children, Waiters, Citizens.

ARGUMENT "La Bohème" is a picture of happy-go-lucky artist life in the Latin Quarter of Paris, with its lights and shadows, comedies and tragedies. It is the most popular of the Puccini operas, in America, by reason of its skillful blending of the gay, lighthearted moments of student life with the pathos and tragedy of blighted love.

Act I *A Garret occupied by Four Bohemians.* Rudolph, a poet, Schaunard, a musician, Marcel, a painter, and Colline, a dreamer, live together in a Parisian attic in a state of chronic poverty yet in perfect harmony and good fellowship. The poet and the painter are discovered, when the curtain rises, sitting in the bare and comfortless room, both cold and hungry. They feed one of Rudolph's manuscripts to the stove in the effort to extract a little warmth. Enter Colline also to warm up, and he is followed by a boy bringing in fuel and materials for a feast. While they are overjoyed at this windfall, Schaunard arrives with a wonderful tale of how he has lined his pockets and thus can afford to give the spread. All fall to with gusto, but at this moment Benoit, the landlord, arrives seeking to collect his long-overdue rent. They ply him with wine until he begins to tell libertine stories, when they pretend to be greatly shocked and thrust him out of the door. The rent money is divided for a further carouse in the Latin Quarter. Rudolph alone remains under a plea that he wants to finish some writing. Presently a timid knock is heard. He opens the door to see a girl, who says: "Excuse me, sir, but my candle is gone out." He aids her to relight it, but a current of the air again extinguishes it. Through the garret window one can see the snow on the roof. She shivers and drops her key. As he picks it up, their hands meet. "How cold your little hand is!" he cries in the first of the tender passages between them. (Tenor aria, "Che gelida mamina!"). He tells her something about himself: "I am a poet" (Sono un poeta); and she replies by giving him her name: "My name is Mimi" (Mi chiamano Mimi)—one of the finest flights for the soprano voice:

A no-less lovely duet follows: "O, lovely maiden!" (O, soave fanciulla!). They decide to cast their lot together and depart to join their friends as the melody follows them down the stairs.

Act II *A Public Square in the Latin Quarter.* The four friends are spending Schaunard's money right and left. Rudolph buys Mimi a hat, and all seat themselves at a café table and order lavishly. While they are dining, Musetta, an old flame of Marcel's, enters with a wealthy admirer, Alcindoro. Musette no sooner sees Marcel than she tries in every way to attract his attention, and also to get rid of her aged suitor. She finally sends the latter out to buy her a new pair of shoes, under a pretext that her old ones hurt her feet, and then rushes over and embraces Marcel. The Bohemians find that they have spent all their money and cannot pay the dinner bill, but Musetta tells them not to worry, that she will add it to her own and leave it for Alcindoro to pay. All disperse as a party of guards comes by, and Alcindoro upon returning finds a bill of such huge proportions that he falls in a heap on his chair.

The high point in this Act is the waltz song by Musetta, where she dissembles her affections.

Act III *At a Gate of Customs.* It is still winter, and the customs officers examine the passports of all who enter the city. Mimi, who is suffering from consumption, comes to the gate to ask for Marcel who is doing some work hard by. When he appears she tells him that she is miserable as she cannot live with Rudolph and also cannot live without him. They have quarreled. Marcel goes to summon Rudolph, and Mimi hides behind a tree. The poet tells his friend why he has left Mimi. She coughs and reveals her presence, and he takes the sick girl in his arms. Meanwhile Marcel becomes jealous of Musetta, whom he accuses of flirting in the inn.

Another operatic gem is heard when Mimi bids farewell to her lover: "Farewell, then, I wish you well" (Addio, senza rancore)—

Act IV *The Garret as in First Act.* Marcel and Rudolph are at work when the other two Bohemians arrive with materials for a scanty dinner. They make merry, however, over the repast, pretending that it is a banquet. Musetta comes in, saying that Mimi is extremely ill. All bustle to help the invalid. They place her upon a cot and hasten out to pawn their clothing if necessary to buy her food and medicines. Rudolph alone remains, and the two lovers are again reconciled and resolve never to part again.

The closing moments abound in beautiful melody: Rudolph's soliloquy, "Ah, Mimi, false one!" (Ah, Mimi, tu più); the "Song of the Coat" by Colline; and the voices of the reunited lovers, "Have they gone?" (Sono andati), and "Oh God, Mimi!" (Oh Dio, Mimi!) "I only wanted to be with you, Beloved," she whispers. "Do you remember?" And the violins and wood instruments echo the strains in this Death Music of their first meeting. "How cold your hands are!" And, "They call me Mimi."

Their friends now enter bringing food and aid, but it is too late. They can only stand silently by the bed of death. With a last despairing cry, "Mimi, Mimi!" Rudolph sinks across her couch.

LA TOSCA

(*La Tos'-ca*)

Tragic Opera in Three Acts. Music by Puccini. Book by Illica and Giacosa, after the drama by Sardou. Costanzi Theatre, Rome, January 14, 1900; London the same year; New York, February 4, 1901. In the latter cast were Scotti and Ternina.

SCENE: Rome.
TIME: Circa 1800.
CAST MARIO CAVARADOSSI, *a painter* (Tenor).
BARON SCARPIA, *Chief of Police* (Baritone).
CESARE ANGELOTTI, *an escaped prisoner* (Basso).
FLORIA TOSCA, *a singer* (Soprano).
SPOLETTA, *a police officer* (Tenor).
Churchmen, Police, Jailer, Shepherd Boy, Servants.

ARGUMENT "La Tosca," founded upon Sardou's tragedy, is an intense plot of passion and revenge, unrelieved by any lighter themes. Its music, brilliant and somber, closely fits the text.

Act I *Interior of the Church of Sant' Andrea, Rome.* The painter, Mario Cavaradossi, is busily engaged upon mural decorations within a church when he is appealed to for aid by Cesare Angelotti, an escaped political prisoner. The painter promises to assist him to escape and meanwhile hides him in the church. Tosca, a singer, and the painter's sweetheart, comes in at this moment and believes that she has discovered evidences of the painter's fickleness, especially since he has been using another woman as the model for his "Magdalen." He reassures her. The sacristan and choir-boys enter, and, later, Scarpia, the Chief of Police, in search of the fugitive. He finds a fan dropped by the model and shows it to Tosca in order to excite her jealousy. He wishes her to betray her lover, and he is also in love with her on his own account.

Three crashing chords from the orchestra denoting the sharp sinister action which is to follow greet the rising of the curtain on Act I. The song by the painter, Cavaradossi, "Strange harmony" (Recondita armonia), follows in praise of his lady.

Then comes a fine interlude of choir singing; the impassioned passages between him and Tosca; and the final thrilling outburst of harmony with Scarpia and the choir: "Te Deum"—

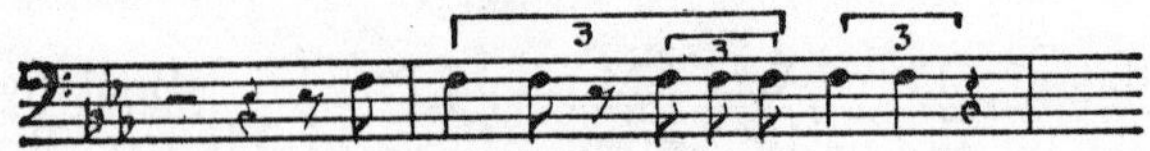

Act II *Scarpia's Offices in the Farnese Palace.* Scarpia's men have not been able to catch Angelotti, but still suspecting Cavaradossi they bring him before their chief. Scarpia questions him sharply without being able to obtain any information, and then remands him to the torture chamber. He has sent for Tosca, who now appears. At first she is silent to all his questions, but when he tells her that her lover is being tortured, and proves this by opening the door to the inquisition chamber, she cannot withstand the strain and reveals Angelotti's hiding-place. The painter reproaches her for the betrayal as he is taken away to prison. Scarpia now tells her that her lover will be condemned to death unless she is willing to make a sacrifice to save him—the sacrifice of her honor. He, Scarpia, loves her and under no other condition can the painter be saved. Tosca recoils from this proposition, but when word is brought that Angelotti has poisoned himself to avoid recapture she fears Cavaradossi will do likewise and says she will consent. The police officer draws up a passport for the prisoner and at the same times gives orders for his execution by a volley of musketry. He carefully explains that it will be a mock-execution, only blank cartridges being used, for the sake of appearances. He advances to Tosca with the passport and endeavors to embrace her. She seizes it and quickly stabs him to the heart. Then piously composing the body, with lights at the head and feet and a crucifix on its breast, she hastens away to the prison.

The supreme number in this Act, and one of the finest in modern Italian opera, is Tosca's exquisite song: "Art and love—these I have lived for" (Vissi d'arte)—

Act III *Battlements of the Prison.* The squad of soldiers prepare to obey the order which they have just received for the execution of Cavaradossi. He is led out to an open court overlooking the battlements, and is there overjoyed to find Tosca, who tells him of the passport which she carries. The execution will only be pretended, she tells him, but he must fall as though slain. The file of soldiers now take their position and fire their volley. The prisoner sinks in a crumpled heap, but when Tosca rushes to his side she finds that he is really dead—pierced by actual bullets. Tosca cannot at first realize the horrible truth, then gives way to despair. The guards now rush in to seize her for the murder of Scarpia, but she evades them.

In the early part of this Act a fine aria for the tenor voice is heard, as Cavadarossi sings a farewell to his beloved: "When the stars are brightly shining" (E lucevan le stelle)—

His final song, "The sting of death I only feared for thee, dear" (Amaro sol per te), comes before he faces the firing squad. Her impassioned, "Now, Mario, all is safe!" is a glad note, all too soon to be followed by her grief when she finds him a corpse. Then amid somber chords from the instruments she leaps from the battlements to her own death—and freedom.

MADAM BUTTERFLY

Dramatic Opera in Two Acts, later Three Acts. Music by Puccini. Italian text by Illica and Giacosa, after the stage play by David Belasco and John Luther Long. Produced unsuccessfully as a two-act opera in La Scala, Milan, February 17, 1904; revised and presented in three acts, at Brescia, May 28, 1904, with success. Covent Garden, London, the next season, in English, Washington, October, 1906; and in Italian at the Metropolitan, February 11, 1907, with Farrar, Caruso, Scotti, and Homer.

SCENE: Nagasaki, Japan.
TIME: The Present.

CAST MADAM BUTTERFLY (Cho-Cho-San), *a Japanese woman* (Soprano).
SUZUKI, *her servant* (Mezzo-Soprano).
PINKERTON, *a lieutenant, U.S. Navy* (Tenor).
KATE PINKERTON, *his wife* (Mezzo-Soprano).
SHARPLESS, *U.S. Consul* (Tenor).
GORO, *a Japanese marriage broker* (Tenor).
YAMADORI, *a Japanese nobleman* (Baritone).
THE BONZE, *uncle to Cho-Cho-San* (Basso).
A baby boy, Relatives of Cho-Cho-San, Villagers, etc.

ARGUMENT "Madam Butterfly" is interesting on several counts. Sung in Italian, its setting is Japan and it also has a strong American flavor, in fact, had its origin on the American stage. The composer has introduced several distinct Japanese melodies, but also artfully contrives to give the work a cosmopolitan touch. For these reasons as well as the dramatic and pathetic story itself, "Butterfly" has remained a favorite on both sides of the Atlantic.

Act I *A Japanese Villa.* Lieutenant Pinkerton, U.S.N., finding that he will be stationed in Nagasaki for some months, desires to contract a Japanese marriage. He is assured by the marriage broker who transacts the business for him that this marriage will be binding only so long as he consents to live with his wife, and that afterwards she can marry again. But Cho-Cho-San, the girl who agrees to marry the lieutenant, has fallen deeply in love with him and believes she is entering into a life contract. She goes so far as to renounce her religion, thus severing all connection with her own people. Sharpless, the American consul, tries to prevent the match by telling his friend Pinkerton how seriously the girl considers it. The lieutenant has further proof of this when a fanatical bonze, or priest, an uncle of hers, appears, as the wedding party is seated at the feast, and heaps curses upon her head for renouncing her faith. All her relatives thereupon desert her, but Cho-Cho-San, though sorrowful, clings to her husband, and he soon calms her fears. The scene closes in mutual protestations of love.

The music, quaint and charming throughout, reaches its climax near the close of this Act in the duet between Cho-Cho-San and the lieutenant. Beginning with the quiet, "Evening is falling" (Viene la sera), it gradually rises in passion to "O, night of rapture!" (O quanti occhi fisi)—

Act II *Scene 1. The Villa. Three years later.* After a short but blissful wedded life, Lieutenant Pinkerton has been recalled to America. He leaves Cho-Cho-San (who is now called "Madam Butterfly") in Japan, promising to return "when the robins nest again." Despite his long absence and silence she still trusts him. Her maid, Suzuki, is not so sure and Butterfly chides her in the famous aria, "Some fine day he'll come!" (Un bel di vedremo)—

As a matter of fact, Pinkerton is returning to Japan, but with no intention of rejoining her. Instead he writes Sharpless, the consul, telling him that he now has an American wife and asking the consul to break this news to Madam Butterfly. The consul brings her the letter, but she is so overjoyed at seeing a missive from him that she pays no heed to its message and the consul has not the heart to disturb her faith. She also turns a deaf ear to Goro, the marriage broker, who comes to arrange a match between her and a Japanese nobleman. When he says that Pinkerton's desertion is equivalent to a divorce she answers proudly: "That may be so in Japan, but I am an American!" Then she brings out her baby boy born of her union with the Lieutenant and asks, "Can this, too, be forgotten?" She bids "Trouble," her boy, not to listen to the bad man. The consul leaves, shaking his head; the sound of a cannon in the harbor is heard, and with a glass Butterfly spells out the name of her lord's ship. In a fever of excitement she and her maid decorate the house. The "Letter Scene" followed by the "Flower Duet" between the two women are particularly charming. But all their preparation is in vain. The night draws slowly by. "Trouble" falls asleep; then the maid; only Butterfly sits erect—watching—waiting—while exquisite music of the night outside brings the fall of the curtain.

Act III (*Also presented as the Second Part of Act II.*) *Setting same as foregoing.* Dawn is breaking as the curtain rises on the little group. Another fine bit of oriental melody greets the rise of the curtain known as the "Vigil Theme":

Butterfly has not closed her eyes. Now Suzuki awakes and persuades her wearied mistress to lie down and rest. She does so, in order that she may look well when "he comes." After she has retired the consul arrives with Pinkerton and his American wife. When Pinkerton hears from Suzuki of Butterfly's devotion and trust he is overcome with remorse and cannot remain to face the deserted bride. Suzuki is commissioned to tell her that Mrs. Pinkerton will care for the child, but Butterfly, entering at this moment, hears it from the American lady's own lips. She retains her composure by a great effort, congratulates Mrs. Pinkerton politely, and says that if they will return in half an hour they may have the child. When the Americans return at the specified time they find that Madam Butterfly has slain herself with her father's sword, on which is inscribed: "Die with honor, when you can no longer live with honor."

The orchestra sounds the final notes, deep, mournful, thunderous—a requiem for a noble love and a sin that never could be expiated.

THE GIRL OF THE GOLDEN WEST

(La Fanciulla del West.) Romantic Opera in Three Acts. Music by Puccini. Book by David Belasco. World premiere at the Metropolitan, New York, December 10, 1910. The cast included Destinn, Caruso, and Amato.

SCENE: A California Mining-camp.
TIME: 1848.

CAST MINNIE, *a Western girl* (Soprano).
JACK RANCE, *the sheriff, a gambler* (Baritone).
JOHNSON, *alias Ramarrez, an outlaw* (Tenor).
DICK, *a servant* (Tenor).
LARKINS (Baritone).
HARRY (Baritone).
Miners, Bandits, Servants, Indians, etc.

ARGUMENT "The Girl of the Golden West" is a romantic and colorful picture of Western pioneer life, which was successful as a drama, before being given a musical setting. The days of the gold fever on the Pacific slope and of the rough-and-ready justice there accorded are here illustrated.

Act I *The Polka Bar.* Minnie, a resourceful "girl of the Golden West," left an orphan, continues to run her father's barroom for the benefit of the miners who flock to the newly discovered gold diggings of California. Minnie herself can gamble and shoot with the best of them if necessary, but she is treated as a sort of ward by the camp whom it would be sudden death to insult. While her friends, the miners, are congregated at her bar, a wandering minstrel halts outside and sings of the "Old Folks at Home," moving some of them to tears. Then Minnie sings a love song which also arouses the sentiments of her hearers. During the singing, Jack Rance, the sheriff, who is also a gambler and who has long loved Minnie, enters. He makes love to her, but she will not listen to him.

The mountains back of the camp have been overrun for some time by a band of outlaws under the leadership of Ramarrez. The miners have offered large rewards for their extermination, but the outlaws are so bold and careless that they plan a robbery in the camp. Their leader comes, under the name of Johnson, to the Polka bar in order to look over the ground and, in the evening, give the signal to his men. But becoming fascinated by the girl, he lingers to make love to her and offers to escort her to her home. She is also interested in him and accepts his attentions.

Act II *Interior of Minnie's Cabin.* The two Indian servants of Minnie crouch in one corner, while she listens, pleased, to Johnson's declarations of love. A noise is heard outside the door and Minnie discovers Rance at the head of a posse. Not caring to have them find a man at her home she conceals Johnson, who is only too willing to go into hiding; then she opens the door. Rance tells her that they are searching for a notorious bandit who, they have reason to believe, is concealed on the premises. Minnie indignantly disclaims knowledge of any such person, but after the posse has gone away she turns upon Johnson and upbraids him for deceiving her. The outlaw tells her that he has been reared to this life, but after seeing her he is ready to reform. She will not listen to him, however, and he leaves the cabin. A few paces from the door a shot is heard. Rance has remained in hiding and now seriously wounds him. Johnson drags himself back to the cabin and Minnie, touched by his plight, conceals him in the loft. Rance returns and demands the fugitive. Minnie again denies knowledge of his whereabouts, but a few drops of blood trickling down from above betray him. In desperation Minnie offers to play a game of poker, the stakes to be the outlaw against her love. The gambling spirit of Rance is aroused and they play. Minnie cheats with the cards and wins. Rance respects his agreement and departs.

Act III *In the Redwood Forest.* Minnie nurses Johnson back to health, and he promises to disperse his gang and go to another state, there to live an honest life. Rance, hearing that he has recovered from his wound and is now on his way to join the outlaws, summons his posse and captures him. The miners promise him short shrift at the end of a rope, and are preparing to lynch him from the first convenient tree, when Minnie rushes forward. She pleads with the miners telling them of Johnson's reformation, and by her influence persuades them to spare his life. Later Rance aids her to effect his escape and she departs with Johnson for an eastern state where they are to be married and begin life anew.

It must be admitted that there has been more interest in the plot than in the music, so far as the American public is concerned. To link up a robust western story with Debussy-like phrases and recitative passages was a task beyond even Puccini's great abilities. There is not enough variety in the orchestration, nor many of the dramatic heights for solo voices. The best of these is perhaps the aria by Johnson, who is facing death: "Let her believe that I have gained my freedom." (Ch'ella mi credo.)

LA RONDINE

(Lah Rone'-dee-neh)

(The Swallow.) Lyric Opera in Three Acts. Music by Puccini. Book by Giuseppe Adami. Monte Carlo, March 27, 1917. At the Metropolitan, New York, March 10, 1928.

SCENE: Paris and Nice.
TIME: The Second French Empire.

CAST MAGDA, *a demi-mondaine* (Soprano).
RAMBALDO, *a banker* (Baritone).
RUGGERO, *a student* (Tenor).
PRUNIER, *a poet* (Baritone).
Lisette, Bianca, Yvette, Perichaud, Gobin, Crebillon, and other Guests, Servants, etc.

ARGUMENT A sentimental work with lilting music and a theme reminiscent of "La Traviata."

Act I *Salon of Magda's Paris House.* Magda, who lives a life of ease, under the protection of the rich banker, Rambaldo, holds sway over a Bohemian circle, ranging from poets and artists down to demi-mondaines. During one such levée, the conversation turns on love, and Prunier, a decadent poet, reads an essay which maintains that old-fashioned love is reviving. Derisive laughter. Magda, however, grows pensive; she recalls an idyllic love of her youth. The poet thereupon reads her palm and tells her that she is like the swallow: she will try her wings on romance, only to fly back home again. At this juncture a young stranger is announced—Ruggero, a man from out of town, whose father is an old friend of Rambaldo's. The latter greets him pleasantly, and offers him a guide to the "Bal Bullier," where he can see other night life.

Act II *The Bal Bullier.* Magda has been attracted by the young visitor, and decides to follow him to the Bal. She does so and has a further opportunity to see him, and discovers for him a love which she has long since believed dead. He, unsophisticated, sees in her the beautiful and pure girl of his dreams. They are happy and when the banker appears on the scene and wants to take her back with him, she repulses him.

Act III *A Rustic Cottage at Nice.* Ruggero and Magda have run away to an idyllic existence. She is content at last, while he writes to his mother asking permission to make the girl his wife. She consents, provided that Magda is all that he has depicted. When Magda learns of this, she realizes that it would be unjust to marry Ruggero. She gives him up and—like the swallow—flies back home to her banker.

A soprano solo (sung by Lucrezia Bori) "Ore dolci e divine," is in record form.

GIANNI SCHICCHI

(*Gee'-ah-nee She'-chee*)

Humorous Opera in One Act. Music by Puccini. Book by Gioachino Forzano. Milan, 1918; Metropolitan, New York, December 14, the same year, together with two other shorter works by Puccini, "Il Tabarro" and "Suor Angelica." None of the three has had many performances in recent years, although "Gianni" seems to have more en during qualities.

SCENE: Florence.
TIME: 1299.

CAST GIANNI SCHICCHI (Baritone).
LAURETTA, *his daughter* (Soprano).
The Relatives of Buoso Donati
ZITA, *"the Old Woman"* (Contralto).
RINUCCIO, *Zita's nephew* (Tenor).
GHERARDO, *Buoso's nephew* (Baritone).
NELLA, *his wife* (Soprano).
GHERARDINO, *their son* (Soprano).
BETTO OF SIGNA, *a cousin to Buoso* (Baritone).
SIMONE, *a cousin to Buoso* (Basso).
MARCO. *his son* (Baritone).

La Ciesca, *Marco's wife* (Mezzo-Soprano).
Master Spinellocchio, *physician* (Baritone).
Amanti di Nicolao, *notary* (Baritone).
Pinellino, *shoemaker* (Tenor).
Guccio, *a dyer* (Basso).

ARGUMENT This little opera is pure sparkling comedy. The story of the dead man's relatives scheming to obtain for themselves the property he has willed to the Church, and being outwitted by the clever rogue they have called to their aid, is full of humor. Puccini's brilliant music is thoroughly attuned to his theme.

Scene: Buoso Donati's Bedroom. The relatives of Buoso are kneeling round the bed upon which his body lies. Their utterances are choked with feigned sighs and tears. Each hopes that he is his relative's principle legatee. When Betto suggests that rumor has credited the Church with the major share, their simulated grief is thrown aside and a frantic search is made for the will. At last it is found, and their worst fears are realized. Buoso's wealth is to go to the Church. In their dilemma Rinuccio suggests asking advice of Gianni Schicchi, with whose daughter Lauretta he is in love. Schicchi proposes that he shall impersonate Buoso and dictate a will to a notary and two witnesses, pretending that his hands are too paralyzed to write. This scheme appeals to the relatives, and they decide to adopt it. The smaller possessions are apportioned between them without difficulty, but there remain the mule, the saw-mills at Signa, and the palace in Florence. Each in turn privately offers Schicchi a bribe for the legacy of these, and each is reassured. He is arrayed in nightgown and nightcap and bundled into bed before the notary and witnesses enter. The pretended Buoso in the quavering voice of an old man dictates his will. To the Church he leaves five liras, to the relatives the smaller properties as arranged. Then comes the disposition of the mule, the saw-mills, and the house in Florence. All hold their breath as he speaks. He leaves them—to his dear friend, Gianni Schicchi! The relatives fume, but they are helpless and dare not give themselves away. When the notary and witnesses are gone they pillage the room and set upon Schicchi, but he defends himself effectively with Donati's cudgel and pursues them downstairs. The young lovers, Rinuccio and Lauretta, are seen on the terrace clasped in each other's arms as Schicchi returns laden with loot. He glances at the lovers, and appeals to the audience to know if Buoso's hoards could have been put to better use, and asks for a verdict of "not guilty."

Two musical numbers are recorded: the tenor aria, "Firenze e come un albero fiorito," and the soprano, "O mio babbino caro."

SUOR ANGELICA

(Sister Angelica.) Romantic Opera in One Act, for female voices. Music by Puccini. Book by G. Forzano. Produced, with "Gianni Schicchi," in New York, December 14, 1918.

SCENE: Near Florence, Italy.
TIME: Seventeenth Century.

CAST SISTER ANGELICA (Soprano).
THE PRINCESS, *her aunt.*
THE ABBESS.
THE MISTRESS OF NOVICES.
THE SISTER MONITOR.
Other Nuns and Novices.

ARGUMENT Because of a youthful, indiscreet love affair, resulting in a child, Angelica has been forced into a convent by the wealthy Florentine family to which she belongs. For seven years she does penance, but meanwhile longs for tidings of her child. Her aunt, who pays her a visit, tells her coldly that the child is dead—although, she says, no care was spared. Angelica goes into the garden, prays the Virgin to forgive her, and ends her life by a drink of poison. As she is dying, a miracle takes place. The walls of the cloister shine with unearthly light, and the Virgin herself appears, leading the child, which she places in the mother's arms.

There is a lovely intermezzo in this opera, and a song for the soprano voice, "Senza mamma."

IL TABARRO

(*Eel Tah-bah'-ro*)

(The Cloak.) Tragic Opera in One Act. Music by Puccini. Book by Giuseppe Adami, after the story by Didier Gold. Produced, with "Gianni Schicchi," in New York, at the Metropolitan, December 14, 1918. Revived, January 5, 1946, with Tibbett and Albanese as the barge owner and his wife; Jagel as "Luigi."

SCENE: Paris.
TIME: The present.

CAST MICHELE, *owner of a barge* (Basso).
GIORGETTA, *his wife* (Soprano).

TALPA, *a longshoreman* (Baritone).
FRUGOLA, *his wife* (Contralto).
LUIGI, *a longshoreman* (Tenor).
TINCA, *a longshoreman* (Baritone).

ARGUMENT The entire action takes place on board a barge, on the River Seine. Michele, owner of a barge, has for some time suspected his wife of infidelity and sets a trap for her and her lover, Luigi. At the end of a day's work all leave the boat except the woman and her lover. Luigi persuades Giorgetta that when all is quiet and it will be safe for him to return to her, she shall strike a match as a signal. When Michele returns he reminds her of their old courtship days and shows her the cloak under which he has sheltered her. She is indifferent and retires. Michele, left alone with his thoughts, strikes a match as if to light his pipe. The lover, mistaking it for Giorgetta's signal, climbs up the side of the barge. He is throttled by the indignant husband, who then covers the body with his cloak. When Giorgetta reappears there is a stormy scene between the two, which reaches its climax when Michele triumphantly lifts his cloak revealing the corpse of Luigi.

The music is a blending of themes only incidental to the action One of the freshest songs is sung by an outside vendor of ditties, with its refrain, "This is the story of Mimi." An organ-grinder comes by and plays a lively air while tipsy bargemen dance to it. There are few solos by the principals, one being by Luigi in praise of love and wine; and another along the same vein of drinking, by Tinca; a duet between the guilty lovers; and a dramatic bass aria by Michele, before committing the final crime.

TURANDOT

(Too'-rahn-doh)

Lyric Drama in Three Acts. Music by Puccini. Book by Giuseppe Adami and Renato Simoni. The score was incomplete at the time of the composer's death, and the last duet and the finale were completed by F. Alfano. La Scala, Milan, April 25, 1926; Metropolitan, New York November 16, 1926.

SCENE: Peking.
TIME: Legendary.

CAST ALTOUM, *Emperor of China* (Tenor).
TURANDOT, *his daughter* (Soprano).

TIMUR, *the dethroned Tartar King* (Basso).
CALAF, *the Unknown Prince, his son* (Tenor).
LIU, *the slave girl of Timur* (Soprano).
PING, *the Grand Chancellor* (Baritone).
PANG, *the General Purveyor* (Tenor).
PONG, *the Chief Cook* (Tenor).
A MANDARIN (Baritone).
THE PRINCE OF PERSIA (Baritone).
THE EXECUTIONER (Baritone).
Guards, Attendants, Wise Men, Priests,
Mandarins, Musicians, Citizens, etc.

ARGUMENT "Turandot" is a love story employing the familiar device of the riddle to be solved, under penalty of death. The scene is China, but a China of legend and fantasy. The music marks a progression along modern lines, especially in intricate harmony, and while hailed by critics has not won lasting popular appeal.

Act I *The Walls of the Great Violet City—Peking.* The square in front of the palace is peopled by a picturesque throng who listen to a proclamation read by a Mandarin. It is to the effect that the Princess Turandot has consented to become the bride of him of royal blood who shall solve three enigmas; but that if he shall fail, his head shall be forfeited. Already several have suffered death and the latest victim is the young Prince of Persia. He is to be beheaded at the rising of the moon. The crowd grows unruly and in the tumult an old man falls to the ground. A slave girl calls for aid in his behalf, and a young man hastens to their side. He recognizes the fallen man as his father, Timur, the former sovereign of Tartar. The son has chosen to remain incognito and is styled the Unknown Prince. He is known only to his father and to the slave girl, Liu, who secretly loves him.

Meanwhile two assistants to the Executioner appear upon the battlements and whet the huge sword which is to decapitate the luckless Persian Prince. The crowd grows more and more ferocious, but when presently the victim appears, handsome and with a dreamy look in his eyes, the hatred of the mob turns to pity, and they clamor to the Princess Turandot to show mercy. In answer to their cry she appears on the loggia, so divinelike in her beauty that the crowd grow silent and prostrate themselves upon the ground. Only the Unknown Prince remains standing. The funeral procession passes on, leaving him with Timur and Liu alone in the square. Then, despite Timur's remonstrances, the Prince announces his intention of himself trying to solve the riddles and win the Princess. As he approaches the gong he encounters three officials, Ping, Pang, and Pong, who also try to dissuade him. Liu adds her entreaties, and the ghosts of other princes slain in the endeavor appear to him. As a final warning, the Executioner appears with the gory head of the Prince of Persia. But undeterred, the Unknown Prince rushes to the gong and strikes it three times, exclaiming, "Turandot! Turandot! Turandot!"

Act II *Scene 1. Pavilion in the Imperial Palace.* This scene is restricted to a colloquy among the three ministers, Ping, Pang, and Pong, who recount China's ancient glories and bemoan the present situation. They mournfully tell of the thirteen unlucky suitors who have offered the Princess their hearts, and only lost their heads.

Scene 2. Square in Front of the Imperial Palace. The curious throng watches the preparations being made for another test—that of the Unknown Prince. Mandarins and Wise Men enter, the latter bearing the scrolls on which the answers to the enigmas are inscribed. A flourish of trumpets announces the entrance of the Emperor, who seats himself on a throne at the top of an outside staircase. At its foot stands the Unknown Prince. A Mandarin reads the proclamation ending with the sentence of death. At its conclusion Turandot appears and tells why she has set this severe test. It is to avenge the fate of a princess, her ancestress of centuries agone. Looking menacingly at the Prince she says: "The enigmas are three; Death is but one!" "No, Princess," he replies; "The enigmas are three; Life is but one!" She then propounds the riddles and he answers each in turn with the words, "Hope," "Blood," and "Turandot." The throng acclaims the Prince, but Turandot appeals to her father to save her from this stranger. The Emperor replies: "Sacred is the oath." While Turandot still rebels, the Prince in turn gives her a chance to escape. He says that if she will tell him his name before the rise of dawn she shall be free and he will lay down his life.

Act III *Scene 1. The Garden of the Palace.* Heralds announce that by order of Turandot none shall sleep that night. The Prince's name must be disclosed under penalty of death. The crowd in terror supplicate the Prince to reveal his name. The three ministers try to bribe him. But he is adamant. Timur and Liu are seized and brought before the Princess, as being the only persons who know the secret. Timur is on the point of being tortured, but Liu springs in front of him and exclaims that she alone knows the stranger's name Then before they have had time to make good their threat to torture her, she seizes a dagger and stabs herself. The crowd is moved to tenderness by her self-sacrifice, and even Turandot stands in wonderment at this unseen power. The Unknown Prince seizes this moment to plead to her heart of ice. As she still defies him he takes her in his arms and kisses her. The embrace frees her pent-up emotions and she admits herself vanquished. As dawn breaks he generously whispers to her his name—"Calaf, the son of Timur." On hearing the fatal secret her pride is rekindled, and she haughtily says that she will take him before the people and proclaim his identity—which means death.

Scene 2. Exterior of the Palace. Again are seen the crowd surrounding the Emperor and his dignitaries. Turandot ascends the staircase, saying: "August Father, I know the name of the stranger." Then turning and looking straight at Calaf who awaits his sentence, she murmurs: "His name . . . is Love!" The Prince rushes up the staircase and enfolds her in his arms, while the throng scatter flowers and shout with joy.

ALBERTO FRANCHETTI

A modern Italian composer, born in Turin, September 18, 1860. Franchetti studied at Italian conservatories, and his music is of a somewhat traditional type. He is known in this country for two operas, "Christopher Columbus" and "Germania." He died in Viareggio, August 4, 1942.

CHRISTOPHER COLUMBUS

An historical Opera in Three Acts and an Epilogue; music by Franchetti; text by Luigi Illica. Produced at Genoa (Columbus' birthplace) in 1892—a quadricentennial.

SCENE: Spain and America.
TIME: Circa 1942.

The story and characters of "Christopher Columbus" follow the general lines of history. Columbus obtains aid from Queen Isabella for his voyage of discovery. Incidents of the voyage and with the Indians in America are depicted; and the epilogue shows the aged voyager lying at the tomb of his patron queen.

GERMANIA

(Ger-mah'-nia)

Dramatic Opera in Four Acts. Music by Franchetti. Book by Luigi Illica. Milan, 1902. At New York, the Metropolitan, January 22, 1910.

SCENE: Various parts of Germany.
TIME: 1806.

ARGUMENT "Germania" is a picture of the upheaval in Germany caused by the Napoleonic wars.

Act I *An Old Mill at Nuremberg.* The revolutionists have converted an old mill at Nuremberg into a printing shop for their literature. Palm, the author of some of this, is sought by the police, but unsuccessfully. Meanwhile, books and pamphlets are sent out as bags of flour. Carl Worms, who is in charge of the press, is visited by Ricke, a Nuremberg girl, who accuses him of betraying her. She is especially downcast as a letter announces the return of Loewe, her lover.

Act II *The Black Forest.* Loewe, Ricke and others seek refuge in a hut, Loewe having been among those proscribed by the victorious Napoleon. Ricke has consented to marry Loewe. Worms then summons him to attend a meeting of the secret brotherhood. Ricke, in terror, flees, leaving a note telling the man she has just wed not to follow her. The bewildered Loewe finally learns the truth from Ricke's little sister Jane.

Act III *A Secret Hall at Koenigsberg.* The patriots meet with the utmost secrecy and lay plans to defeat the invader of their country. Only one standing apart, masked, jeers at their motives. He proves to be Loewe, who now challenges Worms to fight. The latter, however, refuses to defend himself, and others interpose to stop the quarrel.

Act IV *The Battlefield of Leipzig.* The plain is covered with prostrate forms after the great battle has been fought. Ricke seeks among them for the husband she has deserted, and finally finds him not far away from the corpse of Worms. Loewe is barely alive and soon expires in Ricke's arms, but she makes no outcry as she lies down beside him. In life all things conspired to keep them apart; but in death they can be united.

PIETRO MASCAGNI

Mascagni, famous around the world as the composer of one brilliant operatic jewel, was born in Leghorn, Italy, December 7, 1863. He came of humble stock, his father being a baker, and the first years of his life were an unending struggle against hardship. His father wanted him to study law, but the boy had set his heart upon music. An uncle helped him financially; and he studied for two years at the Milan Conservatory, under Ponchielli. After leaving there he made a meager living as a conductor of operas, and finally settled in Cerignola where he conducted an orchestra and taught music. In 1888 while at work on an unfinished opera, he learned of a prize offered for a one-act opera, by Sonzogno, the publisher. On an impulse he wrote "Cavalleria Rusticana" and sent it in. It received the prize, and was performed at the Constanzi Theatre, Rome, in 1890. It aroused the audience to a frenzy of enthusiasm and made the composer famous overnight. His native city, Leghorn, welcomed him home with a torchlight procession. Medals were struck in his honor, and the King conferred upon him the Order of the Crown—all this at the age of twenty-seven. He had "found himself" but never again succeeded in repeating his success, although he lived to eighty-two. His last years were impoverished, due to the ravages of war in his land. He died in Rome, August 2, 1945. Other operas of moderate success include: "Friend Fritz" (1892), "Iris" (1898), "The Maskers" (1901), "Zanetto" (1902), "Isabeau" (1911), and "Lodoletta" (1917).

CAVALLERIA RUSTICANA

(*Cah-vah-lee-ree'-ah Rus-tee-cahn'-a*)

(Rustic Chivalry.) Dramatic Opera in One Act. Music by Pietro Mascagni. Book by Targioni-Tozzetti and Menasci, after the story by Giovanni Verga. Constanzi Theatre, Rome, May 20, 1890. Chicago, 1891, and the Metropolitan, New York, December 30, 1891. By this time, "Cavalleria" was being performed all over the world.

SCENE: A village of Sicily.
TIME: The Present.

CAST Turiddu, *a farmer* (Tenor).
Lucia, *his mother* (Contralto).
Alfio, *a carter* (Baritone).
Lola, *his wife* (Contralto).
Santuzza, *a peasant girl* (Soprano).
Peasant Neighbors and Villagers.

ARGUMENT The theme of "Rustic Chivalry" is well described by its title and still better by the impassioned music which follows closely the simple story to its tragic close. The music fits the theme so closely and is of such continuing loveliness that it seems invidious to single out special excerpts. The Prelude sounds its keynote in three significant passages: the grief and despair of Santuzza; the dialogue between her and Turiddu where she implores him to remain true to her; and an aria in Sicilian folk-style sung by him backstage as a serenade to Lola. As his voice dies away, the curtain rises.

A Village Square in Sicily. The old triangle of love is present. Turiddu, a young farmer, has had a sweetheart, Lola, but is called to military duty. While he is away she marries Alfio, a carter. Turiddu turns for consolation to Santuzza, a peasant girl who loves him not wisely but too well. Becoming tired of this easy conquest, he turns again to Lola, despite the fact that she is wedded. This is the state of affairs as the curtain rises on a peaceful village scene. It is Easter, and the devout peasants are going to church. While the bells chime, the peasants sing of their joy in a new springtime. The swelling tones of the organ follow them. They fall upon their knees while Santuzza leads in the lovely canticle: "Let us sing of our Lord ris'n victorious!"

While the people enter the church, Santuzza lingers outside. She meets Lucia, her lover's mother, and tells her of her trouble in a pathetic melody, "Well, do you know, good mother" (Voi lo sapete). Lucia is sympathetic, but can do nothing beyond going into the church to offer up her own prayers. Santuzza stays behind, feeling unworthy to go in, and next meets the faithless Turiddu. A dramatic dialogue ensues, again interpreted by expressive music. At its height the carefree voice of Lola is heard backstage singing about her "King of Roses." With it still upon her lips she enters and takes in the situation at a glance. A dialogue of bitter irony between the two women ensues. Turiddu again spurns Santuzza and goes with the triumphant Lola into the church. Driven to desperation, Santuzza next confronts Alfio, the carter, and tells him of Lola's conduct. Alfio gives vent to a terrible outburst of rage: "Revenge I'll have upon them this very day!"

The stage is empty, but the curtain does not fall, as the service within the church continues. The storm without suddenly gives way to calm. The first notes of the Intermezzo pray for peace. It is as if the angels on high were adding their voices to this plea.

All too soon the violence of human passion reasserts itself. Church services over, the merry villagers throng the square, meeting and greeting. Cups are passed and Turiddu sings a rollicking drinking song. Alfio returns at this moment and is invited to drink. Instead he refuses and challenges Turiddu to fight, giving this challenge in the Sicilian form of biting his enemy's ear. The two retire, after Turiddu has bidden his mother farewell and asked her to care for the wronged Santuzza, and fight their duel behind the scenes. A short, terrible pause ensues, followed by running messengers, and a cry from the women, "Turiddu has been slain!"

L'AMICO FRITZ

(Lah'-mee-co Fritz)

(Friend Fritz.) Sentimental Opera in Three Acts. Music by Pietro Mascagni. Book by Suaratoni, after the story by Erckmann-Chatrian. Rome, 1891, and Dresden, 1892. At the Metropolitan, New York, January 10, 1894.

SCENE: Alsace.
TIME: The Present.

CAST FRITZ KOBUS, *a rich bachelor* (Tenor).
DAVID, *a Rabbi* (Baritone).
FREDERICO, HANEGO { *friends of Fritz* { Tenor. Tenor.
SUSEL, *a farmer's daughter* (Soprano).
BEPPE, *a Gypsy* (Soprano)
CATERINA, *a housekeeper* (Contralto).

ARGUMENT "Friend Fritz" was the composer's single incursion in the field of Light Opera. While it has many lilting melodies, it has not won a permanent place in the repertory of either English or Italian singers. The story deals with the capitulation of a dyed-in-the-wool bachelor.

Act I *Home of Fritz.* Fritz Kobus, a wealthy farmer and confirmed bachelor, on his fortieth birthday invites his friends to dine with him. Among the guests is Susel, his tenant's pretty daughter, who presents him with a nosegay, and sits beside him. For the first time he realizes a woman's charm. Rabbi David, a confirmed matchmaker, thereupon wagers with Fritz that he will soon be married, but the latter is obstinate.

After a musical melange of greetings and congratulations on the part of Fritz's friends, Susel sings a lovely flower song, one of the most tuneful bits in the opera. Others in this Act are: Beppe's song with violin accompaniment; and a stirring march taken from a popular Alsatian melody.

Act II *A Garden.* Fritz, however, cannot dismiss Susel from his mind. He makes a pretext of visiting her father. The girl mounts a ladder in the garden, picks cherries, and throws them down to Fritz, who is enchanted. When Rabbi David appears and tells him that he has found a suitable husband for Susel, Fritz cannot help revealing his own chagrin.

Susel's charming ballad, under a cherry tree, "Handsome cavalier!" is followed by a duet between her and Fritz, "Lovely Susel," ending with her own vivacious bird song. Other numbers include: an orchestral scherzo, "The Arrival of Biroccino," a diverting version of the story of Isaac and Rebecca, as interpreted by David and Susel; and a turbulent aria by Fritz.

Act III *Home of Fritz.* Back at his own home again, Fritz finds no peace and doesn't know what is the matter with him. The scheming David tells him Susel's marriage has been decided on. Fritz loses his temper, and says he will forbid the bans. At this moment Susel, pale and sad, comes in with a basket of fruit. When her wedding is mentioned she bursts into tears. Fritz tries to comfort her, and presently the girl is in his arms. David wins his wager, one of Fritz's vineyards, which he promptly bestows upon Susel as a wedding gift.

This Act has for prelude an instrumental number, which has some of the charm of the Intermezzo from "Cavalleria." It was as though the composer were striving again to catch the immortal vision. Two other noteworthy numbers are: an impassioned song by Fritz, "O, love!", and a duet between the two principals, "I love you!"

IRIS

(*Ee'-ris*)

Tragic Opera in Three Acts. Music by Mascagni. Book by Luigi Illica. Theatre Constanzi, Rome, November, 1898, and in revised form the next year, in Milan. At New York, the Metropolitan, December 16, 1907. In the cast were Eames, Caruso, and Scotti.

SCENE: Japan.
TIME: Recent.

CAST
CIECO, *a blind man* (Basso).
IRIS, *his daughter* (Soprano).
OSAKA, *a wealthy libertine* (Tenor).
KYOTO, *keeper of a dive* (Baritone).
A GEISHA (Soprano).
A PEDDLER (Tenor).
A RAG-PICKER (Tenor).
Girls, Villagers, Rag-Pickers, etc.

ARGUMENT "Iris" is an Oriental opera, telling the tragedy of a lost soul—a Japanese girl who fell into evil ways through no fault of her own, and who passes through the uttermost depths to the light of a happier world beyond.

Act I *A Japanese Garden.* The scene opens with a colorful hymn to the Sun as the Lord of Life. Iris, as an innocent child, is playing with her doll, and her blind father hears her chatter with much contentment. This idyllic scene is disturbed by the entrance of Osaka, an unprincipled man of the town, who has seen the beauty of the young girl and desires her. He arranges with Kyoto, a procurer for an evil resort, to abduct her. The girl goes with other maidens to do their washing at the river brink, and is attracted by a puppet show devised by the crafty Kyoto. She is seized by the men, who leave a purse of gold to make their transaction legal. Geishas dance around her to prevent a rescue, and her father is told that she went willingly. He curses her and their shattered home.

Act II *A Room in the Yoshiwara, or Home of the Geishas.* Iris lies asleep while other girls hum a soft melody. Osaka enters, asking for her, but is informed by Kyoto that her price is high. The libertine agrees, for, as he says, she is a "creature with a soul." When Iris awakens she believes herself in Paradise, her surroundings and gifts are so lovely, and when Osaka approaches she greets him as a "Son of Light." He answers cynically, and at last, wearied by her innocence, he bids Kyoto take her away. The keeper orders the geishas to robe her in transparent garments and expose her to the gaze of the street crowd. Osaka relents and tells Kyoto he shall have his own price for her. During this brutal haggling over the ignorant girl, who still does not know her whereabouts, her father appears in the crowd below and calls to her. She answers joyfully, but he hurls mud upon her and greets her with contempt and curses. Crazed, the girl casts herself into a deep vault, and is given over for dead.

Act III *A Dump Heap on the Outskirts of the City.* Ragpickers are searching over the refuse of the city, in the hope of finding articles of value. They discover the body of Iris, still clothed in its finery. While they try to secure the dress, the body seems to revive. This scatters the ragpickers, who run away in a panic. In a state of semi-consciousness Iris again hears the voices of the world—Osaka telling her that she has perished as a flower that sheds its fragrance in death—her father justifying his brutal act. Still Iris does not understand it all, and murmurs "Why? why?" Why should her simple life at the cottage be destroyed? As if in answer, the sun bursts forth, and she is reminded of her earlier hymn to "My Lord, the Sun!" Flowers spring up around her, enfold her in their expanding petals, and lift her body heavenward.

LODOLETTA

(Lo-do-let'-ta)

Tragic Opera in Three Acts, by Mascagni. Words by Gioacchino Forzano, after Ouida's novel, "Two Little Wooden Shoes." Rome, April 30, 1917. At New York, the Metropolitan, January 12, 1918. In the cast were Caruso and Farrar.

SCENE: A Dutch Village.
TIME: The Second French Empire.

CAST ANTONIO, *a peasant* (Basso).
LODOLETTA, *his foster daughter* (Soprano).
FLAMMEN, *a painter* (Tenor).
FRANZ (Basso).
GIANETTO (Baritone).
A MAD WOMAN (Mezzo-Soprano).
VANNARD (Mezzo-Soprano).
MAUD (Soprano).
A VOICE (Tenor).
A Letter-carrier, an old Violinist, Villagers, Guests, etc.

Act I *A Village Street.* Lodoletta, foster daughter of old Antonio, and now grown to be sixteen, desires very much to own a pair of wooden shoes, but Antonio cannot afford to buy them. Flammen, a painter from Paris, offers to purchase a picture of the Madonna on the wall of their cottage. Antonio accepts the gold piece and with it buys the coveted shoes. Shortly after, he is killed by the fall of a tree.

Act II *The Same.* The painter has conceived a deep affection for the lovely girl and gets her to pose for his pictures. Their friendship is innocent, but neighbors regard it with suspicion. To shield her, the artist returns to Paris, but finds that he cannot forget his model. Later, when he returns to find her, she has disappeared.

Act III *Flammen's Villa.* Friends of the artist gather at his home for New Year's festivities. While the celebration is at its height, Lodoletta enters the garden in rags. She looks through the window at the merry company, then falls exhausted in the snow. Later, after his guests have departed, Flammen finds two sadly-worn little shoes on his threshold. Looking further, he discovers his sweetheart frozen to death.

FRANCO LEONI

A contemporary Italian composer, born in Milan, October 24, 1864. He studied music at the Milan Conservatory, one of his teachers being Ponchielli. Of his four operas, "Rip Van Winkle," "Raggio di Luna," "Ib and Little Christina," and "The Oracle," only the last named is familiar to American music-lovers. Leoni died in Dover, England, November 11, 1938.

L'ORACOLO

(Lo-rock'-o-lo)

(The Oracle.) Tragic Opera in One Act. Music by Franco Leoni. Book by Camillo Zanoni, after the play, "The Cat and the Cherub," by Chester B. Fernald. Covent Garden, London, June 28, 1905. Metropolitan, New York, February 4, 1915.

SCENE: Chinatown, San Francisco.
TIME: The Present.

CAST Win-Shee, *a learned doctor* (Baritone).
Chim-Fen, *keeper of an opium joint* (Baritone).
Hoo-Tsin, *a wealthy merchant* (Basso).
Win-San-Luy, *son of Win-Shee* (Tenor).
Ah-Yoe, *daughter of Hoo-Tsin* (Soprano).
Hua-Quee, *a nurse* (Contralto).
Chinese Men, Women and Children, Opium Smokers, Policemen, etc.

ARGUMENT An attempt is made in this tragic piece to depict certain phases of Chinese character—the episodical bits in daily life hidden beneath the surface from the passer-by, which, however, are of the most vital importance to the Chinaman himself.

Hatchet Row, in the Chinese Quarter. It is early dawn on the Chinese New Year. Lights gleam from the opium den of Chim-Fen, and the sound of revelry is heard. The keeper ejects one of the most unruly inmates and pauses on his way back to shake his fist at the lighted window of his wealthy neighbor, Hoo-Tsin, the merchant. Why should he work so hard when his neighbor rolls in wealth? The nurse employed in Hoo-Tsin's house approaches, and he demands of her that she obtain a fan given by San-Luy to the merchant's beautiful daughter, Ah-Yoe. Frightened by his threats, she promises. Presently the learned Win-Shee passes. Chim-Fen exchanges New Year's greetings with him, and the Doctor takes opportunity to reprove him for the sort of business he conducts. A policeman passes by, and Win-Shee cautions the other not to notice the "American dog" by word or sign but to pretend to be in earnest conversation. After they have parted company, the Doctor's son, San-Luy, appears beneath the window of Ah-Yoe, where he sings a serenade. The lovers exchange greetings. Now it is broad day and Chinese hail the neighbors everywhere in greeting. Chim-Fen takes this opportunity of general fraternizing to ask of Hoo-Tsin the hand of Ah-Yoe in marriage. The only answer, he receives is the ironical wish, from Hoo-Tsin: "May all the opium in Chinatown pass through your hands!" At this second rebuff that day Chim-Fen is in a rage which is heightened when the crowd reviles him.

As part of the New Year's ceremony, the infant son of Hoo-Tsin is brought in by the nurse, and the oracle is consulted. Part of it is favorable, part unfavorable. Before the child can be taken home, it is kidnapped by Chim-Fen and hidden in a cellar. He then tells the distracted father that he will try to find the child, and makes a bargain with him that it shall be at the price of Ah-Yoe's hand. San-Luy also makes the same bargain. He traces the child to the cellar, but when he attempts to enter he comes to blows with Chim-Fen, and the two fall struggling down the cellar steps. In the outcome San-Luy is killed. When news of the murder is spread abroad there is a great confusion, and the heartbroken Ah-Yoe mourns for her sweetheart. His father, Win-Shee, likewise is disconsolate, but determines to avenge the bloody deed. At nightfall in his wanderings he discovers and rescues the child; then encounters Chim-Fen, whom he reproaches and finally slays. A policeman approaches. Quickly adopting his own advice of the morning, Win-Shee props up the dead body and pretends an animated conversation with it until the officer goes by. Justice has been done according to the Chinese code, so why should the foreign dogs interfere?

The music is not altogether successful in conveying the oriental atmosphere. It relies upon descriptive and dramatic passages familiar to the later Italian school. One of the more delightful numbers is the song of Ah-Yoe on her balcony, in greeting to the new day. Win-Shee also has some good opportunities for the baritone voice.

UMBERTO GIORDANO

Giordano is a contemporary Italian composer of some note. He was born at Foggia, August 26, 1867, and studied at the Naples Conservatory under Serrao. One of his earlier works was the one-act opera, "Marina," which was entered for the Sonzogno prize that Mascagni won with his "Cavalleria Rusticana." This was followed by "Mala Vita," which was produced at Rome, in 1892; "André Chénier" (1896); "Fedora" (1906); "Siberia" (1908); and "Madame Sans Gêne," his most successful work (1915). Giordano died in Milan, November 12, 1948.

ANDRÉ CHÉNIER

(An-dray Shain-yay)

Tragic Opera in Four Acts. Music by Umberto Giordano. Book by Luigi Illica. La Scala, Milan, March 23, 1896. Academy of Music, New York, November 13, 1896. At the Metropolitan, March 7, 1921.

SCENE: Paris.
TIME: The French Revolution.

CAST André Chénier, *a poet* (Tenor).
Charles Gerard, *a Revolutionist* (Baritone).
Countess de Coigny (Soprano).
Madeleine, *her daughter* (Soprano).
Bersi, *her maid* (Mezzo-Soprano).
Roucher, *friend of Chénier* (Basso).
Mathieu, *a Revolutionist* (Baritone).
Madelon, *an aged woman* (Soprano).
Fleville, *a writer* (Tenor).
The Abbé (Tenor).
Schmidt, *jailer at St. Lazare* (Basso).
A Spy.
Guests, Servants, Pages, Peasants, Soldiers, Judges, Prisoners, Mob, etc.

ARGUMENT This opera in plot follows the familiar lines of the heroine willing to sacrifice honor, then life, for the man she loves. The story is of a poet who gets into the toils of his enemies during the French Revolution. Although based upon a character of history, the librettist has taken many liberties with his actions. The real Chénier was both poet and patriot. The music alternates between tender, lyric passages, and others of high emotion, leading up to "set" numbers of the later Italian school.

Act I *Ballroom in a Château.* Prior to the Revolution, Gerard, a revolutionist, is secretly in love with Madeleine, the Countess' daughter. A ball is given, and among the guests is André Chénier, a poet with revolutionary tendencies. Madeleine asks him to improvise a poem on love, but he sings of the wrongs of the poor. Gerard appears with a crowd of ragged men and women, but the Countess' servants eject the intruders.

The song of the poet, a tirade against Church and State, is the principal number in this Act: "Once o'er azure fields" (Un di all' azzurro spazio).

Act II *Café Hottot in Paris.* Some years later, Chénier has offended the Revolutionists by denouncing Robespierre. A spy is watching Bersi, Madeleine's old nurse, and sees her hand Chénier a letter. It is from Madeleine, who begs him come to her aid, and arranges a rendezvous.

Robespierre enters with citizens. Gerard, now high in favor, wants to possess Madeleine, who has come to meet Chénier. They are about to flee, when Gerard interferes. The rivals fight and Gerard is wounded. The lovers escape.

Act III *Revolutionary Tribunal.* Chénier has been captured, and Gerard brings formal charge against his rival. Madeleine pleads for her lover, finally promising to give herself to Gerard if Chénier is spared. Gerard, moved by the girl's love, agrees to save Chénier if he can. At the trial he declares that the indictment is false. But the mob, thirsting for blood, demands the poet's death.

Gerard's inner conflict between lust and honor is admirably depicted by both voice and instruments. The latter introduce a hint of the "Marseillaise." His song is a favorite one with baritones: "An enemy of his country" (Nemico della patria).

Act IV *Prison of Lazare at Midnight.* Madeleine and Gerard visit Chénier. She has bribed the jailer to allow her to take the place of another prisoner. If she cannot live for her lover, she can, at least, die with him. Together she and Chénier go to the scaffold, to pay the last penalty.

In the opening of this scene the poet is discovered writing his last verses. They are in praise and trust of his sweetheart and give opportunity for a fine lyric for tenor: "As some soft day in May" (Come un bel di Maggio).

MADAME SANS GÊNE

(Ma-dam' Sahn Zhayn)

(Madam Don't Care.) Historic Opera in Four Acts. Music by Giordano. Book by Renato Simoni. After the Comedy by Victorien Sardou and E. Moreau. Metropolitan, New York, January 25, 1915. In the cast were Farrar, Amato, De Segurola, and Martinelli.

SCENE: France.
TIME: Days of Napoleon.

CAST
NAPOLEON (Baritone).
CATERINA HUBSCHER ("Catherine," "MADAME SANS GÊNE"), *a laundress* (Soprano).
TONIOTTA, *a laundress* (Soprano).
GIULIA, *a laundress* (Soprano).
LA ROSSA, *a laundress* (Soprano).
LEFEBVRE, *sergeant, then marshal* (Tenor).
FOUCHÉ, *patriot, then minister of police* (Baritone).
COUNT OF NEIPPERG, *an Austrian* (Tenor).
VINAIGRE, *a drummer* (Tenor).
QUEEN CAROLINE (Soprano).
PRINCESS ELISA (Soprano).
GELSOMINO, *valet* (Baritone).
LEROY, *tailor* (Baritone).
DE BRIGODE, *court chamberlain* (Baritone).
MADAME DE BOULOW (Soprano).
ROUSTAN, *head of the Mamelukes* (Baritone).
Citizens, Soldiers, Huntsmen, Ladies of the Court, etc.

ARGUMENT This colorful opera is unique in its attempt to make Napoleon the central figure of a romantic drama—giving him as well as his attendants a singing part. It is full of figures and action, and crosses a considerable period of time.

Act I *Catherine's Laundry, Paris, August 10, 1792.* Catherine Hubscher, a pretty Alsatian, has earned by her saucy manner the popular nickname of "Madam Don't Care." Her laundry is, on this historic morning, a storm center, as the mob is attacking the Tuileries—this is one of the red-letter days of the French Revolution. Fouché, a patriot, enters in great trepidation at the doings of the crowd. He is followed by Catherine, who rallies him for his lack of courage. She herself has great tales to tell of what she has witnessed in the street. Fouché says that it is his ambition to become minister of police. She replies tauntingly that he has about as much chance to become that as she has to become a duchess. A great uproar proclaims that the palace has been taken. So riotous is the street that the laundress prudently barricades her shop. Presently she sees a wounded man, and admits him. It is the Count of Neipperg, an Austrian, who has come to grief in trying to rescue the Queen. Catherine hides him in her room. Her lover, Lefebvre, a police sergeant, enters. He discovers the concealed man and at first is jealous; then believes Catherine and aids her to effect the Count's escape.

The lively action is sustained by both singers and orchestra, without any outstanding single numbers in this Act. A pleasing dance of girls, "La Fricasee," is followed by Catherine's aria on the rudeness of the soldiers. The music then leads up to the curtain in martial strains, the roll of drums, the feet of marching men, and the strains of the "Marseillaise."

Act II *Château of Compeigne.* Nineteen years have passed by. The obscure Napoleon has become a world conqueror, and many of his followers have been ennobled. Lefebvre has been made the Duke of Danzig, and Catherine, his wife, is really a Duchess. But she is still sharp of tongue and bourgeois of action, so much so that the Emperor counsels Lefebvre to divorce her. This the latter laughingly repeats to his wife, and says he doesn't intend to do anything of the sort. Their old acquaintance, Count Neipperg, now enters. He has been dismissed from Court for his too open admiration of the Empress. He is in despair and asks his friends to procure for him a last interview with her. Fouché, now minister of police, enters to announce the royal ladies, for whom the Duke and Duchess are to give a reception. The flunkeys try to tell Madame Sans Gêne how she is to deport herself, but give it up in despair. The reception which follows is conducted without decorum. The hostess flouts her guests to their faces, and it is with open joy they hear that she is summoned to appear before Napoleon, to answer for her conduct.

The music here has more the flavor of Light Opera, as the action alternates between the dramatic and the humorous. The interweaving melody with an unusually vigorous plot keeps the senses quickened.

Act III *The Emperor's Cabinet.* Napoleon receives Madame Sans Gêne, and reproaches her for failing to shed luster on his Court. She should grant her husband a divorce and retire to private life. She retorts that her husband would not exchange her for the proudest princess. Then waxing eloquent she recites the glories of the army life, which she herself has followed. She calls to mind their early days of struggle, and even shows Napoleon his own unpaid laundry bill of nineteen years before. Touched by her naïveté, the Emperor forgives her and stoops to kiss the scar on her arm, received in battle. As she is about to retire, Neipperg enters on his way to the Empress' apartment. There is a sharp encounter between him and the Emperor. As officers rush in, the irate Napoleon orders that he be shot at sunrise.

The musical passages between the former Corporal and laundress are delightful.

Act IV *The Same.* The stage is undisturbed, but a dying fire and gutting candles indicate that the night is far spent and the last hours of the condemned man are running out. There is a brief scene between Catherine and Lefebvre, in which they deplore their own helplessness. Napoleon re-enters in much agitation. Catherine pleads with him to spare the Count, but Napoleon sternly orders her, as a test, to knock at the Empress' door and announce Neipperg's presence. She does so tremblingly. The door opens slightly and a note is handed out. It dismisses the Count and completely vindicates the Empress. The Count's life is spared, and the scene ends amid general felicitations. "As for your divorce," says the Emperor to Lefebvre with mock sternness, "forget it." He tweaks Catherine's ear. "Thank heaven for giving this woman to you!"

A fanfare of hunting horns and a spirited chorus bring the final curtain.

FEDORA

Tragic Opera in Three Acts. Music by Giordano. Book by Colautti, after the play by Sardou. Milan, November 17, 1898. At New

York, the Metropolitan, December 5, 1906, with Cavalieri, Caruso, Alten, and Scotti.

SCENE: Paris and Switzerland.
TIME: Latter part of Nineteenth Century.

CAST PRINCESS FEDORA (Soprano).
COUNT LORIS (Tenor).
COUNTESS OLGA (Soprano).
DE SIRIEX, *a diplomat* (Baritone).
GRECH, *a police officer* (Basso).
DMITRI, *a groom* (Contralto).
CYRIL, *a coachman* (Baritone).
BOROV, *a doctor* (Baritone).
BARON ROUVEL (Baritone).
Servants, Attendants, etc.

ARGUMENT An opera of love and intrigue, the scene of which is laid in Russia; based on a drama by Sardou.

Act I *Home of Count Vladimir, in St. Petersburg.* The lovely Princess Fedora impatiently awaits the coming of her accepted suitor, Count Vladimir. He is brought in, in a dying condition, by De Siriex, a diplomat, and suspicion points to Count Loris as the murderer. Fedora swears by a jeweled cross she wears that she will be avenged.

Act II *Fedora's Apartments in Paris.* At a splendid reception given by the Princess in Paris, she exerts all her wiles upon Loris, in the hope of obtaining from him a confession. Meanwhile, however, she finds herself falling in love with him. She fights this emotion unavailingly; and Loris in his turn avows his love. Then he tells her that the real reason behind his act of vengeance was that fact that Count Vladimir had betrayed his bride and brought her to the grave. The Princess embraces him and shields him from Grech, the police officer whom she had previously stationed outside.

The music in this Act rises to fine lyric heights, as the Count pleads with the reluctant Princess. His aria is a sustained cantanina: "My love compels me" (Amor ti vieta non amar).

Act III *A Swiss Villa.* Although Fedora and Loris have escaped to Switzerland and are now happily married, nemesis pursues them. The police are on Loris' trail, and he receives word that his brother has been put in prison, and his mother has died of grief. On top of this comes word that it is none other than Fedora who has put the police after him. He is ready to kill her when, in her own despair, she swallows poison. Stricken with remorse, he pleads with her to live for his sake; but she dies in his arms.

The music here reaches its climax when the Count, torn by conflicting emotions at news of his mother's death, sings a pathetic aria, "My dear old mother!"

ITALO MONTEMEZZI

Montemezzi is one of the later group of Italian composers, who established his standing by a single opera, but that a powerful one. He was born in Verona, in 1875, and studied in Italian schools. One of his earliest compositions was a choral, "Cantico dei Cantici," produced at the Conservatory of Music in Milan, in 1900, which attracted attention to his gifts. An opera, "Giovanni Gallurese," was given in Turin, in 1905; and "Hellera" at the same place, in 1909. But it remained for "The Three Kings" to bring him to international fame. Montemezzi lived for some years in Beverly Hills, California, but visited in Verona, Italy, where he died on May 15, 1952.

THE LOVE OF THE THREE KINGS

(L'Amore Dei Tre Re.) Tragic Poem in Three Acts. Music by Italo Montemezzi. Book by Sem. Benelli, La Scala, Milan, April 10, 1913. At the Metropolitan, New York, January 2, 1914. In both Paris and London, the same year.

SCENE: A remote castle of Italy.
TIME: The Middle Ages.

CAST ARCHIBALDO, *an aged king* (Basso).
MANFREDO, *his son* (Baritone).
AVITO, *Prince of Altura* (Tenor).
FLAMINIO, *an attendant* (Tenor).
FIORA, *wife of Manfredo* (Soprano).
SERVANT GIRL (Soprano).
YOUNG GIRL (Soprano).
OLD WOMAN (Contralto).
Court Attendants, Mourners, Villagers of Altura.

ARGUMENT Fiora, formerly loved by Avito, Prince of Altura, has been given as the price of peace to the conqueror of that country. The story is the struggle of this princess between her old love and her loyalty to her new lord—the tragedy of jealousy and broken faith. The composer's style is abrupt rather than flowing—a succession of musical phrases set in eloquent, declamatory style.

Act I *Spacious Hall in the Castle.* Archibaldo, the aged King of an Italian country, has conquered, in earlier years, the neighboring state of Altura. As the price of peace he receives the maiden, Fiora, whom he bestows upon his son, Manfredo, for wife. Manfredo tenderly loves his young wife, but is often away at the wars. His father is suspicious as to her conduct, and having become blind is all the more distrustful. In the opening scene, he enters with Flaminio, and questions him as to her whereabouts. He then retires, after having had a signal lantern extinguished. Fiora enters from her apartment and is met by Avito, her former lover in Altura. He renews his love-making, but is warned of danger by the fact that the lantern is extinguished, and turns to flee as the blind Archibaldo returns. The latter questions Fiora sharply as to whom she has been with, and her trembling replies convince him that she is untrue to his son. He sends her to her room, as the sound of trumpets announce the return of Manfredo. The Prince is not informed of his father's fears, the latter murmuring, "O Lord God, let me not see—let me be blind—be blind!"

The music is eloquent in this tense scene. As the blind King enters, his groping steps are mirrored by the orchestra. At his questioning of Flaminio, the latter replies: "There is no one, my lord. All is quiet!" (Tutto è pace!). Fiora's song to her lover, "Give me thy lips" (Dammi le labbra) is a central theme:

The extinguishing of the lantern, and the King's suspicious, "I hear thee breathing!" are other tense moments in the music.

Act II *A Circular Terrace on the Castle Walls.* Manfredo, recalled to his troops, bids his wife a kind and affectionate farewell.

He does not demand anything of her—only that she will cheer him and his troops, as they ride away down the valley, by waving a scarf. Touched by his unselfish devotion she promises, and is minded thereafter to be a faithful wife to him. But alas for her good resolutions!—the first person she encounters upon the castle walls is Avito, disguised as a guard. She bids him go, saying that she is "conquered by kindness." He refuses, and makes such ardent love that she is once more overcome and yields to him. When the servants bring a casket containing Manfredo's scarf, she will not let her lover touch it, but waves it wearily to the distant horsemen. Archibaldo again surprises the lovers. Avito is ready to stab him with his dagger, but is prevented by Flaminio in a silent gesture. The King demands to know who is there. Flaminio shields the Prince, and is dismissed by Archibaldo, who rages at his own helplessness. In a fit of frenzy he throttles Fiora, because she withholds the name of her lover, while confessing her guilt. Manfredo returns, alarmed at the cessation of his signal, the waving scarf, and finds the old King crouching beside the dead body of Fiora. Archibaldo tells why he committed the deed, and Manfredo retires, overcome with grief. He is followed by the blind King, carrying the body.

The orchestra gives a vivid tone picture of Manfredo's cavalry riding down the valley. Then comes another frenzied scene between the two guilty lovers. "How art thou trembling, beloved!" sings Fiora in a low voice; to be answered by his triumphant, "Look up! We are in heaven!" (Siamo in cielo.) But the idyllic scene is rudely broken. The aged King again enters with vengeance in his hands. The hoofbeats of the returning Manfredo also spell tragedy. The closing music of the scene pulsates with grief.

Act III *Crypt in the Castle Chapel.* In the center lies the body of Fiora, clad in white, on a bed of flowers. A choir and various single voices sing lamentations. They disperse upon the entrance of Avito, who bows and shields his face as before a shrine. He bemoans his loss and in farewell kisses her upon the lips. A violent pain seizes him and he arises tottering. Manfredo approaches in the shadow. He recognizes the Alturian, and tells him that the girl's lips were poisoned as a trap to catch him, and his moments are numbered. More in sorrow than in anger Manfredo asks: "Did she love thee?" "More than the life they took from her!" replies Avito, and falls dying. Manfredo supports him, crying, "Why cannot I hate!" Overcome with remorse he casts himself upon the bier and in turn presses the poisoned lips of his dead wife. Archibaldo gropes his way in, to find his son dying. The love of the three kings has brought only death in its wake.

The culminating cry of despair is from the lips of Avito: "Fiora! Fiora! There is naught but silence!" (E silencio!)—

ERMANNO WOLF-FERRARI

A German-Italian composer born in Venice, January 12, 1876. He took his name from both parents, his father being a celebrated German painter, August Wolf. Ermanno took naturally to music and was self-taught until seventeen, when he was placed under Rheinberger's instruction, at Munich. His composition, however, has revealed the Italian rather than the Teutonic influence. His operas include: "Cenerentola" (1900); "Le Donne Curiose" (1903); "I Quattro Rusteghi" (1906); "Il Segreto di Susanna" (1910); "I Giojelli della Madonna" (1911); and "L'Amore Medico" (1913). Three of these, to give them their more familiar English titles, "The Inquisitive Women," "The Secret of Susanne," and "Dr. Cupid," are of lighter texture. His one serious work, "The Jewels of the Madonna," bids fair to remain longer in repertory. He died in Venice, January 21, 1948.

THE JEWELS OF THE MADONNA

(I Giojelli della Madonna.) Dramatic Opera in Three Acts. Music by Wolf-Ferrari. Book by C. Zangarini and E. Golisciani. Berlin, December 23, 1911, with German title and text. Chicago in the original, January 16, 1912; and the Metropolitan, New York, March 5 following.

SCENE: Naples.
TIME: The Present.

CAST MALIELLA, *adopted daughter of Carmela* (Soprano).
CARMELA, *Gennaro's mother* (Mezzo-Soprano).
GENNARO, *a blacksmith* (Tenor).
RAFAELE, *chief of the Camorrists* (Baritone).
Camorrists, Street-sellers, Townsfolk, etc.

ARGUMENT The scene of action is modern Naples. The plot hinges on the rivalry of Gennaro, a blacksmith, and Rafaele, a Camorrist leader, for the love of Maliella. The opening curtain is heralded by an orchestral prelude of Neapolitan folk music, with a hint of the gay dances which enliven a melodramatic plot.

Act I *A Small Open Square by the Sea. Afternoon.* A merry crowd in a small public square awaits the festival procession in honor of the Holy Virgin. Maliella escapes from her house with disheveled hair and disordered dress, protesting against the restraint of her foster-mother. After some banter with Gennaro she sings a challenging song, inviting the assembled crowd of youths to kiss her. An impromptu dance ensues, she is whirled in and disappears, but soon returns followed by Rafaele. She repels him, and when he seizes her to kiss her, stabs him in the hand with a pin drawn from her hair. He hesitates, then kisses the wound, swearing she shall be his, and, as she replaces the pin in her hair, thrusts a flower in her bosom, which she snatches forth and flings to the ground. The procession comes in sight, and he stays by her, pleading. As the Madonna passes, he offers to risk his soul for her, by placing the jewels of the Madonna round her neck. Terrified at the thought, she shrieks, while Rafaele and his fellow-Camorrists laugh. As she is about to enter her home again, Rafaele throws her the flower she has rejected, and this time Maliella places it between her lips and goes within.

Musical numbers include: the blacksmith's song as he works at his anvil and offers a prayer to the Virgin: "Madonna, tears and sighing" (Con sonspiri); Maliella's rebellious story of another girl's love, "Thus sang poor Cannatella"; a touching duet between Carmela and Gennaro, her son; and the chorus of hymns, with bells and guns in the background, announcing the procession of the Virgin.

Act II One of the gems of the opera is the lovely intermezzo which introduces this Act. Its warmth of melody and sensuous appeal form a haunting picture of a typical Neapolitan night.

Garden of Carmela's House. Evening of the same day. Maliella is with Carmela and Gennaro; the festival is not yet over. Carmela leaves them, and Gennaro begins to plead with Maliella, but she complains of the monotony of her life and threatens to leave her home. Gennaro begs for a farewell kiss, and losing control, clasps her in his arms and pours out his passion for her. Maliella escapes from him and proclaims her love for Rafaele, tauntingly repeating the Camorrist's offer to risk his soul for her by robbing the Madonna of her jewels. She returns to the house and Gennaro breaks down. The thought of Rafaele's boast possesses his mind, and his distraught fancy leads him to imagine that only by himself obtaining these jewels can he hope to win Maliella's love. He takes keys and tools with him and locks the garden door after him. Rafaele comes with his fellow-Camorrists to serenade Maliella. She enters the garden and he embraces her through the bars till warned away by the approach of Gennaro, who enters looking like a ghost. In answer to her cry he responds "For you!" and discloses the stolen jewels of the Madonna. She screams, but Gennaro assures her that the Virgin has already forgiven his crime. Fascinated by the jewels glittering in the moonlight, she moves slowly toward them and clasps them about her head, neck and wrists. The sight of the gems calls up the vision of Rafaele to her mind and possesses her utterly; all thought of Gennaro fades and, as if in a trance, she yields herself to him.

The chief music of this Act is the chorus of men's voices in the distance, followed by Rafaele's entrance with his Camorrist friends. He sings an appealing serenade to the accompaniment of mandolins and guitars. The love duet which follows is sustained by the orchestra "with passion," but soon gives way to the more violent scene when the blacksmith claims her.

Act III A second intermezzo is the curtain-raiser for the final Act—and again marks one of the compelling points of an otherwise ordid story. It re-echoes the theme of Rafaele's serenade in the preceding Act, with its graceful waltz rhythm. A scene of wild revelry is hown, with Apache dances and general vulgarity—a fitting prelude to vhat follows.

Meeting Place of the Camorrists. It is the night of the festival. ome of the Camorrists lie about sleeping, others come in from various xpeditions. Rafaele enters and is boisterously greeted. After he has aten he sings of the charms of Maliella, which piques the Camorrist vomen, and they begin a wild, bacchic dance, that by degrees degenrates into an orgy. Suddenly there is a loud knocking, and Maliella ursts in, disheveled, pallid and bareheaded. Rafaele forces her terible secret from her, and at the first mention of Gennaro's name comnands his comrades to bring him his rival, alive or dead. Furious at the derision of his fellows following Maliella's confession, Rafaele spurns her brutally, and she falls to the ground, disclosing the jewels. Gennaro rushes in, pursued by the Camorrists, and seeing Maliella cries her name. Filled with consuming hatred, she shrieks that he is accursed, tells how he robbed the Madonna, and, flinging the jewels at his feet, rushes out, crying despairingly, "To the sea!" The wind, whistling through the den, blows out the candles one by one. The company flees, filled with superstitious terror, and Gennaro is left alone. He, not having obtained death from the hands of the Camorrists, crawls to a rude altar beneath a fresco of the Virgin and, craving pardon for his sacrilege, stabs himself. A crowd, armed with various weapons, bursts into the den, seeking vengeance on the sacrilegist. At the sight of Gennaro dead before the Virgin they halt, awe-stricken, on the threshold.

RICCARDO ZANDONAI

Born at Sacco, Trentino, May 28, 1883, Zandonai was a pupil of Gianferrari, at Rovereto; and later of Mascagni. He wrote half a dozen operas, among them, "Conchita" (1911), and "Melenis" (1912). His best known work, however, is "Francesca da Rimini." Zandonai died in Rome, June 19, 1944.

FRANCESCA DA RIMINI

(Frahn-ches'-ca da Rim'-e-nee)

Grand Opera in Four Acts. Music by Riccardo Zandonai. Book by Tito Riccordi, after the drama by Gabriele D'Annunzio. Reggio Theatre, Turin, February 4, 1914. At New York, the Metropolitan, December 22, 1916, with Alda, Martinelli, Amato, and Mason.

SCENE: First act, Ravenna, then Rimini.
TIME: The Thirteenth Century.

CAST GIOVANNI, *the lame* } *sons of Malatesta da Verrucchio* { Baritone.
PAOLO, *the beautiful* } { Tenor.
MALATESTINO, *the one-eyed* } { Tenor.
OSTASIO, *son of Guido Minore da Polenta* (Baritone).

SER TOLDO BERARDENGO, *a notary* (Tenor).
A JESTER (Basso).
A BOWMAN (Tenor).
TOWER WARDEN (Baritone).
FRANCESCA, *daughter of Guido and sister of Ostasio* (Soprano).
SAMARITANA, *sister of Francesca and Ostasio* (Soprano).

BIANCOFIORE	*attendants to Francesca*	Soprano.
GARSENDA		Soprano.
ALTICHIARA		Mezzo-Soprano.

DONELLA (Mezzo-Soprano).
SMARADI, *a slave* (Contralto).
Bowmen, Archers, and Musicians.

ARGUMENT An opera written around one of the world's famous tales of unrequited love—the story of Paolo ınd Francesca.

ıct I *The House of Polentani, Ravenna.* Francesca, the beautiful daughter of Guido da Polenta, is to be given in marriage to ;iovanni, a son of Malatesta. There are two other sons, Malatestino, ı one-eyed fellow, and Paolo, a handsome young man. Knowing that he maiden would refuse to wed Giovanni, who is a cripple, Paolo is sent o represent him at the betrothal. Francesca falls a victim to this plot vhich has been hatched for political reasons, and falls in love with 'aolo at first sight—a passion which he reciprocates.

The music in this opening Act is of lyric mood. There is a quartet f women's voices which is effective, that of maids attending upon Franesca. This is followed by the aria of a jester, who tells of "Tristan and solde," as a sort of prologue to the tale that is to unfold here.

.ct II *Tower Room in the Castle of the Malatestas.* Francesca has been tricked into marriage with Giovanni, who is called ;ianciotti the Lamester, and nurses in her heart a deep grudge against aolo for his share in the deception. Paolo seeks her and pleads forıveness. He does not attempt to conceal his love for her, and now ould welcome death. The Malatesta castle is being besieged by the ıemy at this moment, and the tower room is the center of warlike activy. Paolo steps out on the parapet to confront his foes, leaving off his elmet and shield. But Francesca, forgetting all save her love for him, ıshes out to shield him from danger with her own body. Neither of ıem is injured; their foes are driven off; and Gianciotti enters the room tell his brother that he, Paolo, has been appointed to an important ›st in Florence, for which city Paolo departs.

The music takes on a furious tone as the battle rages around the castle. Gone for the time are the tender moods, even when the lovers again meet. Tragedy is imminent—the instruments uniting with the voices in a tumult of sound.

Act III *Apartment of Francesca.* In her sumptuous room, Francesca is beguiling her loneliness by reading aloud to her women, from an ancient tome, the story of "Lancelot and Guinevere." During the reading, Paolo is announced, and the attendants retire. He has been unable to remain away at Florence. He and Francesca still make every effort to conceal their mutual passion. They take up the old love story and begin to read it together. But when they come to the passage where Queen Guinevere "takes him by the chin and slowly kisses him on the mouth," they suit the action to the words.

Again the mood of the music is peaceful, tender. Francesca's women sing of the delights of Spring: "March comes and February goes." The greeting between the lovers is restrained. "Welcome, my lord!" she sings. "Paolo, give me peace," she next voices. However, the music takes on a more intimate tone as they read together from another love story.

Act IV *Scene 1. Hall of the Castle.* Malatestino, the one-eyed brother, has also become infatuated with Francesca, and tells her that he would go to the length of poisoning Gianciotti. She re pulses him in horror. They hear a disturbance from a neighborin dungeon, in which a political prisoner is held. Malatestino says he wil silence his noise, and goes and kills the prisoner. When his elde brother reproaches him for his act and his attentions to Francesca, Mala testino diverts attention from himself by hinting at improper conduc on the part of Paolo and Francesca.

Scene 2. Francesca's Apartment. It is night, but Francesca canno sleep soundly. She dreams that harm threatens Paolo. Her wome try to soothe her. A gentle knock is heard at the door, and Paolo's voic calls, "Francesca!" She flings open the door and they embrace. As the sit talking together, a violent knock is heard and the deformed hu band demands entrance. Paolo hastily hides by going down a tra door. The angry husband discovers him, drags him back into th room, and forces him to fight. Francesca rushes between them and re ceives Gianciotti's sword thrust in her own breast. With another sa age thrust Gianciotti pierces his brother's heart; and the two lovers di in each other's arms. Slowly their executioner breaks his bloodstaine sword across his knee.

The climax of the music now grown violent again is reached in the inal scene. Francesca's wild dream and outcry are followed by the oothing song of the women. It is but a brief calm before the final torm. The last meeting of the lovers is shown in impassioned phrases nd a rising tumult of orchestral strings. The rage of the fighting men, s the sword strikes its victims, is mirrored in the orchestra and ends in hords of grief and remorse—a requiem of sorrow.

FRANCE

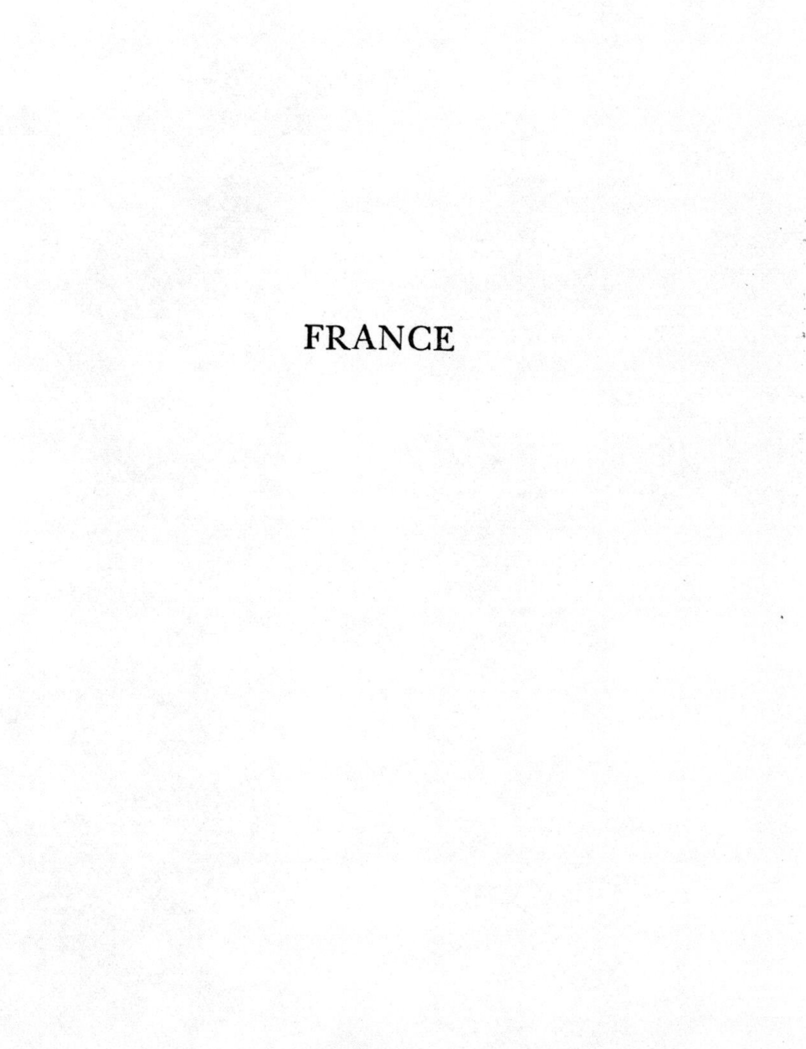

HISTORICAL PREFACE

In tracing the rise of opera in Europe, the student of the French school will encounter many tangled threads. The influence of both the Italian and the German schools is deep and recurring. It was the custom of young French musicians to study in Italy. We have seen how in the French court at Naples, as early as the year 1285, a pastoral with incidental music was performed; and how one of the earliest operas by Peri was given before Henry IV of France, in 1600.

Operas were produced in Paris by foreign composers long before a definite native school was established. The works of Gluck and Mozart vied with those of Rossini and Spontini to such an extent that it was hard for a young Frenchman to get a hearing. Such a one, for example, was Rameau (1683–1764) who had the ill luck to have his "Castor and Pollux" and other works outshone by the German, Gluck. And it was an Italian, Lully, who founded the Grand Opera in Paris, in 1672, and is consequently called the father of French opera.

Early French musicians whose work is still known include: Étienne Nicholas Méhul (1763–1817), whose opera, "Joseph in Egypt," is still studied; François Adrien Boïeldieu (1775–1834), whose "Caliph of Bagdad" is still remembered for its delightful overture; Daniel F. E. Auber (1782–1871), who achieved immortality with at least one light opera, "Fra Diavolo"; Louis F. J. Herold (1791–1833), of whose opera, "Zampa," only the overture remains in popular esteem; and Jacques Halévy (1799–1862), whose "La Juive" still remains in repertory.

The first commanding figure, however, is Meyerbeer. Though considered the real founder of modern French opera, Meyerbeer was born in Berlin and studied in both Germany and Italy. His earlier work shows the influence of Rossini. But his life work was done in Paris and after the sensational success of his great opera, "Robert le Diable," he became the idol of the French music world. This and succeeding works from his pen made both his own fortune and that of the Grand Opera House in Paris, which was placed soundly on its feet.

Thereafter works by native composers came thick and fast. The reader of this book is referred to later pages for the most notable names and examples. Nevertheless, the few great figures can be numbered with the fingers almost of one hand. When we have called the names of Meyerbeer, Gounod, Offenbach, Saint-Saëns, Bizet, Massenet, and Debussy, we have enumerated the chief ones who represent French opera in other lands. In some instances, also, a composer will be known to fame for a single masterpiece. Witness "Faust," one of the most melodious and popular of all operas; "The Tales of Hoffmann"; "Samson and Delilah"; "Carmen"; "Pelléas and Mélisande"; or the haunting melodies of "Mignon," by Thomas.

French opera, like that of its two great neighbors, Germany and Italy, is characterized by certain elusive yet definite qualities. There is a verve, a brilliance, an elegance, which stamp it with a definite hallmark. Even the more ephemeral elements such as the ballet are yet distinctive.

The work of later composers has run the gamut from light to serious, but always with an unmistakable Gallic quality. In the section devoted to Light Opera we take notice of several typical French composers in this field, beginning with Auber and Lecocq, fifty years later, and continuing often on the border line of grave and gay. "The Tales of Hoffmann," for example, is always classed with Grand Opera, but betrays many traits of the lighter medium.

Among outstanding names of the past century one must mention Massenet, who first won fame by his comic opera, "The Great Aunt," before taking up more serious themes. Later he produced a dozen or more dramatic operas, most of which are familiar to American opera-goers. Charpentier belongs to a more modern school. Witness his "Louise" and its sequels. Debussy is one of the most radical of later composers, but each year sees his fame more secure. Erlanger, Dukas, Rabaud, Fevrier, and Wolff, are among the most promising of contemporary French musicians.

No résumé of French opera would be complete without mention of Opera Comique. (See Light Opera section in this volume.) Here again the Italian influence is seen in Opera Buffa, but the French have made this field peculiarly their own. The true definition of Grand Opera is that in which all conversation is set to music. The more frivolous of the French composers early began to break down this artificial barrier and add other touches such as the ballet. Note, for instance the technique of Auber or of Offenbach. In still gayer mood, Planquette, in "Chimes of Normandy." This trend we have taken up in detail in the Light Opera section. The field is inviting and will reward the music student, whether he approaches it from the Grand or the Lighter side. It is one of the definite and important trends of the French school.

JACOB MEYERBEER

Meyerbeer is generally considered a French composer and the founder of the so-called school of modern French opera, although he was born in Berlin (September 5, 1791) and studied the piano in Germany. He first came into prominence as a brilliant pianist. Meyerbeer came of a Jewish family. His real name was Jacob Liebmann Beer. He prefixed "Meyer" at the request of a wealthy relative who made him his heir. He was a pupil in pianoforte of Clementi; also studied under Abbé Vogler, being a fellow pupil of Weber. His first operas were German. In 1815 he went to Italy and composed a series of operas in the style of Rossini. Going to Paris in 1826, he became "immersed in the study of French opera, from Lully onward." The first result was "Robert le Diable" (1831). This was followed by "Les Huguenots" (1836); "Le Prophète" (1849); "L'Etoile du Nord" (1854); "Dinorah" (1859). Meyerbeer died May 2, 1864, in Paris. His "L'Africaine" was produced the year following his death.

ROBERT LE DIABLE

(Ro-bair leh Dee-ah-bleh)

(Robert the Devil.) Grand Opera in Five Acts. Music by Meyerbeer. Book by Scribe and Delavigne. Grand Opera, Paris, November 22, 1831, where its tremendous success insured the fortune of the Grand Opera itself. In English, Park Theatre, New York, April 7, 1834; Academy of Music, November 30, 1857.

SCENE: Sicily.
TIME: The Thirteenth Century.

CAST
ROBERT, *Duke of Normandy* (Tenor).
ALICE, *foster sister of Robert* (Soprano).
ISABELLA, *Princess of Sicily* (Soprano).
THE ABBESS.
BERTRAM, *the Unknown* (Basso).
RAIMBAUT, *a minstrel* (Tenor).
Knights, Monks, Nuns, etc.

ARGUMENT A legendary story involving the tempting of human characters by an archfiend, who may be regarded as the prototype of Mephistopheles in "Faust." Although the opera is seldom produced now, it is still of great interest as a forerunner of the romantic school. Its first enormous success was due to striking scenic effects, to which the plot lends itself, brilliant orchestration, dramatic recitatives, and a running thread of bright melody.

Act I *A Castle in Palermo.* Raimbaut, a wandering minstrel, tells the story of Robert the Devil to a group of listening knights. It seems that Robert is the son of an archfiend by a human woman. The fiend has roamed the earth under the name of Bertram. The son is naturally of wild and ungovernable disposition, being still under the secret control of his father. One of the auditors to whom the minstrel tells this tale is Robert himself. He is so incensed by this disclosure that he wishes to make away with Raimbaut, but the latter is saved by Robert's foster-sister Alice, who is in love with the minstrel.

Act II *The Palace of Isabella.* Robert is enamored of Isabella, the Princess of Sicily, and has come hither to wear her colors in a tournament. Bertram lures him away, and he fails to meet his opponent, thus losing his honor as a knight and his lady's hand in the bargain.

Act III *Scene 1. Rocky Cavern of St. Irene.* The evil spirits hold high carnival, and to them comes Bertram, who promises a recruit in his son Robert. They meet Alice, who has had a tryst with Raimbaut, and she seeks to rescue Robert.

Scene 2. A Ruined Cloister. In order to strengthen his hold on Robert, Bertram calls to life a group of nuns who in life forgot their vows. They tempt the knight and finally tell him he can win Isabella if he steals the mystic cypress from the tomb of St. Rosalie.

In this Third Act some of the more memorable musical numbers are heard: the wild dance of the ghostly nuns; and the two duets between Robert and Bertram, "Our meeting-place" (Du rendezvous), and "Our pleasure lies in constant change" (Le bonheur est dans l'inconstance).

Act IV *Isabella's Chamber.* Armed with the magic talisman, Robert enters Isabella's room. He threatens to abduct her, but yields to her entreaties, spares her, and breaks the cypress branch, destroying the spell.

In this Act we hear the famous aria by Isabella, where her pleadings awake her suitor's better nature: "Robert, whom I love!" (Robert, toi que j'aime).

Act V *A Cathedral Aisle.* Robert comes to the doors of a cathedral seeking divine mercy for his past misdeeds. For the last time his fiendish father seeks to entice him away; but aided by Alice he repulses him. As the fiend flies, the cathedral door swings open, revealing his bride, Isabella, who is awaiting him.

The final Act brings in a medley of conflict for both voice and instrument, ending in a particularly lovely trio by Alice, Robert, and Bertram.

THE HUGUENOTS

(The Hu-gee-nots)

Dramatic Opera in Five Acts. Music by Meyerbeer. Book by Eugene Scribe. Académie, Paris, February 29, 1836. Astor Place, New York, June 24, 1850; Academy of Music, March 8, 1858; and revived at the Metropolitan, in 1901. On account of its length, the opera is often cut to Three Acts. Patti sang in this opera, at the Academy of Music, in 1883. A "Star" performance was given at the Metropolitan, December 18, 1893, with Jean and Edouard de Reszke, Nordica, and Scalchi.

SCENE: Paris and Touraine.
TIME: 1572.

CAST
MARGUERITE DE VALOIS, *the Princess* (Soprano).
COMTE DE ST. BRIS, *a Catholic nobleman* (Basso).
VALENTINE, *his daughter* (Soprano).
RAOUL DE NANGIS, *a Huguenot nobleman* (Tenor).
MARCEL, *his servant* (Basso).
DUC DE NEVERS, *a Catholic nobleman* (Baritone).
URBAIN, *a page* (Mezzo-Soprano).
BOIS ROSÉ, *a Huguenot soldier* (Tenor).
Catholic and Protestant Noblemen and Soldiers, Courtiers, Attendants, Citizens.

ARGUMENT The Massacre of St. Bartholomew's Eve forms the historic groundwork of "The Huguenots." The stormy love affair of two young persons belonging to the warring factions is its theme.

Act I *Dining Hall in De Nevers' Château.* In the interests of peace between the warring Catholic and Protestant parties of France, the Duc de Nevers entertains Raoul de Nangis at a banquet of Catholic noblemen. While at table, the diners are asked to toast their ladies, and Raoul tells of a fair unknown, whom he had once rescued from a band of roistering students, and whom he has since searched for in vain.

Raoul's servant Marcel, now enters and warns him of impending danger. Meanwhile, De Nevers has been called from the room, and Raoul, looking out of the window, perceives him in conversation with the very lady whom he has been toasting. He now thinks that he has discovered a liaison between the lady (Valentine) and the noble, when in reality she has come only to ask her release from a promise of marriage. The arrival of a page at this juncture brings in an unexpected element. In a melodious song he informs Raoul that he is to accompany him, blindfolded, to an unknown destination.

The song by Urbain, the Page (taken by a woman with mezzo-soprano voice) is noteworthy: "Noble sirs, I salute you!" (Nobles seigneurs, salut!)—

Another song for basso voice, by Marcel, intones Martin Luther's "Ein feste burg," followed by a fierce Huguenot battle song.

Act II *Garden of Marguerite de Valois.* Marguerite, like De Nevers, is working for peace, and to this end has invited Raoul to her presence. She is willing to arrange a match between him and Valentine de St. Bris, thus uniting two warring houses. To this end, Valentine has broken her betrothal with De Nevers, but is doubtful as to her father's consent. The princess promises to arrange matters with St. Bris. Raoul is received at court blindfolded, and when unblinded is delighted with his cordial reception. Catholic and Protestant nobles pledge amity, and Valentine's hand is promised to Raoul. But when he discovers in her the same lady that he saw in De Nevers' garden, he thinks that the duke's discarded mistress is being bestowed upon him, and refuses the alliance. St. Bris and De Nevers both wish to avenge this insult, and immediate bloodshed is only averted by the presence of the princess.

In this Act, which is often produced as the second scene of the preceding, Marguerite sings a difficult and beautiful aria for coloraturas, "O, lovely land of Touraine!" with a brilliant passage, "At this word all Nature revives" (A cet mot)—

This is followed by the seductive "Bathers' Chorus" sung on the river bank by women; another song by Urbain in rondeau form: "No, no, no, you never heard it!"; and a charming duet between Raoul and Marguerite, after his bandage has been removed and he sees the glittering court and gracious lady: "Beauty divine!"

Act III *Banks of the Seine near Paris.* Valentine has again accepted the faithful De Nevers and preparations are forward for their wedding. Raoul has sent a challenge to St. Bris, and the latter's friends urge him to involve all the Protestants in the quarrel. Raoul is warned of treachery through Marcel and Valentine, but keeps his appointment with St. Bris. Marcel thereupon calls upon all the Huguenots in a neighboring inn, while St. Bris summons all the Catholics. A general fight is averted only by Marguerite, and as she is in doubt as to whom to believe, Valentine tells her the whole story. Raoul now learns for the first time of his unjust suspicions, but his knowledge comes too late, as De Nevers appears in a boat to conduct his bride away.

A spirited chorus by the soldiery opens this Act. As they sing they imitate the beating of drums with their hands and sing the lively "Rataplan." The vocal protests of the Catholic maidens which follows provides an effective contrast. Just before the duel, a spirited sextet is sung; "On my good cause relying." The fall of the curtain is heralded with an exceptional musical and scenic climax, a military band supporting the orchestra.

Act IV *Room in De Nevers' Mansion.* It is the Eve of St. Agnes. Raoul has come to bid farewell to Valentine. Her grief is voiced in the song, "Amid my tears." A brief scene between them is interrupted by the entrance of St. Bris and his men. Raoul hides behind a screen and is the unwilling auditor of a powerful "consecration of the swords," in which the voice of St. Bris leads. They will wipe out their Huguenot foes. "With sacred zeal let now your soul be flaming," he sings. As soon as the soldiers have departed on their bloody quest, a final, affecting parting duet is sung by the two lovers. It begins with Raoul's impassioned, "Danger presses and time flies!" and reaches to a sublime, "Thou hast said it; thou dost love me!" (Tu l'as dit)—

The close of this touching scene is punctuated by the tolling of bells in the city. The massacre has already begun. The girl clings to her lover and begs him not to go; but Valentine gently thrusts her aside. Finding that she has locked the door, he leaps from the balcony to meet his fate.

Act V (Usually Omitted.) *Marguerite's Audience Hall.* Raoul escapes, wounded, to Marguerite's court and begs her protection for the Huguenots. It is too late, however. Murder is afoot and will not cease till the whole party has perished. Valentine now rushes in and begs him to abjure his faith and thus save himself; but Marcel tells him to remember his oath. The two Huguenots go out to meet their enemies, and Valentine declares she will turn Protestant and die with them.

As stated above, the work usually ends with Act IV, and the audience is given the impression that Raoul falls to his death. The opera is further shortened by the compression of the two first Acts into one. The work is not often produced because of its exacting demands upon the singers. The Metropolitan performances of the season of 1901 were called "the nights of the seven stars," as the most famous singers of the day united in the cast.

LE PROPHÈTE

(Luh Prof-ait)

(The Prophet.) Grand Opera in Five Acts. Music by Meyerbeer. Book by Eugene Scribe. Grand Opera, Paris, April 6, 1849. New Orleans, April 2, 1850. New York, Niblo's Garden, November 25, 1853. Sung in German at the Metropolitan, December 17, 1884.

SCENE: Holland and Munster.
TIME: 1534–35.

CAST
JOHN OF LEYDEN (Tenor).
FIDES, *his mother* (Mezzo-Soprano).
BERTHA, *his bride* (Soprano).
JONAS, *Anabaptist* (Tenor).
MATTHISEN, *Anabaptist* (Basso).
ZACHARIAS, *Anabaptist* (Basso).
COUNT OBERTHAL (Baritone).
Nobles, Citizens, Anabaptists, Peasants, Soldiers, Prisoners, Children.

ARGUMENT An opera with an historical setting, but the chief motif being the power and beauty of mother love

Act I *Count Oberthal's Castle.* John of Leyden has won the hand of Bertha, a village lass. His mother, Fides, who keeps an inn at Dordrecht, approves of the match, but permission must also be obtained from the Count, as lord of the domain. The two women now come to seek it. The Count, however, is so pleased with the girl that he refuses his consent and tries to abduct her. Meanwhile a diversion has been caused by the entrance of three Anabaptists, who are zealots urging the people to rise up against their tyrants.

The music in the First Act includes: a lively chorus by the villagers; a cavatina by Bertha in the joy of her courtship, "My heart beats wildly"; a contrasting, gloomy chant in Latin by the Anabaptists; the plea of John's mother to the Count, "One day in the waves of the Meuse"; and his gruff refusal.

Act II *The Inn at Dordrecht.* In his mother's tavern a group of John's friends rejoice with him over his approaching wedding, with a chorus and dance. But the gloomy Anabaptists again appear. They have been struck with his resemblance to David, their guardian saint, and they seek to persuade him to be their new leader. John then tells them of a dream he has had. "Under the great dome of a splendid temple," is the theme of his song. "What does it mean?" he asks. They reply that he is destined to become a king. But he will not give up Bertha, even for a throne. Scarcely have they gone when she rushes in, wildly. The Count had abducted her, but she has escaped. He tries to conceal the weeping girl, as the Count enters in pursuit. He has seized Fides, John's mother, as hostage, and states that she will be slain if he does not relinquish his sweetheart. Torn between the cruel decisions, John at last gives up Bertha. Fides voices her gratitude in one of the sublime arias of all the Meyerbeer operas: "Ah, my son, my son! May you this day be blessed!" (Ah, mon fils!)—

After the triumphant Count has departed, the Anabaptists return and find John a willing instrument to their desires. He now thirsts for revenge against Oberthal. To further their plot, they stain some of his garments with blood and leave them behind in order that his mother and friends may think him dead.

Act III *The Anabaptist Camp.* The Anabaptist soldiers have captured a party of noblemen, who are forced to pay ransom.

All make merry, and the famous ballet on the ice forms part of the amusement. In the background is Münster, still in the hands of Oberthal's father, who refuses to surrender it to the enemy. They resolve to storm it, a resolution which is heard by Oberthal, who has come disguised to the Anabaptists' camp. He is recognized and is about to be killed, when John hears from him that Bertha has escaped. He bids the soldiers spare Oberthal's life, that he may be judged by Bertha herself. John has already endured great pangs of conscience at seeing his army so wild and bloodthirsty. He refuses to go further, but hearing that an army of soldiers has broken out of Münster to destroy the Anabaptists, he rallies. Praying fervently to God for help and victory, inspiration and fresh enthusiasm come over him and are communicated to his soldiers. They resolve to storm Münster.

The well-known ballet of the skaters with its rhythmic, graceful music forms a pleasant interlude to the underlying tragedy. This is followed by a stirring battle song by Zacharias, in which he prays that his foes, "though numerous as the stars," may yet be overthrown. A trio by the three Anabaptists when they recognize the Count follows. The climactic point in action and music here is reached when John and his followers sing the fine "Triumphal Hymn," beginning with the line, "Ruler of Heaven and of Angels!" As it reaches its high point in ecstasy, the sun comes from behind the clouds, as a harbinger of victory.

Act IV *Public Square in Munster before the Cathedral.* Fides thinks her son dead and, reduced to poverty, is on the public square begging for food. Bertha, who also thinks John dead, meets her and in a despairing song they vow vengeance upon the Anabaptists, who, they think, slew him. Meanwhile, the city has been captured by John and his party and he is even now on his way to the cathedral to be crowned king. His "Coronation March" is one of the finest of its type in all opera:

But John's triumph is menaced by the presence of the two women. No sooner than he begins to speak, when Fides recognizes him and cannot restrain an impetuous cry, "My son!" Again he is caught between two currents. With hands upraised he confronts her. He tells his followers that they can run him through his bared breast, if he is an impostor. This woman must be insane. Fides tearfully recants; her old eyes must have deceived her. John absolves her and the crowd exclaim, "A miracle!" thinking it yet another example of their Prophet's divine powers.

Act V *Scene 1. The Crypt of the Palace.* A counterplot by the three Anabaptists against John is being hatched. They plan to deliver him over to the German emperor, as the price of their own pardon. Meanwhile, John has had his mother brought to him in secret. As the men lead her through the gloom of a dungeon she exclaims: "O priests of Baal, whither do ye lead me?" (O, Prètres de Baal!)—

This is the beginning of a cavatina and aria well liked by mezzo-sopranos, by reason of its tumult of emotions, and is known as the "Prison Scene." At first the grief-stricken mother calls down vengeance upon her son, then relenting prays for his forgiveness. When the entrance of the Prophet is announced, her voice rises into an exultant coloratura strain: "He comes!" The meeting between the two is highly dramatic. He pleads her forgiveness, telling her that his bloody deeds have been to avenge Bertha. At this moment they are joined by the girl herself. Her joy at meeting her lover is speedily clouded over, as she learns for the first time that he and the loathed Prophet are one and the same. She is so shocked that she plunges a dagger into her heart.

Scene 2. A Banquet Hall. The Prophet's enemies are closing in on him. Bertha had aided them by lighting a fuse leading to a powder magazine. John no longer seeks escape. When the Count comes with the command, "You are my prisoner," he replies, "Nay, ye are all my captives!" He joins a party at the banquet table; smoke and flames rise through the floor. Before the final catastrophe, Fides rushes wildly to his side. "My son!" "My Mother!" they cry in a last reconciliation. "Welcome, sacred flame!" their voices blend as the walls crash down upon them.

DINORAH

Romantic Opera in Three Acts. Music by Meyerbeer. Book by Barbier and Carré. Opéra Comique, Paris, April 4, 1859. Academy of Music, New York, November 24, 1864; revived at the Manhattan Opera House, 1907. At the Metropolitan, February 26, 1908, with Tetrazzini as "Dinorah."

SCENE: Brittany.
TIME: Nineteenth Century.

CAST DINORAH, *a peasant girl* (Soprano).
HOËL, *a goat-herd* (Baritone).
CORENTINO, *a bagpiper* (Tenor).
Shepherds, Goat-herds, Villagers, etc.

ARGUMENT The composer's idea here was to write a pastoral opera. The plot, however, has been considered so banal that the occasional bits of fine music have not sufficed to keep it alive. As in his preceding "Star of the North," it is now remembered on account of one famous aria—"The Shadow Song."

Dinorah's home has been destroyed by a storm, and her suitor, Hoël, in order to help her father rebuild it, goes to seek a fabled treasure hidden in the mountains. A soothsayer tells him that he must live there for a year. Meanwhile, Dinorah, saddened by her lover's inexplicable disappearance, wanders into the hills seeking a lost goat. She is half demented and her experiences form the chief part of the story. Hoël, Dinorah and Corentino, a bagpiper, occupy the stage in the first act. In the second, Dinorah, again alone, sings her famous "Shadow Song." As a prelude she sings, "The Ancient wizard of the mountains." Then as the bright moon casts shadows upon the glade she imagines them to be living partners and sings and dances with them: "Light, flitting shadow, companion gay, go not away!"

A storm arises. Hoël and Corentino again enter. The former is still seeking the treasure, but the piper is afraid to touch it, lest he die. In a flash of lightning Dinorah sees her pet goat crossing a ravine by means of a fallen tree. She rushes after him and is carried down the gorge by the flood. In the third act, she is shown to have been saved, although at first Hoël thinks her dead. When she revives and her reason also is regained, Hoël thankfully gives up his foolish quest, and the two happily plan for their wedding.

There are other fine musical moments, such as Dinorah's lullaby to her goat (First Act); and a trio at its end; a "Legend of the Treasure," sung by Dinorah; and the villagers' "Pardon Hymn."

L'AFRICAINE

(Laf-ree-cain)

(The African.) Tragic Opera in Five Acts. Music by Meyerbeer. Book by Eugene Scribe. Grand Opera, Paris, April 28, 1865. Academy of Music, New York, December 1, 1865. At the Metropolitan, 1888.

SCENE: Lisbon; a ship at sea; Madagascar.
TIME: The Sixteenth Century.

CAST VASCO DA GAMA, *an officer in the Portuguese Navy* (Tenor).
DON PEDRO, *President of the Royal Council* (Basso).
DON DIEGO, *Member of the Council* (Basso).
DON ALVAR, *Member of the Council* (Tenor).
INEZ, *daughter of Don Diego* (Soprano).
ANNA, *her attendant* (Contralto).
SELIKA, *an African Queen, held as a slave* (Soprano).
NELUSKO, *a slave* (Baritone).
GRAND INQUISITOR (Basso).
Priests, Inquisitors, Councillors, Sailors, Indians, Attendants, Ladies, Soldiers.

ARGUMENT "L'Africaine" was Meyerbeer's last opera, and considered by him his masterpiece. He did not, however, live to see it produced. It is an elaborate work in its scenic setting, and has a quasi-historical background.

Act I *Royal Council Chamber, Lisbon.* The famous voyager, Vasco da Gama, who has been sent to trace a route around the Cape of Good Hope, has not returned, and is given up for lost. Admiral Diego, believing this true, wishes to bestow the hand of his daughter Inez on another suitor, Don Pedro. At this juncture Vasco returns, having been the only one of his ship's party to escape shipwreck. He brings with him two strange captives. He shows the Council maps of the African coast and endeavors to prove to them the existence of other lands to the East. He pleads for ships and funds to start a new voyage of conquest and discovery. But his rival for the hand of Inez discredits him with the Council. He asserts that Da Gama's contentions are heretical and contrary to the Holy Word. Instead of being given credence and assistance, the Council throws the voyager into prison.

Soon after the first curtain, Inez sings a tender ballad, "Farewell, my beloved shore," to the birdlike accompaniment of the flute. It recurs in the Fourth Act. In the climax of the First Act, Vasco dramatically throws down the gauntlet to the powerful Council, culminating in a stirring chorus.

Act II *A Prison Cell.* Vasco languishes in prison. With him are the two captives he has brought from Africa, Selika and Nelusko. Selika watches over him devotedly. She was a Queen in her own land, but is now content to be the slave of this proud foreigner who has saved her and her companion from a slave ship. But Vasco is thinking only of Inez, and Nelusko, who honors in Selika not only his Queen, but the woman of his love, tries to stab Vasco, the Christian, whom he hates with a deadly hatred. Selika prevents him and rouses the sleeping Vasco, who has been dreaming of another voyage to the unknown country. Selika now shows him on the map the way to her native isle, and he vows her eternal fealty. But presently Inez enters to announce that Vasco is free. She has paid dearly for her lover's deliverance, however, for she has given her hand to Don Pedro, who, having got all Vasco's plans and maps, is commissioned by the Council to set out on the voyage of discovery. On her part, Inez has been told that Vasco has forgotten her for Selika the slave. In order to prove his fidelity to Inez, our ungrateful hero immediately presents her with the two slaves, and Don Pedro resolves to make use of them for his exploration.

Early in this Act we hear the lovely slumber song of the slave queen, Selika: "On my knees, child of the Sun!"; Nelusko's baritone salutation to her: "Daughter of kings, my homage!"; and, for finale, a sextet without instruments.

Act III *On Board Don Pedro's Ship.* Nelusko has been made pilot, but his actions are open to suspicion. Two ships of the fleet have already been lost, but Don Pedro continues to sail on. At this moment a Portuguese vessel is seen approaching. It is in command of Vasco da Gama, who has fitted it out at his own expense. Although Don Pedro is his enemy, he comes aboard the admiral's ship to warn him that the vessel is on a wrong course and likely to meet with disaster. Don Pedro, however, accuses him of desiring only to see Inez, who is on the vessel. At his command, Vasco is seized and bound. A few moments later, however, a violent storm breaks over the ship. It is driven upon a reef. Savages, for whom Nelusko has signaled, clamber up the sides of the vessel and massacre all save a few, who are spared by orders of their Queen, Selika.

The musical feature in this Act is Nelusko's impressive invocation: "Adamastor, ruler of the trackless deep!"—a fine baritone aria—

Other numbers are: a pleasing chorus of women: "The swiftly sailing ship"; a sailors' prayer: "O, mighty St. Dominique!" and the orchestration of the storm and battle scene.

Act IV *A Temple and Palace, on Madagascar.* This opera fairly outdoes itself in scenic display, and here in sharp contrast to the violent episodes on shipboard, we are translated to a stage of barbaric splendor. Selika has been restored to her throne. Vasco, with Inez, has been rescued from the ship and now finds himself on the island he has vainly sought. He voices his amazement at the superb scene with a song, "Oh, Paradise!"—

He has just witnessed an Indian march and ballet with its exotic strains, and his aria to woodwind accompaniment, first in exaltation, then in martial spirit, is a favorite with tenors. Vasco is brought in a prisoner and Selika, in order to save him, asserts that he is her husband. She prevails upon the faithful Nelusko to bear witness to this fact, and the marriage is celebrated according to native rites. Vasco is touched by Selika's devotion to him after his past faithlessness, and again vows that he will remain true to her. But alas! he hears the voice of Inez who is being led away to execution, and he cannot conceal his emotion. The duet between the Queen and the explorer, "Oh, transport! Oh, sweet ecstasy!" contains music closely allied to the tender scene.

Act V *Gardens of Selika's Palace.* Selika divines the cause of Vasco's emotion, and sends for her rival, resolving to put her to death. But again her magnanimity conquers her passion. She sets both her captives free and provides a ship for them to return to their native land.

As the ship sails away, Selika watches it from a promontory, shaded by the deadly manzanilla tree. The odor of its blossoms is poisonous, but she gladly inhales it, as she has bid an eternal farewell to the king of her heart. Her parting soliloquy is filled with poignant grief: "From here I gaze upon a boundless deep." For her the deep is eternity. A few moments later, Nelusko finds the lifeless body of his beloved Queen and resolves to join her in the land of the shades.

JACQUES HALÉVY

Halévy was of Jewish extraction, born in Paris, May 27, 1799. His musical education was completed in the Paris Conservatory and at Rome. In the latter city he devoted himself to church music, as did his pupil Gounod, and strove to interpolate it into his first operas, "The Bohemian" and "Pygmalion." His first success was "Clari" (1828). A comic opera, "The Dilettante Avignon," the next year, was also successful, and the two paved the way for "The Jewess" (1835), which made him famous, and on which his fame still rests. He wrote eight or ten other operas which are now forgotten. Halévy exercised great influence over later musicians, among them Gounod and Bizet, through his teaching at the Conservatory. He died in Nice, March 17, 1862.

LA JUIVE

(La Zhoo-eeve)

(The Jewess.) Tragic Opera in Five Acts. Music by Halévy. Tex by Eugene Scribe. Académie de Musique, Paris, February 23, 1835 New Orleans, the following February. At the Metropolitan, Ne York, in German, in 1887. A notable revival here was on Novembe 22, 1919, when Caruso achieved an "historic triumph." Others wer Ponselle, Orville Harrold, and Rothier.

SCENE: Constance.
TIME: 14[illegible]

CAST ELEAZAR, *a Jewish jeweler* (Tenor).
RACHEL, *his foster-daughter* (Soprano).
CARDINAL DI BROGNI (Baritone).
PRINCE LEOPOLD (Tenor).
RUGGIERO, *a judge* (Baritone).
PRINCESS EUDORA, *the Emperor's niece* (Contralto).
Courtiers, Soldiers, Citizens, Jews, etc.

ARGUMENT A tense and dramatic opera involving a conflict of creeds, racial prejudice, and filial love. "La Juive" found great favor with contemporary critics and composers, among them, Wagner, who is said to have been enthusiastic over it. Its plot is dramatic and the role of Eleazar was for long a favorite with tenors. It was sung by Caruso on his last public appearance, in December, 1920. Of recent years it has been seldom performed.

Act I *A Street.* The Catholic party is celebrating a victory over the Hussites, a heterodox party. They decide to take equally stern measures with the Jews, and all their shops are ordered closed, under pain of death. But Eleazar, a prominent jeweler, keeps his open. He is seized and sentenced to death, when Cardinal di Brogni intercedes for him and protects him from the anger of the crowd. The Cardinal has a secret liking for the Jew and his daughter Rachel, and hopes that the Jew can give him some intelligence of his own long-lost daughter. But despite his favor, Eleazar mistrusts him.

Rachel has a suitor who has won her affections under the name of "Samuel," but who is in reality the powerful Prince Leopold. He also is able to save her and her father from the mob, at a later time, to her own great surprise, as she still does not know his true rank.

The scene opens with a stately "Te Deum" at the Cathedral. Later comes a fine cavatina by the Cardinal, in which he asks the pardon of Heaven upon unbelievers—a baritone song demanding a wide range of voice.

Act II *Home of Eleazar.* The Jews have gathered around a table in a religious festival. Eleazar leads in the singing of their invocation: "Oh, God of our fathers!" Leopold, posing as a Jew, is present, but quietly thrusts the bread aside. There is a knock at the door and the communion is hastily hidden; but the newcomer is the Princess Eudora, who wishes to purchase a chain for her prospective bridegroom, Prince Leopold—for these nuptials have been commanded by the Emperor. On hearing this, "Samuel" is filled with dismay. After the others have gone he confesses to Rachel that he is a Christian, and persuades her to flee with him. The entrance of Eleazar prevents their escape. He orders "Samuel" to marry his daughter, but the latter declines. He leaves amid the curses of the old Jew and the grief of the girl.

Act III *An Imperial Banquet Hall.* The nuptials of Prince Leopold and Princess Eudora are being celebrated with much festivity. The bride brings the golden chain which she has purchased. She is accompanied by Rachel who recognizes in the groom her faithless lover. She openly denounces him, and the Cardinal pronounces upon him the curse of the Church, and consigns him to prison, together with the Jew and his daughter.

The orchestra unites with the voices in this highly dramatic scene. Rachel's avowal of her faith, and scorn of her faithless lover are swiftly followed by the Cardinal's stentorian curse: "You who have outraged Heaven are now by Heaven denounced!"

Act IV *A Dungeon.* Eudora visits Rachel and pleads with her to pardon Leopold. The Jewess relents and resolves to die alone in order to save her lover. Meanwhile, in an interview with the Cardinal, Eleazar tells him that his daughter is still alive, but refuses to divulge more. Brogni pleads with him for tidings, and also promises to save Rachel if she will recant, but both refuse.

It is here that the old Jew sings his fine aria, in which he prays God for guidance in his difficult decision. He can still save his foster-daughter, whom he loves as his own, but he cannot forswear his faith: "Rachel, when the grace of the Lord entrusted thee to me" (Rachel, quand du Seigneur)—

Act V *Court of the Prison.* The Jews have been sentenced to a frightful death by being plunged into a cauldron of boiling oil Eleazar and Rachel march to their doom with firm steps. She has forgiven her lover. Now when the old man asks her if she would renounce the Jewish faith to save her life, she answers with a resolute, "No!" Just as she is hurled into the cauldron, Eleazar points to her, then to the Cardinal. "Behold your daughter!" he announces sternly, and plunges after her. Overcome with horror and grief, the Cardinal tears his princely robes and falls fainting to the ground.

Again a medley of voice and instruments depict the scene, rising to a crash as the curtain falls.

HECTOR BERLIOZ

This French composer was educated for the profession of medicine, but turned aside to the more congenial paths of music. He was born in La Cote-Sainte-Andre, near Grenoble, December 11, 1803. At the age of twenty-seven he won first prize in the Paris Conservatory of Music, for his cantata, "Sardanaple." After a few months' study in Italy, he turned seriously to the production of opera, and also to musical criticism in prose. The operas which first brought him fame were "Benvenuto Cellini," "Beatrice and Benedict," and "The Trojans." Strangely enough, he is remembered today for "The Damnation of Faust," which originally was not an opera at all, but a dramatic cantata. Berlioz was also the composer of orchestral symphonies, such as "Episode in the Life of an Artist," in which the various instruments take the part of speaking or singing characters. He may thus be regarded as a pioneer in the school of "chamber music." He died in Paris, March 9, 1869.

BENVENUTO CELLINI

Opera in Three Acts. Music by Berlioz. Book by Du Wailly and Barbier. Grand Opera, Paris, September 3, 1838.

SCENE: Rome.
TIME: 1532.

CAST
CARDINAL SALVIATI (Basso).
BALDUCCI, *Papal Treasurer* (Basso).
TERESA, *his daughter* (Soprano).
BENVENUTO CELLINI, *a goldsmith* (Tenor).
ASCANIO, *his apprentice* (Mezzo-Soprano).
FRANCESCO, *artisan in Cellini's workshop* (Tenor).
BERNARDINO, *artisan in Cellini's Workshop* (Basso).
FIERAMOSCA, *sculptor to the Pope* (Baritone).
POMPEO, *a bravo* (Baritone).

ARGUMENT Cellini is a famous goldsmith of Rome, in the sixteenth century, who is commissioned by the Pope to make a certain statue. It is carnival time, and his attention is distracted not only by this fact, but also by the love of Teresa, the Papal Treasurer's daughter. After a tangle of cross purposes, the statue is finished triumphantly. It proves to be "Perseus," one of the historic art treasures of Florence.

The overture and "Carnaval Romain" have been recorded from this opera.

THE DAMNATION OF FAUST

Dramatic Opera in Four Acts. Music by Berlioz. Book by Berlioz, Gerard and Gandonniere. Paris, 1846, as a dramatic cantata. In its entirety in Manchester, England, 1880; New York, February 12, 1880; the Metropolitan, December 7, 1906.

SCENE: A German Village.
TIME: The Eighteenth Century.

CAST FAUST, *a philosopher* (Tenor).
MEPHISTOPHELES, *the tempter* (Basso).
BRANDER, *a convivial friend* (Basso).
MARGUERITE, *a peasant girl* (Soprano).
Peasants, Troopers, Roysterers, Students, Sylphs, Fiends, Angels.

ARGUMENT This version of the Faust legend is remarkable for its dramatic intensity and the passion of its music. It also forms an interesting parallel with Gounod's popular opera on the same theme.

Act I *The Open Fields.* Faust, a learned philosopher, wanders out into the sunrise, tired of books for the nonce and pondering the mysteries of Nature. He observes a group of peasants who take great delight in a parade of marching soldiers, but he only wonders at their enthusiasm.

The high moment in this scene is the soldiers' march, which is a favorite orchestral number known as the "Rakoczy March"—

Act II *Faust's Study.* The philosopher returns to his books more than ever weary of them and of all the world. Somehow with all his learning his heart is empty and unsatisfied. He resolves to end it all with a dose of poison, but the sound of Easter music stays his hand. Now comes the fiend, Mephistopheles, to tempt him with the pleasures of the world, and Faust yields and goes with him to a tavern. The coarse songs and jests of the roisterers soon disgust him, however, and Mephistopheles takes him to a beautiful garden where he is lulled to sleep by soft music and dreams of a charming peasant girl, Marguerite. Sylphs dance about him as he awakes, filled with desire to find the girl of his dreams. Soldiers and students pass by singing their rollicking songs, and Faust feels the love of the world once more surging through his veins.

The music which the fiend employs in the garden, and the dance of the sylphs, are the occasion for the most exquisite melodies of the work —the "Ballet of the Sylphes"—

Act III *Marguerite's Chamber.* The fiend conducts Faust to the home of his unknown sweetheart, and Faust conceals himself in her room. Marguerite also has dreamed of Faust and enters the room musing upon her vision while she braids her hair. Meanwhile, Mephistopheles sings a mocking song without. Faust reveals himself to the startled girl and pleads his love so ardently that she is finally persuaded to give herself to him. Their love scene is interrupted by the fiend who comes to warn them that Marguerite's mother and friends are near at hand. Faust is dragged away unseen by the exultant demon, while the villagers threaten the defenseless girl.

The song of Marguerite is followed by a mocking invocation by Mephistopheles, and a "Dance of the Will-o'-the-Wisps." There is a love duet, which becomes a trio as the fiend's urgent voice joins in.

Act IV *Scene 1. Marguerite's Chamber.* Marguerite sits alone and grief stricken, sorrowing for her own sin, for her mother's death, and for the absent Faust. Her aria, "Love, devouring flame," is an eloquent confession. It is broken by the martial singing of soldiers outside her window, which grows fainter as "Retreat" is sounded. The unhappy girl falls unconscious.

Scene 2. A Mountain Gorge. Both music and setting are turbulent. Faust likewise has been yearning for Marguerite and lamenting their interrupted tryst. His soliloquy is titled, "Nature, vast, impenetrable!" The fiend appears and tells him he can save the girl only by surrendering his own soul. The panorama of grinning devils and imminent inferno is depicted musically in the "Ride to Hell"—

Faust's efforts to save Marguerite are thwarted by the demon. She is haled to prison for the murder of her mother, to whom Mephistopheles had given too heavy a sleeping powder and, while Faust descends to Hell, is herself condemned to death.

Epilogue *The Prison Cell.* The unhappy and penitent Marguerite is saved and ascends with angels to Heaven.

BEATRICE AND BENEDICT

Opera in Two Acts. Music by Berlioz. Book by the composer after Shakespeare's comedy, "Much Ado About Nothing." Baden Baden, 1862.

The characters follow those of the Shakesperian play. The plot preserves its spirit, also, except for deleting the intrigue which involves Claudio and Hero. It centers on the spirited interplay between the proud Beatrice and the witty Benedict. The music forms a lively interlude to their quarrels and ends pleasingly as the two decide to "make up."

THE TROJANS

(Les Troyens.) Title given by Berlioz to two lengthy operas, which are now known only to students of music. Text of both by Berlioz.

PART I: "THE CAPTURE OF TROY"

Produced in Karlsruhe, 1890. Characters those of Homer's *Iliad.* Three Acts. I. The Greek camp in front of Troy. The people of that city are rejoicing at the supposed lifting of the siege. Some stand in awe of the gigantic wooden horse left behind by the Greeks. They do not heed the warning voice of Cassandra, the clairvoyant. II. A grove near by. While the Trojans celebrate, Aeneas runs in with the tidings hat Laocoon has been throttled by a serpent because he tried to prevent he entrance of the horse into the city. III. Aeneas is sleeping in his ent. Hector's ghost appears to warn him that Troy has fallen. Aeneas nust sail away to a far land to found a new kingdom.

PART II: "THE TROJANS IN CARTHAGE"

Produced in Paris, unsuccessfully, in 1863; revived in Karlsruhe, in 890. This opera in five acts follows closely the later adventures of Aeneas with Dido, in Carthage. The action ends as the unlucky Queen hrows herself upon her funeral pyre, while Aeneas and his men sail on or Italy.

Recorded music: overture; "Chasse royale et orage"; and the tenor ria, "Inutiles regrets."

CHARLES AMBROISE THOMAS

A French composer, born in Metz, August 5, 1811. He entered the aris Conservatory in 1828, winning three prizes there in successive ears—for piano playing, harmony, and musical composition, the last eing the Grand Prix. Before he had reached the age of twenty-six he had written pieces for the piano, violin, orchestra, and a cantata. His first successful opera was "The Double Ladder" (1837), followed during the course of a long life by many other operas and cantatas, the best known operas being "Mina" (1843); "Betty" (1846); "A Midsummer Night's Dream" (1850); "The Carnival of Venice" (1853); "Mignon" (1866); "Hamlet" (1868); and "Francesca da Rimini" (1882). In 1871 he became Director of the Conservatory. He died in Paris, February 12, 1896.

MIGNON

(Meen-yohn)

Romantic Opera in Three Acts. Music by Charles Ambroise Thomas. Book by Barbier and Carré, after Goethe's "Wilhelm Meister." Opéra Comique, Paris, November 17, 1866. Academy of Music, New York, November 22, 1871; the Metropolitan, October 21 1883.

SCENE: Germany and Italy.
TIME: The Eighteenth Century.

CAST
WILHELM MEISTER, *a German student* (Tenor).
BARON FRIEDRICH (Tenor).
LAERTES, *a strolling actor* (Baritone).
PHILINA, *an actress* (Soprano).
LOTHARIO, *an aged minstrel* (Basso).
GIARNO, *leader of the Gypsies* (Basso).
MIGNON, *a girl of the Gypsies* (Mezzo-Soprano).
Gypsies, Peasants, Servants, etc.

ARGUMENT The story of a girl captured by Gypsies and foun to be the long-lost daughter of a nobleman is nc new to opera, but the present story, based upon Goethe's "Wilhelr Meister," is one of the most pleasing. Despite the widespread popu larity of the song, "Knowest thou the land," and a charming dance, an intermezzo, "Mignon" is not presented frequently. Its plot may b thought too ingenuous, its themes too simple, yet to many opera-goe it is a refreshing change from plots steeped in gloom, or difficult score The Overture with its brilliance and charm is a favorite concert piec with orchestras all around the world.

Act I *Courtyard of an Inn, Germany.* While the strolling actor Laertes and Philina, are resting in the courtyard of a waysid

:avern, a band of Gypsies also stop there. They are footsore and weary from a long journey, but despite this fact the leader, Giarno, orders Mignon, a young girl, to dance for the amusement of other tavern guests. She refuses from weariness and ill-treatment, and Giarno rushes forward to beat her. An old harper tries to protect her, and would himself have been beaten, but is shielded by a young German student, Wilhelm Meister. Mignon is dressed as a boy, and Wilhelm, ignorant of her identity, takes her with him as a page. Meanwhile, Wilhelm has become infatuated with Philina, although Laertes warns him that she is fickle. His rival is the Baron Friedrich, whose uncle has invited the players to visit his castle; and much against the Baron's will, his rival and Mignon go with them.

In this Act while Wilhelm is questioning Mignon about herself and her past, she sings the nostalgic song which is now recognized as one of the most beautiful of its type in all opera: "Knowest thou the land where the orange blooms? . . . 'tis there! 'tis there I'd live!" (Connais-tu le paye?)—

There is also a pleasing duet between her and the old minstrel, Lothario, as he bids her farewell: "O, swallows lightly gliding!"

Act II The Second Act is preceded by a dainty Intermezzo, which has remained deservedly popular; it is in gavotte form:

Scene 1. Boudoir in the Baron's Castle. Philina is making herself very much at home, "prettying" herself and dreaming of further conquests. The voice of Laertes is heard without, in a madrigal to her: "Fair one, have pity on me!" He enters with Wilhelm and Mignon, and the latter jealously looks on from a corner while her beloved pays ardent court to the actress. When the other two finally leave the room, Mignon wonders if she might equal her rival's charms, and tries on some of her dresses and "make-up," meanwhile singing to herself: "I know

a poor fellow." As she thus busies herself in an adjoining apartment, Baron Friedrich enters in search of Philina. He sings the familiar tenor gavotte, "Here am I in her boudoir!" (Me voici dans son boudoir)—

Wilhelm unexpectedly returns and the two men quarrel and are ready to draw swords, when Mignon interposes. The Baron recognizes her borrowed costume and departs laughing. Wilhelm on his part tries to quiet her, in another charming aria, "Farewell, Mignon, take courage do not weep!"

Scene 2. Garden of the Castle. Mignon is so distressed over he false situation that she is on the point of throwing herself into a lake when the notes of Lothario's harp soothe her. She goes to the old min strel for counsel, and in her agitation calls down vengeance upon th castle and its occupants. In the meantime the players are giving a per formance from "Midsummer Night's Dream" on the terrace. Philin is gorgeous in her costume as Queen Titania. The music of the danc is in polonaise rhythm, again a high point in the work; and with it dashing accompaniment Philina sings the brilliant coloratura aria "I'm fair Titania"—

During the pageant Philina misses the flowers that Wilhelm has se her and, willing to pique Mignon, sends her into the castle in search them. Before the girl can return, flames burst from the window The aged Lothario has interpreted Mignon's curse too literally and s fire to the castle. Wilhelm rushes into the building and at great per rescues Mignon, whom he carries forth unconscious in his arms.

Act III *A Castle in Italy.* Lothario takes Mignon, who seems ill i body and mind, to Italy. They are followed by Wilhelr who has discovered her love for him and reciprocates it, after casti off his passion for the fickle Philina. In Italy the mystery of Mignon's birth is cleared. She is the daughter of Lothario, whose real title is the Marquis of Cipriani. Ever since his daughter had been stolen by the Gypsies he has wandered in search of her, and now proves her identity. He bestows her hand with his blessing upon Wilhelm.

The final Act has its fine musical moments, as when Wilhelm sings to the distressed Mignon: "Soothed is now her sorrow"—a lullaby which soon gives way to a more passionate outburst from him as he at last realizes all she means to him. "Ah, little thought the maid!" Before the final curtain a trio is sung by the two lovers and Lothario, with its recurring refrain, "Knowest thou the land?"

HAMLET

Grand Opera in Five Acts. Music by Thomas. Book by Michel Carré and Jules Barbier, after the play by Shakespeare. Grand Opera, Paris, March 9, 1868. Academy of Music, New York, March 22, 1872. Revived unsuccessfully, twenty years later, by the Chicago Opera Company.

SCENE: Denmark.
TIME: Antiquity.

ARGUMENT While ranking high in France among later operas, "Hamlet" has never won lasting regard in America. The plot takes many liberties with the play by Shakespeare and does not make use of the bard's fine verses. Much of its text is banal. Nevertheless, it has fine dramatical passages and several of its arias are highly esteemed by musicians—notably the spirited Drinking Song, "O, Wine, dispel this gloom!"—a tour-de-force for baritones.

The characters are the same as in the original play, and the action follows its general lines. Hamlet broods over his mother's hasty marriage with Claudius, King of Denmark, and is urged on to revenge by his father's ghost. He then seeks to fasten the guilt of his father's death upon Claudius. The final acts deal with the madness and death of Ophelia, and the vengeance of Hamlet upon the usurping King.

Recorded music: "Doute de la lumiere," sung by Sembrich and Emilio de Gogorza; "Chanson Bachique—O vin dissipe la tristesse" (John Charles Thomas); "Scene de folie," a soprano aria, by Norena, Galli-Curci, and Melba; and "Comme une pale fleur," a song for basso (Tita Ruffo. and Mattia Battistini).

CHARLES FRANÇOIS GOUNOD

Although one of the most popular and voluminous of French composers, Gounod's fame will rest largely upon one opera, "Faust." Gounod was born in Paris, June 17, 1818, and studied at the Paris Conservatory, where he won first prize for composition at the age of twenty-one. He was sent to Rome to complete his musical education, where he specialized on church music, a field in which he was interested all his life. We find traces of this predilection in "Faust." He published many masses, hymns, motets, and sacred songs. In 1851 he produced his first opera, "Sappho," at Paris. This was followed by a comic opera ("The Physician in Spite of Himself," based on Molière's comedy); and "Faust," in 1859. The latter at once brought Gounod to commanding notice, and still remains one of the most popular of all operas. Other operas by him are "Philemon and Baucis" (1860); "The Queen of Sheba" (1862); "Mireille" (1864); "Romeo and Juliet" (1867); "Polyeucte" (1878); and "The Tribute of Zamora" (1881). Gounod died in St. Cloud, France, October 18, 1893.

FAUST

(Fowst)

Tragic Opera in Five Acts. Music by Charles Gounod. Book b Barbier and Carré, after Goethe's drama. Lyric Theatre, Paris, Marc 19, 1859. Academy of Music, New York, in Italian, November 2 1863; and, in 1883, with Nordica as "Marguerite." At the Metropol tan on its opening night, October 22, 1883, in French, with Nilsson a "Marguerite."

SCENE: A German Village.
TIME: The Eighteenth Century.

CAST FAUST, *a philosopher* (Tenor).
MEPHISTOPHELES, *the evil one* (Basso).

VALENTINE, *brother of Marguerite* (Baritone).
BRANDER, *a student* (Baritone).
SIEBEL, *a student* (Soprano).
MARGUERITE, *a village girl* (Soprano).
MARTHA, *her servant* (Contralto).
Students, Soldiers, Citizens, Servants, Fiends, Angels.

ARGUMENT This version of the Faust legend so brilliantly interpreted by a French composer has far outranked n popularity any other opera, even from the original German source. ts wealth of melody and sustained exaltation have kept it in continuus repertory. It is probably one of the first ten most frequently heard.

ct I *Faust's Study.* The philosopher Faust has spent his lifetime in study, and now feels that he is growing old and that there is othing else to live for. He resolves to end it all with a dose of poison, ut his hand is stayed by the sound of Easter carols. Mephistopheles nters and promises him a new lease of life and many joys which he has issed, if he will sell his soul. The fiend then shows him a vision of Iarguerite. Faust consents to the compact and is transformed into a andsome youth.

The music in this opening Act is largely colloquy between the two, nding with a spirited duet: "For me life's pleasure!" (A moi les laisirs!).

ct II *An Open Square.* A festival is in progress, and students, soldiers, and citizens wander about singing and making merry. alentine has enlisted as a soldier, but dislikes to go away leaving is sister, Marguerite, unprotected. Siebel, a boy, promises to be her iampion. Mephistopheles now joins the throng of merry-makers and ouses popular interest by telling fortunes. He jests with Siebel on e subject of Marguerite, and Valentine overhears and resents his slurng remark. They draw their swords, but the fiend traces a circle of e around himself. Valentine and his friends hold up their swords ke crosses and the evil one slinks away. The dance continues, and aust enters and offers his arm to Marguerite, but she repulses him.

This Act opens with a chorus of the villagers, who celebrate "Keress" or festival day. Its fine harmony is well known. Next comes a ng for baritone voice of breadth and fervency, in which Valentine ks the favor of Heaven upon his sister while he is away: "Even bravest art" (Avant de quitter)—

An ironical bass sung by the fiend, "The Calf of Gold," is succeeded b a dramatic orchestral score, "The Sword Scene," where Valentine con fronts the fiend. A chorus of triumph over the latter then gives wa to the Kermess dance, known the world around as "the waltz fron Faust"—

Marguerite's voice is now heard in a short reply to her new suitor: "Nc my lord, I do not need your arm."

Act III *Marguerite's Garden.* Siebel brings a bouquet to Margu rite, but the flowers fade until he dips them in holy wate He then leaves them on the doorstep and departs. Faust and Mephi topheles now enter, the fiend urging Faust to press his suit. Seeing th flowers, Mephistopheles departs to purchase a finer present. He soo returns with a casket of jewels which he places beside the flowers an both retire. Marguerite enters pondering over the handsome youn gallant she saw in the market place. She finds the casket and is d lighted with the glittering gems, but does not wish to keep then Martha, her companion, sees them and tells her she would be foolis to reject them. The fiend and Faust return, and the former beguil Martha into a retired corner of the garden, leaving the coast clear f Faust, who woos Marguerite so ardently that she promises to meet hi again on the morrow. But the fiend is persistent. "Wait? Why wai you dreamer? Hear what she tells the stars!" They pause under h open window, and while the woodwinds hint of rapture, the girl agai appears. "Hasten thy return, beloved," she sings. With an answerin cry, "Marguerite!" Faust hastens to her. Darkness falls, punctuated l the sardonic laughter of the fiend.

The entire Act is chockful of melody. The first song is that of Sieb (soprano) "Speak to her of love"—the "Flower Song." Faust's fine apostrophe is heard: "All hail, thou dwelling pure and holy!" (Salut demeure)—

Marguerite at her spinning-wheel sings a quaint oldtime melody, "The King of Thule." But when she discovers the casket, her voice rings out in the magnificent "Jewel Song" (Air de Bijoux) —

A ravishing duet between the lovers completes this brilliant Act.

Act IV *Scene 1. A City Street.* The soldiers return victorious from war, among them Valentine. But his joy at seeing his sister again gives way to fury when he learns that she has been betrayed. At dusk, Mephistopheles and Faust approach Marguerite's home and the fiend sings a mocking serenade. Valentine rushes out to avenge his sister's wrongs and crosses swords with Faust, but the latter, aided by the evil one, gives Valentine his death blow. People rush in, and Marguerite bends over her dying brother, only to hear him curse her with his last breath.

Scene 2. Interior of the Church. Marguerite goes to the church and endeavors to pray, but the mocking fiend intrudes even here and tells her she is damned forever. She falls, overcome, upon the floor.

The "Soldiers' Chorus" heard on the curtain rise is yet another of the familiar numbers; the brass and drums accompanying the male voices: "Glory and love to the men of old!"—

By sharp contrast comes Mephistopheles' mocking serenade beneath the girl's window: "Where is thy wedding ring? Ha, ha, ha ha!" A trio between Valentine, Faust and the fiend, "Give double strength, great God!" is the prelude to the fight and the death of Valentine.

Act V *Scene 1. Walpurgis Revel.* Mephistopheles conducts Faust to the witch revels of Walpurgis night, and for his further tempting conjures up the famous courtesans of antiquity—Lais, Helen of Troy, Cleopatra, and others—who appear in an elaborate ballet. This music is quite familiar, but the scene itself is often omitted. In the midst of this revelry Faust has a vision of Marguerite with a noose around her neck, and at once commands the fiend to transport him back to her rescue.

Scene 2. A Prison Cell. Marguerite has been condemned to death for the killing of her child. Her mind wanders and snatches of the Kermess music reveal her thoughts of an innocent past. Faust enters and implores her to flee with him. Mephistopheles awaits impatiently without, and the trampling of horses' hoofs is heard. But Marguerite refuses to go, saying that she will submit to the will of Heaven. A superb trio follows, in which the girl's voice rises above the others: "Angels, pure and bright!"

Her voice on a last, triumphant note ends in death. "Condemned!" cries Mephistopheles. "Saved!" proclaim angelic voices, as the rear wall of the prison parts, and in a glory of light and sound Marguerite is carried Heavenward; while the fiend claims Faust as his own.

ROMEO AND JULIET

Tragic Opera in Five Acts. Music by Gounod. Book by Barbier and Carré, after the play by Shakespeare. Théâtre Lyrique, Paris, April 27, 1867. Academy of Music, New York, November 15, 1867. The Metropolitan, December 14, 1891.

SCENE: Verona.
TIME: The Fourteenth Century.

CAST THE PRINCE OF VERONA (Basso).
COUNT OF PARIS, *his kinsman* (Baritone).
CAPULET, *a nobleman* (Basso).

JULIET, *his daughter* (Soprano).
GERTRUDE, *her nurse* (Contralto).
TYBALT, *nephew of Capulet* (Tenor).
ROMEO, *a Montague* (Tenor).
MERCUTIO, *his friend* (Baritone).
STEFANO, *page to Romeo* (Soprano).
BENVOLIO, *friend of Romeo* (Tenor).
GREGORIO, *servant to Capulet* (Baritone).
FRIAR LAURENCE (Basso).
Friends of Capulet and Montague, Retainers of the Prince, etc.

ARGUMENT Gounod's opera follows closely the accepted version of the story of "Romeo and Juliet," following the plot, by acts, of Shakespeare's drama. Still earlier versions were the French tale of Boisteau and the Italian novel of Bandelio.

Between the Veronese houses of Capulet and Montague exists a bitter enmity. Open warfare of their retainers has continued, until the Prince threatens the banishment of the next person to engage in the quarrel.

Act I *Reception Hall in the Mansion of Capulet.* The head of the house of Capulet gives a fête in honor of his daughter, Juliet. Romeo, a Montague, comes unbidden to the house and immediately falls desperately in love with the fair young heiress. She likewise has eyes for none but him. Tybalt, a kinsman of Capulet, discovers the intruder's identity and wishes to draw upon him, but is prevented by the host who will not override the laws of hospitality.

Juliet's delight over her party is voiced in the familiar Waltz Song: "Fair is the dream of youth" (Dans ce reve)—

Romeo's impassioned, "Adorable angel!", and her reply are the occasion of a charming duet.

Act II *Capulet's Garden.* Romeo lingers beneath the balcony of Juliet, and is overjoyed to hear her come forth and confess her love for the young stranger, to the moon and stars. He makes his presence known, and the two pledge their love. Servants of Capulet interrupt them, but only temporarily. They plan a speedy marriage.

With the curtain rise we hear the fine serenade by Romeo: "Ah, fairest dawn, arise!" (Ah, leve toi soleil). With her appearance, a delightful interchange of pledges is reflected by the music.

Act III *Scene 1. Friar Laurence's Cell.* The two lovers meet clandestinely in the cell of Friar Laurence, and he consents to unite them, thinking that this will bring about peace between the warring families. The Friar's prayer, "God, who made man in Thine image," is a notable song for basso. There is also a quartet by the Friar, Gertrude, and the lovers.

Scene 2. A City Street. While walking abroad with his friends, Romeo is accosted by Tybalt, who rails at him for having gone to the Capulet home. Romeo is doubly anxious to keep the peace at this time, and answers him softly. But soft words will not satisfy either party. Mercutio, a Montague, draws upon Tybalt and is slain by the latter. Romeo, in just vengeance, then crosses swords and slays Tybalt. The Prince orders his immediate banishment from the city.

Act IV *Juliet's Bedchamber.* Romeo comes to bid his bride farewell; he cannot tarry on pain of death. When he is gone, Capulet enters to inform his daughter that a wedding has been arranged between her and the Count of Paris. She pleads for delay but unavailingly, and she dares not tell her father of her existing marriage. In despair she consults the Friar, who gives her a sleeping potion which causes the semblance of death. She is to be entombed, and Romeo is to be informed of the stratagem and rescue her.

The chief numbers in this Act are: a duet between Romeo and Juliet: "Night hymneal"; the lingering parting between them; and a quarte where their voices are joined by those of Gertrude and the Friar.

Act V *The Tomb of the Capulets.* Before Romeo can receive wor from the friar as to Juliet's feigned death, he hears that she i really no more. He hastens back to Verona and the tomb where sh lies. At the gate he encounters Paris and strikes him to the ground Within he finds his bride apparently lifeless. He drinks a vial o poison and casts himself upon her bier. At this moment she awaken from her trance and learns what he has done. He perishes in her arms and she seizes his dagger and stabs herself.

There is an effective prelude in the music of the final Act. Romeo thinking her dead, voices his sorrow in the lament, "O, my dearly be loved!" The death music between the two is poignant and gripping.

JACQUES OFFENBACH

The earlier fame of Jacques Offenbach rests upon his operettas in the French opera bouffe school. Born in Cologne in 1819, he went as a lad in his teens to Paris, where he spent his life. From his fertile pen poured a long list of delightful works in this vein; but longing to write an acknowledged masterpiece, Offenbach began his score of "The Tales of Hoffmann" in the spring of 1880. By the time it was completed he became fatally ill and never lived to see it produced. He died on October 5 of that year, leaving this, his greatest musical legacy.

THE TALES OF HOFFMANN

(Les contes d'Hoffmann.) Fantastic Opera in a Prologue, Three Acts and an Epilogue. Music by Jacques Offenbach. Book by Jules Barbier, after three tales by E. T. A. Hoffmann. Opéra Comique, Paris, February, 1881. Fifth Avenue Theatre, New York, October 16, 1882. At the Metropolitan, February 14, 1911, by the Chicago Opera Company, with Renaud, Dalmores, Sylva, Zeppilli and Di Angelo.

SCENE: Various parts of Europe.
TIME: The Nineteenth Century.

CAST HOFFMANN, *a poet* (Tenor).

OLYMPIA, GIULIETTA, ANTONIA, STELLA } *his sweethearts.* Four successive parts usually taken by one person (Soprano).

LINDORF, COPPELIUS, DAPERTUTTO, DR. MIRAKEL } *his evil genius.* Part taken by one person (Baritone).

NICKLAUS, *friend of Hoffmann* (Tenor).
SPALANZANI, *an Italian savant* (Basso).
KRESPEL, *father of Antonia* (Basso).

SCHLEMIL, *admirer of Giulietta* (Baritone).
ANDREAS, *servant of Stella* (Tenor).
LUTHER, *an Inn-keeper* (Baritone).
Several small singing parts, such as Students, Servants, Messengers, Friends, etc.

ARGUMENT "The Tales of Hoffmann" was derived from the fantastic and mystical tales written by the German author E. T. A. Hoffmann, which attained a wide popularity in France. The opera is really a musical medley uniting several different episodes.

Prologue *Luther's Wine Tavern at Nuremberg.* The poet Hoffmann, who has traveled widely and had many adventures, is now seeking his latest flame, Stella, who is singing in a theater near by. His rival, Lindorf (who is really the evil genius of the poet) plans to get Hoffmann tipsy and unpresentable, and then bring Stella on the scene With Hoffmann are a group of his student friends who ask him to relate his adventures. He at first refuses, but as he begins to drink, his memory is unlocked and he tells the stories of three love affairs. The three succeeding acts each reveal one of these tales.

Act I *The Home of Spalanzani.* An Italian savant, Spalanzani, is reputed to have a remarkable daughter, Olympia, who dance and sings divinely. Hoffmann and his friend, Nicklaus, attend the large coming-out party. Coppelius, a trickster (the evil genius who thwarts the poet in each adventure) sells Hoffmann a pair of eyeglasse for the occasion, and through these the young poet sees a vision of sur passing beauty. Olympia sings to the delighted throng, and among others straight to Hoffmann's heart. He declares his passion to her a the first opportunity and she responds, although in monosyllables. Sh dances, however, better than she talks, and accepts Hoffmann as a partner. They dance faster and faster until he can no longer keep up with her flying feet and falls exhausted. She flits from the room and a crashing noise is heard. Coppelius returns with a wrecked female figure it is Olympia, who was only an automaton! The figure had been con structed by the savant, aided by Coppelius, who now claims that Spalan zani deceived him as to payment. They quarrel while Hoffman mourns for his lost love.

The tour de force in this Act is Olympia's "Doll Song," an extremel clever simulation of whirring mechanism with a birdlike aria. At on of the loveliest high notes, the doll seems to run down, then the soun of a winding spring is heard, and up soar the notes again.

Act II *Giulietta's House in Venice.* Hoffmann's next passion is for a beautiful Venetian woman, and he goes to make love to her, although his friend tries to dissuade him, hinting that she is not all she ought to be. But Hoffmann's love blinds him to any defects in her morals. He finds her surrounded by a gay set, her favored admirer being Schlemil, who treats Hoffmann disdainfully. Now both Schlemil and the woman are in the power of Dapertutto (the evil genius under another name). Through Giulietta the evil one has become possessed of Schlemil's shadow (in other words, his soul) and he plans to obtain Hoffmann's in the same manner. The poet falls a victim to her wiles and is promised the key to her room if he will challenge Schlemil who now possesses it. He meets Schlemil and they fight. The latter falls, but when Hoffmann hastens to her balcony he sees her gondola gliding away and the coquette laughing in the embraces of another man.

It is at the beginning of this Act that we hear the famous Barcarolle, as Nicklaus and Giulietta sing to the gentle swaying of a boat on the canal: "Oh, Night of Love!" (Belle Nuit!)—

If this work had been entirely forgotten as a whole, the Barcarolle would still be played and sung as long as there are lovers in the world.

Act III *The Home of Krespel.* The next love of Hoffmann's is a pure one, its object being the lovely but delicate daughter of Krespel. Her mother, who has been a famous singer, has died prematurely from consumption, and the young girl inherits both the talent and the physical weakness. For this reason her father does not wish her to sing; but Dr. Mirakel (again the evil genius) who has treated her mother, secretly plans to hasten the daughter's demise. Hoffmann knows nothing of her disability and urges her to sing. She refuses. Then Dr. Mirakel conjures up a vision of her dead mother, who also seems to join in the request. Antonio yields and sings divinely, but the effort has been too great and she falls from weakness into her lover's arms, where she dies.

Epilogue *The Tavern, as in Prologue.* The tales are ended and Hoffmann's friends have departed one by one leaving him alone with his bottle. His head sinks forward upon his arms as he falls asleep. In his dreams the Muse of Poesy appears saying, "All your earthly loves have forsaken you; henceforth follow me." As he sleeps, the door softly opens and Stella, his last flame, enters upon the arm of Lindorf. The latter, the triumphant evil genius, points to the poet scornfully and leads Stella away.

CAMILLE SAINT-SAËNS

Saint-Saëns was born in Paris, October 9, 1835. He began his musical education at the age of two and a half years. At twelve he studied the organ under Benoist—an instrument on which he later specialized and attained world fame. At sixteen he wrote his first symphony. His first opera, "The Yellow Princess," was given in 1872; followed by "Samson and Delilah," in 1877; "Henry VIII," in 1883; "Ascanius," in 1890; "The Barbarians," in 1901; and "Dejanire," in 1911. Of these, "Samson and Delilah" is far and away his masterpiece. Saint-Saëns' fame as a composer rests upon this opera and his orchestral and church music. He died in Algiers, December 16, 1921.

SAMSON AND DELILAH

Dramatic Opera in Three Acts. Music by Camille Saint-Saëns. Book by Ferdinand Lemaire. Weimar, December 2, 1877. New Orleans, January 4, 1893. The Metropolitan, New York, in 1915.

SCENE: Gaza and Vicinity, in Palestine.
TIME: 1150 B.C.

CAST Samson, *a prophet of Israel* (Tenor).
Delilah, *a Philistine woman* (Mezzo-Soprano).
Abimelech, *a Philistine officer* (Basso).
High Priest of Dagon (Baritone).
A Philistine Messenger (Tenor).
Hebrews, Philistines, Priests, Maidens, etc.

ARGUMENT The Biblical story of Samson and Delilah is faithfully reproduced in this opera, which depicts in both text and music the dramatic scenes in the life of Israel's warrior-prophet whose power was wrested from him by a woman's wiles.

Act I *An open Square in Gaza.* The people of Israel have been overcome by their enemies the Philistines, and now pray for deliverance. Samson, their leader and a man of mighty deeds, advises them to be patient. During their devotions Abimelech, the satrap of Gaza, comes out of the temple and ridicules them and their God. Samson turns upon him, wrests the sword from his hand, and kills him with one blow. Other Philistine soldiers rush to their leader's aid, but Samson easily withstands them all. The High Priest urges them forward, but they answer that they cannot overcome Samson; he is invincible. Samson bids his people arm and avenge themselves. They sally forth and a messenger reports that they are everywhere victorious. As the strong man returns, maidens come forth from the temple, led by Delilah, a Philistine woman. She praises Samson and says that she can resist him no longer. They dance about him, and his eyes follow every motion of the seductive Delilah.

Before the rise of the first curtain, a chorus of Israelites behind the scenes is heard bewailing their fate and beseeching Jehovah to intervene. There are some fine choral and fugue passages here. Toward the close of the scene, Delilah exerts her first blandishments on the hero in her "Spring Song"—"Spring voices are singing" (Printemps qui commence)—

Act II *House of Delilah in the Valley of Sorak.* Delilah, gorgeously attired, awaits the coming of Samson. He is tardy and she grows impatient. It was not thus when he was first in her power, but now he is seeking to break the shackles of love. While she waits, the High Priest enters. She must aid them to lay hold upon the warrior, he says; and he offers her wealth if she will deliver him into their hands. Delilah refuses the gold, replying that her hatred is enough. The High Priest departs and sets a secret guard about the house. After a time Samson appears but with reluctance and shame. His God commands him to break off this unholy alliance and lead Israel out of bondage. Delilah makes use of all her wiles to bring him again under her power, singing the bewitching song, "My heart at thy dear voice" (Mon coeur s'ouvre a ta voix)—

What man could resist such passion and pleading? Not Samson. As he capitulates, she asks him to tell her the secret of his strength. He refuses, and she leaves him, but he runs after her into the house. While she has been singing, the mutterings of a storm are heard; now it breaks in all its fury, cloaking the advance of Philistine soldiers upon the house. Delilah opens a window and beckons to them in triumph; while Samson is heard in a terrible cry, "Betrayed!"

Act III *Scene 1. The Prison of Gaza.* Samson has been shorn of his long hair, the secret of his strength, his eyes have been put out, and like a blind ox he trudges around a mill wheel. His captors mock him, while from without his people sing in reproach: "For the love of a woman he sold his power—and made us captive!" Presently he is seized and led forth in chains to grace a triumphal procession.

Scene 2. Interior of the Temple of Dagon. Before a great assemblage of Philistines, their High Priest assisted by the triumphant Delilah makes an offering to their god, Dagon. "Dagon, be ever praised!" they sing:

As the flames flash up from the altar, a wild bacchanale is danced by maidens, as the wood instruments wail out an exotic cadenza. It is a riot of voluptuousness. Unnoticed for the moment, the old warrior prays to Jehovah: "Lord, thy servant remember now. For one moment make him strong again!" Delilah turns and taunts him with his helplessness. She even sings passages from her old love song. All laugh—he is huge sport for them. He is standing between two great pillars which hold up the roof of the temple. His sightless eyes turn toward his tormentors. Then a sudden quickening of his muscles informs him that his prayer has been answered. With one last supreme effort he winds his arms about the columns—they yield—they break—with a rending of timbers the roof crashes down—his enemies are buried beneath the ruins—and with them Samson—and Delilah!

LEO DELIBES

Delibes was born February 21, 1836, at St. Germain du Val (Sarthe), and died January 16, 1891, at Paris. His chief works are "Coppelia," a ballet in three acts founded upon Hoffmann's story of "The Sandman"; "The King Has Said It," a comic opera in three acts, and "Lakmé," a romantic opera. Delibes is at his best in ballets and light operas, his music being of singularly graceful, intriguing character.

LAKMÉ

(*Lack-may'*)

Romantic Opera in Three Acts. Music by Leo Delibes. Book by Gondinet and Gille, based upon the story, "The Marriage of Loti."

First produced at the Opéra Comique, Paris, April 14, 1883. At the Academy of Music, New York, March 1, 1886. At the Metropolitan, New York, in the spring of 1890, when "Lakmé" was sung by Patti. Now seldom produced.

SCENE: India.
TIME: Circa 1880.

CAST NILAKANTHA, *an Indian priest* (Basso).
LAKMÉ, *his daughter* (Soprano).
MALLIKA, *her slave* (Contralto).
GERALD, *a British officer* (Tenor).
FREDERICK, *a British officer* (Baritone).
MRS. BENSON (Contralto).
ROSE (Mezzo-Soprano).
ELLEN (Soprano).
British Officers, Englishwomen, Natives, etc.

ARGUMENT "Lakmé" has been a favorite of divas in the past for its fine opportunities in coloratura, chiefly the "Bell Song." Its oriental plot, a slight, fanciful one, is saturated with exotic, sensuous melody—perhaps an overdose. If this work could be compressed, say within the limits of "Cavalleria" or "Pagliacci," it might rank with them in continuing popularity.

Act I *A Garden in India.* The aged Hindu priest, Nilakantha, has a hearty dislike for all foreigners, the English in particular. Nevertheless, a party of British officers enter his private garden, where they discover some jewels left by Lakmé, the priest's daughter. Gerald, one of the officers, is so delighted with them that he remains behind to sketch them for his fiancée, Ellen, who has come with them but now gone with the others. Gerald's song, punctuated by notes of admiration, "Idle fancies" (Fantaisie aux divins), is a well-known tenor aria.

Lakmé comes upon the intruder, and the two are mutually attracted, but the girl warns Gerald of her father's antipathy and possible vengeance.

Act II *Street Scene in India.* The old priest has found a broken fence in his estate and suspects an interloper. He now bends his cunning to find and punish him. Ordering his daughter to follow him, they disguise themselves as penitents and mingle with the crowd at a sacred festival. The priest believes that when his daughter's voice is heard, one of the British officers will betray himself; so she is ordered to sing. Her song, which is recognized as one of the most difficult and exacting of coloratura arias, begins with a legend of a Pariah's daughter: "In the Forest" (Dans le Forêt). "A young girl forward runs; a ring in her grasp she holds tightly, whence tinkles a bell." The singer imitates the notes of a small bell with her voice, in the famous "Bell Song"—

The old man's ruse works. Gerald starts with pleasurable surprise; the priest recognizes him in turn, stabs him, then escapes. The horrified girl rushes to the wounded man as, with a burst of oriental music, still lacking in the dramatic, the curtain falls.

Act III *A Hut in the Forest.* Gerald is being nursed back to health by the faithful Lakmé. They confess their love and she goes to procure a sacred potion which will render it deathless. But while she is gone, Frederick, a fellow officer, enters and chides Gerald for his inaction. The soldiers are on the march and his duty is with the colors. Martial music is heard in the distance, as Frederick leaves, and the girl returns with the potion. Gerald, however, refuses to drink it. Lakmé, heartbroken, gathers for herself some deadly datura blossoms. Nilakantha rushes in upon them and again would slay Gerald, but the dying Lakmé warns him that her lover has drunk the sacred draught and cannot be harmed. She dies in the arms of the man she has again saved.

GEORGES BIZET

Georges Bizet was born in Paris, October 25, 1838. He studied music under Halévy, and later at the Paris Conservatory. He composed many pieces of music, long and short, but is chiefly remembered for five operas: "Vasco da Gama" (1863), "The Pearl Fishers" (1863), "The Fair Maid of Perth" (1867), "Djamileh" (1872), and "Carmen" (1875). The last is by far his most famous work, and has remained a prime favorite with opera-goers. Bizet died near Paris, June 3, 1875.

THE PEARL FISHERS

(Les Pecheurs des Perles.) Romantic Opera in Three Acts. Music by Bizet. Book by E. Cormon and M. Carre. Théâtre Lyrique, Paris, September 29, 1863. Thirty years later, in Philadelphia, August 25, 1893. The Metropolitan, New York, January 11, 1896.

SCENE: The Isle of Ceylon.
TIME: Barbaric Period.

CAST LEILA, *a priestess* (Soprano).
NADIR, *a pearl fisher* (Tenor).
ZURGA, *a chief* (Baritone).
NURABAD, *the high priest* (Basso).
Fishermen, Fakirs, Priests and Priestesses, Islanders.

ARGUMENT "The Pearl Fishers" is a rapidly moving opera, woven around a simple theme and involving only four leading characters.

Act I *On the Seashore.* A semi-barbaric tribe meet to elect a chief and to hold an annual festival and vigil to frighten away the evil spirits. They choose Zurga as their chief. While the festival is in progress, Zurga's former friend, Nadir, appears from the forest. The two had become estranged on account of their rivalry for the hand of a beautiful woman who had mysteriously appeared on their shores a year before. Each year she comes to pray for the tribe, and none dares molest her or look upon her face. While the two reunited friends converse, a boat draws near and the fair stranger is again announced, accompanied by Nurabad, the high priest. The people draw near her in awe, asking her to intercede for them. She promises to keep lonely vigil for them, and Zurga promises in his turn that, if she is true to her trust, he will bestow upon her a pearl of great price, but that if she is untrue, death shall be her portion. Nadir is a deeply interested spectator, as he recognizes the voice of the woman he so passionately loved a year before. After all the rest have departed he lingers below the rocks where she is holding her vigil.

In the early part of this Act, a notable duet for tenor and baritone is heard, as Nadir and Zurga reaffirm their friendship: "In the depths of the temple" (Au fond du temple). Near the end, Nadir tells his reawakened love for Leila in a song of poignant beauty: "I hear as in a dream" (Je crois entendre encore)—

Act II *Ruins of a Temple.* Nurabad, the high priest, installs Leila in her position as priestess of the tribe. He tells her that she must remain in silent watch and prayer throughout the night. She is fearful of the forest sounds, but promises. Nurabad departs. As Leila trembles at the roar of wild beasts, she is suddenly reassured by the sound of a human voice. It is Nadir singing to her in the distance. She answers, and Nadir, overjoyed, tells her of his love. They embrace, but are surprised by the high priest, who has been in hiding. He calls the people together, telling them that their priestess has been false to her vows. The tribesmen are ready to slay her, but Nadir shields her with his body. Zurga, in order to protect his friend, commands the pearl fishers to disperse. Nurabad tears away Leila's veil, and Zurga then recognizes her as the same woman over whom he and Nadir had formerly quarreled. A storm arises and the people pray to the gods while the priests lead Leila away. Nadir is sentenced to death.

Chief musical numbers: Leila's song, "A fugitive one day" (Comme autrefois); and an impassioned duet between her and Nadir, "You have not understood" (Ton coeur n'a pas compris)—the effect of the latter being emphasized by a raging storm outside the temple ruins. Voices, stage setting, instruments, unite in great dramatic effect.

Act III *The Camp of Zurga.* Zurga is torn between conflicting emotions of his love for Leila and his friendship for Nadir. In the midst of his inner struggle, Leila comes, guarded by two pearl fishers, to intercede for her lover. Zurga declares his own love for her, but she disdains him. She is ready to die if Nadir dies. She gives him a chain which she had formerly received as a guerdon. Zurga, much moved, departs, and the tribesmen cluster around their prospective victims, Leila and Nadir, and begin their tribal dance. As they are at last on the point of stabbing the victims with their knives, Zurga re-enters, telling them that their camp is in flames. They hasten away, while Zurga boasts that he is the incendiary and has chosen this method of saving the captives. He strikes off their shackles, while Nurabad, who has overheard, hastens away to the people, to obtain aid in preventing the escape. Nadir and Leila, however, have time to make their way to the cliffs and safety. Zurga remains behind to shield their flight, and is slain by the knives of his followers.

CARMEN

Romantic Opera in Four Acts. Music by Bizet. Book by Meilhac and Halévy, after the novel by Prosper Merimée. Opéra Comique, Paris, March 3, 1875. Academy of Music, New York, October 23, 1879. The Metropolitan, New York, December 20, 1893, when Calvé made her memorable début.

SCENE: Seville.
TIME: Early part of Nineteenth Century.

CAST
ZUNIGA, *a lieutenant* (Basso).
JOSÉ, *a sergeant* (Tenor).
MORALES, *a sergeant* (Basso).
ESCAMILLO, *a bull-fighter* (Basso).
DANCAIRO, *a smuggler* (Tenor).
REMENDADO, *a smuggler* (Baritone).
CARMEN, *a Gypsy girl* (Soprano).
FRASQUITA, *A Gypsy* (Soprano).
MERCEDES, *a Gypsy* (Contralto).
MICHAELA, *a peasant girl* (Soprano).
Gypsies, Peasants, Citizens, Cigarette Girls, Soldiers.

ARGUMENT "Carmen" is a colorful opera, founded upon Merimée's brilliant romance depicting Spanish Gypsy and peasant life. The central figure is a heartless coquette who lives only for the passion of the passing moment. Here again is an example of a composer of several operas who is known to fame for a single, striking work. And yet, so discouraging was its first reception that Bizet died, three months later, disheartened and depressed over the failure of his beloved "Carmen"—now in continuous repertory around the world.

Act I *A City Square.* A troop of soldiers under the command of Don José, together with town idlers, throng the open square during the noon hour. Especially are they interested in the pretty girls who work in a neighboring cigarette factory. Only the officer, Don José, is indifferent to these coquettes as they jest with the men. Seeing his indifference, Carmen, the Gypsy girl and the greatest flirt of them all, practices her wiles upon him and flings him a red rose. Don José's blood is finally fired, but the girls return to their work, and Michaela, a gentle peasant girl from his home village, arrives with a message for him. The officer is about to throw the Gypsy's rose away when a commotion is heard within the factory and the girls rush out. Carmen has quarreled with another girl and stabbed her. The assailant is brought forward and pinioned to prevent further mischief, but she so bewitches the young officer that he connives at her escape.

There is such a wealth of "quotable" music, that it is hard to particularize. Soon after the curtain rise we hear the ever-popular march of the soldiers as they change the guard:

Carmen's entrance is followed by her captivating song, "Love is a rebellious bird" (L'Amour est une oiseau rebelle)—with its intriguing "Habanera" rhythm—

Near the close, her equally coquettish song, "Near the walls of Seville," making use of another familiar Spanish dance tempo, the "Seguidilla," enables Carmen again to hoodwink the gullible males:

Act II *A Tavern Room.* Carmen has returned to her nomadic life and we find her with her companions singing and carousing in a road house. The famous bullfighter, Escamillo, enters, and Carmen is greatly fascinated by him and also makes him aware of her charms. The inn is closed for the evening, but Carmen and two of the Gypsy men who are smugglers await the arrival of José. The latter is deeply in the girl's toils, and when he appears she urges him to desert the army and join the Gypsy band. At first he refuses, but when a superior officer appears and orders him out, swords are drawn. Carmen summons the Gypsies, who overpower the officer, and all, including José, escape to the mountains.

A brief prelude by the orchestra precedes the rise of the curtain. Then comes the sparkling little Gypsy song, "Ah, when the gay guitars ring out," by Carmen to the accompaniment of these instruments. A lively dance of the Gypsies is supported by full orchestra. When the bullfighter enters, to the shouts of greeting, he struts to the center of the stage, throws out his chest, and sings the unforgettable bravura: "Toreador, on guard! Love is the prize awaits thee, ah, Toreador!"

A fine song for tenor is heard near the end, when José tells Carmen, "You must hear me! This flower you once gave me is dishonored!" It is known as "The Flower Song" (Air de la Fleur).

Act III *Mountain Retreat of the Smugglers.* The smugglers have been busy and successful, aided by José who is still wildly in love with Carmen. She, however, is growing cold to him. He sees this and is deeply dejected by it and at the thought of his perfidy. Carmen's latest conquest, Escamillo, now appears seeking her, and José, wildly jealous, would spring at his throat but for the intervention of the Gypsies. The faithful Michaela again finds José and beseeches him to hasten with her to the bedside of his dying mother. After a struggle between duty and desire, duty prevails and he departs with her.

The Third Act is also given an orchestral prelude marked by delightful, pastoral passages, with harp notes—a calm before the coming dramatic storm. The arrival of the smugglers, after curtain rise, is the occasion of a stirring "Smugglers' March." Carmen's defiant song, "In vain I sort the cards!" is followed by a more pathetic one from the scorned girl, Michaela, who comes seeking the recreant José. "I shall find the guilty one!" she cries. There is a reconciliation between the two, but even as they depart, José calls to Carmen; and the boastful song of the toreador is heard in the distance.

Act IV *Exterior of the Bullfighting Arena.* All Seville is hastening to one of the great fights of the season, where their favorite toreador, Escamillo, is to appear. Carmen has accompanied him, despite the warnings of her friends that the furious José is seeking her. Amid great pomp Escamillo enters the arena, but before she can follow him, her discarded lover appears. At first he pleads with her to return to him. She refuses, and the enraged José stabs her to the heart just as the victorious fighter returns from the arena.

Stirring strains of music herald the final Act. The pace is being quickened to the climax. The street scene is one of a lively ballet. "Viva, Escamillo!" they shout. The music changes. José makes one last plea to the flirt. "Let me pass!" she cries. With a crash of chords, the gates of the arena are thrown open. Escamillo and his friends stop in horror as they see Carmen's lifeless body. José stands by her side. "Yes, I slew her. I am your prisoner." Then with a stricken cry he throws himself beside her. "Carmen, Carmen, how I have loved you!"

JULES MASSENET

One of the most prolific of latter-day composers, Massenet was born in Montaud, France, May 12, 1842. At the age of twenty-one he won the "Prix de Rome" for composition and had already made a name for himself in orchestral work. Three years later began his flood of operas, which were successful almost at once, beginning with two light operas, "The Great Aunt" and "Don Caesar de Bazan." "The Furies," a dramatic work, and an oratorio, "Mary Magdalen" followed. Other operas include: "Herodias" (1881); "Manon" (1884); "Le Cid" (1885); "Werther" (1892); "Thais" (1894); "Cendrillon" (1899); "Griselidis" (1901); "The Juggler of Notre Dame" (1902); and "Don Quixote" (1910). Many of these have been produced in America. Massenet died, August 13, 1912.

HERODIAS

(Herodiade.) Dramatic Opera in Four Acts. Music by Massenet. Book by Paul Milliet and Henri Gremont. Théâtre de la Monnaie,

Brussels, December 19, 1881. The first American production was in New Orleans, February 13, 1892. In New York, Manhattan Opera House, November 8, 1909, with Cavalieri as "Herodias."

SCENE: Palestine.
TIME: 30 A.D.

CAST HEROD, *the tetrarch* (Basso).
HERODIAS, *his wife* (Mezzo-Soprano).
SALOME, *her daughter* (Soprano).
PHANUEL, *a Chaldean* (Tenor).
JOHN THE BAPTIST, *a Prophet* (Tenor).
VITELLIUS, *a Roman consul* (Baritone).
HIGH PRIEST (Baritone).
Jews, Romans, Soldiers, Priests, Dancers, Servants, etc.

ARGUMENT "Herodias" presents another version of the character of Salome from that given in the Strauss opera, based upon the Wilde play. Both, of course, go back to the Biblical account for their slender historical setting.

Act I *Courtyard of Herod's Palace.* While servants labor under the direction of Phanuel the Chaldean, Salome enters seeking her mother, whose identity she does not know. Phanuel promises to aid her, but warns her against the intrigues of the palace. They depart. Herod now enters, seeking this maiden whose dancing has already enslaved him. Herodias meets him and complains of a rough-looking prophet who has bitterly denounced her in public. She wishes to be revenged, but Herod counsels caution. John, the prophet, enters at this moment repeating his denunciations. Both Herod and Herodias leave hastily. Salome runs to greet him, her heart won by his former kindnesses; but he refuses her proffered love.

A lovely aria is heard near the beginning, when Salome tells Phanuel how a man of the desert had befriended her as a child: "He is kind, he is good," she sings (Il est doux, il est bon).

Act II *Scene 1. Herod's Chamber.* The tetrarch reclines at ease watching his dancers; but Salome is not among them and he is unhappy. Phanuel enters to warn him against this life of luxury. But Herod cannot get the vision of the dancing girl from his mind. He drinks a philter brought mysteriously by a slave, and sings of his desire: "Fleeting vision!" (Vision fugitive)—

Scene 2. A Public Square. Urged on by Phanuel, Herod appears before the people haranguing them to throw off the Roman yoke. But they are interrupted by the sound of trumpets announcing the arrival of the Roman consul, Vitellius. The suspicions of the consul are lulled by Herod, who says that the priests desire that their Temple be restored to them. Vitellius says it shall be done. John appears, followed by Salome and others, and the consul is told by Herodias that the prophet is a disturber anxious for power. John retorts that all power is from God.

Act III *Scene 1. An Inner Room.* While Phanuel, the Chaldean, is consulting the stars, Herodias seeks him to know about the future. She is especially desirous to know how to win back Herod's love, and also as to the whereabouts of her lost daughter. For reply, Phanuel shows her Salome who is crossing the court with the dancers. "That my daughter?" exclaims Herodias. "No, my rival!"

Scene 2. The Temple. Salome is in the depths of despair because John has been cast into prison. Herod meets her and offers her his love, but she repulses him. Vitellius enters proclaiming the power of Rome. The priests appear before him urging the condemnation of John. He refers them to Herod. John is brought forward and questioned. Salome throws herself before him begging Herod to pardon him; but this only infuriates Herod, who sentences him to death.

Act IV *Scene 1. A Dungeon.* While John awaits his sentence, Salome enters. Her fortitude and devotion touch him and something like human love enters his heart. But he bids her flee and save herself. The High Priest secretly offers John a pardon if he will use his influence for Herod against Rome, but John refuses.

Scene 2. Audience Hall in the Palace. While Herod, Herodias, and Vitellius hold an audience and are entertained by dancers Salome appears at the special command of Herod. He turns a deaf ear, however, to her requests for John's pardon, and the executioner presently appears with a bloody sword, as a sign that the prophet is dead. Salome turns in fury upon Herodias, saying "This is your deed!" and is about to stab her. Herodias, in fear, cries out: "I am your mother!" "Then take back the life you gave me!" replies Salome, and stabs herself to the heart.

MANON

(*Ma'-non*)

Dramatic Opera in Five Acts. Music by Massenet. Book by H. Meilhac and P. Gille, after Marcel Prévost's "Manon Lescaut."

Opéra Comique, Paris, January 19, 1884. At the Academy of Music, New York, December 23, 1885. Metropolitan, January 16, 1895, with Jean de Reszke, Plancon, and Ancona in the male roles; and Sybil Sanderson as "Manon."

SCENE: Amiens, Paris, Havre.
TIME: 1721.

CAST COMTE DES GRIEUX, *a French nobleman* (Basso).
CHEVALIER DES GRIEUX, *his son* (Tenor).
LESCAUT, *a guardsman* (Baritone).
MANON LESCAUT, *his cousin* (Soprano).
GUILLOT MORFONTAIN, *a minister of finance* (Basso).
DE BRÉTIGNY, *a nobleman* (Baritone).
POUSSETTE, *an actress* (Soprano).
ROSETTE, *an actress* (Soprano).
JAVOTTE, *an actress* (Contralto).
Innkeeper, Citizens, Actresses, Soldiers, Servants, etc.

ARGUMENT "Manon" is a picture of French life among the gay set, drawn from Prévost's well-known story "Manon Lescaut," which is the same source made use of, some years later, by Puccini in his opera of that name.

Act I *A Tavern at Amiens.* Manon Lescaut is a gay and volatile French woman whose spirits her parents very wisely seek to curb by placing her in a convent. On the way thither, escorted by her cousin, she stops at an inn where Morfontain is entertaining some friends. The old roué immediately begins to make advances to her but is repulsed. Not so, young Des Grieux, who has been destined for the priesthood. He finds Manon so attractive, and she him, that they both forsake their prospective vows and run away to Paris.

Manon's opening song is a mixture of the demure and the impish: "I am a simple maiden" (Je suis encore étourdie). Her cousin Lescaut, warns her of pitfalls in his baritone song, "Now give good heed" (Regardez-moi). She speedily forgets the warning, however, as soon as she meets the handsome chevalier. To his question, "If I but knew your name?" and her reply, "I am called Manon"—ensues the usual impassioned duet, "To you, my life and soul!" (A vous ma vie et mon ame). The Act ends with their lively, "We're on our way to Paris!"

Act II *Des Grieux's Apartments in Paris.* Manon and the chevalier live quietly in Paris and he writes to his father the Count, ask ing permission to marry her. Her cousin, Lescaut, comes to demand satisfaction from the chevalier for the abduction. The latter then shows him the letter that he is about to mail to his father, as proof of his honorable intentions. Lescaut seems satisfied, but a new danger threatens. While the two talk, another nobleman has entered, De Bretigny, who takes Manon aside and tells her that the chevalier is on the point of being seized by his father, to prevent this match. She would be wiser to go with him—De Bretigny—who can offer her safety and a life of luxury. She is left alone on the stage to wrestle with this new temptation, and the chevalier on his return from mailing the letter finds her in tears. Seeking to console her, he describes the little dream house he is planning for them: "The Dream" (La reve)—

A sudden knock interrupts their idyl. Manon starts guiltily; she has not warned her lover. Now he goes to the door; she interposes halfheartedly; he is taken by his captors; and she awaits her new lover.

Act III *Scene 1. A Parisian Boulevard.* Manon is the center of a laughing crowd of actresses and boulevardiers. True to his word, De Brétigny maintains her in luxury. But she overhears the Count des Grieux telling a friend that the chevalier, disgusted with Manon's conduct, was about to become a monk. She seeks further information, but the Count, guessing her identity, will not say more. She resolves to seek her former lover.

Scene 2. The seminary of St. Sulpice. The Count does not wish his son to enter the priesthood and endeavors to dissuade him. Afterwards, Manon enters, but the chevalier only reproaches her with her faithlessness. She says that she still loves him, and after much argument persuades him to come back to her.

In this second scene the chevalier sings a fervent song of renunciation: "Depart, fair vision!" (Ah, fuyez, douce image!), but despite his resolution he cannot drive her image from his mind and as if in answer to his secret desires that fickle vision comes back in the flesh. He upbraids Manon that she has been faithless, and tells her that he is seeking solace in a religious brotherhood. A chanting chorus in the background is heard. But the chameleonlike woman only answers: "Ah, look at me! Am I no longer Manon?" (Ah, regardez moi!) The religious chant and his own fine resolutions are unheeded. "Ah, Manon, I love thee!" he cries; and an impassioned duet of reconciliation marks the fall of the curtain. The clash of contending emotions is faithfully reflected in the tumultuous music.

Act IV *A Gambling House in Paris.* In order to maintain Manon in the style to which she is accustomed, the chevalier frequents the gambling houses. He wins large sums, especially from Morfontain. The latter accuses him of cheating and, by way of revenge upon Manon, who jilted him, has both Des Grieux and Manon arrested. The Count also joins forces against her and plots to have her deported where she can do no further mischief.

As the chevalier sweeps in his winnings and the croupier shouts, "Make your plays, gentlemen!" Manon sings a joyous: "Music of Gold" song. However, their joy soon ends with the descent of law. "Oh, despair! Now are our lives parted forever!" she voices her grief.

Act V *The Open Road near Havre.* Manon is being escorted out of the country by a guard of soldiers. The chevalier asks Lescaut, her cousin, to aid him in rescuing her. They try bribery. She has a short interview with Des Grieux, begging his pardon for wrecking his life; but even in her last moments a hint of the selfish, fickle woman asserts itself. "What lovely jewels!" she sighs, as she dreams of former luxury. Then she turns repentant to her chevalier. "Forgive me! I love but thee! Take this last kiss—it is all I have left—" As he clasps her in his arms, she dies.

WERTHER

Tragic Opera in Four Acts. Music by Massenet. Book by Blau, Milliet, and Hartmann, after the story, "The Sorrows of Werther," by Goethe. Imperial Opera House, Vienna, with the composer directing, February 16, 1892. At the Auditorium, Chicago, March 29, 1894. In New York, the Metropolitan, April 19, 1894.

SCENE: Wetzlar, Germany.
TIME: 1772.

CAST WERTHER, *a poet* (Tenor).
CHARLOTTE, *his cousin* (Soprano).
ALBERT, *her husband* (Baritone).
FATHER of Charlotte (Bass).
Friends, servants, etc.

ARGUMENT This story which closely follows that of Goethe was at first hailed as one of Massenet's greatest works. It contains some of his most persuasive melodies, but as a whole has failed to keep a place in active repertory.

Act I *A Terrace in front of the Bailiff's House.* Werther, a young poet of highly romantic disposition, is in love with Charlotte, his cousin, who reciprocates. Her father, the bailiff, however, has planned to carry out her dead mother's wishes and marry her to Albert, an old friend of the family. Charlotte tells Werther that she feels in honor bound to go through with this marriage, and Werther replies, "If you do so, I shall die."

Act II *Square before the Inn.* The ensuing action takes place three months later. Albert and Charlotte are now man and wife. Albert knows of Werther's love for his wife, but trusts him. The poet, unable to hide his sentiments, finally goes away.

Act III *Albert's Home.* Werther has remained away from his beloved until life becomes unendurable for him. He goes back, in spite of himself, and finding Charlotte at home alone, he begins to read to her a poem by Ossian; but the lines serve only to betray his own passion for her. His song of great intensity, "Do not wake me," is generally called, "Chant d'Ossian"—

Her own agitation reveals her love for Werther, but she entreats him to leave her forever. He departs. Later Albert comes in with a note from him, saying that he is going on a long journey and requesting the loan of his pistol. Charlotte, filled with dread misgivings, hastens to Werther's apartments.

Act IV *Werther's Apartments.* Charlotte finds her worst fears are realized. She finds Werther lying upon the floor, mortally wounded. She reproaches herself for his death, but now at last they can confess all their love for each other. As she holds the dying man in her arms, the voices of children are heard, singing a Christmas carol.

THAIS

(Tah'-ees)

Romantic Opera in Three Acts. Music by Jules Massenet. Book by Louis Gallet, after the romance by Anatole France. Grand Opera,

Paris, March 16, 1894. Manhattan Opera House, New York, November 25, 1908, by the Chicago Opera Company, headed by Mary Garden (her New York début) and Renaud. At the Metropolitan, February 16, 1917, with Farrar and Rothier.

SCENE: Upper Egypt.
TIME: Early Christian era.

CAST ATHANAEL, *a monk* (Baritone).
THAIS, *a courtesan* (Soprano).
NICIAS, *a wealthy Alexandrian* (Tenor).
PALEMON, *the head monk* (Basso).
ALBINE, *an abbess* (Mezzo-Soprano).
LA CHARMEUSE, *a dancer.*
CROBYLE, *a slave* (Soprano).
MYRTALE, *a slave* (Soprano).
Monks, Nuns, Citizens, Servants, Dancers, etc.

ARGUMENT The theme of "Thais" is the struggle between the lower nature and the higher; it personifies the eternal conflict between the beast and the angel, in the human race Like Mascagni's "Cavalleria," "Thais" has won enduring fame by reason of its Intermezzo, which has become a favorite with violinists.

Act I *Scene 1. The Theban Desert.* Withdrawing from luxury and sin, a small band of Cenobite monks dwell in the desert near Thebes. Athanael, a young enthusiast of the order, has just returned from a mission to Alexandria, and he gives a gloomy account of the vice rampant in that city. It is under the control of a beautiful courtesan named Thais, who rules by the power of her charms. Athanael cannot get the vision of her loveliness out of his head, and he thinks it would be a great victory for the Church if he could convert her. Palemon, the head of the order, rebukes the idea as foolish, but in his dreams, Athanael witnesses again the lovely woman posing before the populace as Aphrodite, and being acclaimed as a goddess. He awakes, saying that he must return on this mission, although Palemon and the other monks endeavor to dissuade him.

The music in the opening scene reflects the sober, severe life of the Cenobite monks. After a quiet but resonant chorus, Athanael enters and recites dramatically his past experiences in the city and vision of Thais. His song, "Let us have pity in our hearts," is followed by the arguments of the leader and others, to dissuade a further visit to the city of sin.

Scene 2. The House of Nicias, at Alexandria. Nicias, a wealthy leader of fashion, is just now the favored admirer of Thais, although he ruefully admits he is paying extravagantly for the distinction. To his house, Athanael directs his steps, and finally gains admittance there. When he unfolds his plan to Nicias, the latter laughs at it, but good-naturedly promises to aid him. Thais is to be present at supper that very evening, and the young monk must make a good appearance. The leader of fashion looks approvingly at Athanael's fine head and athletic figure, and bids his slave array the guest in rich attire. A great acclamation is heard and Thais enters amid a throng of her adorers. The young monk alone stands aloof and she notices his attitude. "Who is he?" she asks. "One who has come for you," Nicias replies jestingly. "Bringing love?" she asks simply; for to her love is all in all. "Yes, love that you know not of," answers Athanael sternly, coming forward; and he tries to tell her of the higher life. She cannot understand him. He reproaches her and the company interfere. Then Thais, piqued, tries to subdue him by her charms. He retreats, but promises to come to her apartments and talk further. It is her challenge which he accepts, confident of his own integrity.

The music here is in striking contrast with the somber first scene. Now all is gaiety, frivolity, sensuality, but with an undertone as the austere monk strives to oppose it.

Act II *Scene 1. Interior of the Palace of Thais.* In a luxuriously appointed room Thais awaits the coming of one whom she thinks will be her next victim. Meanwhile, she prays to Aphrodite for a continuance of youth and beauty, her only weapons. As she contemplates her loveliness in a mirror, she sings the fine aria, "Tell me that I am beautiful" (Dis-moi que je suis belle)—known as the "Mirror Song"—

Athanael pauses at the door, at first spellbound by the vision of loveliness; then advancing, he tells her that the love which he offers is from God and is for her salvation. They argue, she trying upon him all her coquetry, but he is able to resist temptation. This new type of man impresses her even more than his message. The voice of Nicias is heard calling her, and Athanael departs, saying he will wait for her outside the palace. She must follow him if she would find the new and higher love. "On thy threshold till dawn I shall await thy coming," he tells her sternly. The curtain descends and now is heard the hauntingly lovely strains of the "Meditation"—the vigil of the monk, the awakening of a woman's soul. To a harp accompaniment a solo violin is heard in a strain of pure melody—

Scene 2. Outside the Palace. Moonlight floods the open court, while through the lighted windows come the sounds of revelry and feasting. Athanael lies upon the stone step. Presently the door opens and Thais emerges bearing a lighted lamp. She tells him she has decided to leave all and follow him. "Then break your image and set fire to your belongings," he replies, "for you cannot take any of these things with you." She returns within and obeys him, reappearing in a simple garb, bearing a torch. Meanwhile, Nicias and his friends come forth and order dancers to entertain them. In the midst of the revelry Thais appears, but they recognize her despite her rough dress, and try to detain her. Nicias diverts the crowd's attention by scattering handfuls of gold, and the two pilgrims depart while the palace burns.

Act III *Scene 1. An Oasis in the Desert.* Thais is half-dead from the fatigue of this unaccustomed journey, but presses on without murmuring. She wishes to find the higher love. Athanael's heart is stirred by her sufferings and fortitude. He bids her rest beneath the shade of a clump of palms and brings water to bathe her feet, kissing them. His destination is a convent in the desert, now near at hand. The abbess and her nuns are heard singing as they approach. Athanael commends the new convert into their keeping and stands silent until they have gone. Then he utters a cry of anguish. He has conquered, but now he is alone.

Scene 2. The Cenobite Monastery. Athanael returns to the monasery, where the monks congratulate him upon his success. But he is inifferent to their praise. The vision of Thais still haunts his dreams nd he finds that he is miserable since she has gone out of his life.

Scene 3. The Garden of the Convent. Thais is dying, and has sent or Athanael. He comes and the abbess leads him to her cot in the pen court. The sisters extol her saintly life, but the monk does not eed. He kneels by her side and begs her to come back to him. It is ot the heavenly love which fills his heart, now, but the earthly. She pens her eyes but does not understand him; for visions of heavenly liss already possess her. Deaf to his entreaties, she calls upon the ame of God as she dies, while he grovels upon the ground in despair.

The closing moments between the two are marked by some of the nest passages: his despairing cry to her, and her incoherent answers; ie sorrowful chants of the nuns; then again an echo of the celestial rains of the "Meditation," as her soul wings its way upward with the iusic.

THE JUGGLER OF NOTRE DAME

(Le Jongleur de Notre Dame.) Miracle Play in Three Acts. Music y Massenet. Book by Maurice Lena. Monte Carlo, February 18, 902; Paris, 1903. Manhattan Opera House, New York, November 7, 1908.

SCENE: Cluny, near Paris.
TIME: Sixteenth Century.

CAST JEAN, *a juggler* (Tenor).
BONIFACE, *a cook* (Baritone).
PRIOR OF THE MONASTERY (Basso).
POET, *a monk* (Tenor).
PAINTER, *a monk* (Baritone).
MUSICIAN, *a monk* (Baritone).
SCULPTOR, *a monk* (Basso).
Two Angels, apparition of the Virgin, Monks, Cavaliers, Citizens.

ARGUMENT "The Juggler of Notre Dame" is styled by its librettist a "Miracle" play, but is only such in the nse that it requires a miracle to give value to its denouement. Its eme is medieval and monastic, ignoring love or other affairs of the ntler sex.

Act I *The Cluny Market Place.* During a market day in which al the villagers gather to barter and make merry, Jean the juggle wanders about forlorn and hungry. His tricks are time-worn, his song weak, and when he presently tries to perform for the crowd, they onl jeer at him. Finally, to arouse them he sings a sacrilegious song, "Alle luia to Wine," in which they roar out a chorus. The Prior of a neigh boring monastery is shocked and comes out to anathematize the crowd All scatter, leaving Jean, who is really a goodhearted fellow, to bear th blame of the Church. The Prior is finally touched by his penitence and pardons him, but urges him to join the band of monks. Jean doe not wish to relinquish his liberty, but the sight of the Cook's donke going by with panniers laden with food is too much for his hungr stomach and he consents.

Act II *The Monastery Study.* The busy monks each labor at thei chosen vocation—poets, musicians, painters, scribes, sculptor and what not—but Jean feels himself out of it. He cannot even pra to the Virgin because he knows no Latin, and he fears that she will no listen to any other tongue. Meanwhile, the other monks have bee quarreling as to which of their vocations has the most merit. The Coo alone consoles Jean by relating to him the legend of the humble sag plant, useful in cooking. The quaint story is that the child Jesus wa once refused shelter by the rosebush, but the lowly sage offered its pr tection and has since been valued among herbs. The Cook's son "The Legend of the Sage" (Légende de la sauge) is a favorite with bar tones—

Jean listens to the song open-mouthed and takes new heart. He hir self must have something that would be acceptable to the Church ar the Blessed Virgin.

Act III *The Chapel.* Jean lays aside his monastic dress and puts c his juggler's apparel. He goes before the life-size figure the Virgin, in the Chapel, and since he does not know anything els he prepares to offer to her his little stock in trade—a juggling perfor ance! Spreading out his shabby outfit, he performs his tricks and sin his songs, first begging pardon if they do not suit her. In the midst his performance, the monks enter to celebrate high mass. They rec in horror at this sacrilege and are ready to lay violent hands upon t poor juggler, when suddenly a miracle happens. The image of t Virgin becomes animated, the face smiles, and the arms stretch out protection and benediction. The monks draw back in awe, and Jean, radiant, exclaims, "Now at last I shall know Latin," and dies. Angels appear and the Prior crossing himself says: "We have had a saint among us!"

DON QUIXOTE

(Don Kee-ho'-teh)

(Don Quichotte.) Romantic Opera in Five Acts. Music by Massenet; text by Henri Cain, after the play by Jacques La Lorrain, based on the romance of Cervantes. Monte Carlo, February 19, 1910. New Orleans, January 27, 1912. At the Metropolitan, New York, February , 1914.

SCENE: Spain.
TIME: The Middle Ages.

CAST
DULCINEA (Contralto).
DON QUIXOTE (Bass).
SANCHO PANZA (Baritone).
PEDRO, *burlesquer* (Soprano).
GARCIAS, *burlesquer* (Soprano).
RODRIGUEZ (Tenor).
JUAN (Tenor).
TWO VALETS (Baritone).
TENEBRUN, *chief, and other bandits, friends of Dulcinea, and others.*

ARGUMENT "Don Quixote" is based upon the famous novel of Cervantes and depicts phases in the life of the last of the knights-errant.

Act I *Square in Front of the House of Dulcinea.* A throng praises the beauty of Dulcinea. Into the company ride Don Quixote and his comical companion, Sancho. Night and moonlight. Don Quixote serenades Dulcinea, arousing the jealousy of Juan, a lover of the professional beauty, but the latter appears and prevents a duel. She is amused by the avowals of Don Quixote, and promises to become his beloved if he will recover a necklace stolen from her by brigands.

Act II *On the Way to the Camp of the Brigands.* Here occurs the famous tilt with the windmill.

Act III *Camp of the Brigands.* Don Quixote attacks them. Sancho retreats. The Knight is captured. He expects to be put to death. But his courage, his grave courtesy, and his love for his Dulcinea, deeply impress the bandits. They free him and give him the necklace.

Act IV *Fête at the House of Dulcinea.* To the astonishment of all Don Quixote and Sancho put in their appearance. Dulcinea is delighted to have her necklace returned. The Knight pleads with her to marry him. Dulcinea is so touched by his devotion that she confesses her past life to him, and entreats him to forget her.

Act V *A Forest.* Disillusioned and weary, Don Quixote lies down to die. He bequeaths to his faithful squire the most beautiful of all islands, "The Island of Dreams." It is his proudest possession. As his mind wanders, he beholds the beautiful Dulcinea again. He extends his arms to her, and falls back lifeless.

Critics are agreed that if the music of the first four Acts measured up to that of the last, "Don Quixote" would be frequently heard. As the old hero sings of his "Island of Dreams," the orchestra sustains the powerful basso notes with a delicate, wandering melody (first popularized by Chaliapin). Then the voice of Dulcinea is heard, singing of love and joy. He thrills to it, and his last moments are blissful. Only the faithful Sancho is left disconsolate.

ANDRÉ MESSAGER

Messanger was born in Montlucon, December 30, 1853. He belongs strictly to the modern school and has written many shorter musical pieces; but is known in this country for only one opera, "Madame Chrysanthème." Messager died in 1929.

MADAME CHRYSANTHÈME

(Ma-dam Kris-an-thaym)

Lyric Comedy in a Prologue, Four Acts, and Epilogue. Music by Messager. Book by Hartmann and Alexandre, after the story by Pierre Loti. First produced at the Opéra Comique, Paris, January 26, 189[illegible] In New York, the Metropolitan, by the Chicago Opera Company, January 28, 1920.

ARGUMENT This little love story of a temporary romance in Japan is a rather close parallel to "Madame Butterfly."

Pierre, a French naval officer, confides to his attendant, Yves, that while their ship is stationed in Japanese waters he proposes to contract a temporary marriage with some pretty girl of Nagasaki. He meets Madame Chrysanthème. Kangourou, a matrimonial agent, arranges matters, and the bridal veil is handed to her. While Pierre and his temporary bride are enjoying their honeymoon, his comrades arrive with their own feminine charmers and serenade him.

In the Third Act, a festival is in progress, and Chrysanthème is among the gayest of the gay. But Pierre becomes jealous, thinking she is flirting with Yves, and flies into a rage. Peace is later restored between the young couple, but their happiness is short-lived. The boom of guns aboard ship calls the lieutenant back to duty. Chrysanthème does not cry her heart out, but bears up bravely.

The epilogue is again between the lieutenant and Yves, who mourn for Chrysanthème. Pierre tosses the lotus flowers she has given him into the sea, and prays the gods for forgetfulness.

GUSTAVE CHARPENTIER

Gustave Charpentier is chiefly known for his single opera, "Louise." He was born in Dieuze, Lorraine, June 25, 1860, and received his training in the French schools. He describes "Louise" as a musical romance, saying: "Because in a romance there are two entirely distinct sides, the drama and the description, in my 'Louise' I want to treat these different sides." Charpentier died in 1956.

LOUISE

Dramatic Opera in Four Acts. Music by Gustave Charpentier. Book by the Composer. Opéra Comique, Paris, February 2, 1900. Manhattan Opera House, New York, January 3, 1908. Metropolitan, January 15, 1921.

SCENE: Paris.
TIME: The Present.

CAST Louise, *a sewing girl* (Soprano).
Her Father (Baritone).
Her Mother (Contralto).
Julien, *an artist* (Tenor).
Irma, *a sewing girl* (Contralto).
The King of Fools, *a Bohemian* (Baritone).
Errand Girl (Mezzo-Soprano).
Forewoman (Contralto).
Sewing Girls, Bohemians, Peddlers, Rag-pickers, Grisettes, Gamins, etc.

ARGUMENT "Louise" may be regarded as a bit of canvas belonging to the varied panorama of Paris. It depicts home life among the lower working classes as they come in daily contact with the underworld of the great city. Louise herself personifies the struggle between love and duty; between the instincts of virtue and the desire to be free.

In France "Louise" has achieved greater popularity than any opera since "Carmen." Its cross section of Parisian life, no less than its vivacious, dramatic music, have endeared it. It is also of interest in America as providing the first vehicle for the talents of Mary Garden. As an unknown singer she made her début in it, in Paris, April, 1900, and won fame overnight.

Act I *Garret of a Paris Tenement.* Louise, a sewing girl, has fallen in love with Julien, a young artist whose studio balcony adjoins her window. Julien sings charming serenades, but is an improvident bohemian, like the rest of his class. He nevertheless wishes to marry Louise and has written to her father asking permission, but her mother, a hard-working, practical woman, is violently opposed to the match. She overhears the lovers making plans from their adjacent windows and parts them without ceremony. Louise's father returns home wearied from his day's work, but after supper and a pipe he feels in good humor with the world. He reads Julien's letter and the girl pleads her lover's cause, while her mother as strongly berates it. They quarrel, but the father endeavors to act as peacemaker, although he points out to his daughter the improvidence of Julien. Louise is downcast but promises to try to forget him.

A fine song for tenors is heard early in this Act when Louise asks Julien how he happened to fall in love with her. He replies: "A long, long time I have lived in this room" (Depuis longtemps j'habitais cette chambre)—

Act II *Scene 1. The Road to Montmartre.* It is early morning and Paris is waking up. The last of the prowlers—beggars, thieves, bohemians and street-walkers—are still to be seen. Rag-pickers and newsboys are busy. Servants open windows and shake rugs. Presently Julien and some of his bohemian friends appear. He is planning to elope with Louise, since he cannot obtain her father's consent. Meanwhile she comes by on her way to the shop, escorted by her mother. Julien conceals himself until the latter has gone away, then endeavors to persuade the girl to come with him. She refuses and continues on her way to work.

Scene 2. A Dressmaker's Workshop. Louise and many of her companions are seen busily at work sewing and fitting garments over lay figures. They ply their needles and machines and sing carelessly. One or two tell Louise that she does not look well. Presently a serenader's voice is heard; it is Julien, who will not go away. At first the girls applaud, and then his continued singing grows monotonous. Finally Louise complains of being ill and leaves the room, but the others laugh maliciously as they notice that she is going up the street with Julien.

Act III *A Cottage on the Montmartre.* Julien and Louise have set up an establishment for themselves without consent of either parents or the church. But they justify their conduct on the score of love. They are children of the great city and have a right to be free. Louise voices her joy in a lovely aria, "Ever since the day" (Depuis le jour)—

A group of laughing bohemians pause before the doorway. One of them hangs lanterns from its door and windows. The crowd gathers and the lovers are summoned forth. Then the King of Fools makes an address and crowns Louise as the Muse of Montmartre. In the midst of this revelry a woman pushes her way through the throng, which scatters to right and left. It is Louise's mother come to plead with her daughter. She no longer quarrels, but she says that the father is ill and only Louise's presence can help him. Afterwards she will be allowed to return to Julien. The lovers separate upon these terms, and the girl goes with her mother.

Act IV *The Garret Room.* Louise finds, after she returns home, that she is being held a prisoner. She must sew at home. Her father still treats her affectionately, but insists upon her remaining with them. She says she is a grown woman and has the right to be free. He points out that the freedom she claims is the first step to ruin. In a tender scene between father and daughter, he tries to recall to her the carefree days of her childhood, in a Lullaby (Berceuse) of haunting loveliness—

But his pleas are in vain. Louise cannot forget her lover and the little cottage. At last she seizes her shawl and bursts past her parents to the door. Her mother rushes to the window to call her, while her father pursues her as far as the staircase. But she is gone out of their lives. The old workman shakes his fist at the city which has claimed another victim. "Oh, Paris!" he cries out, heartbroken.

CLAUDE DEBUSSY

Claude Achille Debussy was born in Saint-Germain-en-Laye, near Paris, in 1862. He entered the Paris Conservatory at the age of eleven, and won the Grand Prix de Rome, in 1884, with his one-act cantata, "L'Enfant Prodigue." In Italy he produced a symphonic suite, "Printemps," with only moderate success. This was followed with other suites; then his symphonic poem, "L'Apres-midi d'un Faun" (Afternoon of a Faun) came out, in 1902, to establish him firmly as one of the latter-day French composers to be reckoned with. Three years later came his three symphonic sketches, "La Mer." Ballets followed. His one opera, "Pelléas et Mélisande," extended his fame around the musical world. Debussy died March 26, 1918.

PELLÉAS AND MÉLISANDE

(Pel-lay-as and May-lis-sand)

Lyric Drama in Five Acts. Music by Debussy. Book by Maurice Maeterlinck. Opéra Comique, Paris, April 30, 1902. At the Manhattan Opera House, New York, February 19, 1908, its première in America, with the role of "Melisande" winning acclaim for Mary Garden. Jean Perier sang that of "Pelleas."

SCENE: Allemonde.
TIME: Antiquity.

CAST
ARKEL, *King of Allemonde* (Basso).
GENEVIEVE, *his daughter-in-law* (Soprano).
GOLAUD, *her elder son* (Baritone).
PELLEAS, *her younger son* (Tenor).
MELISANDE, *wife of Golaud* (Soprano).
YNIOLD, *son of Golaud* (Soprano).
A PHYSICIAN (Baritone).
Servants, Blind Beggars, etc.

ARGUMENT "Pelleas and Melisande" is a mystic drama of passion and fate, both text and music being freighted with inner meaning.

Act I *Scene 1. A Fountain in the Forest.* Golaud, a grandson of aged King Arkel, while out hunting discovers a maiden wandering lost and weeping in the forest. She will not tell anything about herself or whence she came, but Golaud, whose wife is dead, persuades her to go with him to the King's court.

Scene 2. Genevieve, daughter of King Arkel, informs him that her son Golaud has taken the strange maiden to wife. He has written his brother, Pelleas, to this effect and asks permission to bring her to court. If it pleases the King a light is to be shown from the tower window; otherwise he will go away. Pelleas is ordered to display the light.

Scene 3. The Castle Gardens. Genevieve shows Melisande (for that is the name given by the strange maiden) the gardens of the castle, but the girl merely shudders and says that it is all old and dark. To divert her mind, Pelleas points out the beacon lights along the shore. She sees a ship sailing away and exclaims that it is her ship. Pelleas, depressed, says that he also is going away. She answers with the plaintive cry, "Why must you go?"

The music so subtly interweaves throughout the action that it is almost impossible to differentiate, or to single out special themes. The composer's style is distinctively his own.

Act II *Scene 1. A Fountain in the Park.* Pelleas cannot tear himself away from this strange girl. He walks with her one day in the park and she seats herself by the edge of a deep pool. She takes off her wedding ring, which she plays with carelessly. It falls into the depths of the water, and Pelleas says that it cannot be recovered. The clock strikes twelve.

Scene 2. Golaud's Chamber. By a curious coincidence, Golaud has met with an accident at the precise moment when the wedding ring fell into the pool. His horse stumbled and fell upon him. Melisande nurses him back to health. He notices that the ring is missing from her finger, and asks her where it is. She answers that she lost it in a cavern by the sea while gathering shells for little Yniold (his son). He commands her to go at once, even though it is nightfall, and search for it. Pelleas can go with her.

Scene 3. The Cavern. Pelleas and Melisande visit the cavern so that the girl will be able to describe it to Golaud. They meet three blind men wandering there and Melisande is frightened. It portends ill fortune.

The instruments as well as the voices again give a vivid picture of setting and action. In the first scene of this Act, the rippling waters of the fountain as they fall into the depths of the pool are mirrored by the orchestra. In the second scene, Golaud describes his accident in the song, "Ah, ah! Tout va bien." Melisande's childish, evasive replies to his questioning follow. Before the last scene there is an orchestral interlude, where we hear again the rippling waters of the fountain. The terrifying roar of the sea sweeps over it.

Act III *Scene 1. Outside Melisande's Balcony.* Melisande combs her long tresses while leaning out of the window and the hair falls in a shimmering mass nearly to the ground. While she combs it she sings an old-time legend which gives the names of the saints who have watched over her. Pelleas comes up a path and stops to fondle the wonderful tresses. He tells her again that he must go away (Il fait beau cette nuit). She begs him again not to desert her, but more in the tones of a child than of a woman. Golaud surprises them, but chides them for acting like a pair of children.

Scene 2. The Castle Vaults. The music takes on a tragic tone, as the "Fate" motive rings out from the orchestra; the interlude closing with a note of "Vengeance." By way of covert warning, Golaud takes his brother Pelleas to the vaults of the castle, showing him the deep silent pits from which no victim could escape.

Scene 3. The Gardens. They return to the gardens and Golaud bluntly cautions Pelleas to be less attentive to Melisande. Pelleas, however, still seems unmindful of his danger. As he comes back into the fresh air again, he exclaims, "Ah, I can breathe again!"

Scene 4. Outside the Window of Melisande's Chamber. It is evening, and the still watchful Golaud questions his little son, Yniold, as to the relations of Pelleas and Melisande. The child replies that they are often together, though they have kissed only once. Golaud lifts the boy up on his shoulders so that he can peer in at the lighted window. Yniold says that Pelleas is there but is not near Melisande. They only look at each other with tears in their eyes. Golaud grasps his son so tensely that the child exclaims in pain.

Act IV *Scene 1. A Corridor.* Melisande agrees to meet Pelleas for a farewell interview by the fountain. She is encountered by the aged King, who speaks kindly to her. But after he is gone, her husband enters, greeting her rudely and violently.

During this change of scene a lengthy interlude is played. The "Fate" motive again rings out dramatically; with moments of tenderer passages identified with Melisande. The music becomes gloomy and heavy with despair as the curtain rises.

Scene 2. The Fountain. Pelleas and Melisande meet by the fountain and Pelleas pours forth a torrent of love. Melisande listens half hysterical. Something moves in the shadows behind them. She is sure that it is her husband, but she clings to her lover in despair. Golaud rushes forward and transfixes Pelleas with his sword, and then turns to pursue the fleeing Melisande.

Act V *Melisande's Bedchamber.* Melisande has given birth to a child, but her life hangs upon a thread. Golaud attends upon her, remorseful for what he has done. She does not seem to remember. He questions her about Pelleas, but she returns evasive replies. She has loved him, but she is innocent of wrong-doing. Arkel and the physician bid him cease troubling her. She is shown her child, but is too weak to hold it. The servants enter silently. Golaud bids them begone, but they only fall upon their knees in prayer. The physician looks at his patient and says that they are right. Melisande is dead.

L'ENFANT PRODIGUE

(Lon-fant Pro-deeg)

(The Prodigal Son.) A "lyrical episode" by Debussy. Words by Ernest Guiraud. Sheffield Festival, England, 1908. Covent Garden, 1910. Boston, 1910.

SCENE: Village on Lake Gennasereth.
TIME: First Century.

CAST LIA (Soprano).
SIMEON, *her husband* (Basso).
AZÄEL, *their errant son* (Tenor).

ARGUMENT This "lyrical episode," with which Debussy won his first prize, is much more conventional and influenced by tradition than are the later, more typical compositions by which the composer took his place as the founder of the impressionist school of music in France. None the less, there are here traces of that marked originality of conception and courage in method which were to set the composer in the very front rank while he was still a comparatively young man.

The hour is early in the morning; the season is the time of harvest. Far off, joyful chants are heard. Lia enters alone, inconsolably mourning her son Azäel, who has left home, and whom she hardly dares to hope that she will ever see again on earth. Simeon comes, and rebukes her for this unavailing and untimely sorrow. A pageant of youths and maidens appears, followed by servants bearing garlands of flowers, fruits, and horns of plenty. They perform a choric dance and then, headed by Simeon and Lia, depart, their singing dying slowly away in the distance. When the stage is clear, Azäel enters, footsore, travel-stained, and weary. He has watched the dance from the shelter of the low-swung boughs, and has recognized his brother and sister among the dancers. Overwhelmed with remorse, he thinks of the days of his innocence, when he used to sit by this same lake with his head against his mother's heart. He will lie down here and die, within sight of the well-remembered village which he has neither the courage nor the strength to enter.

Lia now returns. She cannot bear the tumult of rejoicing, which frets her stricken spirit. Catching sight of Azäel on the ground, she thinks at first that he is a poor wayfarer, and goes to help him. Then she recognizes her long-lost son and folds him in her arms, with passionate words of love, and pity, and pardon. The servants reappear, and she tells them that this is the son of their master. Then Simeon himself returns, but, less ready to forgive than his wife, he stands looking down in silence at the prostrate form of his son, uttering only a hurried prayer to Heaven for guidance. Lia throws herself at his feet, imploring forgiveness for their child, and the father relents. He bids the servants make the glad tidings known with sounds of cymbal and tabor, and orders that the wine jars shall be filled and the fatted calf slain. Then Azäel rises, he and his parents are folded in one another's arms, and all three voice an exultant song of thanks to the Lord God of Israel.

CAMILLE ERLANGER

Erlanger was born May 25, 1863, at Paris; and died in the same city, in 1919. He studied under Leo Delibes at the Paris Conservatory, and won the Grand Prix de Rome, in 1888, for his cantata "Velleda." He wrote numerous short pieces, cantatas, and four operas: "Kermaria," (1897); "Aphrodite," (1906); "Noel," (1906); and "L'Aube Rouge," which had its première at Rouen, in 1912.

APHRODITE

(Aph-ro-dy'-te)

A lyric drama in five acts and seven scenes, after the story by Pierre Louys. Adapted by Louis de Gramont. Music by Erlanger. Opéra Comique, Paris, March 23, 1906, with the American singer, Mary Garden, achieving fame both for herself and the opera. She sang the role of "Aphrodite" also at the American première, in the Metropolitan, February 27, 1920. Edward Johnson, in his first season at "the Met," supported her, in "Demetrios."

ARGUMENT An opera rich in scenic possibilities. Its appeal is directed as much to the eye and the æsthetic sense, as to the ear. The scene is Alexandria; the time, 50 B.C.

The curtain rises to disclose a busy hour of ancient Egypt, upon a crowded wharf at Alexandria. There are citizens of every grade and calling. Some ply their trades, others are there merely for diversion. Rhodis and Myrto play their flutes while Theano dances. All make way for Demetrios, the famous sculptor. A Jewish fortune-teller reads his hand, predicting crime and tragedy because of a woman. At this juncture the beautiful courtesan, Chrysis, enters. Demetrios pays her attention, but she tells him that, to win her favor, he must bring her three precious gifts—the mirror of Bacchis, the ivory comb of Touni, and the pearl necklace of Aphrodite. The sculptor has become so infatuated that he determines to obtain them.

Acts II, III, and IV relate his adventures in quest of these treasures. The people are especially angry at the spoliation of the necklace of Aphrodite. In a fit of compunction Demetrios asks Chrysis if she will wear her trophies in public. She consents. Act V is in two scenes:

Scene 1. The Lighthouse. While the throng gathers to discuss the three crimes that have closely followed each other, and pray the goddess for forgiveness, they suddenly perceive a female figure standing out in relief on the balcony of the lighthouse. She wears the comb in her hair, the necklace around her throat, and holds in her hand the mirror. At first they think it is Aphrodite come to them in person, but soon realize that it is Chrysis. She is seized and thrown into prison.

Scene 2. A Prison. Chrysis is condemned to death, and a poisoned cup is sent her to drink. Demetrios arrives only after she has died. In a vision Demetrios himself sees his fate at the hands of Aphrodite.

PAUL DUKAS

Dukas is a modern French composer, who was born at Paris, October 1, 1865. His only opera that reached the American stage is "Ariane et Barbe-Bleue." Dukas died in Paris, May 17, 1935.

ARIANE ET BARBE-BLEUE

(Air-ee-an ā Barb-bluh)

(Ariane and Bluebeard.) Dramatic Opera in Three Acts. Music by Paul Dukas. Book by Maurice Maeterlinck, after the tale of "Blue Beard." Opéra Comique, Paris, May 10, 1907. New York, March 3, 1911.

SCENE: A Medieval Castle.
TIME: Middle Ages.

CAST BLUEBEARD (Basso).
ARIANE, *his sixth wife* (Mezzo-Soprano).
NURSE (Contralto).
Bluebeard's five earlier wives:
SELYSETTE (Mezzo-Soprano).
YGRAINE (Soprano).
MELISANDE (Soprano).
BELLANGERE (Soprano).
ALLADINE (Silent).
Three Peasants, Crowd of Rustics, etc.

ARGUMENT The old story of Bluebeard and his wives has been embellished by Maeterlinck with touches of mysticism, which are reflected in the music of the opera. Ariane, the determined wife, may be called a foretype of the New Woman.

Recorded music: "Oh! mes clairs diamants" from Act I; and "Ah! ce n'est ce pas encore la clarte veritable," from Act II.

Act I *Great Hall in Bluebeard's Castle.* Despite the ugly reputation of Bluebeard, he has found a new wife in Ariane. She has heard that he has done away with five wives, but cannot believe that he has murdered them; it is her mission to discover his secret. As the curtain rises, the angry roar of the crowd outside is heard. They do not want the ogre to have another victim. Unmoved by all this clamor, Ariane enters with her nurse. She has been entrusted with seven keys. Six are of silver, and the last is of gold. It unlocks the one forbidden door. The nurse opens one after another the six silver locks, and in each room finds a delightful surprise—jewels of rare beauty gush out in streams. But Ariane is not satisfied. Her mission is to find what is behind the forbidden door. The nurse begs her to desist, but she turns the golden lock. The door opens and they hear the distant groans of women. Before they can close it, Bluebeard enters, saying coolly, "You, too!" He tells her he will yet forgive her if she will desist, but she defies him. Enraged, he bids her follow him, but the nurse, hearing the renewed tumult of the crowd outside, rushes to the door and admits them. Bluebeard draws his sword and prepares to defend himself from their attack, when Ariane interposes, telling the rioters to disperse, her husband is doing her no harm. They fall back before her and she closes and fastens the door.

Act II *An Underground Chamber.* Still braving Bluebeard's anger, Ariane and the nurse have been left in the vault leading from the seventh door, but Ariane is undismayed; she is determined to rescue her husband's victims. By the light of the flickering lamp, carried by the nurse, she discovers the forms of women lying huddled upon the floor. They prove to be the five missing wives, who are still alive, but leading a wretched existence. Ariane encourages them, and looks about for some avenue of escape. The lamp goes out, but they see a faint glow at one end of the chamber. It proves to be a door leading to the outer world, which they break through, and the whole party pass out to liberty.

Act III *Great Hall in the Castle.* The castle and grounds are enchanted, so the wives cannot escape. They wander back into the great hall and amuse themselves by dressing up in the finery which they find lying about in profusion. Ariane is showing them how to regain their lost beauty. Presently the nurse enters in terror to say that Bluebeard, who has been absent, is on his way back to the castle, and that the villagers are lying in wait for him. It is as she fears, and although he has a bodyguard, they are overcome in the mêlée and Bluebeard is wounded. The crowd seize him and bind him hand and foot, and are about to throw him into the moat, when Ariane and the other women interpose. She persuades the villagers to bring him into the hall, stating that she is the one most concerned and should have the decision of his fate. In the end they leave him and withdraw. Ariane stoops and cuts his bonds, although the others are fearful. Then she dresses his wounds, which prove slight. He rises and looks slowly from one to another of the group, but makes no effort to molest them. Ariane approaches and bids him farewell; her mission is ended, now she will leave him. He tries to detain her, pleading his love, but she persists in her decision. The other women are given an opportunity to go with her, but they decide to cast their lots with Bluebeard.

HENRI FEVRIER

Fevrier was born in Paris, October 2, 1876. He studied in the Conservatory there under Faure and Massenet. He wrote shorter pieces for voice and orchestra, and, in 1906, won attention for his opera "Le Roi Aveugle." "Gismonda" was produced in 1915; "La Damnation de Blanche-Fleur," in 1920; "Aphrodite," in 1920; "La Femme Nue," in 1932; and several operettas. His chief fame in America, however, rests upon his best work, "Monna Vanna." He died in 1957.

MONNA VANNA

(Mo-na Van-na)

Romantic Opera in Four Acts. Music by Fevrier. Book by Maurice Maeterlinck. Paris, 1909. First time in America, at Boston, 1913. New York, 1914, by the Manhattan Opera Company headed by Mary Garden and Lucien Muratore.

SCENE: Pisa.
TIME: The Fifteenth Century.

CAST PRINZIVALLE, *Commander of the Florentine Army* (Tenor).
GUIDO COLONNA, *Commander of the Pisan forces* (Basso).
BORSO, *Pisan sub-officer* (Baritone).
TORELLO, *Pison sub-officer* (Baritone).
VEDIO, *Secretary to Prinzivalle* (Tenor).
TRIVULZIO, *an envoy* (Baritone).
MARCO VANNA, *a Pisan* (Basso).
MONNA VANNA, *his daughter, wife of Colonna* (Soprano).
Citizens, Soldiers, etc.

ARGUMENT The plot of "Monna Vanna" is rather thin, but is based upon an historical incident. It is a counterplot of chivalry and jealousy.

Act I *Office of the Pisan Commander.* Pisa is being besieged by a Florentine army under the command of Prinzivalle. The garrison is in sore straits for food and ammunition. Prinzivalle informs Colonna, the Pisan general, that he will deal leniently with the Pisans if Colonna will send his beautiful wife, Monna Vanna, for an overnight visit to Prinzivalle's tent. She is informed of these terms and professes herself ready to go, to help her city.

Act II *Prinzivalle's Tent.* A plot by Trivulzio, an enemy of Prinzivalle, is thwarted. Monna then enters as agreed. She states that her only purpose is to save her city. The general respects her intentions and treats her as an honored guest.

Act III *A Square in Pisa.* Monna Vanna returns, but her husband distrusts her. His rage is kindled further when he discovers Prinzivalle in the city. The latter has had to flee from treachery in his own camp, but Colonna thinks it is because of an intrigue with Monna. The latter sees that she can save Prinzivalle only by falling in apparently with her husband's evil designs. Prinzivalle is accordingly cast into prison.

Act IV *A Dungeon.* Monna goes to free Prinzivalle from prison. They confess their love for each other, and flee forth into the world together.

GISMONDA

An opera in four acts, which had its first American performance in Chicago, in 1919 with Mary Garden and the Chicago Opera Company. It was brought to New York as the opener for the Lexington Theatre, January 27, 1919. It was only moderately successful. The story follows the play by Sardou.

Gismonda, Duchess of Athens, promises to become the wife of anyone who will rescue her son from the pit of a tiger, into which he has been thrown by a conspirator, who thus plans to help another man, Zacario Franco, seize the Duchy. But after Almerio, a falconer, slays the beast and brings her the boy, she recants from her promise; she will instead spend a night with him, as reward. Zacario spies upon her; she kills him; Almerio to shield her says that he is the slayer; and the repentant lady clears him of guilt and proclaims him as her husband.

ALBERT WOLFF

Albert Wolff, born in 1884, in Paris, is known as both conductor and composer. After studying at the Conservatory he showed such aptitude with the baton that, at the age of twenty-seven, he was appointed second conductor at the Opéra Comique, to which post he returned after the First World War. He was conductor of French repertoire at the Metropolitan Opera House (1919–1923), then resigned to return as first conductor and musical director of the Comique in Paris. His chief operas are: "Le Marchand de Masques" (Nice, 1904); and "L'Oiseau Bleu" (New York, 1919).

THE BLUE BIRD

(L'Oiseau Bleu.) Lyric Opera in Four Acts and Eight Scenes. Music by Wolff. Book by Maurice Maeterlinck. Metropolitan, New York, December 27, 1919. In the cast were Florence Easton, Leon Rothier, Mary Ellis, and Raymonde Delaunois.

SCENE: Fairyland.
TIME: The Present.

CAST MYTYL / TYLTYL { *The woodcutter's children* { Tenor. / Soprano.
FATHER TYL, *a woodcutter* (Baritone).
MOTHER TYL, *his wife* (Contralto).
BERYLUNE, *a fairy* (Soprano).
GRANDMOTHER TYL (Contralto).
GRANDFATHER TYL (Basso).
MATERNAL LOVE (Soprano).
JOY OF UNDERSTANDING (Soprano).
LIGHT (Soprano).
FATHER TIME (Basso).
BREAD (Tenor).
MME. BERLINGOT (Mezzo-Soprano).
A Little Girl, Two Lovers, Joy of Being Just, Joy of Seeing the Beautiful, Fairy, Night, Cat, Dog, Happiness, a Child, Sugar, Fire, Other Children, etc.

ARGUMENT Maeterlinck's allegorical story for children and those of larger growth, "The Blue Bird," which was originally brought out as a play, has been utilized in this pleasing opera. The plot follows the book faithfully, only making certain omissions required for a musical setting.

Act I *Scene 1. Room in the Woodcutter's Cottage.* It is Christmas Eve, and the two children of the woodcutter, Tyltyl and Mytyl, awake during the night and sit up in bed to watch the festivities in the great house across the way. Suddenly the door latch is lifted; a little, humpbacked woman enters, who introduces herself as the Fairy, Berylune. She tells the children that her little daughter is ill and unhappy, and asks them if they will go in quest of the Blue Bird of Happiness. They agree, and she gives Tyltyl a green cap with a diamond which, turned one way, enables him to see the future. Tyltyl turns the diamond and immediately everything in the cottage is transformed. The furniture comes to life; the door of the clock opens, and the Hours come out and begin to sing and dance. The loaves of Bread become endowed with souls which, in the forms of little men, are pursued by Fire, a sullen, malicious fellow. The Cat and Dog are changed into persons. The Spinning Wheel hums madly. Water flows from the sink tap and begins to fight with Fire. The Lamp falls from the table with a crash, and its flame turns into a fairy of great beauty; she is Light.

Just then a loud knock is heard. It is the woodcutter returning. Tyltyl quickly reverses the diamond and the enchantment ceases. Berylune asks who will accompany the children on their mission to seek the Blue Bird. All except the Dog and Light refuse; but the time is so short that all have to go. The room grows dark, and when Daddy and Mummy Tyl enter they find the children sound asleep.

Scene 2. The Land of Memory. As the mists lift, the children see a peasant's hut and their dead grandparents sitting on a doorstep. Their little brothers and sisters come out of the house to greet them. Tyltyl catches a Blackbird which at first seems blue, but soon grows dull black. They regretfully go on their way.

Act II *Scene 1. The Palace of Night.* Light shows them the way to the Palace of Night. Tyltyl challenges Night and demands the Blue Bird. Night gives him the keys to gloomy caverns wherein dwell the spirits of evil. Tyltyl opens a forbidden door to Destiny, and sees a beautiful garden. Myriads of blue birds hover about, but when the children catch some of them and show them to Light, the birds are lifeless. As they go into the forest, the Oak tree threatens them with death because they have presumed to catch the Blue Bird—the secret of man's happiness. Light comes to rescue the children.

Scene 2. The Garden of Happiness. In a fabulously sweet garden of peace and serenity they are greeted by a band of little Joys which laugh and dance, but do not aid them. Other greater Joys appear, among them the Joy of Understanding and the Joy of Being Just.

Act III *The Cemetery.* The children enter alone in the darkness. At midnight Tyltyl turns the magic diamond, and the grave stones become changed to a fairly dell—the kingdom of the Future where they meet with the souls of children waiting to be born. Fathe Time summons them one by one. Light now tells the children that sh has secured the Blue Bird and it is safely hidden under her cloak. Sh bids Tyltyl turn the diamond again so that they can escape.

Act IV *Scene 1. Doorway of the Woodcutter's Home.* The tim has come for leave-taking between the children and their com rades, Dog, Cat, Bread, Light, and all the rest. They have come back to the home of Tyltyl and Mytyl, but without the Blue Bird. Light and the other souls bid the children farewell.

Scene 2. Room in the Woodcutter's Cottage. It is morning. Mummy Tyl comes in to awaken the children. They begin to tell her of their strange adventures, and she is alarmed, fearing they are ill. As they talk, a neighbor comes in to ask the children if they will not lend their pet bird to her little girl who is sick. Tyltyl climbs up on a chair to get the dove, and exclaims, "Why it's blue! It's our Blue Bird!" Nevertheless he gives it to her; and later the neighboring child brings it back. She is well and happy. But as they play, the bird escapes and flies away. The children ask the audience, if they find it, to please give it back. "We need it to be happy later on," they say entreatingly.

RUSSIA

HISTORICAL PREFACE

Although the roots of Russian opera reach back as far as the eighteenth century, the western world has become familiar with it only within the past fifty years. Few of the works have come to our stages, the Russian ballet making us familiar with Slavonic music, technique and acting before their operas. The composers were merely names in reference books, and even with foremost composers, only one or two works have been performed abroad. Rachmaninoff is authority for the statement that thirteen works by Rimsky-Korsakoff still await production in America.

The pioneer in the Slavonic school was Glinka (1804–57), who wrote a patriotic opera, "A Life for the Czar," which won such lasting regard at home that it is said to have been performed regularly as a season-opener in Moscow and St. Petersburg so long as there was an imperial house. His "Russlan and Ludmilla" is also marked by national and folk touches. Glinka's influence upon later composers has been profound.

With Dargomijsky (1813–68) we reach the threshold of modern Russian opera. His "Russalska" followed a patriotic theme. His "The Water-Sprite" and "The Stone Guest"—the latter reminiscent of Mozart's "Don Giovanni"—are still heard occasionally in Russia.

Rubinstein (1829–95), more famous abroad as a pianist, was the composer of several operas quite successful in their day. His "Feramors" and "Nero" are still remembered; while others such as two Biblical works, "The Tower of Babel" and "The Maccabees," are forgotten.

Borodin (1834–87) won renown as a chemist as well as musician. His "Prince Igor" was one of the first of Russian operas to win and hold attention in other countries.

César Cui (1835–1918) is still unfortunately little known in America, although he lived to an old age and wrote much for the stage. He was also an authority on engineering, teaching this subject in military schools and writing textbooks on fortifications. He championed the cause of the Young Russians and won the nickname of "Musical Nihilist." His operas include: "William Radcliff" (1869); "Angele" (1876); "The Prisoner of the Caucasus" (1883); "The Saracen" (1899); and others ending with "The Captain's Daughter" (1909).

Moussorgsky (1839–81) has become increasingly known to Europe and America. A sketch of his life is given in later pages.

With Rimsky-Korsakoff (1844–1908) we come to the most dominant influence of the modern school. This is due both to the versatility of his talent and the poetry of his themes, which are not overshadowed by the (often gloomy) Slavonic tradition. His "Sadko" stretches its wings as far off as India. He wins agreeable fame, likewise, for the ready aid he gave his contemporaries.

The single figure who challenges his supremacy is Tschaikowsky, a composer of great fecundity and brilliance. His worldwide fame, however, rests upon his symphonies and shorter pieces, rather than his operas. Only one or two of the latter, such as "Eugéne Onégin" and "Pique Dame" have thus far reached an American stage.

More recent composers are still only names to us. We find such men as Napravnik, an organist and director who has guided the production of Imperial Opera, but not make striking contributions of his own; "Harold" being one of his best, followed by "Francesca da Rimini" and a few others. Blaramberg wrote five operas in all, including "The Mummers," a comic opera, and the more ambitious, "The Roussalka-Maiden." Arensky's work is more highly regarded at home. His "A Dream on the Volga" and "Raphael" won the praise of critics and fellow musicians. A more familiar name to us is Rachmaninoff, but as a distinguished pianist and composer for that instrument. He wrote a one-act opera, "Aleko," which had the honor of being produced at the Imperial Opera in Moscow, in 1873.

A more modern figure is that of Igor Stravinsky (b. 1882) who is more famous for his orchestral works in advanced style than for operas. In fact, his works for the stage are more frequently ballet and pantomime. Still another contemporary is Serge Prokofieff (b. 1891). Further notice of these two will be found in later pages.

There are still others in the list, some of whom, we hope, will become more than names to us in succeeding years. The last to challenge attention is Shostakovich, a contemporary writer of symphonies who has achieved sensational success in that field. His opera, "Lady Macbeth," produced in Russia, in 1940, has been hailed as "the most successful written thus far by a Soviet-Russian composer."

The examples of Russian opera included in the present volume are those most likely to appear in our repertory. For convenience they are all included under Grand Opera, and such classification is not wide of the mark, for it is only rarely in the earlier works that one encounters lighter moments on their stage. The roots of Slav music under centuries of oppression were sad, often tragic. Doubtless in the days of troubadours and minstrelsy, the peasantry delighted in their songs and dances—even as they do today. But both Church and State frowned upon any frivolity. In the first centuries of the Christian era, so earnest were the monks in their strife against paganism that songs, dances, and spectacles were anathematized. It is said that as late as the seventeenth century such things were excluded even from the Czars' coronations.

Professor Milioukhov, in his "Sketch for a History of Russian Culture," quotes from one of these medieval moralists the following cheerful thought: "Laughter does not edify or save us; on the contrary, it is the ruin of edification. Laughter displeases the Holy Spirit and drives out virtue, because it makes men forget death and eternal punishment. Lord, put mirth way from me; give me rather tears and lamentations." So effective was this dread teaching, that another monk records with sour satisfaction: "There was silence in all the land of Russia!" No wonder there was, when such propaganda was added to the burden of daily life undergone by the serfs and peasantry.

And yet, perhaps because it was officially forbidden, mirth and laughter did not die. It was "bootlegged" into the remoter districts by wandering bands of musicians—the "Guslee" or guzli players; and the "Skomorokhi" or actors. These were welcomed by common folk and nobles alike, to while away the tedium of the long winter nights. Plays, puppet shows, ballets, and other such entertainment followed, some of it crude, some coarse, and some, strange to say, spiritual; but as a whole pointing the way to a lighter form of stage play, interpreted with and without music.

The clergy, however, were still so intolerant that, when Czar Alexis Mikhailovich summoned musicians to his Court and encouraged a national theater, the Patriarch Joseph hurled the curses of the Church at him (1649) and ordered all the musical instruments in Moscow to be seized and burned in the market place. Only those belonging to the Czar were spared. The Czar Alexis, undismayed, continued to encourage the stage, and there is a record of 1664 which says: "Our Musique-master composed a Handsome Comedie in prose, which was acted in our house." Another play ordered by this Czar dealt with the Biblical story of Esther.

It required another hundred years for the Russian stage to take on what may be termed a native form, and for its musical side to receive any consistent development. The operas which gradually took shape were of Biblical, legendary, or historical trend, with music as savage and violent as the text. One of the first Russian composers to attempt a lighter vein was Fomin (1741–1800). He wrote several operas in the folk style, one being called "The Good Maiden," and another, "The

Miller," which had a wide popular success owing to its folk tunes and dance melodies interspersed with more serious strains. A third, which should have some interest for us, was called "The Americans," but dealt with our Indians, as Russia visualized them.

About this time, the end of the eighteenth century, the Russian Court was overrun with foreign composers, chiefly Italian and French; but as this was a foreign graft, we will not try to chronicle it. However, it did have the effect of putting the leaven in the Russian bread.

We find also on record that the first "opera house" was built by the Empress Anne, in St. Petersburg, but was destroyed by fire in 1749. It was not devoted exclusively to musical plays, however. A new building was opened in the year 1759.

A distinctive feature of the Russian school is that of pantomime. Like the ballet, in which the Russian artists also excel, it provides the dual appeal of bodily motion and instrumental music. Using only these means it produces an extraordinary dramatic power.

The distinguishing trait of Russian opera, as indeed of its songs and other musical expressions, is what may be styled the primal element. It is redolent of the life of the people and of the soil.

MICHAEL IVANOVITCH GLINKA

Glinka, who is of the early modern school, was born near Smolensk, in 1804. He studied the piano and the violin under Russian teachers, then spent four years in Italy, partly on account of health. He is credited with writing the first national opera for his country, in "A Life for the Czar" (1836). In his orchestral compositions he was the forerunner of Tschaikowsky and Rimsky-Korsakoff. His second opera, "Russlan and Ludmilla" (1842) is noteworthy in its introduction of oriental music, a practice followed by other Russian composers. He lived in Spain from 1845 to 1847, there writing two Spanish overtures: "Jota Aragonesa" and "Noche en Madrid." Other works are for the piano. Glinka died in 1857.

RUSSLAN AND LUDMILLA

Russian Opera in Five Acts. Music by Glinka. Text based upon a poem by Pushkin. St. Petersburg, 1842.

ARGUMENT Although this opera has not yet been produced in America, its brilliant and colorful overture has long been esteemed by orchestras. This and a "Patter Song," popularized by Chaliapin are familiar to listeners of recordings.

The curtain rises upon a scene of festivity. Prince Svetozar is giving a reception to suitors for the hand of his daughter, Ludmilla. The visitors include: Russlan, a native nobleman; Ratmir, a Tartar prince; and Farlaf, a Varangian chief, but a coward at heart. Ludmilla favors Russlan; the god of love, Lel, is invoked; but just then a clap of thunder is heard, and the lights go out. When they return, the Princess is missing. Her father promises her hand to the one who will bring her back unharmed.

The Second Act takes place in the cavern of Finn, the wizard. Russlan learns from him that the maiden is in the clutches of Chernomor, a villainous dwarf. The evil fairy, Naina, may also interfere with him, says Finn. In a second scene, Russlan searches for magical weapons on a battlefield, which will aid him to free Ludmilla.

The Third Act is laid in the enchanted palace of Naina. She has promised her aid to the timorous Farlaf. To aid her plot, she has imprisoned Ratmir, the Tartar prince. Three Persian damsels sing to him a siren song. He is also visited by Gorislava, a former sweetheart whom he has abandoned, and she now pleads with him to return. Russlan, too, is in danger of listening to the songs of the three sirens, but Finn shields him.

In the Fourth Act, the dwelling of the dwarf Chernomor, Ludmilla is seen a prey to despair. A ballet is danced to divert her. It is interrupted by the entrance of Russlan, who employs his magical sword to overcome the dwarf. But the Princess has been sent into a trance-like slumber, from which Russlan cannot awaken her. He carries her away, still unconscious.

In the Fifth Act, Russlan makes use of a magic ring. As he places it upon Ludmilla's finger, she awakens; her father again bestows her hand upon the knight of her choice, and the curtain falls amid melody and rejoicing.

Recorded music: overture; Farlaff's "Rondo," sung by Chaliapin; and an aria by Gorislava, "O, my Ratmir!"

ALEXANDRE BORODIN

Borodin was born in St. Petersburg, Nov. 12, 1834, and died there Feb. 28, 1887. He was equally famed as a scientist and musician, being professor of chemistry, Academy of Medicine, St. Petersburg. As he said: "In winter I can only compose when I am too unwell to give my lectures. At Christmas (1886) I had influenza, so I stayed at home and wrote the Thanksgiving Chorus in the last act of 'Igor.'" He never finished this opera, however. It was completed by Rimsky-Korsakoff and Glazounoff, and presented in 1890, three years after his death. His many other activities prevented Borodin from fully realizing his talents as a composer. He wrote two symphonies, two quartets for strings some shorter pieces for the piano, and only one opera, "Prince Igor," which, however, has maintained high rank among Russian operas.

PRINCE IGOR

(Prince Ee'-gor)

Dramatic Opera in Prologue and Four Acts. Book and Music by Alexandre Borodin. Imperial Opera House, St. Petersburg, October 23, 1890. New York, the Metropolitan, December 30, 1915.

SCENE: Russia and Siberia.

TIME: 1185.

CAST PRINCE IGOR SVIATOSLAVITCH (Baritone).
JAROSLAVNA, *his second wife* (Soprano).
VLADIMIR, *his son by his first wife* (Tenor).
PRINCE GALITSKY, *brother of Prince Igor* (Basso).
KONTCHAK, *a Khan of Tartar* (Basso).
KONTCHAKOVNA, *his daughter* (Contralto).
OVLOUR, *a Tartar soldier* (Tenor).
SCOULA, *a minstrel* (Basso).
EROCHKA, *a minstrel* (Tenor).
NURSE (Soprano).
YOUNG TARTAR GIRL (Soprano).
Russians, Tartars, Soldiers, Courtiers, etc.

ARGUMENT A tale of early Russian history, which is more concerned with manners and customs than with historic incident. The opera is full of color and sentiment, and furnishes the composer with an excellent medium for contrast between native life and oriental, which are often closely allied. Folk music, exotic dances, comedy, tragedy alternate.

The Overture is marked with spirit and fire. An impressive allegro movement is followed by a rapid folk dance; then a lovely, more subdued aria, "No sleep, no rest," heard later in the score; all leading up to a crashing climax as the curtain rises.

Prologue *Market Place of Poultvle, the seat of Prince Igor.* Just as Prince Igor of Seversk is starting out at the head of his army to crush the Tartars, an eclipse of the sun occurs. This is regarded as a bad omen, and the people urge him to postpone his expedition, but he is determined to proceed. He takes with him his son, Vladimir, and commends his wife to the care of his brother, Prince Galitsky, who is also left at the head of the government.

Act I *Scene 1. Courtyard of Prince Galitsky's Mansion.* No sooner has Prince Igor departed, than the regent, Galitsky, tries to overthrow him. There is feasting and carousing as Galitsky sings a wild song telling his followers what he would do for them, if he were Governor: "Song of Prince Galitsky"—

Some timid girls approach to beg him to release one of their number who has been abducted; but he boasts that he himself is the abductor, to their further fright. His scoundrelly rule is aided and abetted by the minstrels, Scoula and Erochka.

Scene 2. Apartment in Palace of Prince Igor. While her husband is away at the wars, the Princess Jaroslavna contemplates sadly her own loneliness and the dissoluteness of the court under Igor's brother's reckless misrule. Her mood is reflected in an expressive aria, "Song of Jaroslavna"—

The same group of maidens enter, who had pleaded with Galitsky to release one of their friends; they ask her protection. When her brother-in-law enters the room she upbraids him bitterly for his perfidy and in a stormy scene orders him from her presence. At this moment a messenger enters with the news that Igor's army has been defeated, he and his son are prisoners, and the Tartars are marching against Poultvle. The news of this disaster causes the people to renew their loyalty, and rally to the defense of Jaroslavna.

Act II *Camp of the Tartars.* The beautiful daughter of Kontchak, the Tartar prince, has enslaved the prisoner of war, Vladimir, much more completely than his soldiers could have done. Vladimir, indeed, is becoming reconciled to his captivity, since it brings him near to her. He lingers before her tent, singing a serenade. Igor, however is anything but pleased with his fate, although his captor has treated him with every consideration. He is offered a means of escape by Ovlour, a Christian soldier, but declines to take advantage of the Khan' chivalry. The Act ends with an elaborate banquet given by the Tartar prince in honor of his royal captive. Here is heard the familiar "Polovetzki Dance"—at first dreamy and sensuous, but mounting by degree to a savage turbulence:

Act III *Same as Act II.* Victorious soldiers return to camp, bringin trophies from the conquest of Poultvle. At the tidings of th overthrow of his capital, Igor can no longer refuse to escape. While th soldiers are dividing the booty, Ovlour plies them with drink, and in th resulting orgy he and Igor prepare to flee. The Khan's daughter di covers their plans and entreats Vladimir to stay. He hesitates, and eprimanded by his father. However, as the party sets forth, she clings o the young prince and holds him back. Igor and Ovlour depart withut him. When the escape is discovered, the soldiers are ready to kill ladimir, but the Khan accepts the situation philosophically. "Since he old falcon has taken flight, we must chain the young falcon by giving im a mate," he says, and bestows upon him the hand of his daughter.

ct IV *Scene 1. Jaroslavna's Palace.* Jaroslavna sings a touching lament for her lost husband and despoiled country. But as he gazes out over the ravaged fields, two horsemen are seen approachng. They are Igor and his faithful attendant, Ovlour. Husband and ife are reunited, and in the joy of home-coming much of the intervenng sorrow is forgotten. Igor plans to rehabilitate his country.

Scene 2. The Kremlin. As Igor and Jaroslavna enter the Kremlin o give public thanks, they encounter the two rogues, Scoula and rochka, who have been prime movers in the regent's misgovernment. hey know that they will suffer if caught, so forestall discovery by ringng the bells to announce publicly the restoration of Prince Igor. heir audacity prevents their punishment, and the opera ends pleasntly, amid popular rejoicing.

MODESTE MOUSSORGSKY

Moussorgsky was born at Karevo, March 28, 1839. His first lessons n the piano were with his mother. In 1852 he entered a school for nsigns, but retained his interest in music. Later he came in touch ith Borodin and Rimsky-Korsakoff, and with others of a little group ntroduced a new school of Russian music. He wrote chorals, songs, iano pieces, and an orchestra suite, and three operas—"Boris Godouoff," "Khovantchina" and a folk opera, "The Fair of Sorochintzy." ome of his work was left unfinished. Moussorgsky's last years were ent in poverty, due partly to dissipation. He died on his birthday, Iarch 28, 1881.

BORIS GODOUNOFF

(Bo'-ris Go'-do-nof)

Russian National Musical Drama, in Prologue and Four Acts. Book d Music by Moussorgsky. After the historical drama by Pushkin.

St. Petersburg, January 24, 1874. The Metropolitan, New York, November 19, 1913. The early version, which was lengthy, was revised after the composer's death by his friend, Rimsky-Korsakoff. The character of Boris afforded a notable vehicle for the Russian basso, Chaliapin.

SCENE: Russia.
TIME: 1598–1605.

CAST
BORIS GODOUNOFF, *the Czar* (Baritone).
FEODOR, *his son* (Mezzo-Soprano).
XENIA, *his daughter* (Soprano).
NURSE (Contralto).
MARINA, *a courtesan* (Mezzo-Soprano).
PRINCE SCHOUISKY (Tenor).
TCHELLAKOFF, *Secretary of the Duma* (Baritone).
PIMEN, *a monk* (Basso).
GREGORY, *the pretended Dimitri* (Tenor).
WARLAAM, *a vagabond* (Basso).
MISSAIL, *a vagabond* (Tenor).
A SIMPLETON (Tenor).
POLICE OFFICER (Basso).
COURT OFFICER (Tenor).
INNKEEPER (Tenor).
LOVITZKY, *a Jesuit* (Basso).
TCHERNISKOWSKY, *a Jesuit* (Basso).
Citizens, Courtiers, Officers, Monks, etc.

ARGUMENT The theme of this opera is based upon an historical episode, and may be regarded as an epic of Russian life. It involves characters from the highest to the lowest, and the chief figure, the unhappy Czar, is in a sense a lay figure around whom the action revolves.

Prologue *Scene 1. Courtyard of a Monastery.* A mob of people gather about a monastery, in which Boris Godounoff has taken refuge, and clamor for him to become their Czar. Their outcry, however, is instigated by police officers, as it is felt that Boris is a usurper who has been guilty of the murder of Dimitri, the Czarevitch.

A brief prelude by the orchestra brings the first curtain rise. A chorus by the mob outside the walls gives voice to their entreaty: "Why hast thou abandoned us? Have pity, O, Father!"

Scene 2. Square in front of the Kremlin. Boris has yielded to the carefully staged demand on the part of the people, and is publicly crowned amid gorgeous ceremonies. From the portico of the cathedral Prince Schouisky proclaims: "Long live Czar Boris!" And the people answer with a shout: "Glory to Czar Boris!" This is the setting for the lofty Coronation Scene:

ct I *Scene 1. Interior of a Monastery.* The aged monk, Pimen, is engaged in writing the history of the time. He has come to the part dealing with the death of Dimitri and the accession of Boris, when Gregory, a novice, awakens from a sleep, in the corner of the cell, and learns this tragic story. As there seems to be doubt that the prince was actually slain, Gregory inwardly resolves to proclaim himself the lost heir to the throne.

Scene 2. An Inn on the Russian Border. While the hostess of an inn goes singing about her work, a fugitive arrives in haste and demands shelter. It is Gregory, who has escaped from the monastery, and is trying to get over the border, in order to further his plot against the throne. While two monks who have accompanied him are drinking, the police arrive in search of the pretender. They hand a paper to Gregory and ask him to read it for them. He begins it and finds that it is a description of himself, so in the reading he changes it to describe one of the other monks. The latter is seized by the officers, but gets possession of the paper and finds that it applies to Gregory. He, however, jumps through the window and escapes.

ct II *The Czar's Palace.* Xenia, the daughter of Boris, sorrows for the death of her lover, Dimitri. Her nurse sings a song to comfort her, and her little brother, Feodor, also sings a folk song. Boris enters and greets his children. A messenger announces the arrival of Prince Schouisky, who is reported to be in league with the Czar's enemies. When the Prince enters, Boris upbraids him for his duplicity, but the Prince protests that he is loyal. He has seen the pretended Dimitri, in order to learn what manner of man he is. At the mention of Dimitri's name, Boris changes color, and begins to ply him with questions. Finally he dismisses him in order to hide his own terror-stricken condition.

Act III *Marina's Apartments.* Marina, an adventuress in the em-ploy of the Jesuits, seeks to entangle Gregory in her net. Sh knows his true story, but is willing to aid in his plot provided he wil grant her party certain rights. Gregory meets her in her garden, an the two exchange vows of love. In this scene a Polish national dance i staged, while the guests sing: "On to Moscow and to victory!" Th duet between the lovers is punctuated by the seductive mazurka rhythn of the Polonaise.

Act IV *Scene 1. A Street.* A crowd rushes through the streets, clam-oring as loudly for the supposed Dimitri as they had previ-ously shouted for Boris. Gregory arrives and is greeted as the tru Czar, while the mob rushes to storm the palace.

Scene 2. Hall of the Duma. While the Duma is in session, Princ Schouisky arrives and states that he believes Czar Boris to be demente He is interrupted by the entrance of Boris, who violently denounces h enemies and asserts his own innocence. The Prince tries to calm hin by asserting that the monk Pimen is at hand, with a written record the events leading up to his accession. Pimen enters and tells of a su posed miracle which took place at the grave of Dimitri. The latter undoubtedly dead and has become a saint. Boris again grows violen giving evidence of insanity. He restrains himself with an effort, an summons his son Feodor, whom he proclaims his heir. In a voi trembling with anguish he sings, "Farewell, my son!"—

Then, "Hark, 'tis the passing bell!" as the solemn tone of the bells heard without. A choral of great beauty also marks this final scer Boris, growing weaker, cries, "Lord, grant Thy mercy!" And near t end, as he points to Feodor, he tells the people, "Behold your Czar With a final cry of "Mercy!" he falls dead, while the nobles stand wi bowed heads; the music dies away into a requiem, and the curtain fal

KHOVANTCHINA

(Ko-vant-shee'-vah)

Folk Drama in Five Acts. Book and music by Moussorgsky. Marie Theatre, St. Petersburg, November 7, 1911. Philadelphia, April 18, 1928. First performed at the Metropolitan, February 12, 1950.

SCENE: Moscow and environs.
TIME: Seventeenth Century.

CAST SHAKLOVITOFF, *a Boyard* (Basso).
DOSITHEUS, *leader of "Old Believers"* (Tenor).
IVAN KHOVANSKY, *a patrician plotter* (Basso).
ANDREW KHOVANSKY, *his son* (Baritone).
PRINCE GALITSIN, *a reformer* (Baritone).
MARTHA, *an "Old Believer"* (Soprano).
EMMA, *a German girl* (Mezzo-Soprano).
SUSAN, *an "Old Believer."*
The sect of Streltsy; "Old Believers"; citizens, guards, etc.

ARGUMENT Like "Boris," the composer here takes an episode from earlier Russian history, in order to show the life of the Russian people in their struggle against the established order of things. The score was unfinished at the time of Moussorgsky's death, and his friend, Rimsky-Korsakoff, again rendered valuable service, not only to him but to the music-loving world, for thus preserving some fine, typical examples of folk music. After a brief Prelude, an engaging tone picture, the curtain rises.

Act I *The Red Square, Moscow.* A group of the Streltsy, a fierce radical party, is seen near the Kremlin. They boast about a bloody encounter of the previous night. A scribe enters to take up his morning duties; the gang gibes him and then departs. The Boyard Shaklovitoff enters and bribes the scribe to write a letter of denunciation against the house of Khovansky, charging that they are plotting to overturn the throne. Ivan, head of that house, presently comes in, and his proud bearing indicates that the charge has foundation. His son, Andrew, is a libertine. At this moment he is pursuing a German maid, Emma. While she is trying to thrust him off, Martha, a former flame of his enters. Martha is a mystic, and now foretells that he is doomed for his many sins. Ivan re-enters, but instead of reproving his son or shielding Emma, he himself is taken by her charms and quarrels with

Andrew over her; finally ordering her arrest. The entrance of Dositheus, venerable head of the "Old Believers," restores peace.

Act II *Apartment of Prince Galitsin.* Galitsin has been educated in Western Europe and has fine ideas about reform, but is also superstitious. He summons Martha to read his horoscope, but when she foretells that his riches will be of no avail and that his last days will be in sorrow and poverty, he flies in a rage and orders his servants to take her out and drown her. Again old Dositheus comes to quell a quarrel.

Act III *Outside the House of Khovansky.* Martha has escaped drowning and now, seated near the home of the man who has discarded her, sings of her old passion. Susan, a fanatical "Old Believer," chides her for her shamelessness and threatens to denounce her as a witch. Dositheus again pours oil on the troubled waters. With the fall of night on the deserted street, Shaklovitoff enters. In a fine musical soliloquy he exclaims: "Yes, they sleep; the Streltsy sleep. Sleep thou, my Russia . . . but thine enemies are even now plotting thy destruction!" Then he prays for divine guidance to save his beloved country.

He is interrupted by the noisy arrival of the Streltsy, but the latter have antagonists in the persons of their own wives and sweethearts. Their quarrel is broken up by the scribe, who rushes in to say that the revolt against the Czar has been quelled and their cause is lost.

Act IV *Scene I. Country House of Khovansky.* Prince Ivan is seeking diversion in the folksongs of his servants and the wild dancing of a group of Persian slaves: "Dance of the Persian Slaves"—

Shaklovitoff enters to announce he is to attend a council of state; but as the Prince is changing his costume, he is assaulted by a group of conspirators and killed by daggers.

Scene 2. A Square in Moscow. During the change of scene, mournful strains are heard from the orchestra, as if bewailing the fate of unhappy Russia; then with the curtain, a stately processional before a church. Through the sorrowing crowd comes a guard with Galitsin in chains. He is being led away into exile—thus proving Martha's prediction. Dositheus in a fine soliloquy mourns over his country. Martha enters to inform him that a trap has been set for the "Old Believers." He charges her to see to it that Andrew is present at the fateful meeting. Then learning that Andrew and Emma are united, he denounces Martha as a witch and orders the Streltsy to kill her. They, however, have given up their cause and bring in headsman's axes for their own execution. At the fateful moment, word comes that the Czar has issued a general pardon.

Act V *A Woodland near Moscow.* A last meeting is held by the "Old Believers," headed by Dositheus, who urges them to remain true to their beliefs. Martha prays for the soul of Andrew, and is ready to mount the great funeral pyre which the Faithful have decided to use as one great, general sacrifice. But Andrew is smitten with remorse at her devotion, and himself climbs the pyre. Others follow fanatically, while Martha applies the torch. As the flames mount up, soldiers enter, but halt appalled at the catastrophe. The dying chant of the Faithful is heard, followed by a blast of trumpets. Old Russia is passing—a new Russia is at hand.

THE FAIR AT SOROCHINTZY

(La Fiera di Sorocinzi.) Comic Opera in Three Acts. Music by Moussorgsky. Book by composer, after the story by N. V. Gogol. French version, by Louis Laloy, produced at the Theatre of Monte Carlo, March, 1923. At the Metropolitan, New York, in Italian, November 29, 1930.

SCENE: A village in Little Russia.
TIME: Uncertain.

CAST TCHEREVIK, *an old peasant* (Basso).
OKHRIM, *a Cossack, his "Old Crony"* (Baritone).
KHIVRIA, *wife of Tcherevik* (Contralto).
PARASSIA, *his daughter* (Soprano).
GRITZKO, *a young peasant* (Tenor).
IVANITCH, *the Pastor's son* (Tenor).
A GYPSY (Basso).
Youths, Maidens, Gypsies, Vendors, Cossacks.
Jews.

ARGUMENT A rollicking comedy betraying manners and customs of the peasant folk of Little Russia. The music is typically Russian, with folk-songs and native dances.

Act I *The Fair. A hot day.* The market place of Sorochintzy is filled with jostling crowds and littered with wares on display. Tcherevik, an old peasant, enters with his pretty daughter, Parassia, who is at first attracted by all the finery on display, but later by the ardent glances of a young man, Gritzko. The latter believes in striking while the iron is hot; he loses no time in love-making, and soon has his arms around the fair Parassia. The old peasant surprises them, and remarks sarcastically that he seems to know how! Gritzko then tells him that he is the son of an old crony, Okhrim, and that he would like to be his son-in-law. Tcherevik relents and later he and the Old Crony celebrate the prospective match by getting drunk. Fortified by this potion, Tcherevik reels home to tell the good news to his shrewish wife, Khivria. She disapproves so vigorously that the Old Crony beats a retreat. Gritzko, disconsolate, meets up with the Gypsy who, for a consideration, agrees to help him win the girl. Parassia enters, and the lovers plight their troth.

Act II *Tcherevik's Cottage.* While Khivria cooks the evening meal her husband is sleeping off his drink. She bemoans her fate and thinks how much happier she could be, say, with the Pastor's son. She arouses Tcherevik with more abuse, but he only laughs tipsily. She orders him out. Later, who should come in but the Pastor's son, with whom she has evidently had an assignation. They sit down to the well-filled table. Just about the time the man is emboldened to pay compliments to the rather formidable female, her husband and some of his friends return. The guest must perforce take refuge in an attic, which has an indifferent floor. Among the newcomers is the Gypsy, whose shrewd glance takes in the situation. He tells a weird tale, and the others' nerves are further shattered by the dropping of objects down through the rafters. Eventually the Pastor's son is discovered.

Act III *The Village Square.* Due to this disclosure, the sharp tongue of Khivria is silenced and her husband is boss of the house. He tells Gritzko and Parassia that they can marry. When his wife tries to object she is squelched. The villagers join in a wild hopak, or country dance, in honor of the approaching wedding.

PETER ILITCH TSCHAIKOWSKY

The most widely popular of Russian composers, Tschaikowsky was born at Votinsk in Viatka, April 25, 1840. His father was a mining engineer, but Peter showed such an early predilection for music, that he was allowed to begin piano study. In 1862 he entered the Conservatory at St. Petersburg, where he studied under Rubinstein. He was given a professorship of harmony in the Moscow Conservatory, where he remained until 1878. After that date he devoted himself to composition, being remarkably prolific as well as outstanding. In the next quarter-century his name appeared upon eleven operas, three ballets, six symphonies, five orchestral suites, four overtures, besides numerous shorter pieces. His greater fame in America rests upon such works as his Symphony Pathetique, 1812 Overture, and Marche Slav. His best known operas are: "Valouka" (1876); a prize work, "The Oprichnik" (1877); "Eugéne Onégin" (1879); "Pique Dame"; and "Iolanta." He left incomplete an opera which he hoped would be his masterpiece, "Romeo and Juliet," from which some fine excerpts are favorite orchestral numbers. In 1891 Tschaikowsky came to New York to take part in the dedication of Carnegie Hall. He died in St. Petersburg (Petrograd), November 13 (25), 1893.

EUGÉNE ONÉGIN

(Yoo-jane' Oh-nay'-gin)

Russian Opera in Three Acts. Music by Tschaikowsky. Text after Pushkin's tale by Modeste Tschaikowsky, the composer's brother; German text by von A. Bernhard. Moscow, March, 1879. New York, in concert form, Carnegie Hall, February 1, 1908. At the Metropolitan, in Italian, March 24, 1920.

SCENE: Russia.
TIME: Recent.

CAST
LARINA, *owner of an estate* (Mezzo-Soprano).
TATIANA } *her daughters* { (Soprano).
OLGA } *her daughters* { (Alto).
FILIPIEVNA, *a waitress* (Mezzo-Soprano).
EUGÉNE ONÉGIN, *a gallant* (Baritone).
LENSKI, *a poet* (Tenor).
PRINCE GREMIN (Baritone).
A CAPTAIN (Basso).
SARETSKY (Basso).
TRIQUET, *a Frenchman* (Tenor).
Guests, Villagers, Servants, etc.

ARGUMENT This opera may be characterized as a series of "lyrical scenes" which follow so closely the epic tale of Pushkin, that the latter should be studied for a thorough enjoyment of the musical work.

Act I *A Country Estate.* Eugéne Onégin, a young society blade, i called from the social diversions of the city by the death of ar uncle, who has willed to him a country place. Eugéne comes willingl enough, as he has grown sated with city life, and welcomes a period o retirement. He meets in the country a poet, Lensky, who is somewhat o a fanatic; also Larina, a neighboring landowner, and her two daughters One of the girls, Olga, is betrothed to the poet. The other, Tatiana, i an over-sentimental girl who proceeds to throw herself at the feet o this worldly-wise city man. Eugéne, however, will not accept her love and she mopes exceedingly.

Act II *A Ballroom.* Tatiana's birthday is the occasion of a ball at her mother's estate. Thither the two men are invited, but Eugéne is so bored by it all that, as a means of diversion, he begins flirting with Olga, Lenski's sweetheart. The poet, in a fury, challenges Eugéne, who cannot escape the challenge, though treating it all as a cynical jest. But in the duel he has the misfortune to shoot his antagonist. He leaves the country, more cynical and depressed than ever.

In the opening minutes of this Act is heard the brilliant waltz in honor of Tatiana, which has become a prime favorite with orchestras:

Act III *A Hall in Prince Gremin's Palace.* Twenty-six years elapse. Eugéne has wandered restlessly from one country to another, but has never found happiness. Back in St. Petersburg he attends a ball given by Prince Gremin; and in the person of the Princess Gremina recognizes the Tatiana of the country affair. She has grown to be a well-poised social leader. He now finds in her all the qualities she formerly lacked, and begins to court her. She upbraids him for his fickleness, but finally admits that she still cares for him. She remains true to her marriage vows, notwithstanding, and Onégin sadly bids her farewell.

PIQUE-DAME

(*Peek-Dam*)

(The Queen of Spades.) Tragic Opera in Three Acts. Music by Tschaikowsky. Book by Modeste Tschaikowsky, after a story by Pushkin. St. Petersburg, 1890. At the Metropolitan, New York, in German, March 5, 1910.

SCENE: St. Petersburg.
TIME: Recent.

CAST HERMAN, *a gambler.*
"PIQUE-DAME," *a Countess.*
LISA, *her grand-daughter.*
PRINCE YELETSKY.
Gamblers, Society Folk, Servants, etc.

ARGUMENT Herman, an inveterate gambler, is torn between two passions—his love for a girl and his desire to win at cards. The two emotions are exemplified in the persons of Lisa, a young girl, and the Countess, her grandmother—an old dame who is so lucky at cards that she has been nicknamed "The Queen of Spades" (Pique-Dame). She is said to base her phenomenal success on a combination of three cards. Although Herman loves the younger woman, he pays more attention to the older one, in the hope of learning the secret. Lisa also loves Herman, but becomes engaged to Prince Yeletsky. To spy upon the old woman, Herman hides in her bedroom one night. When she sees him the shock kills her, and Herman learns nothing. Half-crazed with remorse Herman is haunted by the old Countess' ghost. The apparition then shows him the three cards that will always win. On the night after her funeral he plays against Prince Yeletsky, and wins twice by the cards shown him by the ghost. Thereupon he stakes everything he possesses on the third card, but he turns up, not the expected card, but the queen of spades. At the same instant he sees a vision of the Countess, smiling derisively. In despair, Herman kills himself.

NICOLAI A. RIMSKY-KORSAKOFF

A Russian composer, born at Tikhvin, Novgorod, March 6, 1844. Both of his parents were passable musicians, and the boy showed early signs of musical aptitude. They planned for him a naval career, bu the removal of the family to St. Petersburg brought to the young man, now reaching maturity, a further opportunity to follow his bent of composition. He studied under Balakiref, while attending Naval College, and although sent on a three years' cruise at the completion of his college course, he could not turn his back upon music. In 1866 he settled in the capital and devoted himself to the piano and composition. He contracted a lasting friendship with Moussorgsky, which was mutually helpful. His first opera to be produced was "The Maid of Pskof" (1873); followed by "A Night in May" and "Christmas Eve Revels." In 1871 he became Professor of Composition in the St. Petersburg Conservatory; and until the year 1890 was a conductor of the Russian Symphony. Several contemporaries including Moussorgsky and Borodin are indebted to him for aid in revising or completing their works. He wrote 13 operas, the more important being; "Snegurotchka" (The Snow Maiden), (1880); "Mlada," (1892); "Sadko," (1897); and "Kastchei," (1902); and "Le Coq d'Or," (1908). He also wrote many orchestral numbers, and was highly regarded both as musical mentor and composer. Rimsky-Korsakoff died near St. Petersburg, now Petrograd, June 8, 1908.

A NIGHT IN MAY

Folk Opera in Three Acts. Music by Rimsky-Korsakoff. Book adapted from Gogol's Malo-Russian tales. Mariensky Theatre, St. Petersburg, January, 1880. Moscow, 1898. Drury Lane Theatre, London, June 26, 1914.

ARGUMENT This is a graceful, humorous and fantastic skit laid in a village of Little Russia. It opens with a dance by merrymakers. The peasants believe that the spirits of unhappy maidens who have met their death by drowning in the near-by lake reappear as water nymphs. The village belle, Hanna, is courted by Levko, the Mayor's son. The father opposes the match, but pays court to the girl, himself. A crowd of roisterers led by Kalennik, the village "cut-up" and drunkard, waylay the Mayor. In retaliation he locks his son, Levko, up. He escapes and wanders disconsolately by the lake singing to the accompaniment of his bandorra. Here occurs the high spot of the opera. He sees a vision of water nymphs, who dance a lovely ballet, as they tell him to "Sing on!" Pannochka, their leader, who, according to legend, had once lived in a castle by the lake, then gives him a sealed letter which, when delivered to his father, brings about a happy ending. The opera is a happy contrast to the more serious Russian music, and reveals the composer as a genuine humorist.

THE SNOW MAIDEN

(Snegurotchka—Snay-goo′-rotch-kah.) Fairy Opera in Prologue and Four Acts. Music by Rimsky-Korsakoff. Book by Ostrovsky. Imperial Theatre, St. Petersburg, January 29, 1882. At the Metropolitan, New York, in French, January 23, 1922.

SCENE: Berendeys, a Russian province.
TIME: Legendary.

CAST SNEGUROTCHKA, *the Snow Maiden* (Soprano).
KING WINTER, *her father* (Basso).
FAIRY SPRING, *her mother* (Contralto).
BOBYL, *a villager* (Baritone).
BOBYLICKA, *his wife* (Contralto).
LEL, *a shepherd* (Tenor).
KOUPAVA, *a village maid* (Mezzo-Soprano).
MIZGUIR, *a Tartar merchant* (Tenor).
THE CZAR.
THE CZAR'S ADVISER.
LORD CARNAVAL.
A Woodland Sprite, Other Spirits, Villagers, Courtiers, Musicians, etc.

ARGUMENT A charming fairy tale is here interwoven skillfully into a melodious score—the whole reflecting one of the lighter moods of Russian folklore.

Prologue *A moonlit night in the "Red Mountain."* In the distance is seen the village of Berendeys, ancient capital of the Czar. Although springtime is near, Fairy Spring confesses to the shivering birds that the cold season is due to her wrongdoing. Some years before, she had fallen in love with King Winter and borne him a daughter, Snow Maiden. Since that time King Winter had lingered ever longer in the north. He warns her to guard their child from the rays of Yarila, the Sun God. The Snow Maiden now enters and bids her father a tender farewell. He leaves her in the care of a shepherd, Bobyl, and his wife.

In this Prologue are heard: the charming song by the Snow Maiden, "To go berrying"; and the rich chorus voicing their farewell to Carnival.

Act I *Outskirts of a Village.* None of the villagers can quite understand the lovely Snow Maiden. She inspires love, but is unable to feel any warmth of heart, herself. The advances of Lel, the shepherd, who sings pleading songs, only move her to tears, but frozen ones. At the betrothal ceremony of Koupava and Mizguir, a rich Tartar merchant, the Tartar is so entranced by the Snow Maiden's beauty that he is ready to leave his bride for her; but the Snow Maiden remains cold, despite the urgings of her foster parents to such a rich match.

In this Act is heard the lovely "Song of the Lark," by the Snow Maiden:

Act II *The Czar's Palace.* The kindly old Czar has been very despondent over the condition of his country. Year by year the winter grows longer and the summer shorter. He is convinced that the Sun God is offended, but does not know how to placate him. At this juncture, the spurned bride, Koupva, comes pleading justice. Mizguir will not take her back, and is banished. The Snow Maiden now enters, and Czar and court alike are spellbound by her beauty and charm. On learning that her heart is frozen within her, the Czar suspects that here may lie the secret of the Sun God's displeasure. He announces a great reward to the successful suitor who shall win her and cause her heart to melt.

The Czar's song, "Full of wonders," has an orchestral accompaniment of unusual charm.

Act III *The Sacred Forest. Night.* On the eve of summer the villagers and court are gathered for a festival to greet the dawning days of warmth. Lel, the singer, is present and, at the Czar's request, he sings a legend of a far-off day when the clouds and the thunder conspired together to bring summer. The Czar is so pleased that he bids Lel choose for himself any one of the maidens for a bride. Much to the inner dismay of the Snow Maiden, he passes her by and selects Koupava. At the gay party's dances, the Maiden sits by dejectedly. Mizguir attempts again to win her, but in vain.

One of the gems of this Act is Lel's song, with pipe accompaniment, "Clouds plotted with thunder."

Act IV *Valley of the Sun God Yarila. Early Morning.* The Snow Maiden comes at dawn to a lonely lake to summon her mother, Fairy Spring. When the latter rises from the water, the girl begs her to bestow upon her the power to love. Her mother finally yields to her entreaties, though sadly, and the girl goes away with a joyous step. Before the Czar and his court she confesses that at last her heart is warm and free, and that she loves Mizguir. Just at that moment a bright ray of sunlight falls upon her. As she sings a plaintive farewell, she slowly melts away before their eyes. Mizguir in despair plunges into the water seeking her, and drowns. But the good Czar tells the people not to mourn; this sacrifice has been necessary to appease the Sun God; and hereafter he will smile upon their land. The plaintive lament, "Death of the Snow Maiden," is a high point.

A moving chorus by the villagers in praise of the Sun God ends the piece. The choruses are often accompanied by guzlis. The music is truly national, although it deals with legend. It is rich in lyrical melody.

SADKO

(Sahd-ko')

Legendary Opera in Seven Scenes. Music by Rimsky-Korsakoff. Book by composer and W. T. Byelsky. Private Opera House, Moscow, December 26, 1897. New York, at the Metropolitan, season of 1929–30.

SCENE: Novgorod, Russia.
TIME: Legendary.

CAST THE KING OF THE OCEAN (Basso).
VOLKHOVA, *his favorite daughter* (Soprano).
SADKO, *a minstrel* (Tenor).
LUBAVA, *his wife* (Mezzo-Soprano).
NEJATA, *a guzli player* (Contralto).
A VIKING MERCHANT (Basso).
A HINDU MERCHANT (Tenor).
A VENETIAN MERCHANT (Baritone).
AN APPARITION (Baritone).
THE TWO ELDERS (Tenor and Basso).
Buffoons, Merchants, Townspeople, Singers, Daughters of the King of the Ocean, etc.

ARGUMENT Again, as in "Snow Maiden," the composer makes use of a native legend to weave a fantasy of tableau and music, of unforgettable charm.

Scene 1 *Guild Hall in Novgorod.* While the merchant princes of Novgorod are feasting and making merry, they ask a guzli player from Kiev to entertain them with a song. He sings of old, heroic days and they vigorously applaud. Sadko, another street singer, now enters and they bid him sing also. But his song is fantastic; he belittles the city's commerce, and says he would transport their ships to the wide ocean and make them all wealthy. As he is down at the heels they laugh him to scorn.

Scene 2 *The Shores of Lake Ilmen.* On a clear summer night Sadko wanders along the lake shore, playing on his guzli. He sings of his unhappy lot and implores aid. A wind ruffles the waves and a group of swans swim toward him. When they reach land they are changed into lovely maidens; one being Volkhova, daughter of the King of the Ocean. She promises him her love, and tells him that he will catch three golden fish and voyage to distant lands.

Scene 3 *Room in Sadko's Humble Cottage.* While Sadko has remained out all night dallying with the Sea Maidens, his wife, Lubava, awaits his return. She sings sadly of her fears. At last with the dawn he returns and her song is changed to one of joy; but he thrusts her roughly aside. The sound of the bell for early mass reminds him that now is the time to greet the people and tell them the great secret he has learned—and away he dashes from the disconsolate Lubava.

Scene 4 *The Port of Novgorod.* An early morning throng of merchants, townspeople, singers, and four buffoons, jostle one another by the side of the quay where large sailing craft are moored. Into the throng comes the excited Sadko, shouting that he has a wonderful secret to tell. He can catch fish of solid gold from the lake. As a roar of laughter greets this statement, he wagers his head against their ships that he can prove his claim. They send him out in a boat, a net is cast, and, sure enough, he catches the golden fish. With the fleet that is suddenly his, he plans to go on a voyage, and summons other men of courage to join him. Then he asks three foreign merchants to tell of their country. In turn, a Viking, a Hindu, and a Venetian praise their land; and Sadko and his band decide upon Venice.

Their songs, among the most typical and popular of this composer's music, are titled: "Song of the Viking Guest," "Song of India," and "Song of the Venetian Guest":

Song of the Viking Guest

Scene 5 *On Board Sadko's Ship, the Falcon.* Twelve years have passed by. Sadko has amassed great wealth, but now lies becalmed, and the superstitious sailors declare it is because they have not shared their wealth with the King of the Ocean. So treasures are cast overboard, but with no result. Then lots are cast, and the lot falls upon Sadko. Undaunted he is sent overboard and floats away on a plank, playing his guzli. His aria is a notable one. He hears Volkhova's voice calling him, and sinks into the deep; while the released *Falcon* sails on her course.

Scene 6 *Undersea Palace of the King of the Ocean.* This entire tableau is a fantasy, filled with sprites, fish, maidens, and elves, dancing before the King and Queen. Sadko, seemingly quite at home, sings at the King's request and so delights him that he gives Sadko the hand of the Sea Princess in marriage. Faster and more furious grow the music and dancing, until great waves are stirred up on the surface above. An Apparition is seen, who strikes the guzli from a player's hands. He then informs the King that Sadko must be allowed to return to his native land.

Scene 7 *The Shores of Lake Ilmen. Early Morning.* Volkhova has returned with Sadko to the lake near his home, but realizes that she must give him up to his home and wife. She sings a Lullaby (Berceuse) beginning, "Sleep came to the shores of the lake"—

She ends by telling him that she will always be near him. Then the rosy light of dawn breaks, the sun rises, and she is changed first into a mist, then into the great River Volkhova. Thus she will always be by his side. Sadko awakening is greeted joyfully by his faithful wife, Lubava, and shares her rapture. The past seems like a dream, but proves a reality when his ships come sailing in, one by one, laden with wealth. His neighbors surround him with songs of acclaim.

LE COQ D'OR

(*Luh Coak Dore*)

("The Golden Cockerel.") Opera Pantomime in Prologue, Three Acts, and Epilogue. Music by Rimsky-Korsakoff. Book by V. Bielsky, based on a poem by Pushkin. Zimin's Theatre, Moscow, May, 1910. New York, the Metropolitan, in French, March 6, 1918.

SCENE and TIME: Legendary.

CAST KING DODON (Baritone).
PRINCE GUIDON (Tenor).
PRINCE AFRON (Baritone).
VOEVODA POLKAN, *the general* (Baritone).
AMELFA, *the royal housekeeper* (Contralto).
THE ASTROLOGER (Tenor).
THE QUEEN OF SHEMAKHAN (Soprano).
THE GOLDEN COCKEREL (Soprano).
Soldiers, Citizens, Fairies, Dancers, etc.

ARGUMENT The author states in the preface to this opera, which is presented by dancers in pantomime, as the singers remain seated: "The purely human nature of Pushkin's 'Golden Cockerel'—that instructive tragi-comedy of the unhappy consequences following upon mortal passions and weaknesses—permits us to place the plot in any region and in any period."

Prologue Before the curtain, the lusty crowing of a cock is heard, mingled with bizarre melodies. An Astrologer steps out to inform his hearers that through his magical powers they will be wafted away to a place in the olden time. Then as the instruments continue with their wild strains, the curtain rises.

Act I *The King's Palace.* King Dodon much prefers his ease on a couch, or a hearty dinner, to the cares of state. His more active enemies take advantage of his lethargy to attack him on all sides. He asks advice of his sons, but they disagree, and Polkan, the General, disdains all their counsel. As they wrangle, an Astrologer brings to the king a Golden Cockerel that has power to foretell events and to give warning of danger. The King is delighted, and has the bird installed in a lofty tower. It is so efficient that the monarch says, "Why worry," and has his bed brought out into the throne room and goes comfortably to sleep. But he is hardly asleep before the cock sounds the tocsin. The enemy is at hand. The King, grumbling, sends his two sons off to war, and finally goes himself.

Act II *A Narrow Defile.* The King arrives too late to aid his sons, and finds their dead bodies. As he reproaches himself he notices a tent on the hillside; and to his astonishment a beautiful woman appears. It is the Queen of Shemakhan. Raising her arms in invocation to the Sun, she sings an exquisite, exotic aria, marked by unusual chromatics: "Hymn to the Sun"—

King Dodon is so overpowered by her beauty and singing, that he is persuaded to dance with her. Almost exhausted, he yet finds breath to propose to her. She seems to hesitate, but finally says she will accept him, if he commands the execution of General Polkan.

Act III *A Public Square.* The King returns to the city with his new Queen, and the populace turns out to welcome them—a gorgeous pageant marked by rich music (Bridal Cortege):—

But the Queen soon tires of this new life and her aged spouse. The Astrologer now returns and claims as a reward for the Golden Cockerel, the person of the Queen herself. Dodon, enraged, kills him with a blow. The magic bird revenges his master's death by attacking the monarch, who falls to the ground as though struck by a thunderbolt. Darkness falls, and when the light returns, both the bird and the Queen have disappeared.

Epilogue Here the Astrologer returns to life and states that the whole thing is a fable.

IGOR STRAVINSKY

Igor F. Stravinsky is one of the most fertile of latter-day Russian composers. His songs, symphonies, and incidental music have made him popular with many discerning musicians. Others, however, find some of his more modernistic works difficult to follow. He was born in Petrograd, June 17, 1882. His ballet-burlesque, "Petrouchka," was produced in 1912. "Le Rossignol" was originally a ballet, as he excels in this type of composition.

LE ROSSIGNOL

(Luh Ro'-seen-yole)

("The Nightingale.") Fairy Opera in Three Acts by Igor Stravinsky and S. Mitousoff, after the fairy tale by Hans Christian Andersen. Originally composed as a ballet, 1909; rewritten as an opera and produced at Paris and Drury Lane, London, 1914. At the Metropolitan, New York, March 7, 1926.

SCENE: China.
TIME: Legendary.

CAST THE NIGHTINGALE (Tenor).
THE KITCHEN-MAID (Soprano).
THE FISHERMAN (Tenor).
THE EMPEROR OF CHINA (Basso).
THE CHAMBERLAIN (Basso).
THE BONZE (Basso).
Japanese Ambassadors, Courtiers, Etc.

ARGUMENT The authors of the libretto have followed closely the delightful fairy tale of Hans Christian Andersen, and have lost none of the whimsicality and tender charm of the original. Even the fact that there is an obvious moral to the little tale fails to detract from its beauty.

Act I *The Edge of a Forest by the Seashore at Night.* A fisherman is singing, and soon the Nightingale's voice is heard. A little group of people appear—a deputation from the Chinese Court headed by the Kitchen-maid, the Chamberlain, the Bonze, and a few courtiers, has come to seek the Nightingale in the hope that his singing may cheer the Emperor in his sadness. The Nightingale agrees to return with them to the Court, though he says his song sounds better in the quiet forest.

Act II *Entr'acte. The stage is veiled by tulle curtains.* The populace beg of the Kitchen-maid, now promoted to Chief Court Cook, a description of the wonderful bird, and are disappointed to learn that he is quite insignificant in appearance.

[*The tulle curtains slowly rise and disclose the fantastic porcelain palace of the Chinese Emperor.*]

At a sign from the Emperor the Nightingale sings. The beautiful song so touches the Emperor that he offers the bird any favor that he may desire, but the Nightingale declares that the tears in the Emperor's eyes are sufficient reward. At this moment Japanese ambassadors enter, bringing to the Emperor of China an artificial nightingale from the Emperor of Japan. The mechanical bird is made to sing, and during its song the real Nightingale flies away. His absence is perceived by the Emperor with annoyance, and a decree of banishment is pronounced, while the artificial nightingale is given a place by the Imperial bedside.

Act III *The Imperial Sleeping Chamber in the Chinese Palace—Moonlight.* The sick Emperor lies upon his bed, and at one end of it sits Death, crowned with the imperial crown and holding the imperial sword and standard in his hands. The spirits of his past deeds speak to the Emperor, who calls for music to drown their cries. His summons is answered by the voice of the Nightingale, who has stolen back from exile and sings to him from the garden. When he ceases Death asks for another song. The Nightingale demands the crown of the Emperor as the price for singing, then the sword and standard. During the last words of the Nightingale's song, Death silently disappears. The Emperor begs the Nightingale to remain at Court, but the bird refuses this, promising instead to return and sing every night. The courtiers enter in solemn procession, thinking to find their Emperor dead, and see him standing in full imperial regalia in the middle of the room. . . . In the distance the fisherman's song is heard.

"Le chant du Rossignol"—chorus with orchestra—is in record form.

PETROUCHKA

(Pa-trooch'-kah)

A Ballet Burlesque by Stravinsky. First produced at Petrograd, in 1912. At the Metropolitan, New York, 1919.

ARGUMENT This is an ironical pantomime given in the form of a puppet show. The puppet master is exhibiting his little figures before a gaping crowd in a public square of Petrograd. When his curtain rises, a dainty dancing girl is seen—and opposite her two men—one of them, Petrouchka, the noble lover, and the other a swarthy and gigantic Moor, whose regard for her bodes no good. A violent quarrel ensues between the two suitors, and naturally the sympathies of the audience are with Petrouchka. But alas! The gigantic Moor overpowers him, thrusts him in prison and—while he bemoans his hard fate and lack of favor with the ballerina—finally kills him. This tragic end to poor Petrouchka's suit causes consternation among the spectators, who are only reassured when the puppet master parts the curtains and shows them that the slain suitor is nothing but a dressed-up doll.

SERGE PROKOFIEFF

Prokofieff (b. 1891) has been styled one of the advance guard in musical futurism. He is a native of Sontsavka, in southern Russia; studied piano at an early age, and made several European tours as a concert pianist—one in the United States, in 1918. He has written works for both the piano and the orchestra, also operas including: "Maddalena," "The Gambler" (Petrograd, 1916), and "The Love for Three Oranges" (Chicago, 1921); a ballet, "Le Bouffon"; and a descriptive piece, "Peter and the Wolf," frequently played.

Prokofieff died March 4, 1953, in his country home a few miles out of Moscow. At one time he was at odds with the Soviet government over some types of his music, but he made his peace with the critics and remained in favor.

THE LOVE FOR THREE ORANGES

(L'Amour des Trois Oranges.) Burlesque Opera in Prologue and Four Acts. Music by Prokofieff. Book by composer, after the tale by Carlo Gozzi. Chicago Auditorium, December 30, 1921, the composer conducting. This also witnessed the American début of Nina Koshetz, as "Fata Morgana." The same company, with the composer wielding the baton, presented it at the Metropolitan, New York, February 14, 1922.

ARGUMENT In the Prologue we are introduced to four opposing groups: first, the Glooms in somber robes, who urge that the forthcoming play shall be a tragedy; second, the Joys in bright robes, who clamor for a comedy; third, the Empty Heads, who ask for a farce; and, fourth, the Jesters, or Cynics, who quell the hubbub, so that some sort of a piece may go on.

The Three Oranges are really three princesses, who are under the spell of the wicked enchantress, Fata Morgana. A Prince desires to free them, but he himself is seemingly ill beyond cure. The court physicians tell the King that the only thing which will make the Prince well is a hearty laugh; but that is impossible, as the young man was born without any sense of humor at all. The ensuing action is the attempt on the part of clowns, masqueraders, magicians, and others to stir the Prince's risibles. The Prince at last bursts out laughing at a silly antic of Fata Morgana, which so provokes her that she invokes a curse upon him. Then she tells him that he will not be happy until he finds and falls in love with one of the Three Oranges, and his love is returned. This at last is accomplished.

Among the best-known musical numbers of this opera are: the extremely modernistic "Waltz Scherzo," as danced by the imps; and a strikingly fantastic "March and Scherzo," played by the orchestra as an entre-acte.

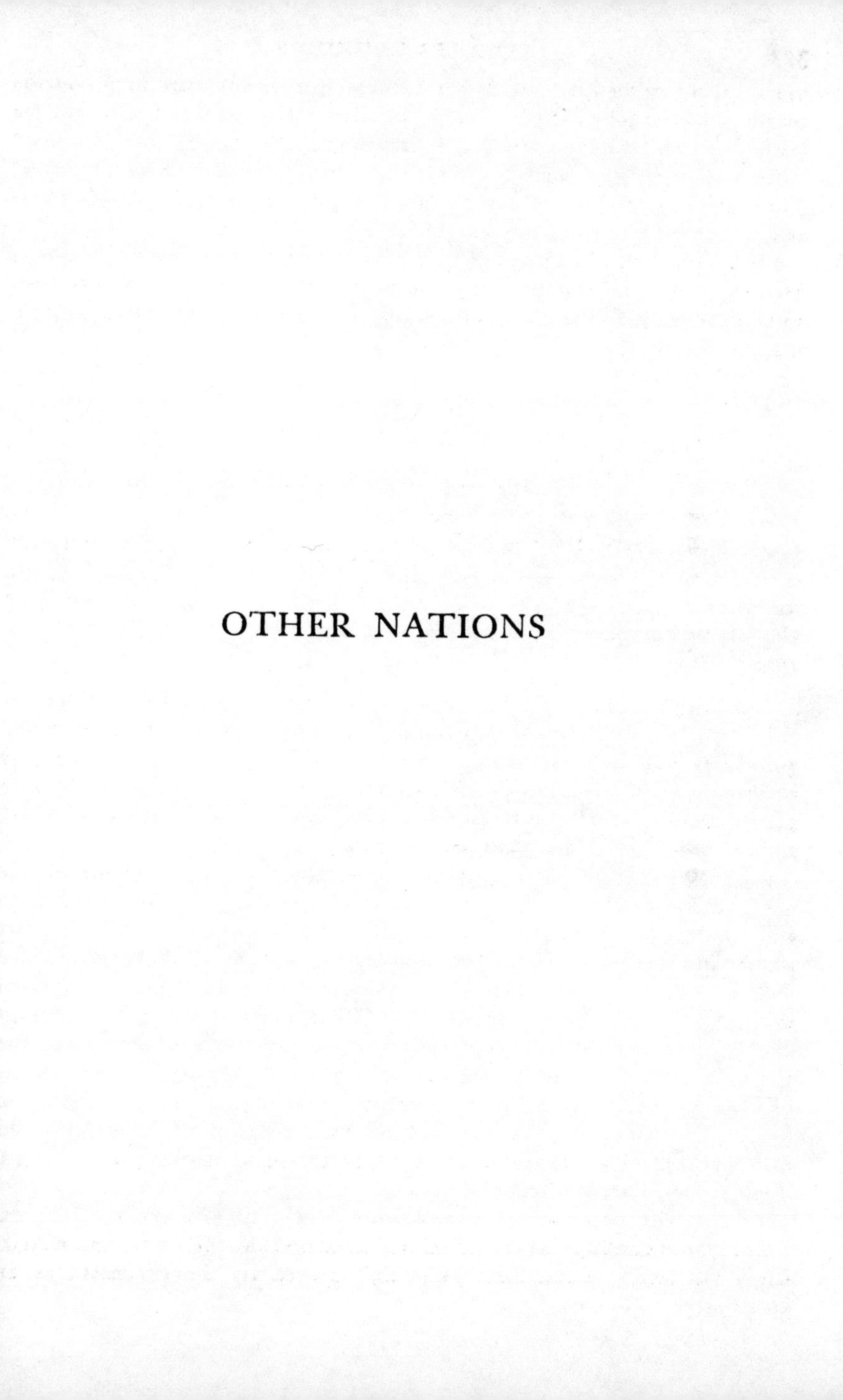

OTHER NATIONS

HISTORICAL PREFACE

It is difficult to make hard and fast distinctions as to country in the case of many composers. While one may be born and receive his musical education in one land, his life work may largely be in another. Such is the case of several whom the reader will find listed in this volume under the United States.

From Spain, however, we have one outstanding name which has remained identified with that country. Enrique Granados in both life and work is typically Spanish. A sketch of him follows.

From Holland comes Richard Hageman, but it will be noted that since 1916 his work and residence have been in the United States.

A Czech composer, Jaromir Weinberger, is another case in point. He has been composing and teaching in America since the year 1922.

The two great world wars have, in fact, profoundly dislocated lodgings and races, and America has continued to be the land of freedom and opportunity. Our listings, therefore, have not been dictated by chauvinism, but as a matter of convenience.

In the case of England, the reader is referred to the Light Opera section, as practically all examples from that country fall more logically there than in the more serious or classic mood we style "Grand."

ENRIQUE GRANADOS

Granados was widely known in his native country before attracting attention abroad. He was born in Lerida, Catalonia, Spain, July 27, 1867. He began the study of the piano at an early age at the Barcelona Conservatory; and later composition at Madrid. In 1900 he founded and conducted the Society of Classical Concerts, Barcelona. He also toured various cities as a concert pianist with success. He first attracted attention in opera with his "Maria del Carmen" (Madrid, 1898) which went the rounds of Spanish theatres. Inspired by the etchings of Goya, he wrote a series of musical studies later incorporated into his "Goyescas." This and his delightful "Danzas Espanolas" are his chief claims to fame. In 1915 he accepted an invitation from the Metropolitan Opera House, New York, to visit that city and superintend the première of "Goyescas." He did so, but with tragic consequences to himself. On his way home, his ship, the *Sussex,* was sunk by a German torpedo in the English Channel, and he perished, March 24, 1916.

GOYESCAS

Folk Opera in One Act of Three Scenes. Music by Granados. Book by Fernando Periquet. Première in New York, the Metropolitan, under direction of composer, January 28, 1916.

ARGUMENT The character studies of the eminent Spanish painter Goya (d. 1828) are the inspiration of this work, hence its name. It is a lively presentation of native life in both scenes and music. For its New York presentation Granados wrote an overture, which is now considered one of his finest works. The story involves flirtations and quarrels, a theme by no means limited to Spain. The text is in Spanish.

Scene 1 *A Street in the outskirts of Madrid.* The citizens are enjoying a fiesta in characteristic fashion. Paquiro, the toreador, is flirting with every woman in sight, and they are smirking and pirouetting in return. The majas and majos are dancing and singing, meanwhile playing a popular game of tossing a pelele, or straw-man, up and down in a blanket. The toreador's flirtations are interrupted by the arrival of Pepa, his reigning sweetheart, in a dogcart, and she is warmly greeted. But, "Make way!" is heard and with much pomp a sedan chair is borne in carrying a lady of society, Rosario, who has agreed to meet an admirer, Fernando, a captain of the royal guards. But the fickle Paquiro, runs to greet her and to remind her that she has once promised him her company at a candle-light ball. Fernando overhears him and, in a rage, informs him that he, Fernando, will be the lady's escort. Pepa also is in a pet and a good, four-cornered quarrel ends the scene.

Scene 2 *The Ball.* The Captain makes good his boast and brings Rosario to the dance. At once his quarrel with the jealous Paquiro flares up again. As they square away at each other, the sensu ous Spanish dance music provides a dramatic foil. The duel is arranged, while Pepa is torn with rage and fear, and Rosario swoons away.

Scene 3. *Rosario's Garden.* Just before he meets the toreador, Fernando pays a visit to Rosario. Their tender avowals are interrupted by the solemn tones of a bell—it marks the hour of the field of honor. Fernando tears himself away, while his sweetheart despairingly follows. The duel is off-stage, but again the music interprets the action. A cry is heard from Fernando, and a shriek from Rosario. She carries him in wounded, and as they sink together on a stone bench, he breathes his last.

Recorded music from this opera: a delightful intermezzo with 'cello solo by Pablo Casals; and a brilliant piano number played by José Iturbi, "La maja y el ruisenor."

JAROMIR WEINBERGER

A Czech composer, born in Prague, in 1896. Weinberger was a pupil of Kricka and Hofmeister. He wrote numerous pieces for the orchestra, such as "Don Quixote"; pantomimes, sonatas, and folk songs. His fame, however, rests on "Schwanda," a close product of the soil. In 1922 Weinberger came to America to accept the professorship in composition in the conservatory at Ithaca, New York. In 1937 his opera, "Wallenstein," was performed in Vienna.

SCHWANDA

(The Bagpiper.) Folk Opera in Two Acts and Five Scenes. Music by Jaromir Weinberger. Book by Milos Karës. National Theatre, Prague, April 27, 1927. At the Metropolitan, New York, November 7, 1931.

SCENE: A Czech Village.
TIME: Legendary.

CAST SCHWANDA, *the bagpiper of Strakowitz* (Tenor).
DOROTA, *his wife* (Soprano).
BABINSKY, *a robber* (Baritone).

A QUEEN (Mezzo-Soprano).
A SORCERER.
A JUDGE.
A HEADSMAN.
THE DEVIL (Basso).
THE DEVIL'S SECRETARY.
Guards, Courtiers, Attendants, Demons, Villagers, etc.

ARGUMENT "Schwanda" is a delightful folk opera based upon the familiar theme of the power of music over humans and demons alike. It is the "Pied Piper" theme handled upon a somewhat broader pattern. The music is thoroughly in keeping with the rustic spirit, one Bohemian dance with its rollicking bagpipe background being a perennial favorite with orchestras. Indeed it seems probable that this dance will remain in repertory long after the entire work may be absent from the stage.

Act I *Scene 1. Schwanda's Farm.* The peaceful morning scene in a Czech farmyard is rudely broken as soldiers enter in search of a notorious robber, Babinsky. Dorota, the good-looking wife of the farmer, avers that she hasn't seen any robber. They go away, and immediately after the coast is clear, Babinsky slides down out of a tree. He makes love to the young woman and urges her to run off with him, but she will not. After a while the farmer himself enters, and the robber tries another tack. He tells him his talents are wasted here; if he will go with him to the court of Queen Ice-Heart, his pipes will win him fame and fortune. While Dorota is in the house, the two men depart. As soon as she finds them gone, she resolves to follow.

Scene 2. The Queen's Court. Queen Ice-Heart is sad. She has sold her living heart to a Sorcerer, who now rules her. Schwanda enters and his merry piping soon dispels her gloom. The Sorcerer goes away defeated. The Queen is so delighted with her cure that she kisses Schwanda and offers him half the throne. Unfortunately, Dorota appears just at this time, and objects. The furious Queen orders the piper's trial and death.

Scene 3. Square outside the City Gate. The luckless Schwanda is about to lose his head, at the hands of a swarthy Headsman who awaits the signal. He is granted a last request. He wishes to play his pipes but they cannot be found; the Sorcerer has hidden them. In despair he resigns himself and down goes the executioner's arm—but instead of his wielding an axe, it is a broom cleverly substituted by Babinsky. The latter then turns over the pipes to Schwanda, and as he begins to play willy-nilly, the Queen and all her train dance back into the city, leaving

Schwanda, Dorota, and Babinsky outside the walls. Dorota chides her husband for getting into this fix, but he says that if he ever kissed the Queen, "may the Devil take him to Hell on the spot!" Instantly the pavement opens and amid a sulphurous flame down he goes. Babinsky tries again to take advantage of the situation and win Dorota, but she is so inconsolable, he agrees to go to Hell and bring the piper back to her.

Act II *Scene 1. Hell.* Schwanda arouses the Devil's ire by refusing to play for him. He is about to be tortured. Babinsky arrives and says that he will play cards with the Devil, staking his own and Schwanda's souls against one-half of the Satanic kingdom. They play and the Devil wins, but the robber proves that he has been cheating and the Devil is declared the loser. Babinsky magnanimously gives back the half kingdom; he doesn't know what to do with it, anyway. Schwanda thereupon plays so merry a tune on his pipes that all the imps and demons dance, and the two humans are released and sent back to earth.

Scene 2. The Farmyard. Babinsky is persistent; he again plots to win Dorota for himself. He tells Schwanda that since twenty minutes in Hell are the same as twenty years, he will not be interested further in his wife; she is now bald and deaf and lame. But Schwanda still wants her. Now Dorota herself hastens up, as blooming and fair as ever. She throws herself into her husband's arms, and the robber, shaking his head, goes gloomily away. Neighbors rush in to greet the reunited pair, and their cries of joy mingle with those of the chickens, ducks and other farm denizens.

Recorded music; orchestral selections; songs for baritone—"Ich bin der Schwanda," and "Wie kann ich denn vervessen?"; and Polka and Fugue.

THE UNITED STATES

HISTORICAL PREFACE

"Opera *in* the United States" is a more exact term, than "of"—since it ıust be admitted that this country has excelled in the production of ɔreign works, while being woefully lacking in native ones. In this we esemble England. One wonders why the genius of the Anglo-Saxon oes not lend itself readily to classic opera. Since the turn of the cenıry and particularly because of the impact of two great wars, New York as become the musical center of the world, in opera, symphony, and ɔncert, yet despite this fact America has still to produce one outstandıg grand opera.

In the formative years of our country it was natural that we should ırn to Europe for inspiration. One of the earliest such examples was n oratorio opera written by Francis Hopkinson, a signer of the Declaraon of Independence. It was titled "The Temple of Minerva," comosed in honor of our alliance with France, and performed in 1781, ith General and Mrs. Washington and the French minister in the ıdience. A few years later during the Presidency of Washington, a ıllad opera with native theme, "Tammany," was written by James ewitt, and performed in the old John Street Theatre, New York, 1794. wo other works of this time were: "The Archers of the Mountaineers," ısed on Schiller's "Wilhelm Tell"; and "Edwin and Angelina," on oldsmith's "Vicar of Wakefield"—both by foreign composers.

Meanwhile companies from abroad were already touring our coast ties. In New Orleans by the year 1810 grand opera had already beme established.

William Henry Fry's "Leonora" is now recognized as the first native ɔera. Written in 1845, from the play by Bulwer-Lytton, "The Lady Lyons," it was performed at the Chestnut Street Theatre, Philalphia, June 4, 1845. Nevertheless Fry was so susceptible to foreign ıditions that he allowed his work to be translated into Italian, and us it was sung in the Academy of Music, New York, in 1858. A secıd work by him, "Notre Dame de Paris," was based upon Victor ugo's story.

In the year 1855 it is refreshing to note a truly native work, "Rip Van inkle," by George Frederick Bristow. Shown at Niblo's Garden,

New York, it won popular acclaim and ran for a month, showing even then how eagerly Americans awaited American opera. Notwithstanding this promising fact, no other outstanding work is chronicled for the next forty years. Then we find Walter Damrosch producing his "Scarlet Letter" with his own company. Damrosch seems to be the John the Baptist of the new era. His lifework as composer, conductor, producer, and interpreter is not finished even as this is written.

The Academy of Music continued to open its hospitable doors to foreign works, and to frown upon native ones. We have already noted that "Leonora" was admitted there only in a foreign translation. The Metropolitan Opera House was thrown open in 1883, but for man years maintained this tradition. Our singers were trained abroad and more than one of them chose foreign-sounding names—plain "Richard" becoming "Riccardo." The dearth of native talents in composition, as well as an opera-going fetich, was to blame for this.

It was not until the year 1910 that the New York temple of music wa persuaded to admit an American work, and that only a one-acter, "Th Pipe of Desire," by Frederick Shepherd Converse. This opera wa awarded a medal by David Bispham, a stalwart exponent of nativ music, but despite the fanfare, the "Pipe" went out after only two per formances. His "The Sacrifice," with a California theme, was pre sented in Boston, the following year.

In 1911, Victor Herbert's "Natoma" was shown, first in Philadelphi then in New York, with an excellent cast and an Indian theme; bu neither this nor his "Madeleine" was continued in repertory—despite the fact that Herbert was, and is, the most illustrious of our composer of operetta. Reginald DeKoven, who also excelled in Light Opera contributed two in the Grand field, "Rip Van Winkle" and "Th Canterbury Pilgrims."

A possible dozen other works comprise the product, and again worl conflicts may be to blame for the poor showing of the past quarte century, for the story is similar in other countries. Horatio Parke has given us "Mona"; Henry K. Hadley, "Cleopatra's Night"; Charl Wakefield Cadman, "Shanewis"; Louis Gruenberg, "The Emper Jones"; Deems Taylor, "The King's Henchman"; John Laurence Se mour, "In the Pasha's Garden"; Howard Hanson, "Merry Mount."

Nor should we overlook some of the lighter works which yet deserv serious consideration, for example, George Gershwin's "Porgy ar Bess," a truly native work which will be sung at least in part, long aft many more ambitious efforts are covered with dust. Other compose also, have filled our ears with tuneful music—Rudolf Friml, Jeron Kern, Sigmund Romberg, Richard Rodgers, come at once to mind. the section of this volume devoted to the lighter vein we shall ha something more in detail to say about them. For in Light Opera and Musical Comedy, at any rate, the stages of the United States are filled to overflowing.

VICTOR HERBERT

Victor Herbert (1859–1924) came of Irish stock, but from the year 1886 his work was identified with America. His fame rests upon his many successful operettas. He made two incursions into the more serious field: "Natoma" and "Madeleine."

NATOMA

(Nah-toh'-mah)

Romantic Opera in Three Acts. Music by Herbert. Book by Joseph D. Redding. Philadelphia Opera House, February 25, 1911. Metropolitan, New York, February 28, 1911. The cast at both places was from the roster of the Chicago Opera Company, with Mary Garden as "Natoma"; Lillian Grenville, "Barbara"; John McCormack, "Merrill"; Sammarco, "Alvarado"; Huberdeau, "Don Francisco."

SCENE: Southern California.
TIME: 1820, during Spanish Occupation.

CAST NATOMA, *an Indian maiden* (Soprano).
BARBARA, *her mistress* (Soprano).
PAUL MERRILL, *lieutenant U.S.N.* (Tenor).
DON FRANCISCO, *Barbara's father* (Basso).
FATHER PERALTA, *a Monk* (Baritone).
JUAN BAUTISTA ALVARADO, *a Spaniard* (Tenor).
JOSÉ CASTRO, *his companion, a half-breed* (Baritone).
PICO, *a Spaniard* (Baritone).
KAGAMA, *a Spaniard* (Baritone).
Spanish Citizens, Indians, American Soldiers, Nuns, Servants, etc.

ARGUMENT "Natoma" is so entitled from the chief character, an Indian maiden, who typifies the higher and poetic side of her people. The opera's plot represents a fusing of three diverse strains, the Indian, Spanish, and American (English), and is also interesting as having an English libretto.

Act I *The Island of Santa Cruz.* Don Francisco, a wealthy Spaniard, has sent his daughter off to a convent on the mainland to perfect her education. She is now expected back and all are eagerly anticipating her arrival: her father, who has sadly missed her; Alvarado, a young Spaniard who has long paid her court, but in vain; and Natoma, her Indian maid and companion, who worships her devotedly. There is still another who awaits Barbara's arrival with some interest—Lieutenant Merrill, of the United States Navy, whose duties bring him to these still-Spanish shores. Natoma has lost her heart to the officer, but he treats her as a mere child of the forest. She launches into a glowing description of her mistress' charms, until she suddenly realizes that this handsome young American will fall a victim to them and forget her, Natoma. Thenceforth, her heart is torn between two emotions, love and loyalty.

Barbara arrives amid great acclamation. She and the lieutenant speedily become interested in each other, just as Natoma had feared. In the evening a dance is given, and Alvarado realizes that he has a formidable rival. He is repulsed by Barbara and plots with Castro, his half-breed servant, to abduct her. Natoma overhears the plot and plans to frustrate it.

Chief musical numbers: the Spring Song, by Natoma: "I list the trill of golden throat"; and Paul's Address, "No country can my own outvie"; and Spanish dances.

Act II *Public Square in Santa Barbara.* It is Fair day at the old Spanish town of Santa Barbara, and interest in the occasion is heightened by a visit from the American marines. A dance is held in the open square, each young Spaniard inviting his lass to join him in the whirling figures. Alvarado attempts to show in public that he has a claim upon Barbara by inviting her somewhat peremptorily to dance. She hesitates, but when her father consents, she reluctantly becomes his partner. His manner angers her and she breaks away from him. He tries to compel her, and when she refuses, watches her like a hawk to seize and carry her away. Castro and several of his accomplices are at hand. To divert the general attention, Castro now challenges any one to join him in the dangerous dagger dance. A circle is formed and he thrusts his dagger in the ground defiantly. After a pause, Natoma rushes forward and thrusts her own weapon by its side. Then they dance warily around, each seeking to become possessed of the other's weapon. Finally, Natoma springs forward like a cat, knocks the half-breed's weapon aside, and dashing across to Alvarado, who is about to abduct Barbara, stabs him to the heart. The villagers crowd forward to seize her, but Merrill and his marines protect her from violence. The priest appears at the church door saying: "Vengeance is mine, I will repay, saith the Lord," and Natoma seeks sanctuary within the walls of the Church.

The "Dagger Dance," sung and acted with two flashing blades, is the high point musically of Act II. The song of the Váquero is also notable.

Act III *Interior of the Church.* Natoma crouches alone in the Church, still torn by an inner conflict. The fierce blood of her ancestors yet courses through her veins and she dreams again of the old life of the forest. She has no remorse for her bloody deed, but she does not wish to give up the lieutenant, even to her beloved mistress. The priest enters and she rails at him, but his stern words of admonition finally reach her heart and she decides to renounce all and enter the Church. The worshipers arrive, among them Barbara and Merrill, but the Indian girl gives them no heed. Mass is celebrated and the sisterhood is seen proceeding through their sunlit garden. Then Natoma bids her mistress farewell and goes through the open doors to take the veil. The "Natoma Theme" with orchestra brings the final curtain.

There are recordings of "The Spring Song" (Alma Gluck), "Paul's Address" (John McCormack) and orchestral numbers.

MADELEINE

(*Mad-lane*)

Lyric Opera in One Act. Music by Herbert. Book by Grant Stewart, after the play by A. Decourcelles and L. Thiboust. Metropolitan, New York, January 24, 1914, with cast of that company, headed by Frances Alda.

SCENE: Paris.
TIME: New Year's Day, circa 1760.

CAST MADELEINE FLEURY, *a prima donna* (Soprano).
NICHETTE, *her maid* (Contralto).
CHEVALIER DE MAUPRAT, *an admirer* (Tenor).
DUC D'ESTERRE, *an admirer* (Basso).
DIDIER, *a painter* (Basso).

ARGUMENT This little lyric piece depicts one day's experience in a public singer's life, and shows that the applause of thousands does not compensate for the loss of a single friend.

Salon of an Opera Singer. It is New Year's Day, and Madeleine Fleury, a favorite diva of the hour, has received many costly presents. Nevertheless she finds difficulty in finding a friend to dine with her. She asks her admirer, the Chevalier de Mauprat, who declines because he has promised to dine at home with his mother. Next she asks the Duc d'Esterre, who makes the same excuse. She cajoles, pleads, and even threatens to ask his rival Fontanges, but without avail. She does, in fact, write to Fontanges, but he pleads the same engagement. In desperation she asks her maid, Nichette, and the latter says the same thing, that she had previously promised to dine at home with her mother that day. Madeleine throws herself upon the sofa in a burst of tears, and is found disconsolate by the poverty-stricken painter, Didier, who has known her since childhood. He states that he also is to dine with his mother, but asks her if she will not join them. Touched, she declines, but he has given her an idea. Nichette presently returns to say that her mother has given her permission to dine with her mistress, but Madeleine excuses her. The singer takes down her mother's portrait from the wall, and places it on the table opposite her plate. She, too, will have her mother's company, and she will not be alone.

"A perfect day," sung by Frances Alda, is recorded.

REGINALD DE KOVEN

De Koven (1861–1920) is more widely known for his light opera "Robin Hood," which was first produced by the Bostonians with grea success, and still remains a standard of this type. De Koven also wrot many successful songs. "The Canterbury Pilgrims," which represent his first successful excursion into the realms of grand opera, was pro duced in New York in 1917. "Rip Van Winkle" followed, three year later, and the month of his death.

THE CANTERBURY PILGRIMS

Dramatic Opera in Four Acts. Music by De Koven. Book by Percy Mackaye, after Chaucer. Metropolitan, New York, March 8, 1917.

SCENE: England.
TIME: April, 1387.

ARGUMENT "The Canterbury Tales" of Geoffrey Chaucer is the foundation of this opera. To quote Mr. Mackaye, the librettist:

"In writing 'The Canterbury Pilgrims' one of my chief incentives was to portray, for a modern audience, one of the greatest poets of all times in relation to a group of his own characters. As a romancer of prolific imagination and dramatic insight, Chaucer stands shoulder to shoulder with Shakespeare. For English speech he achieved what Dante did for Italian, raising a local dialect to a world language.

"In the spring of 1914, at the suggestion of Mr. De Koven, I remodeled my play, 'The Canterbury Pilgrims,' in the form of opera, condensing its plot and characters to the more simple essentials appropriate to operatic production. Thus focused, the story depicts Chaucer—the humorous, democratic, lovable poet of Richard Second's court—placed between two contrasted feminine characters, the Prioress, a shy, religious-minded gentlewoman, who has retired from the world, but has as yet taken no vows; and the Wife of Bath, a merry, sensual, quick-witted hoyden of the lower middle class, hunting for a sixth husband. These three, with many other types of old England, are pilgrims, en route from London to the shrine of Thomas à Becket, at Canterbury.

"Becoming jealous of the Prioress, the Wife of Bath makes a bet with Chaucer concerning the gentlewoman's behavior—a bet which she wins by a trick in the third act, only to lose it in the fourth."

The plot hinges upon the machinations of the Wife of Bath, who decides that Chaucer will serve admirably for husband number six. He, however, entertains a respectful devotion for the Prioress, who is a gentlewoman of the time without Church vows.

Failing to win Chaucer's regard by fair means, the Wife of Bath has recourse to strategy. She wagers with the poet that she will get from the Prioress a bracelet which the latter wears upon her wrist. Should the Wife win, Chaucer must marry her. By underhanded methods, Alisoun wins her wager, and Chaucer is in much distress of mind at the prospect of marrying her. Finally he appeals to his king to settle the contention. Richard decrees that if the Wife of Bath marries again she must choose a Miller—a decision that is greeted joyfully by a certain white-hatted swain who has long cast eyes upon the buxom Wife. The poet and the Prioress are then reconciled.

RIP VAN WINKLE

A "folk" opera in Three Acts. Music by De Koven. Book by Percy Mackaye. Chicago Opera Company, January 2, 1920. In New York by same company at Lexington Theatre, January 30, 1920.

SCENE: The Catskills.
TIME: Eighteenth Century.

ARGUMENT This American opera has an American setting and is thus native in every particular. It is based upon the well-known story by Washington Irving, but with many changes.

Act I *A Village Green.* Rip Van Winkle, a happy-go-lucky idler who is yet beloved by all the children of the village, is to marry Katrina, daughter of Nicholas Vedder. Katrina is a good manager but somewhat shrewish in disposition. Her younger sister, Peterkee, is as irresponsible as Rip, and is a partner with the latter on a truant fishing expedition. Rip has, in fact, totally forgotten about his wedding for the nonce. Katrina hauls him over the coals, while her father settles with Peterkee.

A goose-girl greets the crestfallen Rip, and he soons forgets his woe in a dance with the children. He tells them the story of Hudson and his crew of the *Half Moon,* who visit the Catskills every twenty years for a game of bowling. It is this game which sounds like thunder in the mountains. At the height of his yarn the children are terrified by a thunder clap, and Hudson himself appears. The children flee, but Rip and Peterkee remain and are invited by Hudson to visit his party in the mountains. He promises Rip a magic flask. Katrina enters as the ghostly captain vanishes. She gibes at Rip's story and tells him that if he is not back by the next night she will wed Jan, the schoolmaster's son. Rip and Peterkee set forth for the hills.

Act II *Scene 1.* After the storm Rip and Peterkee leave his hut and continue their way.

Scene 2. They encounter Dirck Spuytenduyvil, mate of the *Half Moon,* carrying two kegs of liquor, which Rip helps him to carry to the top of the mountain.

Scene 3. The Mountain Top by Moonlight. Hendrick Hudson and his ghostly crew welcome Rip and Peterkee to their party of ninepins. Hendrick and Dirck plot to bring about the future wedding of Rip to Peterkee instead of to Katrina, by detaining Rip on the top of the mountain until their return twenty years later. To carry out this design, Peterkee is allowed to win the magic flask in a bowling match with Dirck, who then conducts her down the mountain in safety. Rip, enthused in his game as always, is given a sleeping potion, the ninth draught of which overwhelms him with slumber just as the *Half Moon* comes sailing across space.

Act III *Scene 1. Twenty years later.* At sunrise on the mountain peak, Rip is awakened by sprites, who take flight as he rouses into consciousness. Rising painfully, he is bewildered to find himself old, white-bearded and in tatters. Calling for Peterkee, he hobbles down through the mists which half conceal the ruined chimney and walls of his hut.

Scene 2. Meanwhile, Peterkee, who is now a young woman, comes searching for the magic flask. Finding it in the chimney niche, where she left it, she prays that Rip, so long lost, may yet return. Rip appears before her but she does not recognize the tattered stranger. They are on the point of recognition when her father enters, chiding Peterkee for running away from her approaching wedding.

Scene 3. On the village green a wedding party awaits Peterkee, who, despite her protests, is about to be married to Hans, a younger son of the schoolmaster, Van Bummel. At this moment Rip enters, tattered and torn. He has come to claim Katrina, still not realizing that twenty years have elapsed. She meanwhile has married Jan, and is the mother of a numerous family. Amid the general jeers, Peterkee is the only one who befriends him. She bestows on him the magic flask. Rip drinks and is restored in a twinkling to his lost youth. Hudson and his crew appear, and the hand of Peterkee is bestowed upon Rip.

WALTER DAMROSCH

Although of German extraction, Damrosch has been identified with American music since his youth, and during his later life he came to be recognized as its dean. He was born in Breslau, January 30, 1862, the son of the eminent conductor, Leopold Damrosch. He came to America at the age of nine, with his father, who was conducting at the Metropolitan Opera House. It was not long before he began to assist his father, and, upon the latter's death, took over many of his tasks, although only twenty-three. Damrosch had a long and successful career as conductor of orchestras and oratorio societies. His first opera, "The Scarlet Letter," was produced in 1896. A light opera, "The Dove of Peace," was produced in Philadelphia and New York, in 1912, "Cyrano" in 1913. In addition to these he composed incidental music to various other works. Damrosch died in New York, December 22, 1950.

THE SCARLET LETTER

Opera in Three Acts. Music by Walter Damrosch. Book by George Parsons Lathrop, after Hawthorne. First produced by Damrosch's company in New York, March 6, 1896.

SCENE: Boston.
TIME: Seventeenth century.

CAST ARTHUR DIMMESDALE (Tenor).
HESTER PRYNNE (Soprano).
ROGER CHILLINGWORTH (Baritone).
REVEREND JOHN WILSON (Basso).
GOVERNOR BELLINGHAM (Basso).

Act I *Market Place, Boston.* An angry crowd waits without the prison clamoring against Hester Prynne, adulteress. She is conducted to a scaffold in the public square, with the Scarlet Letter on her breast. Arthur Dimmesdale and the Governor watch the scene from a balcony. Hester is bidden to reveal the name of her paramour, but refuses. The Governor commutes her sentence but bids her leave the community.

Act II *Hester's Hut in the Forest.* As Arthur is on his way to see Hester, who has been shunned by all, he is confronted by Chillingworth, who tries to wrest his guilty secret from him, unsuccessfully. In a pathetic scene between Arthur and Hester the two lovers plan to escape by ship across the ocean. Arthur learns that Chillingworth is her husband.

Act III *Same as Act I.* As Hester is about to take ship she learns with dismay that Chillingworth is advised of their plans and is going on the same vessel. Arthur, who has been in failing health, then summons Hester again to the public scaffold and, despite her protests, proclaims his share in her shame; then sinks down and expires. Hester produces a bottle of poison, drinks it, and proclaims: "Thou shalt not go alone!"

CYRANO

(Sear-ah-no)

Romantic Opera in Four Acts. Music by Walter Damrosch. Book by W. J. Henderson, after the play by Edmond Rostand. Metropolitan, New York, February 27, 1913, with Alda, Martin, and Amato.

SCENE: France.
TIME: 1640.

CAST
CYRANO DE BERGERAC (Baritone).
CHRISTIAN, *a suitor of Roxane* (Tenor).
DE GUICHE, *a suitor of Roxane* (Basso).
ROXANE (Soprano).
Her Duenna (Contralto).
RAGUENEAU, *a pastry cook* (Tenor).
LISE, *his wife* (Soprano).
LE BRET, *friend of Cyrano* (Basso).
MONTFLEURY, *an actor* (Tenor).
Cavaliers, Musketeers, Actors, Cadets, Citizens.

ARGUMENT This story follows fairly closely the play by Rostand, which has achieved such striking success.

Act I *Interior of Hotel de Bourgoyne.* Cyrano, a swashbuckling Gascon with an enormous nose, is displeased by an actor's performance in a small play, and also because the man, Montfleury, has cast eyes on Roxane, Cyrano's cousin. De Guiche interposes and in a duel is slightly wounded by Cyrano. De Guiche musters a company of one hundred, but Cyrano says he will fight them all.

Act II *Ragueneau's Pastry Shop.* Cyrano has never dared to confess his great love for Roxane, on account of his huge nose. However, he gives vent to his feelings in a letter, but just then she enters and dashes his hopes by confessing that she is attracted by Christian, a rather empty-headed gallant. This young man is going to the wars in Cyrano's own company, and the Gascon promises Roxane he will keep an eye on him. He even overlooks some studied insults on Christian's part; and goes so far as to indite his love letters.

Act III *A Square in Old Marais.* Roxane comes from her home near by and is accosted by De Guiche. She dissembles and asks him to keep Cyrano's company from the front. After his departure Christian enters, while Cyrano lingers in the background. The young wooer is so dull that Cyrano is forced to prompt him in his speech. The lovers plan to wed at once, and their ceremony takes place within, while Cyrano halts De Guiche, by pretending to be moonstruck.

Act IV *Scene 1. Camp of the Gascony Cadets.* Cyrano fulfills his promise to both the lovers by writing at least one letter a day from Christian to Roxane. Just before a battle which is imminent a coach dashes up and Roxane appears. Her lover's impassioned letters have so stirred her that she must see him again at any cost. Christian realizes that it is not him, but Cyrano, whom the girl really loves. He goes into battle and is slain. Roxane is prostrated with grief.

Scene 2. A Convent Garden. Cyrano, wounded in battle, seeks shelter in a convent. Two other wayfarers enter—Roxane and Ragueneau. Roxane sorrows over her cousin, but he tries to talk only of Christian. At her request, he reads the last letter she received and, as he reads on, darkness falls, and she realizes that the letter must be his own and not the cadet's. He tries to deny it, but she sees his sacrifice clearly at last. She kisses him tenderly as his soul takes flight.

The Man Without a Country. See page 603.

HORATIO PARKER

Horatio William Parker was born in Auburndale, Mass., September 15, 1863. He graduated at the Royal Conservatory, Munich, in 1885, and became Professor of the Theory of Music at Yale University, in 1894. He was awarded a prize of $10,000 by the Metropolitan Opera Company, in 1911, for the best opera written by an American composer. This was "Mona." Three years later he was again successful in competition, winning a prize for a like sum from the National Federation of Women's Clubs, for his opera, "Fairyland." He was the author of a considerable volume of church music, oratorios, cantatas, and shorter pieces. Parker died December 18, 1919.

MONA

(Mo'-na)

Dramatic Opera in Three Acts. Music by Parker. Book by Brian Hooker. The "Ten Thousand Dollar Prize Opera" of the Metropolitan Opera House, New York. Première, March 14, 1912.

SCENE: Southwestern Britain.
TIME: Circa 100 A.D.

CAST ROMAN GOVERNOR (Baritone).
QUINTUS, *his son, known to the Britons as Gwynn* (Tenor).
ARTH, *a British Tribesman* (Basso).
ENYA, *his wife* (Soprano).
GLOOM, *their son, a Druid* (Baritone).
CARADOC, *chief bard of Britain* (Baritone).
NIAL, *a changeling* (Tenor).
MONA, *Princess of Britain* (Mezzo-Soprano).
Soldiers, Druids, Bards, Britons.

ARGUMENT "Mona" tells the dramatic story of an early princess of Britain, who endeavors to win by war the freedom of her people, and who finds too late that the gentler arts of love which she forswore would have won the prize she sought.

Act I *Interior of Arth's Forest Hut.* While the fiery Britons chafe under the military sway of Rome, the Druids seek a chieftain who shall again lead them against the invaders. They find one in Mona, last of the line of the warlike Boadicea, who has been reared as the foster child of Arth and Enya. Mona is beloved by Gwynn, a man of peace who endeavors to reconcile the Romans and the Britons. Unknown to her he is the son of the Roman Governor by a captive British woman and has more than once stood between the warring factions. He endeavors to persuade Mona to forsake her warlike traits and wed with him, but she feels that her destiny is linked with her country, even as was that of Boadicea.

Act II *A Druidic Temple in the Forest.* The Roman Governor finds that the Druids are again holding their ancient rites, a sign that an uprising is planned. But Gwynn, his son (known to the Romans as Brennius) believes that he can obtain peace for the country by winning the heroic Mona as his wife. The Governor, cynical, lets him try the plan. Mona is found by Gwynn after one of the Druidic conclaves and is compelled to confess her love, after a stormy scene of wooing. But she instantly repents her womanly weakness when Gwynn tells her he is Roman born. She summons her people who take Gwynn prisoner.

Act III *The Forest before a Roman Town.* Nial, the half-witted changeling, and Enya, watch the battle with the Romans at the walls of the town. The Romans have been warned and drive the Britons back. Mona is carried in by the retreating forces but is unwounded. To her aid comes Gwynn, who has been released in the mêlée, and once again offers her his love and protection. He confesses his identity to her but she will not believe. She thinks he has been a spy, and in an excess of mistaken devotion to her country she slays him unresistingly. The Romans pursue the enemy, and Mona is brought face to face with the Governor and learns the truth—that Gwynn was the best friend of Britain and with him perished the hope of peace. Mona realizes that by denying her womanhood she has missed happiness for herself and the true welfare of her country.

FAIRYLAND

Allegorical Opera in Three Acts. Music by Parker. Book by Brian Hooker. Los Angeles, 1915.

SCENE: A Mountainous Country in Europe.
TIME. Circa 1300.

CAST ROSAMUND, *a novice* (Soprano).
AUBURN, *the king* (Tenor).
CORVAIN, *his brother* (Basso).
ROBIN, *a woodsman* (Baritone).
MYRIEL, *the abbess* (Contralto).
Nuns, Soldiers, Foresters, Villagers, Fairies, etc.

ARGUMENT This opera is a combination of allegory and fancy. It does not succeed in either realm, despite some pleasing music.

Act I *A Valley.* Corvain has designs upon the throne of his country and plots to usurp the place of his brother Auburn the king, who is a dreamer. The nuns from a neighboring abbey enter in solemn procession, but Rosamund, a novice, is still longing for the world that she has forsaken. Corvain stands in their path, and the abbess challenges his presence there. Corvain openly boasts his designs upon his brother's throne. While they talk, Auburn enters, and is spurred by the abbess to take action against Corvain. The latter flees, but when night falls he returns, strikes the king down, and seizes the crown. A light gleams in a nearby shrine. Corvain hastens away. A fairy scene ensues, in which Auburn becomes king and Rosamund queen of Fairyland.

Act II *Hall in a Castle.* Corvain is seen attired in the robes of royalty and granting audience. Rosamund enters in sore distress, seeking the way to Fairyland. Auburn also comes in attired as a pilgrim. He does not recall her as his spouse in Fairyland, and when she tries to open his eyes, the abbess seizes her in the name of the Church. When Auburn tries to dispute the throne with Corvain, the latter overmasters him.

Act III *Public Square before the Abbey.* Rosamund has been condemned to death for being untrue to her vows. She stands tied to a stake as the abbey bell rings. The abbess offers pardon if she will recant, but the girl refuses. As the abbess departs, Auburn comes stealthily to her. His eyes are open at last, and he recognizes her as his queen of Fairyland. Corvain arrives with a strong guard. They seize the king and he is tied to the stake also; but when they would kindle the fagots, roses bloom, fairies appear, and the two victims step forth in regal robes as monarchs of Fairyland.

FREDERICK S. CONVERSE

Frederick Shepherd Converse was born in Newton, Massachusetts, January 5, 1871. He graduated at Harvard, and then went abroad to study music, at Munich. He composed various works with considerable success for the piano; and in the vocal field, songs, cantatas, and oratorios. In the realm of opera his achievement was only temporary. His "The Pipe of Desire" (1910) won the distinction of being the first opera by an American to receive its production in America. The following year his opera, "The Sacrifice," was produced, but neither work continued in repertory. Converse died in Westwood, Massachusetts, June 8, 1940.

THE PIPE OF DESIRE

Dramatic Opera in One Act. Music by Converse. Book by George Edwards Barton. Metropolitan, New York, March 18, 1910, with Martin, Homer, Whitehill, and Witherspoon.

SCENE: A Woodland.
TIME: Spring.

CAST IOLAN, *a peasant* (Tenor).
NAOIA, *his sweetheart* (Soprano).
THE OLD ONE (Basso).
Elves, Nymphs, etc.

ARGUMENT The scene of this fairy opera is laid in a sylvan glade; the time is the spring of the year. Elves flit hither and yon, at their various tasks. They are awakening Nature from her winter's sleep. Iolan, a peasant, comes in singing. He is to wed his sweetheart, Naoia, on the morrow, and his heart is glad. He beholds the elves at work, and the latter are reproached by the Old One, who carries the magic Pipe of Desire. He plays upon the Pipe, and it is snatched from his hands by Iolan, who would test its power. The Old One warns him that it has fatal powers. The peasant nevertheless persists, and at last hears entrancing music and beholds a vision of himself in later years rich, with Naoia by his side. He calls her to him, but when she comes she is in rags and wounded. The playing of the Pipe has brought misfortune to her. She soon dies in her lover's arms, and his spirit follows her.

THE SACRIFICE

Dramatic Opera in Three Acts. Music by Converse. Book by Composer. Boston Opera House, March 3, 1911.

SCENE: Southern California.
TIME: 1846.

ARGUMENT "The Sacrifice" is a colorful opera dealing with the transitional period in Southern California when the old Spanish civilization, fostered by the Mexicans, gave way before the aggressive American arms.

Act I *Garden of Senora Anaya's House.* Chonita, a beautiful Mexican senorita, has left her own home to visit her aunt in Southern California—chiefly in order to be near her lover, Bernal, a Mexican officer. Meanwhile the old order of things is passing in this section and American soldiers are in control. Bernal is forced to visit his sweetheart clandestinely. Chonita is also beloved by Captain Burton, an American officer, who calls upon her and makes love to her, while the Mexican hides in a grove nearby. Chonita dallies with him in order to be assured of his protection during the troublous times; but this explanation made later to Bernal only renders him the more jealous and furious.

Act II *Interior of a Church.* The American soldiers have converted a Mission church into a barracks, demolishing shrines and altars. The curtain rises upon a typical camping scene in which the soldiers tell of their last fight. Dancing and singing girls enter and the soldiers follow them to the garden. Chonita and her servant Tomasa now enter to learn particulars of the recent fight. Burton tells Chonita that Bernal has been killed, and learns that the Mexican was her lover. But Bernal was only wounded and presently creeps into the church. Chonita hides him in a confessional. The soldiers suspect the presence of a spy, but Bernal betrays himself by springing upon the Captain when the latter returns to renew his court with Chonita. The girl interposes between the rivals and is accidentally wounded by Burton. The Mexican is captured by the soldiers.

Act III *The Bedchamber of Chonita.* The Mexican girl is conveyed to her room where she lies in a delirious condition. She believes that Bernal is being shot as a spy. A priest has been sent for and presently appears, followed secretly by a band of Mexicans. The priest sends a request to the American officer to allow Bernal to visit the sick girl. Burton brings the prisoner in person, and the two Mexican lovers forget all the others in their joy of meeting again. Burton realizes that he stands between the two and happiness, and is unselfish enough to wish for the girl's welfare at any cost. The way is suddenly cleared when the band of Mexicans, hidden without, charge upon the house. Burton makes no resistance but offers himself to the nearest Mexican weapon and is slain. Chonita understands the greatness of the sacrifice and, supported by her lover, totters over to kneel beside the body and offer a prayer for the noble American's soul.

HENRY K. HADLEY

Henry Kimball Hadley was born in Somerville, Mass., in 1871. He studied music in Boston and Vienna. He is chiefly known as a song writer and composer for the piano, having written over 150 such pieces. He also composed ballets and orchestral numbers, and two operas, "Azora" and "Bianca," prior to "Cleopatra's Night." Hadley died in New York, September 6, 1937.

AZORA

The Daughter of Montezuma. Legendary Opera in Three Acts. Music by Hadley. Book by David Stevens. At the Metropolitan, New York, 1917, by the Chicago Opera Company.

Azora, the lovely daughter of the Aztec ruler, Montezuma, is loved by Xalca, Prince of Tlascala, and she reciprocates. Their evil genius, Ramatzin, an Aztec general, is also desirous of winning the girl. He instigates Canek, high priest of the Sun, to thwart Xalca. An invasion is threatened by the Tarascans, and Xalca leads the army against them; being promised a suitable reward. He returns victorious and demands the hand of Azora, but Ramatzin and Canek again interpose, and Montezuma says the Sun God has demanded their hearts in a human sacrifice. They are bound to the altar and await the fatal stroke, when the sun's rays fall upon it. Just before the fatal moment, Cortez and his Spanish troops rush in, and the lovers are saved.

CLEOPATRA'S NIGHT

(Clee-o-pah'-trah's Night)

Romantic Opera in Two Acts. Music by Hadley. Book by Alice Leal Pollock, after the story by Theophile Gautier. Metropolitan, New York, January 31, 1920, with Frances Alda, Orville Harrold, and Jeanne Gordon.

SCENE: Egypt.
TIME: Antiquity.

Act I *Cleopatra's Summer Palace.* The Egyptian Queen has retired to her baths to rest and refresh herself against the coming of Marc Antony on the morrow. Suddenly an arrow falls close beside her, but it bears only the message, "I love you," on a bit of papyrus. Before the Queen can recover from her surprise at this audacity, a young hunter appears, who confesses that he has shot the love message, and pleads his fierce passion for the Queen by way of excuse. "Do you love me enough to die for me?" asks the Queen. "I do," answers Meiamoun boldly. "Then I will give myself to you tonight," responds Cleopatra, "if you are content to die tomorrow." The young man accepts her terms, although Mardion, a lady-in-waiting who loves him, tries to dissuade him. Unsuccessful, she stabs herself as Meiamoun and Cleopatra float away on the royal barge.

Act II *Terrace of the Palace. Morning.* The young hunter, attired like a prince, is seated by the side of the Queen watching the dancing girls, when a slave enters bearing the poisoned draught. Cleopatra relents and would postpone his doom, but news of the arrival of Antony prevents. Meiamoun drains the cup and falls lifeless.

CHARLES W. CADMAN

Charles Wakefield Cadman has specialized in Indian music and his songs and other compositions in this field have been deservedly popular, since they reflect the spirit of the native American. Cadman has visited Indian reservations and secured phonograph records of the tribal lays. He was born in Johnstown, Pa., December 24, 1881, and studied harmony and orchestration at Pittsburgh. His "Shanewis," an opera in two scenes, was produced in New York in 1918 and 1919. He has written two other operas, "The Garden of Mystery" and "The Red Rivals" (Daoma). Cadman died in Los Angeles, December 30, 1946.

SHANEWIS

(Shah'-nee-wis)

(The Robin Woman.) An American Opera in Two Scenes. Music by Cadman. Book by Nelle Richmond Eberhardt. Metropolitan, New York, March 23, 1918.

SCENE: Western America.
TIME: The Present.

ARGUMENT Shanewis is an Indian girl who has had exceptional advantages in education. She has been befriended by an American lady and thus had the opportunity to cultivate her rich voice. She is called "The Robin Woman." Shanewis falls in love with the son of her patron, not knowing that he is already betrothed to Amy Everton, an American girl. Meanwhile Philip, an Indian suitor, pleads his cause in vain, and urges her to make use of a bow and poisoned arrows, but she disdains him. In anger at his rival's perfidy in keeping Shanewis in ignorance of his other love affair, the Indian grasps the weapons and slays the deceiver.

"The Spring Song of the Robin Woman," sung by Elsie Baker, is recorded.

A Witch of Salem. See page 603.

RICHARD HAGEMAN

Hageman is better known as both pianist and conductor, than as a writer of opera. He was born in Leeuwarden, Holland, July 9, 1882. Until the age of ten he was the pupil of his father, who was director of the Amsterdam Conservatory. He made his debut as pianist at the ripe age of six. Later he studied at the Brussels Conservatory, and became conductor of the Royal Opera House, Amsterdam, in 1904–5. He came on a tour to the United States, two years later, and, in 1916, accepted the post of assistant conductor at the Metropolitan, which he held for five years. He has conducted orchestras in various cities and, since 1939, has lived in Hollywood, writing incidental music for films. He has also become an American citizen. His one opera of note is "Caponsacchi."

CAPONSACCHI

(Cap-on-sah'-kee)

Tragic Opera in Prologue, Three Acts, and Epilogue. Music by Hageman. Originally titled, "Tragedie in Arezzo." English text by A. F. Goodrich, from Browning's "The Ring and the Book." A German text by W. Wolff and J. Kapp was produced at Freiburg, 1932;

Vienna, March 19, 1935, when it bore its present title, "Caponsacchi." At New York, the Metropolitan, in English, February 4, 1937.

ARGUMENT The book follows the story by Browning. Both the Prologue and the Epilogue reveal the trial of Guido, a dissolute Italian, and Caponsacchi, a saintly but quite naïve monk. In the plot, the pawn is the lovely, childlike wife of Guido, Pompilia. He continually abuses her, as her purity of character shames him, and also he cannot get hold of her family's wealth. She is pregnant and now desires above all things to shield her coming child. She appeals to the priest, Caponsacchi, to protect her from her husband; and together they undertake a foolish journey to Rome. Guido lays a trap for them, but when he seeks to surprise the pair, the innocent Caponsacchi disarms him in a duel. In the Third Act matters reach a climax. Pompilia's son is born; she is at the home of her parents; but she is still in deadly fear of her husband. She again sends for the priest, and when a knock is heard at the door, thinks it is he. But Guido rushes in, seeking the whereabouts of the child. When she will not tell him, he murders her father and mother before her eyes. She still defies him, to protect her son. He orders his followers to kill her also; but at this moment Caponsacchi rushes in, ready to slay Guido. He is prevented only by the arrival of the police.

In the Epilogue while the two men are still on trial, Guido's followers outside howl for his freedom, and death for the recreant priest. Caponsacchi's evidence is unsupported by any proof, but when all seems lost, a curtain at the rear parts, revealing the Pope. He has heard all the evidence, and now vindicates Pompilia, condemns Guido, and bestows his papal blessing on the priest.

Helen Jepson has made two recordings of songs: "This very vivid morn," and "Lullaby."

LOUIS GRUENBERG

Although born in Russia, August 3, 1883, Louis Gruenberg came to America as a child and was educated here. He studied piano and composition abroad under Busoni, and made a European tour as a pianist. Later he returned to America and made his home in Brooklyn. He wrote numerous orchestral pieces, concertos, chamber music, and songs. His fairy opera, "Die Hexe," was followed by "Jack and the Beanstalk," the words by John Erskine. It was produced by the Juilliard School, in 1931. His opera, "Emperor Jones," created a sensation during the spring season of 1933.

THE EMPEROR JONES

A musical tragedy in two acts, with prologue and interlude, after the play by Eugene O'Neill. Music by Gruenberg. Libretto by Kathleen de Jaffa. Metropolitan, New York, January 7, 1933, with Tibbett as the "Emperor."

SCENE: An island in the West Indies.
TIME: Recent.

CAST BRUTUS JONES, *Emperor* (Baritone).
HENRY SMITHERS, *a Cockney trader* (Tenor).
AN OLD NATIVE WOMAN (Soprano).
CONGO WITCH DOCTOR (Dancer).
Soldiers, Natives, Ghosts of the Formless Fears, Jeff, Convicts, Planters, Slaves, etc.

ARGUMENT This work may be described as a tragedy with music. The tone effects merely furnish the background for an elemental struggle of a human soul.

Prologue A concealed chorus chants vindictively: "De Emperor, he must die!"

Act I *Room in Palace.* The audience chamber of the Emperor Jones is shown as a large, high-ceilinged room, rather bare and set off in the center by a massive throne. It is deserted. An old woman glides in and is seized, a few moments later, by Smithers, the disreputable, white hanger-on of the Emperor. At first she is sullenly silent, then as he threatens her with the whip she shows him that the palace is without its retinue of servants and that the distant tom-toms presage a revolt. Smithers summons his master, who enters in all the barbaric elegance and swagger of such a potentate. Although sensing that trouble is brewing, Jones maintains his bluster. He says that he has made all plans for his get-away and that no ordinary bullet can harm him; only a silver bullet, and he has provided that for himself. Then he tells of his former lawless life in the States, including jail-breaking and murder, but threatens Smithers with death if he blabs. The cringing Smithers promises silence. As the monotonous tom-toms grow more insistent and Jones realizes that he is deserted and in imminent danger, he says: "I resigns de job of Emperor dis minute!" But even then he saunters off with a great air of bravado, hat cocked on one side, and whistling.

Interlude Again comes the angry muttering of the unseen chorus: "Dis man must die!" This recurs from time to time in the ensuing action.

Act II *The Forest at Night.* Jones enters still whistling but walking rapidly and looking all about as if in search of something. Far-off tom-toms keep their incessant beating. He turns over one white stone after another hunting for a cache of food, but without success. As hunger and fatigue creep upon him he loses his self-assurance. The somber tree trunks with their draperies of moss lend themselves to fantastic shapes, which finally become the Formless Fears. They creep writhingly up toward him until in a frenzy he fires a shot; they vanish. Ere he has recovered from this fright he sees the ghost of Jeff, the pal he has murdered over a crap game. He shoots a second time, and Jeff disappears. Meanwhile, he has stripped himself piece by piece of his royal trappings, and is now naked to the waist. Again his frenzied eyes behold a scene from his past—that of the convict gang and the guard whom he has brained with a shovel. He tries to re-enact this deed, but as the guard stands defiant he fires for the third time, and these wraiths vanish. But he now realizes that his shots have drawn attention to his location, and he begins to run madly here and there, and to sing the Negro spiritual, "It's me, O Lawd, standin' in the need of prayer!" As he crouches in fear and weariness, another scene unfolds—a Southern plantation of ante-bellum days. Fashionably dressed ladies and gentlemen are clustered around a slave block. The auctioneer makes Jones take his place on the block, and in a rage he wastes two more of his precious bullets; the crowd vanishes; but the exultant chorus of spectres chant, "Five bullets gone!" He realizes that only one remains —the silver. As he falls groveling upon the ground, the Congo Witch Doctor appears and dances around his body. Jones stares as though hypnotized. The tom-toms are nearer, more overpowering, as soldiers and natives close in upon the fugitive. Screaming a final prayer to God, he cries, "De silver bullet. You won't git me! I'se Emperor yit!" Then he fires this last missive into his forehead and falls lifeless.

The baritone song (by Lawrence Tibbett) "Standin' in the need of prayer," is recorded.

DEEMS TAYLOR

Deems Taylor has the somewhat unusual distinction of being a native of New York City. He was born there, December 22, 1885. His elementary studies were at the Ethical Culture School, and he graduated from New York University. During his college course he wrote the music for four comic operas, and one of them, "The Echo," was given Broadway representation by Charles Dillingham. His work after college, however, was in journalistic channels; he wrote for the New York *Press,* the *Tribune* (later as war correspondent, 1916–17), *Collier's Weekly,* musical critic for the *World,* and, in 1927, he became editor of *Musical America.* He wrote several successful cantatas and songs, a symphony, "Through the Looking Glass," and incidental music. In 1925, the Metropolitan Board of Directors gave him the great honor of commissioning an opera which, in advance, they agreed to produce. The result was the very successful, "The King's Henchman" (1927). "Peter Ibbetson" (1931) followed; then "Ramuntcho" (1942) by the Philadelphia Opera Co. Taylor has served as broadcaster and interpreter on many music programs and is recognized as one of the foremost American composers.

THE KING'S HENCHMAN

Lyric Drama in Three Acts. Music by Deems Taylor. Book by Edna St. Vincent Millay. Produced by direction of the Metropolitan Opera Company "for its exclusive use," and presented, February 17, 1927. In the cast were Tibbett, as "Eadgar"; Johnson, as Æthelwold"; and Florence Easton, as "Ælfrida."

SCENE: England.
TIME: Tenth Century.

CAST
EADGAR, *King of England* (Baritone).
DUNSTAN, *Archbishop of Canterbury* (Baritone).
ÆTHELWOLD, *Earl of East Anglia* (Tenor).
ORDGAR, *Thane of Devon* (Baritone).
MACCUS, *servant to Æthelwold* (Baritone).
THORED, *Master-of-the-Household to Ordgar.*

HWITA, *cup-bearer to the King.*
ÆLFRIDA, *daughter of Ordgar* (Soprano).
ASE, *servant to* ÆLFRIDA (Contralto).
Lords and Ladies of Eadgar's Court, Retainers, Villagers, Servants.

ARGUMENT Although of American composition, "The King's Henchman" takes for its theme a love story of old England of the Tenth Century. It reveals the struggle between love and duty, as in "Tristan and Isolde."

Act I *Hall of King Eadgar at Winchester.* Eadgar, King of England, is a widower who wishes to marry again. He has heard reports concerning the beauty of Ælfrida, daughter of Ordgar, and wishing to satisfy himself as to the truth of these rumors before asking her hand, he commissions Æthelwold, his henchman, to go in his stead. Æthelwold, who is the foster-brother of the King and his close friend, is reluctant to take this mission, as he is a soldier and unversed in the ways of women. He may not know whether the maiden is fair, and he may not say the right thing. However, his regard for the King overcomes his timidity, and he consents to set forth. He and the King pledge a parting cup, according to old Saxon custom, and he rides forth at dawn followed by his trusty squire, Maccus.

Act II *A Forest in Devonshire.* After an arduous journey of a month the two horsemen near their destination on Hallowe'en. The fog, however, is so thick that they do not know where they are. Tired out, Æthelwold lies down on the ground to sleep, while Maccus goes farther to seek a path. After an interval Ælfrida enters with her maid, Ase. She is obeying an old custom of Hallowe'en, in which a maiden by weaving certain spells may obtain a vision of the man she is to marry. During her song of invocation the fog lifts and she sees the young nobleman lying asleep. She believes him to be a spirit, but is so enraptured that she kisses him. He awakens and thinks in turn she is a sprite, who has cast a spell over him. They soon realize their mutual love, and embrace; but just then Ase is heard calling, "Ælfrida!" and he knows that his dream lady is none other than the one he was sent to claim for the King. As she departs, he is in despair. When Maccus returns, he is told that they must go at once. On their way, the voice of Ælfrida is heard calling him. He bids his squire return to the King and say that Ælfrida is not comely enough for the King; he himself will wed her.

Act III *Ordgar's House in Devonshire.* It is spring. Æthelwold and Ælfrida are wed and happy, but he is tormented with thoughts of his treachery to his lord. She, too, is discontented, as she had thought that her husband would take her to the Court. At last he consents to take her to Flanders. As they make preparations, Maccus announces the King's arrival on a visit. In a panic, Æthelwold asks his wife to stain her face with walnut juice. Her father, however, wishes her to look her best. The two men go out to pay their respects to Eadgar, and as the three return, the door of Ælfrida's apartment opens and she appears radiantly beautiful. Her vanity has gotten the better of her caution. After the first amazed glance, the King sadly reproaches his henchman for his faithlessness. The latter stabs himself. Eadgar does not try to stop him; he rebukes Ælfrida for her part in the tragedy, and bids his men bury the body of his henchman with all honors.

Two baritone arias (by Lawrence Tibbett)—"Oh! Caesar, great art thou!" (Act I); and "Nay, Maccus, lay him down" (Act III) are in record form.

PETER IBBETSON

Romantic Drama in Three Acts. Music by Deems Taylor. Book by Constance Collier and Taylor, from the novel by Du Maurier. Metropolitan, New York, February 7, 1931. In the cast were Johnson, Tibbett, and Lucrezia Bori. The work won an award of Five Thousand Dollars from the Juilliard Foundation.

SCENE: England and France.
TIME: 1840–1887.

CAST PETER IBBETSON, *a gentleman of French and English blood* (Tenor).
COLONEL IBBETSON, *his uncle* (Baritone).
MARY, *Duchess of Towers* (Soprano).
MRS. DEANE, *a wealthy widow* (Mezzo-Soprano).
MRS. GLYN, *her mother* (Contralto).
ACHILLE GREGOUX, *an inn-keeper* (Tenor).
MAJOR DUQUESNOIR, *a veteran* (Basso).
THE PRISON CHAPLAIN (Basso).
PASQUIER DE LA MARIERE, *Peter's father* (Baritone).
MARY PASQUIER, *Peter's mother* (Soprano).
MME. SERASKIER, *Mimsey's mother* (Soprano).
Mimsey and Gogo, Dream Children; Guests, Servants, Prison Officials, etc.

ARGUMENT Based upon a popular novel of its day, "Peter Ibbetson" is a romance of frustrated love which found its true fulfilment on the wings of tragedy and behind prison walls.

Act I *An English Drawing Room.* At a ball given by Mrs. Deane in her country home, Colonel Ibbetson, a middle-aged fop, tries to monopolize attention. He reads a poem which he claims as his own, but his nephew, Peter, arriving late, says the poem is by another. Furiously the Colonel turns upon him, and later tells Mrs. Deane that Peter is his own son, the result of one of his many conquests. Meanwhile, Peter has told her of his own early life in France, and of a childish sweetheart whom he will never forget. Among the last arrivals is Mary, Duchess of Towers. She and Peter exchange glances, wondering if they have ever met before.

Act II *Scene 1. An Inn near Paris.* On a visit to Paris Peter goes to his old home, but finds nothing of his former life. He does meet Major Duquesnoir, but the veteran does not recognize him. Peter chances to see the Duchess of Towers and, puzzled by her effect upon him, falls asleep. The next scene is his dream.

Scene 2. A Garden at Passy. Peter, a boy of twelve called Gogo, plays in a garden with Mimsey, whom he adores. He sees his father and mother. His dream idyll is shattered by the arrival of Ibbetson, who speaks insultingly to Peter's mother. With a cry the boy rushes to her aid. The Duchess stands idly by looking on.

Scene 3. Same as Scene 1. Peter awakens as the Duchess enters the inn seeking shelter from a storm. She recalls having seen him at Mrs. Deane's ball. As they chat they realize that they are the boy and girl sweethearts of long ago. He relates his dream, and she completes it. Their astral bodies have been meeting. However, she now tells Peter she is married to another and must not see him again, even in his dreams.

Act III *Scene 1. Colonel Ibbetson's Rooms in London.* Mrs. Deane and her mother come to the Colonel's home to try to regain some letters. They show Peter one, in which the Colonel claims that Peter's mother was his mistress. The ladies take their leave soon after Ibbetson returns. Peter confronts him with the slander, and in a quarrel strikes him fatally with his cane.

Scene 2. Chaplain's Room, Newgate Prison. Peter has been sentenced to death for the murder of his uncle. He refuses to tell his motive. At dawn, when he is led to the scaffold, Mrs. Deane tells him his sentence has been commuted to life imprisonment. He at first pleads that he be allowed to die; but the lady tells him, Mary bids him continue to sleep and "dream true."

Scene 3. A Lake near Paris. In his second dream, Peter returns to the little lake where he and Mimsey played as children. No one recognizes him. Mary hurries to him, greets him tenderly, and tells him she will never leave him again. Their dream life is the only important one.

Scene 4. A Cell in Newgate. Thirty years have passed by. Peter, still a prisoner and now an old man, lies dying. Mrs. Deane brings him a last message from his beloved, who has just passed on. He does not need to be told this; she has been with him constantly in his dreams, until the previous night; and now in a last vision she smiles upon him. While Mrs. Deane rushes for the doctor, the walls dissolve, and Mary and Peter, young again, step out into the sunshine.

An orchestral suite from this opera is recorded.

RAMUNTCHO

Lyric Drama in Three Acts. Music and book by Taylor, from a novel by Pierre Loti. Philadelphia, by the Philadelphia Opera Co., February 10, 1942.

SCENE: The Basque village of Etchézar.
TIME: Early part of present century.

ARGUMENT The story is that of the love of the young Ramuntcho for a village maiden, Gracieuse. He is a smuggler and, in the opening scene, we find him and his companions engaged in this lucrative but dangerous traffic. They narrowly escape capture by the Spanish customs officers. In the next scene, a village square, our hero is found in a game of pelote. He willingly turns from this pastime to greet his sweetheart, Gracieuse, but her mother, Dolores, is bitterly opposed to the match. Not only is Ramuntcho a smuggler, he is likewise the illegitimate son of an old friend of hers. He tells Gracieuse that if she will marry him, he will give up smuggling and take his three years' service in the army.

The first two scenes of the Second Act witness the parting of the lovers. The third scene follows a lapse of two years. Gracieuse has heard nothing from her lover and wonders what has happened to him. Her mother, Dolores, has been confiscating his letters and burning them. In despair Gracieuse finally enters a convent to "find peace and comfort close to the arms of God."

In the Third Act, a year later, Ramuntcho comes home to find the deception practised upon them. He wants to take his sweetheart away from the nunnery by force, but she respects her vows. She still loves him and is partly reconciled, but she says: "I have taken my vows, Ramuntcho. I belong to God forever."

The music is enlivened by arias, duets, songs by the soldiers, and other "set pieces" in the lyric style. It has no leit-motifs, except for an identifying phrase for Ramuntcho, which appears first in the overture. There is also a limited use of Basque folk songs and dances, skillfully arranged.

JOHN LAURENCE SEYMOUR

Seymour is a California composer, who was born in 1893. He studied composition and the violin in Los Angeles. He was graduated from the University of California in 1917, and two years later received an M.A. degree from the same institution. In 1926 he was appointed Director of the Department of Dramatic Art of the Sacramento Junior College; and in addition to this he has been lecturer on music and dramatics at the University of California. He has written songs and chamber music, and six operas. "In the Pasha's Garden" was his first work to receive Metropolitan recognition.

IN THE PASHA'S GARDEN

Tragic Opera in One Act. Music by Seymour. Book by Henry Chester Tracy after tale by H. G. Dwight. Metropolitan, New York, January 24, 1935. In the cast were Helen Jepson and Lawrence Tibbett.

SCENE: Constantinople.
TIME: Uncertain.

CAST A PASHA (Baritone).
HIS WIFE (Soprano).
HER LOVER, *a Frenchman* (Tenor).
A EUNUCH (Basso).
Servants.

ARGUMENT *A Pasha's Garden.* The unfaithful wife of a Pasha makes an appointment with her lover, to meet her in the kiosk of the garden. They are overheard in their rendezvous by a eunuch, who informs his master. On the Pasha's approach, the woman, in alarm, persuades her lover to conceal himself in a large chest; then to allay her husband's suspicions she suggests that they dine in the kiosk. Acting on covert hints from the eunuch, but giving no outward sign, he obtains the key of the chest from his wife, on a pretext, and then orders his servants to bury it in the garden. Horrified but helpless, the woman stands by and watches her lover being entombed alive.

HOWARD HANSON

Hanson is one of the later American composers, born in Wahoo Nebraska, in 1896. His musical education begun in the West was continued at the Institute of Musical Art, New York. For three years he studied in Europe, as a Fellow of the American Academy, Rome. At twenty-eight he was made Director of the Eastman School of Music Rochester. He has written several orchestral suites and chorals. His first opera, "Merry Mount," was heard in 1934.

MERRY MOUNT

Dramatic Opera in Four Acts. Music by Hanson. Book by Richard L. Stokes, after a story by Hawthorne. Metropolitan, New York, February 10, 1934. In the cast were Tibbett, "Wrestling Bradford," D'Angelo, "Praise-God Tewke," and Gladys Swarthout, "Plentiful Tewke."

SCENE: A Massachusetts Village.
TIME: May, 1623.

CAST FAINT-NOT-TINKER, *a sentinel* (Baritone).
SAMOSET, *an Indian chief* (Basso).
DESIRE ANNABLE, *a sinner* (Soprano).
JONATHAN BANKS, *a dissenter* (Tenor).
WRESTLING BRADFORD, *a preacher* (Baritone).
LADY MARIGOLD LACKLAND

PRAISE-GOD-TEWKE, *an elder* (Baritone).
PLENTIFUL TEWKE, *his daughter* (Mezzo-Soprano).
MYLES BRODRIB, *a captain* (Baritone).
PEREGRINE BRODRIB, *his son* (Soprano).
LOVE BREWSTER, *a young woman* (Soprano).
BRIDGET CRACKSTON, *her grandmother* (Contralto).
Other Puritans, Indians, Fiends of Hell, etc.

ARGUMENT This opera is of interest because it draws its inspiration from one of the earliest American hemes. It depicts the religious intolerance of the first Puritan colony.

ct I *The Village. Noon.* It is a Sabbath day and the Puritan folk are seen emerging from their log church. The central strucure is surmounted by a cannon. One or two Indians are present; and wo white offenders are awaiting punishment—a woman at the whiping post, and a man in the stocks. Wrestling Bradford, still thinking hat more preaching is needful, begins to harangue the crowd. He ops to deal with the man and the woman. He then confesses to Elder 'ewke that while outwardly a man of God, inwardly he is very much a ıan of flesh. Of late he has been tempted by the pagan goddess, Astoeth herself. Tewke advises him to get a wife and offers the hand of his wn daughter, Plentiful. The girl is willing, but Bradford, after emracing her, says that she "has no medicine for his wound." The stern rderliness of the day is disturbed by the entrance of a jester, Jack rence, who has come over from London with some Cavaliers. He lays with the village children, and is soundly reproved by Bradford. ady Marigold enters and is so incensed that she strikes the preacher ith her riding crop. A general mêlée between Cavaliers and Puritans narrowly averted. But Bradford, far from being offended by the lady ho struck him, falls an immediate victim to her charms. She tells im, disdainfully, "Come at sundown and wed me to Lackland." This ıakes Bradford still more determined to have it out with the Cavaliers.

ct II *The Maypole. Afternoon.* A Maypole has been set up on a small hill called "Merry Mount." Indians are present, led by amoset. The pole is a setting for the wedding of Lady Marigold, but ıe Puritans see in it still another mark of ungodliness. Bradford, enering, denounces it as a "staff of Hell," and his men hack it down. In ıe fight the Cavaliers are defeated. Brodrib strikes the Indian chief, amoset, and the latter leaves, nursing revenge.

ct III *Scene 1. The Forest. Twilight.* Bradford makes advances to Lady Marigold and is repulsed. Lackland rushes in to aid er and is killed by the pike-thrust of a guard. Tewke reproaches

Bradford for his treatment of Plentiful and his present conduct. Th preacher tries to pray, but falls into a troubled sleep.

Scene 2. Bradford's Vision. Night. The Valley of Tophet. Th forces of Hell surround Bradford, led by Lucifer. Finally appear Astoreth—and her face and figure are those of Lady Marigold. Wil with desire to possess her, the preacher signs Lucifer's book, forswearin God and cursing the New England colony. The demon then places he hand in his as they sing of the wine of life.

Act IV *The Village. Night.* Samoset and his braves have attacke and set fire to the settlement. The first part of Bradford' curse has come true. As the colonists bemoan their ruined homes, h staggers in. When they ask him to pray for them, he confesses his si and shows the mark of Satan on his brow. Marigold enters bemoanin Gower; she swoons at Bradford's confession. The enraged Puritans ar for stoning them both, but Bradford forestalls human punishment b seizing her bodily and, exclaiming, "Come, drain with me the wine c death!" he leaps with her into the flames.

Recorded music: baritone solo (by Lawrence Tibbett). "'Tis a earth defiled"; and a suite including the overture, children's dance Love Duet, prelude to Act II, and Maypole Dances.

GIAN-CARLO MENOTTI

Menotti offers another example of a foreign-born composer who work is identified with America. Born in Milan, Italy, July 7, 191 he came here when seventeen and became a naturalized citizen. H wrote his own libretti and practically all in English. He studied co position at the Curtis Institute, Philadelphia, and his first oper "Amelia Goes to the Ball," was produced there in 1937. "The O Maid and the Thief," a radio novelty, came in 1939. Other opera "The Island God" (1942), "The Medium" (1946), "The Telephon (1947), "The Consul" (1950).

AMELIA GOES TO THE BALL

(Amelia al Ballo.) Opera buffa in One Act. Music and book by Menotti. First produced at the Curtis Institute, Philadelphia, April 1, 1937. At the Metropolitan, New York, March 3, 1938.

SCENE: Milan.
TIME: The Nineties.

CAST AMELIA, *a society lady* (Muriel Dickson).
HER HUSBAND (John Brownlee).
HER LOVER (Mario Chamlee).
A FRIEND (Helen Olheim).
THE CHIEF OF POLICE (Norman Cordon).
THE COOK (Lucielle Browning).
THE MAID (Charlotte Symons).

ARGUMENT An amusing little farce set to sparkling music. The story concerns the burning desire of Amelia o go to a certain dance. All other considerations are secondary. Vhen the curtain rises, the lady is seen making her toilet. Her husand impatiently awaits her. He is in party dress, but visibly unhappy; e has discovered a compromising note written by another admirer to is wife. She brushes his complaints aside. When he insistently deands the name of her lover, she agrees to tell him, provided their plans or the evening are unchanged. But when she confesses that it is a man iving in an apartment upstairs, her irate husband dashes out armed vith a pistol to shoot him. Amelia is distraught, not at the coming ncounter, but because it may interfere with the ball. The young man ets himself down on a rope and pleads with her to elope with him, but e replies, "some time next week." The husband rushes in, tries to oot, his gun jams, and the two men decide to talk things over. In a uff, Amelia hits her husband over the head with a vase and knocks him ut. Her shrieks bring the Police Chief and his men. To explain way the situation, Amelia tells him that the young man is a burglar ho has assaulted her husband. He is taken into custody—but the lady ill weeps and wails. When the Chief finds that her grief is occasioned y the fact that she will now not be able to go to the ball, he gallantly ys that he will escort her there, himself.

A joyous, bubbling overture sets the mood for the piece, which is in e best traditions of the old opera buffa. Since both plot and score ere by the composer, he has welded genuinely comic situations with elodious interludes. The climactic scene, for example, where Amelia smashes the vase over her husband's head is so cleverly managed in the score that even those familiar with it would get an added thrill. The piece may be described as a satire on womankind, midway between "Cosi fan Tutte" and "The Secret of Suzanne." It should also be noted that Menotti wrote his story originally in Italian. It was translated into English by George Mead, and so sung.

THE ISLAND GOD

Tragic Opera in One Act and Three Scenes. Music and libretto by Menotti. English text by Fleming McLeish. Metropolitan, New York, February 20, 1942.

SCENE: an island in the Mediterranean.
TIME: the present.

CAST
ILO, *a fugitive* (Leonard Warren).
TELEA, *his wife* (Astrid Varnay).
LUCA, *a fisherman* (Raoul Jobin).
A GREEK GOD (Norman Cordon).
VOICE OF A FISHERMAN (John Carter).

ARGUMENT This work has been described as more truly a cantata, than an opera. There is very little action and Virgil Thomson, in the New York *Herald Tribune,* remarked that the composer "proved in 'Amelia' his sense of theatrical values but he has not proved in 'The Island God' that he can do without a plot."

Through the sea fog an exhausted pair stumble on to a desolate sea shore. They are Ilo, a fugitive, and his wife, Telea, fleeing from oppression in their native land. Ilo finds the ruins of a temple, and calls upon an unknown god to come and help him restore it. The god answers his summons and together they begin work. The stage setting remains in succeeding scenes. In the second scene, Luca, a fisherman enters and finding Telea alone tells her that he is ready to bring aid to them, but Ilo on his return declines it. In the third scene, Luca and Telea, now lovers, are fearful of Ilo, who is still busied with his work on the temple. Telea prompted by Luca throws a net over Ilo's head and the two bind him up in it, then flee. The wrathful Ilo reproaches his god, only to learn that the deity is afraid of him; he only exists through the faith of Ilo. The latter throws down the altar—and man and god perish together.

The music interprets the stormy mood of the story, with much blaring of brass and heavy orchestration.

THE OLD MAID AND THE THIEF

Musical farce in One Act. Music and book by Menotti. First produced as a radio operetta, an innovation, by the National Broadcasting Company, April 22, 1939. First stage performance by Philadelphia Opera Company, February 11, 1941.

SCENE: An American cottage.
TIME: The present.

CAST Miss Todd, *an old maid* (Contralto).
Laetitia, *a servant* (Soprano).
Bob, *a tramp* (Baritone).
Miss Pinkerton, *a village gossip* (Soprano).

ARGUMENT The subtitle of this humorous skit well describes the theme: "How a virtuous woman made a thief of an honest man." Miss Todd, a spinster, and her pert maid, Laetitia, are tired of living alone. When Bob, a harmless tramp, seeks shelter, they ask no questions, telling the neighbors that he is a cousin from Australia. Miss Pinkerton, a village gossip, thinks differently and spreads the word that he is an escaped convict. Despite the ugly rumor, Miss Todd and Laetitia are much taken with the man and wait on him hand and foot. When he asks for a drink, Miss Todd, though a temperance leader, raids a liquor store. The theft is laid to the tramp, though he is innocent. He learns that the police are on his trail, so resolves that if he is to be labelled a thief, he might as well be one. He ransacks Miss Todd's house and runs away with Laetitia.

THE MEDIUM

Tragic Opera in Two Acts. Music and book by Menotti. First produced at the Brander Matthews Theatre, Columbia University, May 8, 1946; next by the Ballet Society at the Heckscher Theatre, New York, in conjunction with "The Telephone," by the same composer, May 1, 1947. The two operas then went to the Ethel Barrymore Theatre for a successful run.

SCENE: Parlor of a spiritist medium.
TIME: The present.

CAST Madame Flora, *a medium* (Contralto).
Monica, *her daughter* (Soprano).
Toby, *a deaf-mute.*
Mr. and Mrs. Gobineau; Mrs. Nolan; *clients.*

ARGUMENT Although in two acts, the plot runs consecutively in the parlor of Madame Flora, a spiritist medium. With the aid of her two confederates, Monica, her daughter, and a deaf-and-dumb boy, Toby, she holds fraudulent seances and fleeces her clients. Toby despite his handicap has fallen deeply in love with Monica. During one of the spirit manifestations, the medium herself is terrified by feeling a clammy hand reaching out and strangling her. She screams, the hand ceases its grip, and in her terror she tells her clients it is all a fraud. They refuse to believe her confession, but she now thinks the trick was done by Toby and her life is in danger. She beats the boy unmercifully, in spite of Monica's pleas in his behalf, which only enrage her further. He is turned out of the house. Flora tries to find solace in drink, falls into a stupor, and Toby returns to seek Monica. Her mother, partially sobered but still in a frenzy of fright, draws a revolver and fires into the screen which has been a backdrop for her seances. There is a crash and the body of Toby tumbles out and sinks at her feet.

THE TELEPHONE

Musical farce in One Act. Music and book by Menotti. First produced by the Ballet Society at the Heckscher Theatre, New York, May 1, 1947, as a curtain-raiser for "The Medium."

CAST Lucy (Soprano).
Ben (Baritone).

ARGUMENT: Ben is in despair because his lady love is so addicted to the telephone; the line is always busy. If he calls on her, he has no time to pop the question, for the phone interrupts. At last he calls her number from the neighborhood booth, luckily gets her, and she accepts him. He is going on a business trip, but makes a note of her number and tells her that he will ring her up every day. Presumably the course of true love then runs smoothly.

THE CONSUL

Musical Drama in Three Acts. Music and book by Menotti. Produced at the Ethel Barrymore Theatre, March 15, 1950.

Scene: A city in Europe.
Time: The present.

CAST John Sorel (Conell MacNeil).
Magda, *his wife* (Patricia Norway).

THE MOTHER (Marie Powers).
CHIEF POLICE AGENT (Leon Lishner).
FIRST POLICE AGENT (Chester Watson).
SECOND POLICE AGENT (Donald Blackey).
NIKA NAGADOFF (Andrew McKinley).
THE SECRETARY (Gloria Lane).

ARGUMENT Although titled a Musical Drama, this is Opera and an excellent example of American work. The action is laid "somewhere in Europe," but it is sung in English. The plot is simplicity itself, the harrowing struggle of a wife to join her husband by obtaining a visa in a consulate—an ironical commentary on official brutality and redtape. The Consul himself never appears, but the spirit of the office is represented by a careless and unsympathetic Secretary.

Act I The scenes in this and later acts shift from a shabby apartment to the consulate and back again. The acts are connected by musical interludes and the entire action takes place within a few weeks. John Sorel is a fugitive trying to escape the toils of the police and begin life anew in a land of freedom, presumably America. The police watch his home. In the first scene a crash of tools reveals him hiding from them. He tells his wife, Magda, that he will try to communicate with her, but she is fearful. She goes to the consulate repeatedly in an effort to get her much-prized visa, but is put off indifferently by the Secretary and given endless forms to fill out.

Act II *A month later, evening.* The Grandmother sings a lullaby to Magda's baby who is dying. Later both infant and Grandmother die. Magda has a strange dream where John comes in with his "loving sister"—but she resembles the Secretary and has evil features. After she awakes, the Chief of Police enters with brutal questioning. After her child's death, Magda goes again to the consulate. A fantastic interlude is seen, where a magician and hypnotist, Nika, casts a spell over all present and they imagine themselves in a ballroom and dance wildly until the Secretary coldly stops them and tells them to get their papers ready. The magician rapidly pulls a rabbit and other gimcracks from his clothing, but no official papers.

Act III Magda is warned that she must at all cost prevent her husband from communicating with her, or all is lost. But it is too late. The police have been tipped off and are keeping close watch. Magda makes a last desperate attempt to get aid from the consulate, only again to be thwarted by the Secretary who tells her airily that her case will be attended to "in the morning." As she returns home, her telephone rings repeatedly; she knows the answer; it must be her husband who is in custody. "I never meant to do this!" she moans and turns on the gas in her stove. The final suicide scene occupies fifteen minutes of slow music by the orchestra, some singing, and choreography. The dream of a happier land and the constant frustration and final tragedy are admirably portrayed by the score.

AMAHL AND THE NIGHT VISITORS

Musical play in One Act. Music and book by Menotti. First opera written especially for television and produced by the N.B.C. network, December 24, 1951. Later produced on stage by the New York City Center.

SCENE: a village near Bethlehem; TIME, the birth of Jesus.

CAST AMAHL, *a crippled boy of fourteen* (Soprano). HIS MOTHER (Soprano). KING KASPAR (Tenor). KING MELCHIOR (Baritone). KING BALTHAZAR (Bass). The Page (Bass). Shepherds, villagers, dancers.

ARGUMENT Written especially for use at Christmastime. Amahl, a cripple, lives in poverty with his widowed mother, who is constantly annoyed by his imaginative flights. One evening he has seen a king in gorgeous apparel approaching their poor cottage. She is ready to whip him, but she also sees three richly clad men accompanied by a Page laden with gifts. They tell her they have seen the Star; they are weary and wish to spend the night here. She bids them welcome, although the hovel is bare. The gifts of the Wise Men are Gold, symbol of Power; Incense, symbol of Prayer; and Myrrh, symbol of Death. While her guests rest, Amahl's mother cannot resist trying to steal the gold, to aid her to cure her boy's lameness. The Page seizes her; they struggle. When peace is restored, the boy learns that the treasure is for the Child of Bethlehem, for whom all the world is awaiting. Amahl too wants to give something of his own. He has only his rude crutch. He flings it at the feet of the men. "Let me give this!" he cries; and immediately afterwards he exclaims, "Mother, I can walk!" A miracle has happened, and he begs permission to accompany the kings on their way to the Christ child. While he waves farewell to his mother standing at the door, the curtain falls.

RECENT AND REVISED GRAND OPERA

CHARLES W. CADMAN

A WITCH OF SALEM

Dramatic Opera in Two Acts. Music by Cadman. Book by Nelle Richmond Eberhart. Produced at Chicago by the Chicago Civic Opera Company, December 8, 1926.

CAST ARNOLD TALBOT (Tenor).
SHEILA MELOY (Soprano).
CLARIS WILLOUGHBY (Soprano).
Townsfolk of Salem, Massachusetts.

ARGUMENT The scene is Salem, the time 1692, when the witch-hunt of history rocked the sleepy little town to its foundations. Involved in it are the three principals of this opera. Claris Willoughby is the daughter of a well-to-do Puritan. His ward is Sheila Meloy, lately come over from Ireland, who finds the severe life of the colony foreign to her former life. Sheila had fallen in love, as a girl, with Arnold Talbot, and is embittered to find him engaged to marry her cousin, Claris. When the witch-hunt is at its height, Sheila accuses her cousin of being a witch, and says that there is a red cross upon her breast, a birthmark, in fact, being there. Poor Claris is promptly tried and just as promptly sentenced to hang. While the noose is being adjusted, the remorseful Sheila confesses her wrongdoing to Arnold and tells him that if he will kiss her once, she will go with this upon her lips and take her cousin's place on the scaffold. The rather implausible story is sung and enacted with dramatic force.

WALTER DAMROSCH

THE MAN WITHOUT A COUNTRY

Opera in Two Acts. Music by Damrosch. Book by Arthur Guiterman from the classic story by Edward Everett Hale, of the same title. Metropolitan, New York, May 12, 1937.

CAST Philip Nolan, *a Lieutenant of Marines* (Tenor).
Mary Rutledge, *his betrothed* (Soprano).
Harman Blennerhasset (Tenor).
Aaron Burr (Baritone).
Colonel Morgan (Bass).
Commodore Stephen Decatur (Spoken).

ARGUMENT The plot can be briefly summarized as following the well-known short story by Hale, of the man who in an unguarded moment forswears allegiance to the United States and shouts, "I never wish to hear that cursed name again!" The army officers take him at his word. He is placed on board a Navy vessel and never allowed ashore, while all references to his country are kept carefully from his ears.

The time is 1807; the opening scene in the home of Harman Blennerhassett, on the Ohio River. Practically all of the characters are historic, that of Philip Nolan being fictitional. The intrigue against the United States known as the Aaron Burr plot is fomenting, with its center here. Young Nolan, a lieutenant in the Marines is involved. He is in love with Mary Rutledge, who begs him to have nothing to do with the conspiracy, but he persists. When he is arrested he voices his defiance and thereafter is "the man without a country."

The second act takes place several years later. Of all the wars and rumors of wars, and the growth of his native land, Nolan knows nothing, and his longing for word becomes intense. A new poem by Walter Scott falls into his hands, with the famous lines:

"Breathes there a man with soul so dead
Who never to himself hath said,
'This is my own, my native land.'"

He falters and turns away sobbing. His punishment is complete. At the siege of Tripoli against the pirates, Commodore Decatur relents and lets him take part in the battle. He fights heroically until cut down by a bullet. Dying he hears Mary's voice as in a dream telling him he is pardoned.

OTTORINO RESPIGHI

Ottorino Respighi has come to be regarded as one of the most talented of contemporary composers. Born in Bologna, Italy, July 9,

1879, he studied the violin, played in quintets in European concerts, and in 1932 toured America as a soloist. He earned fame for his numerous orchestral suites, the best known being "The Fountains of Rome" and "The Pines of Rome." He was made a member of the Royal Academy of Italy in 1932. Three operas, "Re Enzo" (1905), "Semirama" (1910), and "La Fiamma" (1934), were little known outside of Italy. His best-known opera, "La Campana Sommersa" ("The Sunken Bell") was produced in Germany and America. Respighi died in Rome, April 18, 1936.

THE SUNKEN BELL

(La Campana Sommersa.) Legendary Opera in Four Acts. Music by Respighi. Book by Claudio Guastalla, based upon the drama by Gerhart Hauptmann of the same title. First performed in Hamburg, in 1927. At the Metropolitan, New York, in November, 1928.

CAST HEINRICH, *the bell-caster* (Tenor).
MAGDA, *his wife* (Soprano).
RAUTENDELEIN, *an elf-child* (Soprano).
THE WITCH, *her grandmother* (Mezzo-soprano).
NICKELMANN, *the old man of the well.*
THE FAUN (Tenor).
THE PASTOR (Bass).
THE BARBER (Tenor).
THE SCHOOLMASTER (Baritone).
Mortals, elves, witches.

ARGUMENT The scene and time of this charming fantasy are in the realm of dreams. By an ancient well is seated a pretty elf-child, Rautendelein, who is troubled over the misfortune that has come to the bell-caster, Heinrich. While taking his latest and best bell up a hillside to the church, a mischievous Faun has overturned his cart and the bell has dropped into a lake. Rautendelein has fallen in love with the foundryman and determines to aid him. While he lies asleep upon the ground she draws a magic circle around him, although warned by the Witch, her Grandmother, that he is a mortal and must die. The Witch then spirits the bell-caster away.

The second act takes place in Heinrich's home. His wife, Magda, listens intently for the sound of the bell, but he rushes in all but dead to tell her that the bell is sunk and he has lost his power to cast another. The Pastor brings a girl into the house, who proves to be Rautendelein, whose love for him gives him new life and courage.

In the third act, Heinrich has abandoned Magda and their children to live in the mountains with Rautendelein. The elves help him to make finer works, but the Pastor urges him to give up this life of sin and return to his family. The bell-caster refuses saying: "If I desist from this work, may the sunken bell ring again." When the wrathful neighbors come to kill him and destroy his new temple on the mountain, he is aided by spirits in defeating them. However, when later the images of his children stand before him bearing an urn containing tears of his dead wife, who has thrown herself into the lake, he repents, regains his mortal self—and the tolling of the sunken bell is heard.

In the final act, same setting as the first, Rautendelein has gone back to her first lover, the old man of the well. Heinrich, deserted by all, comes to see her once more before he dies. The Witch permits him to do so. The elf-child at first reproaches him for having driven her back into the well, then relents and presses a kiss upon his dying lips.

BENJAMIN BRITTEN

British composer born November 22, 1913, Lowestoft, England. He was educated in Gresham's School, Norfolk; later in Royal College of Music, 1930–33. He studied composition under John Ireland; piano under Arthur Benjamin. First public performance in 1934 at the Florence Festival, and then in Barcelona and London. Britten has written widely for the films, stage, radio, piano, symphonic concerts. His "Ballad of Heroes" was given in 1939. Since then he has composed three operas, "Peter Grimes," "The Rape of Lucretia," and "Albert Herring," the first-named being the most important and given in England in 1945 with "considerable acclaim." In December, 1950, New York audiences were given a novelty, "Let's Make an Opera," with music by Britten.

PETER GRIMES

Tragic Opera in a Prologue and Three Acts. Music by Britten. Book by Montagu Slater, from George Crabbe's poem, "The Borough." Composed for the Koussevitsky Music Foundation and performed at Sadler's Wells Theatre, London, June 7, 1945; at the Berkshire Music Center in America, August 6, 1946; at the Metropolitan, New York, February 12, 1948.

SCENE: A Suffolk fishing village.
TIME: Circa 1830.

CAST PETER GRIMES, *a fisherman* (Tenor).
JOHN, *a boy apprentice* (Silent).
ELLEN ORFORD, *a schoolmistress* (Soprano).
NED KEENE, *an apothecary.*
MRS. SEDLEY, *a village gossip* (Contralto).
SWALLOW, *a lawyer.*
CAPTAIN BALSTRODE, *a retired skipper* (Baritone).
REV. HORACE ADAMS, *a rector.*
HOBSON, *a carrier* (Bass).
BEN BOLES, *a fisherman and Methodist* (Tenor).
"AUNTIE," *landlady of "The Boar"* (Contralto).
Her two nieces, townspeople, and fisherfolk.

ARGUMENT The story reveals a cross-section of English village life, a little over a century ago. The central figure, Peter Grimes, is a social misfit, a recluse with a bad reputation. Rumor has it that he mistreats the boys whom he obtains from an orphanage, although he maintains that he cannot afford to hire a man to help him with his nets.

The prologue set in the borough hall shows Peter being cross-examined by Swallow, the lawyer, regarding the mysterious fate of an apprentice. Peter sullenly protests his innocence and through lack of evidence is dismissed with a sharp warning. His neighbors shake their heads. A long, slow-moving melody pervades the prologue, and later harps suggest the glitter of the sea.

Act I *Scene 1. The Beach with exterior of buildings.* Peter has few friends to help him secure another boy. Ned Keene, the apothecary, is willing to give him another chance. His two staunchest allies are Ellen Orford, a widow and teacher, with whom he is in love; and Captain Balstrode, an old salt, who bluntly advises him to leave town and either enter the Navy or become a privateer. But Peter is obstinate. He is going to fish for all the fish in the sea and then marry Ellen. Ellen tells him that she is going with Hobson, the public carrier, to the orphanage to get a new boy.

Scene 2. Interior of Tavern. A storm is raging and the townspeople are huddled inside. Peter dripping enters to await the boy. Word comes that the storm has swept away a portion of the cliff near Peter's hut. However, the carrier arrives safely with the apprentice,

John, much to general disapproval. There is a rousing chanty in this scene, "Old John has gone fishing."

Act II *Village Street outside of Church.* It is Sunday morning and a clear day. People are going to church, while bells chime in with the melody. Ellen notices that the new boy, John, is dressed in clean clothes and allowed to rest on Sunday, as Peter had promised, but she also sees that the boy is unhappy and his neck is bruised. She confronts Peter, who now enters, but the man has one of his irrational streaks and angrily maintains that the boy is now his property and he can do as he pleases; then he seizes the lad and returns home. The people coming from church are furious and threaten to go to the hut and thrash Peter. Balstrode tries to calm them. They march down the street to the beat of Hobson's drum.

Scene 2. Peter's Hut (made from an inverted boat). An orchestral interlude ceases and Peter is shown roughly shaking the frightened boy and telling him to take off those fine clothes and "on with this jersey." A shoal of fish is in the offing and, Sunday or no Sunday, they must after them; he must get rich. Then the beat of Hobson's drum is heard and the angry mutterings of the mob. Alarmed, Peter shoves the boy out a side door and follows him to the cliff's edge. A wild scream is heard. The men burst in to find the hut empty. The Captain peers out the side door; he surmises the truth but keeps his counsel.

Act III *Scene 1. Outside Moot Hall.* The music affords relief from previous tenseness. A dance is going on within, which the crowd watches through the windows; music gay and lively. Ellen and the Captain, however, are much perturbed. They have searched for three days and Ellen reports that she has found the boy's jersey washed up on the strand. Mrs. Sedley, the busybody who has been active in other situations, overhears her and now loudly demands that a further search be made. An interlude notes the passage of several hours.

Scene 2. On the Beach. A heavy fog hampers the seekers. A horn wails dismally. Peter wanders in haggard but sullen. The crowd shouts, "Peter! Peter Grimes!" Ellen and the Captain still try to shield him, but the situation has grown so ominous that Balstrode takes him aside and advises him to get into his boat, go out to sea, and never return. He consents. Dawn breaks; the fog lifts; the villagers take up their daily tasks; Ellen and the Captain sadly leave the scene with, "The sea is so deep, so deep!"

THE RAPE OF LUCRETIA

Tragic Opera in Two Acts. Music by Britten. Book by R. Duncan, from Obey's "Le Viol de Lucrece." Performed at the Glyndebourne Opera House, in July, 1946.

The plot follows the familiar theme, the scene Rome, about 500 B.C. Tarquin the Tyrant while a guest in the house of Collatinus, the General, violates Lucretia, the latter's wife. On the General's return she appears dressed in deep black, tells of her misfortune, and stabs herself. A Chorus after the manner of the Greek tragedies foretells the action.

ALBERT HERRING

Comic Opera in Three Acts. Music by Britten. Book by E. Crozier from a tale by Guy de Maupassant. First performance in 1947.

Turning aside from serious work to this light comedy, Britten is regarded as not successful. Nevertheless there are moments of excellent music. In a sparkling farce of village life, the action hinges upon the vain attempt on the part of a committee to find an acceptable Queen of May. Whenever any local girl is mentioned, a sour old maid smirches her reputation. Who then is pure? In despair they turn from the fair sex and choose a King of May—one Albert Herring who apparently is blameless as he has been tied closely to his mother's apronstrings. Albert is at first dismayed, but being duly crowned and allotted many unaccustomed privileges, he decides to sow a wild oat or two for himself.

LET'S MAKE AN OPERA

Musical Play in Two Acts. Music by Britten. Book by Eric Crozier. John Golden Theatre, New York, December 13, 1950.

On the assumption that audiences like to participate in a show, they are here given full opportunity to do so. The whole first act might be called rehearsal, the folks out front being told what roles they are to assume, whether singing or imitating forest calls. Act II then puts on this dual performance, an operatic skit about an English chimney sweep who is befriended by lads and lasses in England, the time being 1810. As a novelty it attracted attention, but more as a diverting "parlor game."

BERNARD ROGERS

Bernard Rogers is an American composer who was born in New York City, February 4, 1893. He studied at the Institute of Musical Art, New York, and in Cleveland with Ernest Bloch. He has won several awards, the Pulitzer Scholarship, the Guggenheim Fellowship, and the Eastman Award. He is teacher of composition at the Eastman School of Music. His first opera, "The Marriage of Aude" (1931) won the Bispham Medal. He has been on the Editorial Board of *Musical America.* "The Warrior" was written in 1946 and produced in 1947.

THE WARRIOR

Tragic Opera in One Act. Music by Rogers. Book by Norman Corwin. Metropolitan, New York, January 11, 1947.

CAST SAMSON, *a Jewish warrior* (Baritone).
DELILAH, *a Philistine woman* (Soprano).
Other Philistines.

ARGUMENT The story follows that of the Old Testament telling of Samson's betrayal by Delilah. In the opening scene, the siren is shearing off the warrior's locks while he sleeps. A second scene reveals him as a prisoner, mocked and bound and finally blinded by redhot irons. A third episode is his trial in prison where Delilah pours out her scorn upon him. The final scene is the famous last act of the warrior. His hair has grown long again, he seeks forgiveness of Jehovah, and at a great festival of his enemies he thrusts aside the pillars and brings the temple crashing down.

KURT WEILL

Kurt Weill was born in Dessau, Germany, March 2, 1900, the son of a cantor. His musical gifts were shown at such an early age that, at ten, he wrote his first opera, which earned him a scholarship at the Berlin Conservatory where he studied under Humperdinck. At 26, his opera "Protagonist" was produced, and he wrote an opera each year until Hitler's crusade against the Jews forced him to leave Germany, in 1933. In Paris he wrote some ballet music. In 1937 he collaborated with Max Reinhardt with the score for the spectacular pageant of Jewish history, "The Eternal Road." This and other work brought him to America, and he became a naturalized citizen in 1943. He wrote the music for "Johnny Johnson," "The Lady in the Dark," "Street Scene," "One Touch of Venus," and "Lost in the Stars." He was actively associated with the Playwrights Company. Weill died April 3, 1950.

LOST IN THE STARS

Musical Tragedy in Two Acts. Music by Kurt Weill. Book by Maxwell Anderson, based on Alan Paton's novel, "Cry, the Beloved Country." The Music Box, Ocotber 30, 1949.

CAST Stephen Kumalo (Todd Duncan).
John Kumalo (Warren Coleman).
James Jarvis (Leslie Banks).
Edward Jarvis (Judson Rees).
Nita (Elayne Richards).
Grace Kumalo (Gertrude Jeannette).
Linda (Sheila Guyse).
Absalom Kumalo (Julian Mayfield).
Irina (Inez Matthews).
Numerous others, including singers.

ARGUMENT The story follows faithfully the original book by Paton, regarded by critics as one of the most significant and important novels of the past decade or two. It tells of a simple Zulu preacher, a Negro, who goes on a visit to Johannesburg, the metropolis of the gold-mining in the Transvaal. He is seeking his son, Absalom, who meanwhile has gotten into bad company, is implicated in a slaying during a hold-up, convicted, and sentenced to hang. The desolate father and the white man, Jarvis, whose son has been slain, finally come to a mutual understanding and respect. The scenes where Stephen tries to give up his pastorate and the final meeting between him and Jarvis are particularly moving. It is a strong, sincere play of elemental emotions, excellently staged, acted, and sung. The cast is distinctive, headed by Todd Duncan, originally of "Porgy and

Bess," who cancelled a concert tour in Australia to create his role; and Leslie Banks, who came over from England. Most of the company are Negroes, good singers and actors, the chorus especially good. It is hard to particularize, but in the opening scene are the songs, "The Hills of Isopo," "Thousands of Miles," and the resounding, "Train to Johannesburg"; in the second, "The Little Grey House," "Who'll Buy?" and "Trouble Man"; the finale, "Lost in the Stars." In Act Two, "The Wild Justice," Stephen's pathetic prayer, "O Tixo, Tixo, Help Me," the chorus in the prison, "Cry, the Beloved Country"; "Big Mole," a song by a teenage boy, "Alex" (Herbert Coleman) that almost stopped the show; "A Bird of Passage," and the final reprise, "Thousands of Miles."

MARC BLITZSTEIN

Blitzstein was born in Philadelphia, March 2, 1905 He was a student at the University of Pennsylvania, 1921–1923; spent two years at the Curtis Institute, followed by a year in Berlin. He was Guggenheim fellow in 1940; then served overseas with the U.S. Air Force until 1945 and received honorable discharge. Since then his musical career has been identified with New York, composing for radio and motion pictures; a symphony, "Air Borne"; operas including "The Cradle Will Rock" (1937), "No for an Answer" (1941), and "Regina" (1953).

REGINA

Opera in Three Acts. Music by Blitzstein. Book by composer based on "The Little Foxes" by Lillian Hellman. Produced at the New York City Center, April 2, 1953. (See below.)

CAST REGINA GIDDENS (Brenda Lewis).
HORACE GIDDENS, *her husband* (William Wilderman).
ALEXANDRA GIDDENS, *their daughter* (Priscilla Gillette).
BEN HUBBARD (Leon Lishner).
OSCAR HUBBARD (Emile Renan).

BIRDIE HUBBARD, *his wife* (Ellen Faull).
LEO HUBBARD, *their son* (Michael Pollock).
JAZZ (William Dillard).
ADDIE, *cook* (Lucretia West).
CAL, *butler* (Lawrence Winters).
Others in household and musicians.

ARGUMENT The plot of this drama of family life with its jealousies and bickerings follows the Hellman story so closely that it does not require details here. It had been shown previously on Broadway, in 1949, with Jane Pickens in the title role. Several of the principals were retained for the City Center production. The scene is the Giddens home in Bowden, Alabama, in the spring of 1900. It is a picture of easy-going Southern life with cotton pickers and singing of spirituals. This is rudely broken by the entrance of Regina, whose greedy scheming with her two brothers dominates the plot. Horace, her husband, is an invalid and her persecution ends his life. She is apparently the winner in the whole shabby affair, but her daughter, Alexandra, who sees through it, denounces Regina and says she will no longer live with her.

The musical numbers reflect the scene, with a ragtime band and the singing of "Blues," "Greedy Girl," "Summer Day," "Best Thing of All," and the spiritual heard outside, "Certainly, Lord," as the curtain falls.

GIOACCHINO ROSSINI

CENERENTOLA

(Cinderella). Light Opera in Two Acts. Music by Rossini. Book by Jacopo Ferretti. First performed in Rome, January 25, 1817, and popular in Europe for the next ten years or more. In New York it was sung with acclaim by the Garcia Italian company with a good cast including Madam Malibran and Madam Viardot, in 1826. Then laid aside for nearly a century, it was sung successfully in London, in 1934, by the Spanish mezzo-soprano, Conchita Supervia. Produced by the City Center company, New York, April 5, 1953.

CAST PRINCE RAMIRO (Riccardo Manning).
DANDINI, *his servant* (George Gaynes).

DON MAGNIFICO (Richard Wentworth).
CLORINDA, *his daughter* (Laurel Hurley).
TISBE, *his daughter* (Edith Evans).
ANGELINA, *his stepdaughter* (Frances Bible).
ALIDORO (Arthur Newman).
Gentlemen and Ladies of the Court.

ARGUMENT The familiar story of Cinderella is retold with minor variations. Angelina, called Cinderella, is kept a virtual slave by her stepfather, Don Magnifico, an impoverished nobleman, and his two daughters, Tisbe and Clorinda. The latter show their selfishness by turning away a beggar, but the kindhearted Cinderella gives him food and drink. He is Alidoro, the tutor of Prince Ramiro, who is on this secret quest for a suitable wife for the Prince. Alidoro's report is so favorable that the Prince also visits the Don's home, but in disguise as a groom. He and Cinderella are mutually attracted; while Dandini, his servant, dressed in the Prince's attire, is fawned upon by the other sisters.

A court ball is announced, at which time Ramiro will select a bride. Clorinda and Tisbe go in gay attire, but their father will not permit Cinderella to go and threatens to beat her. Alidoro comes to her rescue, provides a costume, and she attends, but pays no attention to Dandini, still posing as the Prince; she is captivated by the supposed groom. She gives Ramiro one of her two bracelets, so that he may identify her again. Ramiro seeks her out at the Don's home, reveals his true rank, and announces that she will be his Queen. The furious sisters and their humiliated father are forced to seek forgiveness.

IGOR STRAVINSKY

THE RAKE'S PROGRESS

Opera in Three Acts, nine scenes, and Epilogue, by Igor Stravinsky. First produced in Venice, September 11, 1951; Zurich, November 24; at the Metropolitan, New York, February 14, 1953, Fritz Reiner conducting; in Boston, May 18, 1953, through the Boston University Workshop, with the composer conducting.

Libretto by W. H. Auden and Chester Kallman is based on the famous cartoons by Hogarth, and depicts life in eighteenth-century England.

CAST Trulove (Basso).
Anne, *his daughter* (Soprano).
Tom Rakewell (Tenor).
Nick Shadow (Baritone).
Mother Goose (Mezzo-Soprano).
Baba the Turk (Mezzo-Soprano).
Sellem, *Auctioneer* (Tenor).
Keeper of Madhouse (Basso).

ARGUMENT The life of a rich libertine in England, with overtones of the Faust legend. Tom Rakewell has inherited wealth from some mysterious uncle, at least so says Nick Shadow his evil genius and prototype of Mephisto. He promises Tom the pleasures of earth for a year and a day. Tom forsakes Anne Trulove, his betrothed sweetheart, goes to London and plunges into debauchery. He weds Baba, the bearded lady of the circus, but life with her soon palls on him. His money is nearly exhausted, and Nick gives him a machine by which he can turn stones into bread. At the end of the year and a day, Nick takes Tom to a graveyard and demands his soul in payment. Tom is given a final chance, to name three cards correctly. The voice of Anne, who is still faithful to him, is heard guiding him, but in the solution of his task he loses his mind.

The score contains arias, duets, recitatives with piano, and music requiring only a small orchestra, with Russian influence. Critical opinion of this modern style composition has been sharply divided.

INDEX OF CHARACTERS

INDEX

APOLLO EDITIONS

A1 Emerson's Essays $1.95
A3 The Lost Americans *Frank C. Hibben* $1.25
A4 Shakespeare's Plays in Digest Form *J. Walker McSpadden* $1.25
A5 The Shakespearean Review Book *Fannie Gross* $1.25
A6 The Shorter Plays of Bernard Shaw *George Bernard Shaw* $1.95
A8 Laugh with Leacock *Stephen Leacock* $1.95
A9 Man's Emerging Mind *N. J. Berrill* $1.95
A13 The Reach of the Mind *J. B. Rhine* $1.95
A16 King Solomon's Ring *Konrad Lorenz* $1.95
A21 Adventures in Nature *Edwin Way Teale* $1.95
A24 The Wisdom of the Living Religions *Joseph Gaer* $1.95
A26 The Twelve Seasons *Joseph Wood Krutch* $1.50
A30 Coming of Age in Samoa *Margaret Mead* $1.75
A31 Thunder Out of China *Theodore H. White and Annalee Jacoby* $1.95
A35 Introduction to Higher Mathematics *Constance Reid* $1.50
A37 No More War *Linus Pauling* $1.75
A38 Strange Sects and Curious Cults *Marcus Bach* $1.75
A39 That's Me All Over *Cornelia Otis Skinner* $1.85
A40 Lewis and Clark *John Bakeless* $1.95
A42 New World of the Mind *J. B. Rhine* $1.95
A44 Giovanni's Room *James Baldwin* $1.75
A47 The New World of Math *George A. W. Boehm & the Editors of Fortune* $1.50
A49 In Quest of the Northwest Passage *L. H. Neatby* $1.95
A56 A Primer of Foreign Relations *A. A. Berle, Jr.* $1.95
A58 Growing Up in New Guinea *Margaret Mead* $1.95
A60 Zen for the West *Sohaku Ogata* $1.65
A61 Great English Short Novels: *Edited and with an Introduction by Cyril Connolly* $2.95